By the same author

The Blue-Coated Worker: A Sociological Study of Police Unionism, Cambridge University Press, 1978

Chief Constables: Bobbies, Bosses or Bureaucrats?, Oxford University Press 1991

Beyond Law and Order: Criminal Justice Policy and Politics Into the 1990s (ed. with Malcolm Cross), Macmillan 1991

The Politics of the Police

Second edition

Robert Reiner
Professor of Criminology
Law Department, London School of Economics

HARVESTER
WHEATSHEAF

New York   London   Toronto   Sydney   Tokyo   Singapore

First published 1992 by
Harvester Wheatsheaf
Campus 400, Maylands Avenue
Hemel Hempstead
Hertfordsire, HP2 7EZ
A division of
Simon & Schuster International Group

Typeset in 10/12pt Times by
Columns Design & Production Services Ltd, Reading

Printed and bound in Great Britain by
Biddles Ltd, Guildford and King's Lynn

British Library Cataloguing in Publication Data

A catalogue record for this book is available from
the publisher

ISBN 0-7450-0958-1 (hbk)
ISBN 0-7450-0959-X (pbk)

---

1 2 3 4 5   96 95 94 93 92

For Toby and Charlotte

CONTENTS

PART III: LAW AND POLITICS

He who lets himself in for politics, that is, for power and force as means, contracts with diabolical powers and for his action it is not true that good can follow only from good and evil only from evil, but that often the opposite is true. Anyone who fails to see this is, indeed, a political infant. (Max Weber, 'Politics as a vocation' (1918), in H. Gerth and C.W. Mills (eds), *From Max Weber*, London: Routledge, 1948, p. 123)

If the Lord does not guard the city, the watchman keeps watch in vain. (Psalm 127, v.2)

PREFACE TO THE SECOND EDITION

The political context of policing has altered dramatically since the first edition of this book was completed. As the Preface to the first edition indicates, the police then stood in the vortex of a storm of conflict between the Conservative government, their champions, and a mounting chorus of criticism from the Left. Nearly eight years later the police remain at the centre of political concern, but party polarisation has diminished. The love affair between the police and the Tories has cooled if not died, whilst Labour in its Kinnockite new realist guise, although seeking to repair broken bridges and lose the stigma of being 'anti-police', remains critical of many aspects of policing. The need for fundamental organisational and cultural reform to restore public confidence in the police is now the shared concern of all police leaders and staff associations. However, the social context for achieving this has seldom been less propitious, with growing unemployment, poverty, inequality, social divisions, and their progeny: record-breaking statistics of crime and continuing disorder.

When this book was initially written it had a twofold purpose. The first was to point out the deplorable consequences for the police and our social order of the polarised conflict then raging. Labour has moved in the direction I was advocating, and this side of the original purpose is now redundant. The Conservative government has continued to deny any link between its economic and social policies and problems of 'law and order', despite plentiful research evidence demonstrating it (Farrington *et al.*,

1986; Box, 1987; Field, 1990). This aspect of the book's original concern – to show how Tory policy is undermining British policing, once considered a major national asset – remains relevant.

The second aim of the book was to be a text synthesising the growing research literature on the police, and this has become even more important. In the second half of the 1980s there has been a veritable flood of research and publishing on the police, largely because of the centrality of policing to the political agenda (Reiner, 1989b, 1992a). The high proportion of references in the bibliography of this edition which date from the late 1980s is testimony to this. There has also been a growth of courses looking at policing, in law, social science and politics degrees, as well as a burgeoning of specialist policing and criminal justice courses at undergraduate and postgraduate level (responding in large part to the post-Scarman enthusiasm for higher education amongst the police themselves). I hope that this book, which sets out to review what this now vast research literature has to tell us, will prove useful to those who have to study or teach on such courses, as well as of some interest to all who are concerned about a public institution of vast importance to the health of our social order.

This second edition is updated throughout, and the conclusions have been revised fundamentally. In particular, full account has been taken of the Police and Criminal Evidence Act 1984, and of the profound alterations to the law and practice of police governance since the mid-1980s. Police powers and accountability have been transformed more in the half decade since the first edition than in any comparable period, and these changes have been incorporated into the book.

In the Preface to the first edition, I set out my intellectual debts in detail, and want to repeat my gratitude to all who are mentioned there. Jerome Skolnick was mentioned as a key influence who I had not then had the pleasure of meeting in person. I am pleased to say that this omission has now been corrected, and the influence of Jerry's work is now as much by personal as published communication. I have also been strongly impressed by making the personal acquaintance of Sir Kenneth Newman and Sir Peter Imbert, whose reform efforts are discussed here. Once again, though, my main debts are to my wife Miki, and children, Toby and Charlotte, without whose encouragement this work would never have been completed (or perhaps started). Finally, I must thank my father and late mother for their original inspiration and impetus. As the Book of Proverbs enjoins, I will endeavour not to forget the law of my father or the moral instruction of my mother.

Robert Reiner
7 January 1992

PREFACE TO THE FIRST EDITION

Policing in Britain has become thoroughly politicised. The high-water mark was reached at the 1984 party conferences. In the first week of October the police were subject to a torrent of bitter, sometimes hysterical, abuse from many speakers at the Labour Party conference, notwithstanding the efforts of the leadership to try to develop a more balanced and rational discussion. Perhaps the nastiest jibe was the rejection by one speaker of Mr Kinnock's comparison of the police to 'the meat in the sandwich' of social conflict. They were not the meat, she said, but the salmonella poisoning. The conference also passed several condemnatory resolutions, including one to give day-to-day control of policing to elected authorities, and another to limit the police role in industrial disputes. The party leadership promptly tried to distance itself from these amorphous if not meaningless proposals, and to concentrate on discussion of the very serious issues raised for civil liberties and police accountability by the miners' strike. But it is small wonder that the chairman of the Police Federation reacted to the vituperation levelled at his members by questioning whether the police would continue to be able to give equally loyal service to a Labour as to a Conservative government (*The Guardian*, 4 October 1984, p. 5; 6 October 1984, p. 14). The Superintendents' Association, sensing the dangers of the Federation's increasingly partisan stance, reaffirmed police loyalty to any elected government, and underlined that their oath of allegiance was to the Queen and country, not the party in power (*Daily Telegraph*, 5 October 1984, p. 2). For their part, the

Conservatives at their conference the following week not only warmed the police with glowing praise, The Home Secretary, Mr Leon Brittan, took the opportunity to pledge the removal of one of the few powers of local police authorities, by making any attempt to suspend a Chief Constable subject to appeal to the Police Complaints Authority (*The Standard*, 9 October 1984, p. 1). These controversies all underline the importance of the topics this book deals with. It is my argument that policing is at a critical watershed. Established in the early nineteenth century in the face of virulent political opposition, the police were able to legitimate themselves to a remarkable extent by the middle of this century. This was the product of the strategies adopted by the architects of the English police tradition in order to depoliticise policing, and the wider historical processes of the incorporation of the working class into the body politic and the pacification of social relations. The growing turbulence of the 1970s repoliticised policing, with important climacterics being the 1981 urban riots and the 1984 miners' strike. These made police strategy and control issues of partisan political controversy for the first time in over a century. Since 1981 and the Scarman Report there has been a strong current of reform in police circles, aimed at restoring their legitimacy. But these efforts to depoliticise policing are threatened both by government policy and the virulence of some radical opposition to the police. This politicisation of policing issues is very dangerous to the police themselves, and to those who are policed. Unfortunately, most discussions of policing now are polarised between the Tory view of them as latter-day saints, and the radical demand for control by elected bodies. The latter is far from being a panacea when those who bear the brunt of policing are vulnerable minorities. Unlike the circumstances in which the police developed, they are not now opposed by the majority of the population. The working class is increasingly divided on ethnic lines, and as a result of the ravages of unemployment. The hope for policing that respects the rights of minorities lies not in democratic control through elected authorities, but in a reassertion of the traditional legal and professional ideals of the police embodying a universalistic and impartial authority, albeit one sensitive to the need for public acceptance.

This argument is based on a consideration of what is now an impressively large volume of research, historical and sociological. I thus hope that the book will not only cast some light on the present crisis but serve as a text for people studying the police in academic courses. In recent years there has been increasing attention to the police in many academic subjects – law, politics, sociology, criminology, history. Despite the burgeoning monographic and polemical literature, I have found no single source that I could refer students to in order to discover conveniently what work has been done. I hope that the present volume might be a useful starting point.

As the references which I have assembled in the text indicate, I owe many debts to a wide range of authors. Of those I have never met, I have gained most from reading the work of Wilbur Miller, Jerome Skolnick and William Ker Muir Jr. I have benefited from hearing valuable lectures by John Alderson, Sir Cyril Philips and Lord Scarman. I gained much from attending the Nijenrode conference on control in the police organisation arranged by Maurice Punch in 1980, and hearing the valuable contributions of Egon Bittner, David Bayley, Lawrence Sherman and the others (collected in Punch, 1983). I have especially benefited at crucial points from reading the work of, and/or talking to, Mike Brogden, Mike Chatterton, Theodore Ferdinand, Nigel Fielding, Simon Holdaway, Michael Ignatieff, Barrie Irving, Tony Jefferson, Tony Judge, Martin Kettle, Mike Levi, Barry Loveday, Peter Manning, Geoffrey Marshall, Cyril Robinson, Paul Rock, Andy Scull, Laurie Taylor, Tank Waddington, Jock Young and Michael Zander. Crucial debts are to: Clifford Shearing and Philip Stenning for many stimulating discussions in the summer of 1983 while I was at the Centre for Criminology at the University of Toronto, during which many of these ideas crystallised; to John Styles for his helpful guidance with recent historical work; and to Michael Banton for getting me started. Needless to say none of the above is responsible for the failings of what follows.

I owe enormous gratitude to my wife Miki and children Toby and Charlotte for tremendous support, above all in the summer of 1984 during which I finished this. They (and our lodger Tess Joseph) have had to put up with too many months in which my mind was stuck in a panda car. Finally, I thank Mrs Pauline Tilley for processing my words efficiently and cheerfully.

Robert Reiner
9 October 1984

POLITICS AND POLICING

The group of words, police, policy, polity, politics, politic, political, politician is a good example of delicate distinctions.

(Maitland, 1885, p. 105)

Most police officers stoutly maintain that policing and politics don't mix. Chief Constables regularly declaim on the political neutrality of the police service and on the dangers embodied in campaigns for enhanced accountability to democratically elected local authorities, denouncing this as an insidious bid for 'political' control. Sir Robert Mark, Commissioner of the Metropolitan Police (Met.) in the early 1970s, claimed the support of a

> long tradition of constitutional freedom from political interference in our operational role . . . the police are not servants of government at any level. We do not act at the behest of a minister or any political party, not even the party in government. We act on behalf of the people as a whole.

The most outspoken of the 1970s breed of pontificating policemen, Sir James Anderton, then Chief Constable of Manchester, put the matter more sharply when he claimed,

> we are now witnessing the domination of the police service as a necessary prerequisite of the creation in this country of a society based on Marxist Communist principles. The current concern over policing

1

being expressed by certain political factions has got precious little to do with better community participation in police affairs, or the improvement of democracy – rather it is the first conscious step manifesting itself towards the political control of the police, without which the dream of a totalitarian, one-party state in this country cannot be realised. (*The Times*, 18 March 1982)

This notion of the political neutrality or independence of the police cannot withstand any serious consideration. It rests on an untenably narrow conception of 'the political', restricting it to 'the administrative apparatus of state and party organisation', a usage which Worsley many years ago referred to as 'a dying conceptual apparatus, the prerogative predominantly of a few formal constitutional and legal theorists' (Worsley, 1964), and one is tempted to add, some senior police officers. In a broader sense all relationships which have a power dimension are political. The police are inherently and inescapably political: 'The civil police is a social organisation created and sustained by political processes to enforce dominant conceptions of public order' (Skolnick, 1972, p. 41).

Their specific role in the enforcement of laws and the maintenance of order is as specialists in coercion. This does not mean, as we shall see, that the police routinely invoke their coercive powers, ultimately the capacity to use legitimate force (Bittner, 1970, 1974; Klockars, 1985). The craft of successful policing is to be able to minimise the use of force, but it remains the specialist resource of the police, their distinctive role in the political order. In this sense the police are actually at the heart of the state's functioning, and political analysis in general tends to underplay the significance of policing as both source and symbol of the quality of a political civilisation.

Some police activities are avowedly concerned with the control of behaviour which is explicitly political in motivation and intended impact. These range from activities defined as 'subversive' (the province of the Special Branch) to the maintenance of order in demonstrations or some industrial disputes. The control of overtly political behaviour is the task of the specifically political police, or 'high policing' (Bunyan, 1977; Turk, 1982a and b; Brodeur, 1983). A characteristic of the English police tradition is the attempted unification of the 'high policing' function of regulating explicit political dissidence with the 'low policing' task of routine law enforcement and street-level order maintenance. In most other countries there is a greater degree of organisational separation, although *de facto* specialised riot control units have developed within the police in Britain.

In his previously cited remarks Sir James Anderton conceded that Chief Constables today could not avoid becoming involved in 'politics with a small p', by which he presumably means the broad sense of politics as the exercise of power. What the Chief Constables are most concerned to claim is that the police are not involved in partisan politics, but impartially enforce the law. This claim is only sustainable in a very narrow sense, if at all (Wilson, 1981). A distinction must be made between partisanship in *intent* and in *impact*. In a society which is divided on class, ethnicity, gender and other dimensions of inequality, the impact of laws even if they are formulated and enforced quite impartially and universalistically will reproduce those social divisions. This is the point encapsulated in Anatole France's celebrated aphorism: 'The law in its majestic equality, forbids the rich as well as the poor to sleep under bridges, to beg in the streets, and to steal bread' (*Le Lys Rouge*, Paris, 1894). In practice, of course, the inequalities of social power are likely to have an impact on the processes of legislation and administration of justice, so that the law will deviate from formal impartiality (Griffith, 1977; Hain, 1984). For both these reasons the *impact* of law and its enforcement in an unequal society will be objectively political even in the narrower sense of partisanship, favouring some groups at the expense of others. But it does not follow from this that the law or its enforcement are partisan in *intention*. This would be a deviation from the legal ideals of impartiality and universalism, and it is this which the Chief Constables are concerned to deny.

As the ensuing chapters argue, the English police tradition has to a large measure eschewed overt partisanship. The constitutional structure within which it operates, autonomous of direct control by elected authorities, is intended to preserve this. Moreover, it must be emphasised that while policing is inherently political and indeed partisan in reproducing social inequalities, at the same time it preserves the minimal conditions of civilised and stable social existence from which all groups benefit, albeit differentially (Marenin, 1983). This Janus-faced nature of policing as expressing social divisions as well as a universal communal interest was nicely captured during the 1984 miners' strike when Arthur Scargill, after months of vituperative condemnation of police tactics, had to be given a police bodyguard because of threats on his life (*Daily Mail*, 12 September 1984, p. 1).

However, if policing is an inherently political activity, it does not follow that it usually is or should be seen as such. Policing may be inescapably political, but it may not be *politicised*, that is, the centre of overt political controversy over its manner, tactics or mode of operation and organisation. Like riding a bike, policing is the sort of activity that is thought about only when the wheel comes off. When things are running smoothly it is a socially invisible, undiscussed routine.

This book will be concerned with the *de facto* politics of policing in terms of its uneven social impact (Chapter 4), the political ideology of police officers and the political role of the police in popular ideology (Chapters 3 and 5), and the *politicisation* of the police, their involvement in overt political conflict (Parts I and III). As Chapter 1 will show, the English police were established in the face of acute political conflict. To gain acceptance, the architects of the British policing tradition constructed an image, organisation and strategy which were intended to defuse the various strands of political opposition. Over the first century and a quarter of its existence the police in England and Wales were largely successful in accomplishing their depoliticisation, and came to be seen as legitimate by the mass of the population.

It should be noted, however, that there are inherent limits to police legitimation in any society. Since policing is centrally concerned with the resolution of conflicts using the coercive powers of criminal law, ultimately resting on the capacity to use force, there is in most police actions someone who is being policed *against*. In this sense the police are inherently dealers in and dispensers of evil and can never command universal love. For policing to be accepted as legitimate it is not necessary that all groups or individuals in a society agree with the substantive content or direction of specific police operations. It means at minimum only that the broad mass of the population, and possibly even some of those who are policed against, accept the authority, the lawful right, of the police to act as they do, even if disagreeing with or regretting some specific actions. Of course, in conditions of relative social harmony, acceptance of judicious policing may be a lot more wholehearted. But as policing is inherently an activity concerned with the ordering of *conflict*, 'policing by consent' cannot imply complete and universal approval. To suggest otherwise is dangerous in that it raises expectations which can never be realised (Fielding, 1991).

However, despite the conflicts and travails at the birth of policing, and the still storming political controversies about the causes and impact of the new police, by the 1950s something like the maximal possible degree of consent had been achieved. This was a result of police strategy against a favourable background context of the pacification of social relations and the in- stitutionalisation of class conflict. After the 1960s a set of interrelated changes once more politicised the police, and by the 1980s political conflict raged about the direction and control of policing. After 1981 and the influential Scarman Report, a number of initiatives developed within the police seeking to depoliticise and relegitimate the force. The competing arguments and strategies will be evaluated in the light of the very substantial body of evidence about police culture, operations and images which is reviewed in Part II. The nub of my conclusion is that the post-Scarman reform initiatives were well grounded in the lessons that can be learned from the research evidence. None the less, there is as yet no indication that they succeeded, or will do so. The chances of Scarmanism's success were gravely lessened by strains resulting from government policies which aggravated the problems of policing by multiplying unemployment, especially among the young and ethnic minorities. The reforms were also threatened by distrust of, and hostility to, the police among large sections of the Left which led them to root-and-branch opposition to the new strategies during the early 1980s.

The problems to which Scarman's analysis and recipes were addressed have multiplied. The police stand at a lower ebb in public trust and esteem than at any time since they were established in the nineteenth century. They have been rocked by scandals revealing gross miscarriages of justice, and appear increasingly less able to protect people from criminal victimisa- tion, which is rising at record speed. Serious disorder, on a scale without precedent since the Second World War, has continued throughout the 1980s, in a variety of contexts, including political and industrial conflict and a miscellany of leisure pursuits from football to 'joyriding'. The militarisation of the police in response to this has undermined police legitimacy without controlling the rise of disorder.

In response to all these problems police and government have pursued a number of reform strategies, and competing ones are on offer from the Left (Reiner, 1992b). Police thinking at policy-making levels is still suffused with the Scarman philosophy (Reiner, 1991, Ch. 6), but with additions from management theory and the fashionable language of consumerism (both in response to pet panaceas of the Conservative government).

In the first half of the 1980s, the police were pigs in the middle of sharply polarised political debate. They were the darlings of the Tories and in conflict with Labour-controlled police author-ities to which the national Labour Party threatened to make them more accountable. Gone were the halcyon days of consensus, when the police stood above the party fray as beloved totems of the nation.

At the end of the first year of the post-Thatcher era, there was good news and bad news for the police. The good news was the return of consensus about policing. The bad news was the new consensus view that the police were failing badly on almost every front, and in need of drastic reform. Once the preserve of the supposedly anti-police 'Loony Left', this was now the received wisdom even of the true blue press and politicians, staunch supporters of law and order (cf. *The Economist*, 14 February 1992; *The Evening Standard*, 18 February 1992, p. 11, 19 February, p. 9). A *Guardian* cartoon on 29 November 1991, just after the Court of Appeal declared the convictions of the 'Tottenham Three' to have been miscarriages of justice, summed it up well. Apologising for being late for a date a man offers the excuse: 'I asked a policeman the time, and he lied'.

For the last years of the 1980s and the first years of the 1990s, news about the police was dominated by scandals involving major miscarriages of justice. At the same time there was a steady background stream of revelations of police abuse, and of failure to deliver adequate services. The news also contained many items which put the police in a much better light. However, these did not balance the impact of the 'bad news' on public perceptions, and indeed were not given equal weight in reporting. The same is true of the many on-going efforts by the police service to improve its practices and image, which in a variety of ways have been steadily pursued since the shock-waves of 1981, the urban riots and the Scarman Report. It is increasingly apparent that the police feel trapped in a time warp. They are intent on reforms (cf. the letter from the Association of Chief Police Officers' President, *The Guardian*, 22 February 1992, p. 22); however, the impact of these on public perceptions of the police is continuously being undercut by shocking revelations of skeletons in the cupboard, as well as unrealistic expectations of performance and probity built up in the bygone era when the lid was shut tight firmly on scandals.

This book sets out to analyse how the police got to their present situation, and what research on their working suggests about the prospects of success for the reforms which are being pursued energetically. The verdict is far from encouraging, largely because the effects of Conservative government policy are to increase social divisions, poverty, injustice, relative deprivation – and the anger these give rise to – the bitter fruits of which the police must cope with. To seek to return to the 'Golden Age' of consensus about policing symbolised by the Dixon of Dock Green myth is chimerical at best. The more pragmatic but attainable target is to achieve public recognition for doing a 'dirty work' occupation as professionally, efficiently and impartially as this can be done in an ever more fragmented and divided society. The review and analysis of social and historical research offered here is intended to further this very urgent objective.

PART I

History

CHAPTER 1

THE BIRTH OF THE BLUES
The establishment of professional policing in Britain, 1829–56

All politics starts with a reading of history. . . . How was it in the past? The question is the prelude to justifying how it should be in the future. History is a subject for study, but also a basis for action.
(Hugo Young, *The Guardian*, 7 January 1992, p. 18)

'I never saw any of them again – except the cops. No way has yet been invented to say good-bye to them.' Philip Marlowe's fatalistic lament, with which Raymond Chandler concludes his classic mystery *The Long Goodbye*, embodies a basic assumption shared even by those who are critical of the police. Welcome or unwelcome, protectors, pigs or pariahs, the police are an inevitable fact of modern life.

A consideration of the process by which modern professional policing in Britain came into being makes problematic this taken-for-granted acceptance. The establishment of the police was a protracted and painful process, in the face of bitter resistance and smouldering hostility. In the late eighteenth and early nineteenth centuries the police idea was a clearly politicised, fiercely contested matter.

Interpretations of police history

Until fairly recently all the available accounts of the origins and development of policing in Britain operated within a framework of palpably conservative assumptions. The police were seen as an inevitable and unequivocally beneficent institution, a cornerstone of national pride, which had been developed by English pragmatic genius as a response to fiercesome threats to social order and civilised existence. There was initial opposition to the police, but it arose from vested interest, malevolence or blinkered obscurantism, and was rapidly dissipated when the benefits of a benign police institution became apparent to all.

This view of police history as the inevitable march of progress came under challenge in the 1970s, as a new revisionist account of the development of the police became dominant. In this the police are seen as a means (together with associated reforms of criminal procedure, punishment, social policy and political representation) of maintaining the dominance of a ruling class against the interests and opposition of the various sections of the working class who constitute the majority of the population.

This revisionist interpretation is already being debated by more recent work (for example, the collection of essays in Cohen and Scull, 1983). There is nothing like a clear 'counter-revisionist' position as yet. But recent research does suggest that both the traditional and the early revisionist accounts embody questionable assumptions (Bailey, 1980, 1981a and b; D. Jones, 1982, 1983; Emsley, 1983; Brogden, 1987; Styles, 1987; Palmer, 1988). A more complex picture of police development is emerging (Emsley, 1991 is an excellent synthesis).

The cop-sided view of history: the orthodox story

The orthodox studies are all more or less informative versions of the same 'ideology as history' (Robinson, 1978).[1] There is a spectrum of sobriety and rigour running from jingoistic eulogies intended for a popular audience (Minto, 1965), through the early pioneering explorations of the English police tradition (Lee, 1901; Reith, 1938, 1940, 1943, 1948, 1952, 1956), to some awesomely detailed and scholarly work (Radzinowicz, 1948, 1956, 1968; Hart, 1951, 1955, 1956; Critchley, 1978). The orthodox interpretation, even in its straightforward form, is far from dead; it still flourishes in local histories (Walters, 1975), 'company' histories (Ascoli, 1979), and even the occasional general history (Stead, 1985). Although the different orthodox accounts vary in analytical penetration and informative detail, they share certain core assumptions. These can be distilled into the answers to ten questions about the 'new' police. The orthodox view can then be contrasted with the revisionist position on these same issues.

(1) What was the source of the need for a new police?

The basic causes of the need for police reform are seen as the twin pressures of urban and industrial revolution. As these spread through the country they brought with them new problems of order which were met by the institution of the new police. The problem was the inability of old control arrangements to cope. 'The breakdown in law and order marched in step with the progress of the Industrial Revolution' (Critchley, 1978, p. 21).

(2) What was wrong with the old policing arrangements?

'The eighteenth-century system was one of very severe penalties . . . but very weak and capricious enforcement machinery' (Philips, 1983, p. 54). The punitiveness of the criminal code was both inhumane and counter-productive. It made victims reluctant to prosecute, and juries loathe to convict. That certainty of punishment was a more effective deterrent than severity was a fundamental axiom of the late eighteenth-century 'classical' criminology of Beccaria and others (Taylor, Walton and Young, 1973, Ch. 1; Roshier, 1989). It was closely tied in with the arguments for police reform proposed by such writers as Colquhoun and Bentham.

The key agents of the 'old' policing system, the constables, watchmen and amateur justices, were widely lampooned by eighteenth- and nineteenth-century advocates of police reform, and their criticisms are retailed by the orthodox view. The office of constable had become so onerous that it became common to hire deputies. Penny-pinching led to the use of men who were 'scarcely removed from idiotism' (Critchley, 1978, p. 18). Many magistrates exploited their offices for fees (the so-called 'trading justices'). The London nightwatchmen, the 'Charlies' (instituted in the reign of Charles II), were said to be 'contemptible, dissolute and drunken buffoons who shuffled along the darkened streets after sunset with their long staves and dim lanterns, calling out the time and the state of the weather, and thus warned the criminal of their approach' (*ibid.*, p. 30). Those members of the old constabulary who were not ineffective were corrupt, milking their offices for rewards and fees. Thief-takers became thief-makers. Their prototype, Jonathan Wild, had subordinates who 'stole on commission, and surrendered what they had taken to Wild who then returned the goods to their erstwhile owners' (Rock, 1977, p. 215). In short, the old system was said to be uncertain, uncoordinated and haphazard, relying on private and amateur effort, and prone to corruption.

(3) What were the motives for police reform?

The large and rapidly growing cities were seen as breeding-grounds of crime and disorder, due to their anonymity. Henry Fielding compared London to 'a vast wood or forest, in which a thief may harbour with as great security as wild beasts do in the deserts of Africa or Arabia', while Horace Walpole wrote of

being 'forced to travel, even at noon, as if one were going to
battle' (Critchley, 1978, p. 21). Rapid urban and industrial
development brought immense social dislocation and disruption
in its wake, engendering demoralisation, crime and social
conflict. 'Civilisation works its miracles and civilised man is
turned back almost into a savage', wrote de Tocqueville after
visiting Manchester (cited in Hobsbawm, 1968, p. 86).

Patrick Colquhoun, the London stipendiary magistrate who
was a major exponent of police reform, attempted in his 1795
Treatise on the Police of the Metropolis to quantify precisely the
number of criminals and the amount of loss engendered by their
crimes (Reiner, 1988a). In 1810 the government began publishing
annual figures of indictable committals for trial in England and
Wales, which showed an apparently inexorable increase (Philips,
1980, p. 180). Even at the time, it was debated whether these
reflected a 'real' increase in offending, as opposed to such factors
as increasing ease of prosecution. But Peel relied heavily on these
statistics in the parliamentary debate before the 1829 Act was
passed.

In addition to the fear of rising crime, the orthodox view
recognises the importance of public disorder as a motive for
police reform. This was a concern about disorder in the double
sense of declining moral standards, and the threat of riot.
Colquhoun and other police reformers waxed loquacious about
moral decay, which was also seen as a source of political conflict
(Philips, 1980, p. 177).

The role of politically motivated disorder in the creation of the
new police tends to be underplayed by the orthodox view (Hart,
1955; Ascoli, 1979; and Philips, 1982 are exceptions to this). The
notorious Peterloo massacre of 1819 does not feature in
Critchley's 1978 book (the standard orthodox reference).[2] It gets
the briefest of mentions in Reith, and is assimilated to the 'crime-
industry' (Reith, 1956, p. 122). The only political disorders which
are featured prominently in the orthodox explanations of the
1829 Act are the Gordon riots, the reactionary anti-Catholic
demonstrations which were the immediate stimulus for Pitt's
abortive 1785 Police Bill, the first attempt to establish a
professional police force. Concentrating on them allows the
problem to be more readily depicted as 'City gangsterdom'
(Reith, 1943, p. 29).

The overall theme of the orthodox histories, then, is that police reform was motivated mainly by fear of crime, but also by moral and mob disorder, all engendered by the problems of rapid transition to an urban industrial society. The early nineteenth century is seen as 'the golden age of gangsterdom' (Midwinter, 1968, p. 14) or 'an epoch of criminality' (Lee, 1901, p. 203).

(4) Who opposed the new police?

Given this picture of the new police as unequivocally necessary to control the evil by-products of industrial growth, the orthodox view is at something of a loss in explaining opposition to the establishment of the police. Not that the weight and power of this opposition can be denied. From the middle of the eighteenth century a growing chorus of voices unsuccessfully urged the creation of a professional police. Instead, a series of expedients was introduced, notably the 1792 Middlesex Justices Act, creating twenty-one paid magistrates controlling seven police offices.

After Pitt's 1785 Act there were several inquiries into the policing of London which considered the establishment of a centralised professional police for the metropolis. In 1798 a Select Committee on Finance, largely influenced by Colquhoun, favoured a new police, but no legislation was introduced. Six parliamentary committees – in 1812, 1816, two in 1817, 1818 and 1822 – were set up to consider London's policing arrangements, but recommended against a new police, before Peel was finally successful.

The orthodox historians' only explanation of this is to impugn the intelligence or integrity of the opponents of the police. The rock upon which Pitt's 1785 Bill had foundered was the opposition of the City to encroachment on their corporate rights, and Peel deftly avoided this problem by excluding the City from his 1829 Act. Much of the resistance to the police legislation from 1785 to 1856 was couched in a rhetoric drawing on the supposed traditional liberties of Englishmen, which was invoked by

aristocratic Tories and working-class radicals alike. The frequently quoted passage from the 1822 Committee Report – 'It is
difficult to reconcile an effective system of police, with that
perfect freedom of action and exemption from interference,
which are the great privileges and blessings of society in this
country' – is dismissed by Critchley as 'thoroughly reactionary'.
    Reith sees the opposition in an even more sinister light: 'It was
the efforts of gangsterdom alone, and the success of its
propaganda, which frustrated for nearly a century every attempt
to end the menace of crime and disorder by creating police'
(Reith, 1943, p. 12). Altogether the orthodox view has no
analysis of the social location and basis of the various currents of
thought concerning the police, and denies the opposition any
meaning or rationality that is not venal.

(5) *How long did opposition to the police last?*

After the new police took to the streets, the orthodox histories
have to account for the opposition of the masses who were not
directly represented in the parliamentary debates. This opposition, although clearly virulent in the early 1830s, is depicted as
rapidly evaporating once the worth and virtue of the new police
became apparent. At first pamphlets circulated exhorting the
populace to 'Join your Brother Londoners in one heart, one hand
for the ABOLITION OF THE NEW POLICE', and attacking 'Peel's
bloody gang'. During the fighting between the police and a
meeting of the National Political Union, a PC Culley was fatally
stabbed. The inquest jury returned a verdict of 'justifiable
homicide'. This clearly indicates the strength of continuing public
opposition to the police, but the conventional view has it that
after a parliamentary inquiry, 'public opinion . . . veered in
favour of the police' (Critchley, 1978, p. 55; for a critique, see
Brogden, 1982, pp. 174–7). In the orthodox narrative, this was
the crucial turning-point. 'The police, though they did not then
know it had won their final and conclusive victory over the
Ultras. More importantly, they had won an even greater victory

in the long term – the seal of "public approval"' (Ascoli, 1979, p. 105). Altogether, in the orthodox view, opposition to the police may have been nasty and brutish, but it was blessedly short.

(6) What was new about the 'new police'?

The orthodox histories argue both that the 'new' police established between 1829 and 1856 was a novel creation in terms of efficiency and integrity, and that it had roots in ancient traditions of communal self-policing.

The 'newness' consisted of the institution of a bureaucratic organisation of professionals, rationally administered and directed towards a policy of 'preventive policing', that is, regular patrols to deter crime, suppress disorder and maintain security. Gradually with the spread of the 'new' police throughout the country, following the Metropolitan 'prototype', a more coordinated network of systematic law enforcement came into being, but without a degree of central direction that would be incompatible with traditional liberties, thus striking a balance 'nicely adjusted to the British genius' (Critchley, 1978, p. 101).

The 'newness' of the Metropolitan Police is also emphasised by stressing the high standards of entry and discipline established by Peel, and the two Commissioners he appointed, Colonel Charles Rowan (of the Light Brigade) and Richard Mayne, a barrister. This meant that few of the old parish constables or watchmen were eligible, and indeed only one-sixth of the original intake of nearly 3,000 men remained in the force 4 years later.

On the other hand, the force's ancient origins in communal self-policing, and the continuity of the office of constable (with its common-law powers theoretically unaffected by incorporation into a bureaucratic body) are also stressed. This argument was pioneered by Lee: 'Our English police system . . . rests on foundations designed with the full approval of the people, we know not how many hundreds of years before the Norman conquest' (Lee, 1901, p. xxvii). It is echoed by Reith, who sees the police as 'directly traceable to the dawn of European history, and to the customs of the Aryan tribes of the Continent whom their leaders made responsible for securing the observance of tribal laws' (Reith, 1943, p. 14; see also Rolph, 1962, pp. 1–10; Critchley, 1978, pp. 1–28; Ascoli, 1979, pp. 1, 9–16). These arguments all go back only as far as the tenth century, by which time there was already a clear-cut feudal hierarchy into which the vestigial kin structure and communal self-policing traditions had been incorporated for order maintenance by a succession of invaders (Robinson, 1979, p. 49, n. 36).

(7) What was the social impact of the new police?

In the orthodox account, the social impact of the police was the clearly benign one of solving the problem of order and checking the spread of lawlessness. 'Three thousand unarmed policemen, cautiously feeling their way against a hostile public, brought peace and security to London in place of the turmoil and lawlessness of centuries' (Critchley, 1978, pp. 55–6). This not only protected individual victims from depredation but stabilised society for future growth within a liberal democratic framework. The reformers' purpose was enunciated most clearly by Colquhoun: 'Everything that can heighten in any degree the respectability of the office of constable, adds to the security of the state, and the life and property of every individual.' The orthodox analysis suggests that this purpose was concretely achieved by the English police system.

Reith waxes loquacious on the splendid advantages brought about by Peel's creation. 'It is an unquestionable historical fact that the appearance of public orderliness in Britain, and of individual willingness to cooperate in securing and maintaining it, coincides with the successful establishment of the police institution' (Reith, 1943, p. 3). The same sentiments are echoed by most of the orthodox histories (Lee, 1901, pp. xxv–xxvii; Gorer, 1955, pp. 294–8, 305–12; Critchley, 1978, p. xvii; Ascoli, 1979, pp. 3–4, 346–9). In the orthodox view the police were not only successful in the more immediate and mundane jobs of crime control and order maintenance; through their efforts they were ultimately to transform the whole national character, and indeed, world civilisation.

(8) Who gained from the new police?

It is a striking theme of the orthodox analysis that not only did the police benefit society as a whole but, contrary to initial fears, their major impact was on the welfare of the working class and the poor. They are the guardians of the weak against the strong. Lee claims the police were 'designed to stand between the powerful and the weak, to prevent oppression, danger and crime' (Lee, 1901, p. xxx). Reith takes up the argument. The 1839 Royal Commission Report on the setting-up of a rural constabulary is said to provide 'a remarkable picture . . . of the sufferings endured by the working classes as the consequences of absence of police' (Reith, 1956, p. 203). Critchley also pursues the theme that the poor had most to gain from the police.

> The wealthy paid gamekeepers to protect their property and slept with arms near at hand, and the middle-class tradesmen formed voluntary protection societies. The poor simply managed as best as they could until the reform of rural police was at last put in hand. (Critchley, 1978, p. 28)

While on the one hand the poor and the working class are singled out by the orthodox histories as beneficiaries of the police, they are also pinpointed as the source of most crime. This follows on from Colquhoun's contemporary analysis linking indigence and crime to the need for police (*Treatise on Indigence*, Colquhoun, 1806). Ascoli also stresses the particular contribution of the poor to the eighteenth-century 'crime problem': 'While the upper and middle classes exploited the financial possibilities of privilege and position, the lower orders – with no such advantages – resorted to crime on an unparalleled scale' (Ascoli, 1979, p. 28). Despite this, by 1837 the new police were 'universally accepted' (Ascoli, 1979, p. 111).

The orthodox historians are thus unanimous in claiming the

universal benefits of the police, but some emphasise the special gains of the poor and the working class. They not only came to be protected from criminal victimisation but were prevented from sinking into crime themselves through the promotion of that 'moral improvement of the labouring classes by the exercise of supervision and restraint', which Colquhoun saw as a prime police function (Radzinowicz, 1956, p. 233).

(9) Who controlled the police?

It is a central claim of the orthodox histories that English police power is only the crystallised power of the people. This is one reason for the eagerness to stress the roots of the police in ancient traditions of communal self-policing. The police are not the police of government but of the community.

> Happily for English liberty there has never existed in this country any police force at the disposal of the central government, powerful enough to coerce the nation at large. Our national police has always been of the people and for the people. (Lee, 1901, p. 61)

Reith emphasises 'the historic tradition that the police are the public and that the public are the police' (Reith, 1956, p. 287).

Critchley more soberly rejects this idea of 'a mystical fusion between the policeman and the ordinary citizen' (Critchley, 1978, p. xviii). But both he and Ascoli emphasise that the new policing arrangements were democratically accountable: 'The device which is most characteristically English has been to arm the police with prestige rather than power, thus obliging them to rely on popular support' (Critchley, 1978, p. xviii).

The Metropolitan Police were made accountable to the Home Secretary as their police authority, to the obvious chagrin of the 'arrogant and inefficient' justices and parochial authorities whose status and power was thus undermined (Ascoli, 1979, pp. 93–5). The relationship between Home Secretary and Metropolitan Commissioner was rapidly negotiated as one in which the minister 'should deem it imprudent' to interfere in the Force's internal working over the head of the Commissioner, or in its '*operational* role' (Ascoli, 1979, pp. 106–12). The Commissioner is

> the servant of the Crown and people, answerable to Parliament, in its capacity of *vox populi*. . . . He, and every member of his force, is subject to the same law of which they are the executive arm. . . . He is, by definition, as impartial in his field as the judiciary.[3] (Ascoli, 1979, p. 11)

Mayne's victory over the attempt of Samuel Phillips, as Under-Secretary at the Home Office, to intervene more closely in police matters is seen as a triumph over 'bureaucratic arrogance'. That it left the path clear for considerable practical autonomy for the professional police Commissioner was no danger. 'Not once did Rowan and Mayne seek to abuse their power nor did they consider themselves anything other than servants of the public, with a statutory duty to preserve the King's Peace' (Ascoli, 1979, p. 112).

A measure of central direction over provincial policing arrangements marched on steadily from the 1835 Municipal Corporations Act (which required all boroughs to institute police forces). It was opposed by a continuing strain of rhetoric, denouncing each step as a sinister French, Russian or Venetian (but at any rate distinctly continental) usurpation of the traditional English rights of self-government, those 'local institutions which had been in existence since the time of King Alfred'. In the end, the 1856 Act expressed a rough balance between the continuing responsibilities of local government and justices, and a measure of central government supervision. This was exercised through the establishment of a Home Office Inspectorate of Constabulary, which had to certify a force as efficient before it could qualify for a new Exchequer grant of 25 per cent of the cost of pay and clothing.[4] In the end this proved to be a wedge with which the Home Office was able to introduce more central direction, and Chief Constables to construct a large measure of autonomy from local control. But it incorporated a balance of nominal power such that the orthodox histories can see the pattern of policing arrangements as embodying the principle of democratic accountability.

The final ingredient in popular control of the police was the strategy governing recruitment and training.

It was a deliberate policy to recruit men 'who had not the rank, habits or station of gentlemen' . . . the police was to be a homogeneous and democratic body, in tune with the people, understanding the people, belonging to the people, and drawing its strength from the people. (Critchley, 1978, p. 52, citing Gash, 1961, p. 502)

Thus the orthodox analysis maintains that the 'people' control the police. Partly this is a matter of formal channels of legal and democratic accountability. But fundamentally it derives from selecting the police in a representative way, and imbuing them with a sense that their powers derive from consent not coercion.

(10) What model of historical explanation underlies orthodox police history?

The orthodox histories operate with a model of explanation which is teleological and unilinear. By 'teleological' I mean that the underlying dynamic driving the development of the police is an assumed 'fit' between the 'new police' model and the order maintenance requirements of an industrialised, liberal-democratic society. This urges on the progressive unfolding and realisation of the police idea. But police development is not just the product of impersonal forces. The structural problems of industrialism and urbanisation constitute merely 'the *demand* for order'. The *supply* of appropriate ideas and institutions to provide the requirements for order without eroding traditional liberties came from a battery of 'far-sighted' reformers who were the per-sonalisation of national genius. The accomplishments of these perspicacious 'pioneers of policing', the Fieldings, Colquhoun, Peel, Rowan and Mayne, are celebrated in the orthodox histories (Stead, 1977). However, the 'correct' ideas of these great men (as well as the 'false' notions of the opposition) are essentially epiphenomenal. At most they oiled (or spoked) the wheels of development and speeded (or retarded) its progress.

The pattern of development is portrayed as 'unilinear', that is, it has one clear direction, and despite temporary spills and setbacks never departs from this trajectory. The irresistible force of industrialisation and its control problems, meeting the immovable object of stubborn English commitment to liberty, could result in only one outcome – the British bobby. Critchley and Radzinowicz emphasise English empirical trial and error, and the absence of tidy logicality, grand philosophical design or 'lofty constitutional principles'. But trial and error is only the specific mechanism by which the path is charted. The implicit explanation of police development is that the model which ultimately emerged (in stages, to be sure) best met the conflicting demands of order and liberty. The implicit explanatory schema is of the mutually conditioning interaction of innovative ideas and social circumstances, a sort of idealist dialectic. The works of Lee, Reith and the other simpler exponents of the orthodox view differ only in having a less complicated and conflict-ridden (i.e. less dialectical) model of straightforward idealist determination.

Having outlined the traditional view of police history, I shall turn to a similar analysis of the 'revisionist' critique which became dominant in historical work of the 1970s, contrasting its answers to the same questions. I shall suggest that while revisionism is an unequivocal advance, specifying much more concrete and precise social bases of political conflict around the police, and relating policing to a wider context, it embodies equal but opposite distortions to the orthodox account. It is a lop-sided rebuttal of cop-sided history. Historical research and understanding of policing, social control, crime and criminal justice are in a state of enormously productive ferment at present, and much more detailed knowledge is accumulating, transcending the limits of either a straightforward 'orthodox' or 'revisionist' model (Brogden, 1987; Styles, 1987; Emsley, 1991).

While the orthodox view has been usefully analysed as 'ideology as history' (Robinson, 1979), and revisionism has undeniably exposed orthodoxy's shortfalls as history, this does not dispose of it as ideology. The Reithian Police Principles (Reith, 1956, pp. 286–7) may not be or ever have been realised in practice. But they have undeniably been a significant reference point for British police thinking. Moreover, as an aspiration for what a police force should be like they ought not be dismissed too readily. A police force with the Reithian ethic as an institutional ideal to which obeisance is paid is preferable to one which is not committed explicitly to the 'transmuting of crude physical force . . . into the force . . . of public recognition' (1956).

A lop-sided view of history? The new revisionism

The model I have constructed of the traditional view is clearly an ideal-type. It synthesises the essential elements of the work of a diverse group of writers, none of whom fits the pure model in every respect. The ideal-type of 'revisionism' I am about to construct is probably even more of a 'one-sided accentuation'.[5]

The essence of revisionism is captured in the quote from Engels that heads Storch's 1975 article, the flagship of the approach.[6] 'Because the English Bourgeois finds himself reproduced in his law, as he does in his God, the policeman's truncheon . . . has for him a wonderfully soothing power. But for the workingman quite otherwise!' How does revisionism answer the same ten questions that the orthodox view addresses?

(1) *What was the source of the need for a new police?*

To industrialisation and urbanisation as the fundamental sources of the demand for a new police, revisionism adds that both processes occurred within a specifically capitalist framework. Crime and disorder, those consequences of industrialism which the traditionalists identified as the basis of the demand for order, are not hard and unequivocal categories. Each is defined variously by different political viewpoints and social classes. At the root of the new problem of order is the shifting and accentuated pattern of class division and conflict associated with the rise of capitalism, in both town and country.

The rapid growth of large cities involved the development of much greater segregation between classes. The poor areas may have generated more crime and disorder as a consequence of anonymity, demoralisation and despair. In any event the upper-class perception of routine crime altered, so that it came to seem symptomatic of a deeper threat to the social order as a whole, stemming from the 'dangerous classes', the rapidly growing urban poor (Silver, 1967, p. 3).

The meaning of collective disorder also changed: 'The market system was more allergic to rioting than any other economic system we know' (Polanyi, 1944, p. 186). Rude and Hobsbawm have both shown how until the early nineteenth century riotous protest was an accepted and mutually understood means by which the politically unrepresented masses communicated grievances to the ruling elite – 'bargaining by riot'. But with the spread of industrial capitalism riot came to be regarded not as a form of proto-democracy, but as a fundamental threat to the social and political order (Hobsbawm, 1959, p. 116; Storch, 1980, p. 34).

Capitalism also required a tighter disciplining of hitherto relatively loosely regulated aspects of social relations. 'A stable public order was a precondition of rational calculation on the part of industrial capitalists' (Spitzer and Scull, 1977a, p. 277).

The development of a formally 'free' labour market meant that the traditional practice of workers retaining some of the produce they handled had to be stopped, and replaced by the 'cash nexus' (Bunyan, 1977, p. 61). Payment in kind was redefined as theft. 'From the outset there was nothing impartial about the police. They were created to preserve for a colonial merchant and an industrial class the collective product of West Indian slavery and London wage labour' (MacDonald, 1973; Brogden, 1982, p. 55). This was part of a broader pattern of change whereby a 'moral economy', in which prices and relationships were seen as subject to traditional conceptions of justice, was replaced by a pure market economy, governed only by the impersonal laws of supply and demand (Thompson, 1971, 1975, 1992).

The new mechanised conditions of factory production also required that the formally free labour force be subject to even tighter discipline in both work and 'leisure' time to fit the rhythms and regimentation of capitalist organisation. This produced 'the criminalisation of traditional street pastimes which were solely recreational' (Cohen, 1979, pp. 120–1). The police officer became a 'domestic missionary' (Storch, 1976), 'the moral entrepreneur of public propriety' (Cohen, 1979, p. 128), charged with converting the folkways and mores of savage street-dwellers to respectability and decency.

Another consequence of stressing capitalism and class conflict over industrialism *per se* is that revisionists are able to distinguish fractions of the ruling class in a significant way. It is not just that industrial cities aggravated the control problems of an unchanged ruling class. The ruling class itself altered, with the industrial bourgeoisie gaining in significance relative to the still dominant landed gentry. The bourgeoisie and their property were more exposed to crime and disorder, less embedded in traditional social networks of deference and paternalistic personalised authority, and more reluctant to give their time or life and limb in voluntary police bodies. This points to the revisionist answer to the second question about the new police.

(2) What was wrong with the old police?

The revisionists challenge the orthodox view that the main problems with the old private enterprise police arrangements were corruption and inefficiency. There is no issue about the widespread corruption of the old justices and thief-takers (Spitzer and Scull, 1977a and b), although this is endemic in detective work and continues today (Cohen, 1979, pp. 133–4; Hobbs, 1988).

The main question, however, is about the alleged inefficiency of the old police. Several critics have discerned a scent of upper-class snobbery and condescension in the traditional knockabout humour at the expense of the old constables and Charlies (Brogden, 1982, p. 53). What is represented by respectable contemporaries as inefficiency or corruption pure and simple may have been fear of the sympathy between the old police and their own communities which made them unreliable as the policing of morality and disorder became politicised (or even in policing routine crime). Above all, the loyalty of a working-class police drawn from the local community could not be depended upon by manufacturers for controlling industrial disputes (Foster, 1974, pp. 56–61; Storch, 1975, pp. 89, 92–3; Leon, 1990, 1991). It has been suggested that similar motives stimulated the later American establishment of state police forces and the 'professionalisation' of city forces in the late nineteenth and early twentieth centuries (Robinson, 1978).

In any case, the revisionists argue that social order in the

eighteenth century was not dependent upon the direct effectiveness of the formal control apparatus (Hay, 1975b). Contrary to
the view of contemporary reformers that the eighteenth-century
criminal justice and penal systems were an antiquated and
irrational mess, a judgement which the orthodox police historians
all share, Hay argues that it was an effective system for
maintaining the stability of the old hierarchical social order. A
combination of rules and rituals emphasised both the majesty and
terror of the law (embodied above all in the 'Bloody Code' and
the ceremonials of sentencing to death and public execution, see
Linebaugh, 1991). This was combined with strict adherence to
legality (so the system symbolised impartial and formal justice).
Despite the proliferation of the death penalty for many new
offences, less than half the people condemned to death were
executed. This was precisely the nub of the utilitarian reformers'
criticism that severe nominal punishments, which were unlikely
to be carried out, were counter-productive as deterrents. Hay
turns the orthodox argument on its head. The moral bonds which
were built up between superiors and subordinates throughout the
social hierarchy by the process of interceding to seek mercy, and
the debts incurred when it was granted, cemented a social order
of small communities based on personal ties more effectively than
an efficient criminal justice system could have done. In the end
the rulers gained most from their own mercy. 'The private
manipulation of the law by the wealthy and powerful was in truth
a ruling-class conspiracy . . . [which] made it possible to govern
eighteenth-century England without a police force and without a
large army' (Hay, 1975b, pp. 52–6).

The old institutions of suppressing riot were, claim the
revisionists, counter-productive rather than ineffective for the
restoration of social stability. The traditional means of responding to collective disorder were the army, the militia (raised by
compulsory ballot of all inhabitants by the Lord Lieutenant of a
county), and volunteer forces, notably their cavalry component,
the yeomanry and special constables (Leon, 1990, 1991). The
militia was politically unreliable, as those selected often employed
deputies, who would be drawn from the same social strata as
rioters. The army was like a sledgehammer. It could only
alternate 'between no intervention and the most drastic procedures – the latter representing a declaration of internal war

with lingering consequences of hate and resentment' (Silver, 1967, p. 12). Moreover, as soldiers were also drawn from the poor they were politically unreliable on occasion (Stevenson, 1977, pp. 33–4). The volunteer forces, especially the yeomanry, had been *politically* dependable. But urban bourgeois manufacturers were less ready to answer a call to arms – 'the classic confrontation of an agrarian military tradition and a pacific commercial and industrial one' (Silver, 1967, p. 10). Not only were the manufacturers less personally valorous than their hunting and shooting rural counterparts. They saw that 'the use of social and economic superiors as police exacerbated rather than mollified class violence' (*ibid.*, p. 10). As the 1839 Royal Commission on the Rural Constabulary put it: 'the animosities created or increased, and rendered permanent by arming master against servant, neighbour against neighbour, by triumph on the one side and failure on the other, were even more deplorable than the outrages actually committed.' This motivated the establishment of a 'bureaucratic police system that . . . drew attack and animosity upon itself, and seemed to separate the assertion of "constitutional" authority from that of social and economic dominance' (*ibid.*, pp. 11–12).

Finally, the new manufacturing and merchant urban bourgeoisie lacked certain protections against crime which the rural gentry enjoyed. They did not have the ecological safeguards of large estates and lack of proximity to the 'dangerous classes' (Brogden, 1982, pp. 49–50). Nor did they enjoy the services of private retainers and guards. Finally their capital took the form of movable merchandise and machinery, much more vulnerable to theft or damage.

In short, the revisionist view emphasises not so much the intrinsic ineffectiveness of the old privatised policing as its growing unsuitability for the new class relations of a capitalist society.

(3) What were the motives for police reform?

The immediate motives for establishing the new police were to the revisionists the same as in the orthodox account, but with the emphasis and prime mover reversed. The basic cause of increasing disorder was capitalist development. This disrupted existing social networks, destroyed moral communities, replaced personal bonds by the cash nexus, and caused immense deprivation and demoralisation. We have noted that the official crime statistics which began to be published in the early nineteenth century register an upward trend, and this continues until a peak in the 1840s. Between 1805 and 1942 the rate of committals for trial went up four and a half times, and the absolute numbers seven times (Gatrell and Hadden, 1972, pp. 372–4). However, the revisionists question how much of this was a genuine increase in criminality, and how much was due to changed sensitivities, penal reform, the availability of police, and other factors leading to a greater propensity to prosecute offences.

What is certainly true is that many respectable and influential contemporary commentators took the figures as indicating that 'the progress of wickedness is so much more rapid than the increase of the numbers of people' that a new police was needed to deal with it. Police reform was part of a much broader rationalisation of the penal code, punishment (the use of prison as the standard mode), criminal procedure and the prosecution process, as well as other aspects of social policy with a control element (Donajgrodski, 1977a and b; Philips, 1980).

But while the crime panic engendered by the rise of capitalism is recognised by the revisionists as a factor in police reform, it is subordinated to the more general demand for moral and political order, reversing the orthodox priorities. 'The existence of the modern police force owes little to the exigencies of combating professional crime and was developed primarily as an instrument of political control and labour discipline' (Hirst, 1975, p. 225).

However, the crucial reason for the creation of the new police is seen as neither crime control, moral discipline nor riot control *per se*. It was the need for a force which could stabilise relations between conflicting social classes as far as this was possible. Therefore the police were charged with an 'omnibus mandate' of regulating all facets of working-class life (Storch, 1975, p. 88; Brogden, 1982, pp. 53–71). In the revisionist view, then, the motive for formation of the new police was the maintenance of the order required by the capitalist class, with control of crime,

riot, political dissidence and public morality being separate
subsidiary facets of this overall mission.

(4) Who opposed the new police?

Opposition to the new police came partly from sections of the
upper class. But this was not irrational obscurantism, as the
orthodox histories imply. The source of ruling-class opposition
was a distinct sector of the class, the landed gentry, and was
perfectly rational in basis. The gentry did not need to support a
public police out of rate-payers' money, when their own security
was adequately protected by privatised means. They could rely
on 'large numbers of personal servants to guard their plate and
their wives' (Hay, 1975b, p. 59). Furthermore, their local
political power-bases would be undermined by a more rationalised and professional police, for they controlled the magistracy
which was the focal point of the old system. This remained a
strong strand of the opposition to each increment of standardisation from 1829 to 1856, and accounts for the form that local
police authorities ultimately took. Furthermore, the development
of a more rationalised system of crime control would rupture the
delicately constructed relationships of deference and condescension which were the microscopic basis of order. The gentry could
expatiate high-mindedly on the threat to traditional liberties
posed by the importation of French, Russian or Prussian-
influenced policing schemes, and scoff at the evidence of the
volume of mere larceny assembled by Colquhoun and Peel
(Palmer, 1976, pp. 11–16).
　But if initial opposition to the police did come from the landed
gentry, this evaporated as the threat of Chartism grew. Later
upper-class opposition was over the specific form and control of
the police rather than the principle itself (Storch, 1980, p. 34;
Brogden, 1982, p. 56).
　The deepest source of opposition to the new police came from
the working class, both before and after the inception of
professional policing. This was only indirectly reflected in
parliament, for the working class did not have the vote. But in
places with class-conscious working-class majorities, such as

Oldham after 1832, and the enfranchisement of the petty bourgeoisie 'who were dependent on working-class custom', pressure could be put upon MPs to achieve a measure of indirect parliamentary representation (Foster, 1974, pp. 52–4). This was used to oppose all the Police Bills of the period, the Oldham MPs invoking the standard libertarian rhetoric about 'tyranny', and describing the police as 'an unconstitutional force so palpably for the express purpose of coercing the people' (Foster, 1974, pp. 69–70).

But the prime arenas for working-class opposition to the police were extra-parliamentary. It was expressed in collective disorder and small-scale street conflicts. Storch has detailed graphically the numerous anti-police riots that followed the coming of the 'plague of blue locusts' to working-class communities in the North (Storch, 1975, p. 94).

(5) *How long did opposition to the police last?*

Whereas in the orthodox histories initial working-class opposition to the police disappeared fairly rapidly after the advent of the new police, the revisionists trace a line of intermittent overt hostility (expressing continuous latent conflict) right down to the 1981 street battles. Conflict was only attenuated, not ended, once the police became established (Storch, 1975, pp. 106–8).

Cohen discerns the same 'ancient tradition of collective self-defence' against police interventions into street life in the London of the early 1900s. During the 1920s, overt physical conflict between the police and the working class as a whole came to be replaced by a perennial hostility between the police and working-class male youth, which continues today (Cohen, 1979, pp. 120–1; see also White, 1986).

Brogden documents a similar

> residue of continuing, if spasmodic conflict between the police institution and the lower orders. . . . For the . . . participants in the street economy . . . attitudes to the police institution throughout the first century of policing remained essentially unchanged. They were subject to continuing, occasional, and apparently arbitrary 'culls'. (Brogden, 1982, pp. 180–1)

He traces a direct line from the nineteenth-century anti-police riots in Liverpool to Toxteth in 1981: 'The composition and objectives of the street combatants of July, 1981 replicates the sentiments of those earlier anti-police demonstrations' (*ibid.*, pp. 241–2). While relations between the regularly employed, respectable and organised sections of the working class and the police were not characterised by open conflict to the same degree, approval was tentative and brittle, with many violent and bitter struggles in the first two decades of this century between police and strikers (*ibid.*, pp. 186–9). Brogden's recent oral history of inter-war policing on Merseyside reveals such conflicts vividly (Brogden, 1991).

(6) What was new about the 'new police'?

To the revisionists, the novelty of the 'new' police was not efficiency or integrity. The revisionists are more sceptical both about the poor press accorded the 'old' police and the laurels heaped on their successors. Individual ineffectiveness, indiscipline and corruption remain endemic amongst modern police officers. The novelty of the 'new' police was that they were a bureaucratically organised force charged with a mandate to 'prevent' crime by regular patrol and surveillance of the whole society (but especially the denizens of the 'dangerous classes' – St James was to be guarded by watching St Giles). Intermittent and spasmodic law enforcement dependent upon private initiative was replaced by continuous state policing financed by the public purse. Control dependent upon legitimation by particularistic traditions of personal deference was displaced by impersonal authority legitimated by values of legal rationality and universalism. '[T]he bureaucratization of police work placed day-to-day operations of the control system in the hands of faceless agents of the state, men who no longer operated in their own self-interest, but (presumably) in the general interest' (Spitzer and Scull, 1977a, pp. 280–1).

With this notion of a sharp break between old and new, the revisionists rebut the orthodox mythology of fundamental continuity between the modern constable and antique traditions of tribal self-policing. His position has been transformed by new legal powers and by becoming a member of a large, disciplined and technologically advanced organisation.

(7) What was the social impact of the new police?

In the revisionist account the advent of modern professional policing transformed the social order into a 'policed society'. This 'is unique in that central power exercises potentially violent supervision over the population by bureaucratic means widely diffused throughout civil society in small and discretionary operations that are capable of rapid concentration' (Silver, 1967, p. 8). The net result was the penetration of society by the political and moral authority of the dominant strata, the construction of an essentially manipulated (and thus vulnerable) consensus.

The new police constituted part of a move to a more centralised social order, in which the state penetrated the depths of society, spearheaded by the police institution. But for the police to operate as the advance scouts of the state implies an imperative of some integration with the policed. The consent which they have to negotiate is perennially tenuous and liable to be disrupted in times of crisis when the coercive reality of the police again comes to the fore (Silver, 1967, pp. 15, 20–4; Storch, 1975, pp. 107–8; Cohen, 1979, pp. 128–36; Brogden, 1982, pp. 236–7). In normal times, however, the police paint a surface gloss of serenity on the rotting fabric of capitalism.

(8) Who gained from the new police?

Revisionism stands on its head the orthodox conception of universal benefits from policing, with special gains to the poor and weak. The beneficiaries of the new police are seen as the bourgeoisie who established them, and the police themselves who have carved out opportunities for social advancement and greater power. The bourgeoisie gained most from the new police, who protected their property, safeguarded their security and stabilised the social order on which their power and position was based (Bunyan, 1977, pp. 63–4; Brogden, 1982, p. 71).

The petty bourgeoisie, particularly shopkeepers, have also been identified as benefiting especially from the new police, who protected them from depredation and economic competition from the lower strata involved in the street economy (Brogden, 1982, pp. 182–3). This particular view is largely shared by the orthodox historians. The middle classes are seen as beneficiaries of policing in all historical work (D. Jones, 1983, p. 165).

Finally, creation of the new police opened up an avenue of social mobility to those working-class men who were prepared to endure the hostility of their erstwhile fellows. As the police occupation gained some measure of professional stability it began to draw in working men who were attracted by the middle-class image of respectability and a career (Cohen, 1979, pp. 134–4; Steedman, 1984, Part 2). The Chief Constables (who in the county forces often were ex-army officers) became powerful figures with a considerable measure of autonomy over an important area of local policy (Brogden, 1982, pp. 70–1; Steedman, 1984, pp. 41–55).

(9) Who controlled the new police?

The one thing on which revisionism is agreed is that 'the people' did *not* control the police. But there is some debate about whether or not the provincial police were controlled by the local elite (or in the case of the Metropolitan Police by the Home Secretary). As has been indicated earlier, the Home Secretary nominally has control over the Metropolitan Police as its police authority. But from early on the Commissioners were conceded a large discretion to determine the conduct of the force. The Commissioners also successfully fended off control attempts from the existing magistracy. However, the relationship between the Home Office and the Commissioner continued (and continues) to be ill-defined, with, for example, a prolonged argument between the Home Secretary and Commissioner in 1886–7 over the issue of the policing of demonstrations in Trafalgar Square (Bailey, 1981b, pp. 94–125).

Most of the discussion among revisionists centres on the degree of control of police by local elites in the counties (through the magistracy) and in boroughs (through the Watch Committee). The two positions on these issues reflect wider theoretical differences between an 'instrumentalist' conception of the police as 'tools' of the dominant class and a 'structuralist' account of policing as a function of the political economy.

Foster implies an instrumentalist view in his description of the struggles over control of the police in Lancashire between the working-class movement and the manufacturers in the first three decades of the nineteenth century. When local constables were controlled by the town vestry in Oldham, or by the Police Commission following the 1826 Oldham Police Act, they were exposed to popular pressure. However, the 1839 County Police Act placed control of the police into the hands of the magistracy, and the police became a weapon of the employers. The rules of conduct for the new force laid down that policemen should be 'non-political', that is, insulated from the earlier form of popular control (Foster, 1974, pp. 56–61).

The clear import of Foster's account is that the police were under the control of the police authorities, and the question was, who dominated the authority? After 1839 power over the police shifted decisively to the bourgeoisie. Storch also suggests an instrumentalist view when he attributes the 'implantation of a modern police in the industrial districts of Northern England' to 'a new consensus among the propertied classes that it was necessary to create a professional, bureaucratically organised lever of urban discipline' (Storch, 1975, p. 86; a similar position is argued in Bunyan, 1977, pp. 60–2).

The structuralist account is put most clearly by Spitzer and Scull (1977a and b), Cohen (1979) and Brogden (1982).[7] One of the main theses of Brogden's book is that, contrary to the weight of both orthodox and radical received opinion, Chief Constables achieved a large measure of autonomy very early on after the establishment of the new police. This was true not only of county forces, whose Chief Constables had overt control over policing, but also of boroughs, where Chief Constables were supposed to be under the direction of the Watch Committee (a similar position is advanced in Jefferson and Grimshaw, 1984b). In the case of Liverpool, Brogden's material indicates that the Head Constable began to show a measure of independence from the Watch Committee as early as 1841 (five years after the force was established), and by the end of the century had achieved 'considerable latitude of decision-making'. However, Liverpool may well have been a special case: it was one of the largest borough forces, and Brogden emphasises the peculiarities of the local political economy. Moreover, it is Brogden's thesis that the organisational autonomy constructed by the Chief Constable was a relative one. Neither Chief Constable nor local elite are regarded as having much freedom of manoeuvre as both were constrained by the exigencies of the political economy. Thus Brogden refers to the oft-cited instance of the 1890 Watch Committee instruction to the Head Constable Captain Nott-Bower to 'proceed against all brothels'. This order is usually invoked to demonstrate Watch Committee control. Brogden argues the episode shows the opposite. Not only was it an isolated occurrence, but the Chief Constable could within a year revert to the old approach because the strict prosecution policy had such damaging effects on trade. But what Brogden illustrates is not so much the autonomy of the Chief Constable, as that both he and the Watch Committee are just bearers of structural imperatives (Brogden, 1982, p. 69).

However, while the revisionists may argue about the precise relations of local elite and police chief, and of both to the political economy, they are united in denying the orthodox claim that the new police were subject to popular control.

(10) What model of historical explanation underlies revisionism?

The revisionist account is just as much a teleological and unilinear one as the orthodox history. This is true of both the instrumentalist and structuralist versions. In the instrumentalist variant, the ruling class is induced to establish the police by the perceived 'fit' between the police and the control requirements of capitalism (as distinct from industrialism *per se*). 'The genius of the British ruling class is that they realised the need to have such a force and set about creating it' (MacDonald, 1973, cited in Bunyan, 1977, p. 62).

In the structuralist account the link between the exigencies of capitalism and police development is not necessarily mediated by a clear ruling-class perception of this purpose. But there is the same notion of an inexorable drive along only one possible trajectory. The working-class resistance which revisionists admiringly celebrate is none the less seen as doomed to romantic failure. The ideas of the opposition (laudable) or the proponents of police reform (oppressive) are ultimately epiphenomenal. The real dynamic is the unfolding requirements of capital. To the idealist dialectic of the orthodox view is counterposed a materialist dialectic of a similarly deterministic kind.

Orthodoxy and revisionism: critique and synthesis

In many respects revisionism constitutes an unequivocal advance in our understanding of the emergence of the new police. Above all, it is located in a broader analysis of the social conflicts and in particular the class and power structure of the eighteenth and nineteenth centuries. This is hardly surprising for it is largely the work of professional historians sharing a wider concern for social, economic and political history. However, the revisionist view is in many respects merely an inversion of the traditional approach. To the latter's uncritical consensus model it opposes an equally one-sided conflict perspective. Just as the orthodox historians, faced with evidence of hostility and opposition to the police, dismiss this as malevolent or misguided, so too the revisionists, confronted with apparent periods and pockets of working-class consent to policing, regard this as manipulated, a brittle skin over a bubbling volcano of resentment. To the revisionists, conflict between police and the working class in a capitalist society has structural roots, so periods of social integration can only be an artificially constructed, temporary truce. On the other hand, in the traditionalist analysis a liberal democratic industrial society is structurally integrated, so social conflict can only be a superficial phenomenon (and is often regarded as manipulated by agitation – a counterpart to the revisionist conception of an artificially constructed ideological consent and creation of false consciousness). I shall critically evaluate the orthodox and revisionist analyses in terms of the ten dimensions in which I compared them, suggesting a more complex picture than the unilinear development of policing implied by both approaches.

I shall start with question 10, the basic model of historical explanation, as the logically prior issue. Both the orthodox and revisionist approaches assume a 'fit' between the type of police system and the control requirements of an industrial or capitalist society. It is these conditions, not of their own making, which call into being the actions of the men who make their own history by creating a new police force. The ultimate question is whether a complex modern industrial society could exist without some sort of police force, in the minimal sense of a body of people mandated to intervene in situations potentially requiring the exercise of legitimate force. This is an essentially metaphysical issue, dependent upon conceptions of human nature, the 'iron laws' of social interaction and organisation (if any), views of morality, justice, and even deeper matters of ultimate ends, meaning and the nature of being – the province of religious belief. Anthropological evidence clearly documents small-scale societies without police, and the police function has complex conditions of emergence (Robinson and Scaglion, 1987). In my judgement it seems utopian to suppose that we could do without a police force in any conceivable large-scale and complex industrial social order, whether or not it was capitalist. (Perhaps I am a victim of 'police fetishism', a special case of 'legal fetishism'; see Collins, 1982, pp. 10–14.) But, even if some police force is seen as necessary in the last analysis, it does not follow that alternative lines of development were impossible (D. Jones, 1983, p. 157). I shall duck the task of constructing a 'counterfactual' history of the police (Emsley, 1983, p. 163); but let us consider just one or two possibilities.

Is it conceivable that Peel might not have been able to pilot the 1829 Act so skilfully through parliament? After all, most histories do express surprise that following so many decades of opposition, the Act was finally passed as smoothly as it was. It may be granted that the metropolis would eventually have needed a new police. But by the time that eventuality materialised, perhaps the reformed parliament would have taken a different view of making the Home Secretary the police authority? Perhaps it would have wanted to include a measure of local elected representation for the police authority – no taxation without representation.[8] This would have greatly altered the pattern of present controversies. Or we can contemplate a rather different counter-factual. Is it not conceivable that those contemporaries who pressed for a more militaristic response to the industrial and political disturbances during the post-Napoleonic War and Reform Bill crises could have carried the day?[9] Then we might not now speak of England's comparative uniqueness in not having a 'third force' explicitly specialised for suppressing riots, and of its relatively benign tradition in crowd control. Once it is conceded that the path of development was not tightly predetermined, then our perspective on all the other questions shifts. Above all, the ideas and arguments of contemporaries assume a new significance as independent sources of influence, not just more or less wise or misguided epiphenomena hastening or hindering, but not diverting, the course of history. Furthermore, while these ideas and arguments are related to class position, and broadly limited by structural constraints generated by the political economy, they are not foreordained by them. Nor are people's strategies necessarily the best for their interests.[10] It is in this light that I shall turn to the other nine questions about the emergence of the police, and try and construct a critical synthesis, which must perforce be tentative in the light of the enormous amount of on-going research on each topic (Emsley, 1991 is a comprehensive, state-of-the-art account of current historical research).

(1) What was the source of the need for a new police?

The police are needed to deal with conflicts, disorders and problems of coordination which are necessarily generated by any complex and materially advanced social order. The orthodox histories (and undoubtedly many police officers themselves) see these as stemming from a perennial and asocial struggle

between good and evil (Robinson, 1979). To deny the reality of
the evil deeds which big city police confront every day would be
to invite the opprobrium that practical police officers, who are in
the 'tomorrow business', rightly heap on armchair academic
utopians. None the less many of the personal or group conflicts
they confront are rooted in structural contradictions and
problems which are inevitable in any advanced society, capitalist
or socialist (Hirst, 1979). The most fundamental difficulty in
analysing and dealing with policing in a capitalist society is that
the police have the inextricably dual function of handling troubles
derived both from the problems of *any* industrial society *and*
from its specifically capitalist form (Marenin, 1983, 1985). The
Reithians neglect the latter dimension, the implication of the
police in structural conflicts associated with particular relationships of class and privilege. But the revisionists push aside the
aspects of policing concerned with universal interests in social
order, cohesion and protection, falsely implying 'that all social
relations can be described in the language of power and
domination' (Ignatieff, 1983, p. 101). This railroads any actually
experienced sense of the morality, justice, necessity or mere
secular usefulness of legal rules and the means of their
enforcement into a falsely conscious acceptance of dominant
ideology. What is needed is a neo-Reithianism which neither
writes off the police as 'conning bastards' nor as all sweetness and
light. Problems of inter-personal offending and political conflict
would be engendered by the pressures of industrialisation and
urbanisation whatever the social framework, but in early
nineteenth-century England they took the concrete form of class
conflict in capitalism – although intra-class victimisation must not
be overlooked. However, this sort of overarching perspective
only has the propaedeutic function of pointing our attention in a
certain direction. To further assist our enquiries we must proceed
to the interrogation of the usual suspects.

(2) What was wrong with the old police?

The orthodox histories depict the old control institutions as
corrupt and inefficient; the revisionists portray them as effective

in maintaining ruling-class hegemony in the eighteenth century precisely through a lack of technical rationality. What seems to be agreed is that the old institutions were ineffective in a direct instrumental sense.

Recent research has cast doubt on the received certainties of both sides of the debate (Storch, 1989). Styles has shown that some at any rate of the provincial justices could be assiduous and effective detectives (Styles, 1982). John Fielding grew impatient at the reluctance of many local justices to cooperate with his schemes to develop a centrally coordinated information system for tracking down fugitives. But he took a purely national perspective, which failed to recognise the rationality and adequacy of the local arrangements for law enforcement, which were a multi-purpose administrative apparatus. 'Thus what appears from one perspective as a characteristically eighteenth-century failure to adopt sensible reforms offering efficient policing, emerges from another as a concern to ensure what is best described as policing appropriate to local circumstances' (Styles, 1983, p. 149).

Nor were the existing forms of riot control as ineffective, either technically or politically, as the orthodox and revisionist cases suggest. In particular, both the army and local magistrates seemed to be quite adept in many instances at cooling down potential disorder, and special constables were enrolled at times of extra pressure (Leon, 1990, 1991). In the longer term, philanthropy and poor relief were often mobilised to reduce the tensions generating disorder. Altogether it might be more appropriate to ask why in the acute economic distress and upheaval of the early nineteenth century, and with the revolutionary ideological example of France, there was not *more* political turbulence than there was. If the fear of riot and the 'dangerous classes' was as acute as both orthodox and revisionist historians suggest, then the long delay in police reform remains a baffling mystery. 'A large-scale police force was not created in England before 1829 because the authorities were confident that they could maintain public order using the old system, with *ad hoc* modifications. In this they were more justified than has often been allowed' (Stevenson, 1977, pp. 47–8).

Hay's analysis of the eighteenth-century criminal justice system has been challenged by recent research. Styles (1977) points out

that the proliferation of new capital statutes (especially the Black
Act) which Hay, Thompson and the other revisionists see as the
spearhead of an 'extending tyranny of exclusive property' were
the least used of all capital statues. Furthermore, Hay and his
associates emphasise those criminal activities 'which involved a
clear conflict of interpretation between authority and local
communities', such as blacking, poaching and smuggling, rather
than the routine thefts and assaults which were the bulk of
prosecuted criminal offences, and over which there might have
been more general consensus. The nub of Styles' critique is that
Hay and his associates have not adequately explored the diversity
and complexity of eighteenth-century criminal activity and public
reactions to it. They are too ready to impart to the eighteenth
century somewhat premature notions of 'class conflict' and
'resistance' (Styles, 1977, pp. 979–81).

Brewer and Styles' important collection confirms Hay's account
of the highly discretionary character of eighteenth-century
criminal law, and the ideological significance of 'the rule of law'.
But they qualify the picture of it as a unilateral weapon of the
ruling class. The judicial process *could* be used as a class tool,
and to legitimate existing social arrangements or changes desired
by the patrician class. As in any legal order, its benefits were
disproportionately available to those with the greatest means.
'But this does not mean that we should regard the seventeenth-
and eighteenth-century legal process as simply an instrument of
an elite, or as serving only a class function' (Brewer and Styles,
1980, p. 19). Men from all classes, apart from the notable
exception of the labouring poor, were involved in the workings of
a citizen judiciary (*ibid.*, p. 20). Even the grievances of the poor
tended to be expressed in terms of authority's dereliction of legal
duty, rather than a challenge to authority *per se*.

King's analysis of prosecutions at Essex quarter sessions in the
late eighteenth century confirms and extends these points. He
finds that 'the key decision-maker in the eighteenth-century
criminal law was the victim himself.' Moreover, those bringing
prosecutions for property crime were overwhelmingly from 'the
middling sort' and artisans, but the unpropertied labouring poor
also resorted extensively to the law as victims of theft and assault.
He suggests that the pardoning prerogative was exercised
according to consistent criteria of merit and justice, rather than

used as an arbitrary or biased tool of the powerful. King is not suggesting that a consensus view of eighteenth-century society should be reverted to, or that the gentry lacked social power. Rather he is presenting a more pluralistic picture of the criminal law 'as a multiple-use right within which the various groups in eighteenth-century society conflicted with, and co-operated with and gained concessions from each other' (King, 1984, pp. 57–8).

Langbein (1983) has launched the most vitriolic onslaught yet on Hay's 'fatal flaws'. He partly relies on his own data from mid-century Old Bailey cases, which suggest that 'we often cross a class line when we move from the offender to his victim, but not a class gulf'. He also points out that part of the reason for the apparently massive increase in separate capital property offences was the low level of principled and systematic codification of English law. Many apparently new laws were really only marginal extensions of existing statutes to closely analogous cases. The over-representation of the poor as defendants is not an indication of the intrinsic class character of the law or criminal justice system, but of the way that universal law impartially applied in an unequal society mirrors that inequality. 'To seize upon that as the *raison d'être* of the criminal justice system is, however, to mistake the barnacles for the boat' (Langbein, 1983, p. 120).

In sum, then, recent historical work suggests a much more complex view of the 'old' policing arrangements than either the orthodox or revisionist police historians do. The eighteenth-century criminal justice system was enormously diverse and discretionary, but not as ineffective as earlier writers have suggested. Nor was it the unilateral weapon of the ruling class portrayed by revisionism. Whatever motivated the establishment of the new police it was not the patent breakdown or inadequacy of the old.

(3) What were the motives for police reform?

The motive stressed by the police reformers, notably Peel in his introduction of the 1829 Metropolitan Police Bill in parliament, was fear of rising crime. But whether or not crime *was* increasing was unclear to contemporary opinion. The official statistics for committals to trial certainly registered an apparently inexorable upward trend. But there were those even in the 1829 debates who challenged the validity of these figures in the light of the greater ease of prosecution since the 1750s (Philips, 1980, pp. 179–80). By the time we come to the debates on the 1839 and 1856 Bills opponents were ready to jump in with the obvious argument that the police reformers were using rising crime statistics to justify the extension of a preventive police, the efficacy of which was called into question by those very figures. Chadwick and the other opponents of police reform were forced to abandon the numbers game (Watts-Miller, 1987, pp. 43–7).

Nor does the contemporary argument that whatever the quantity of crime, it was of a more serious nature – the work of a growing professional criminal class – derive much sustenance from recent evidence. Outside London there is little indication that offending was the work of people rationally exploiting crime for a livelihood, or making rich pickings out of their offences. On the other hand, the revisionist notion of 'social' crime as proto-political protest is also hard to sustain. Recent research suggests that most offences were 'prosaic and undramatic, involving small amounts being stolen, squalid robberies, burglaries and assaults . . . nor are there visible indications of social purpose, still less of the individualistic waging of the class war, behind most "normal" criminal acts' (Philips, 1977, pp. 286–7; see also Bailey, 1980, p. 36).

The 1856 Bill was motivated partly by dread of vagrant criminality associated with the end of the Crimean War and the prospect of a footloose army of unemployed returning soldiers. There was also apprehension that the end of transportation meant that 'an organised race of criminals' released on tickets-of-leave would roam the countryside (Steedman, 1984, p. 25). But these fears were only able to overcome concern about threats to liberty and rate-payers' purses after two abortive Police Bills had been defeated in 1854 and 1855, and after much parliamentary shenanigans and wheeler-dealing. Evidently the threat to social order posed by crime cannot have been so clearly overwhelming as either the police reformers (or the orthodox and revisionist histories) imply.

The same qualifications must be levelled at the fear of political and social disorder, which the revisionists see as the primary motive for police reform. True, reference to riot was not (as the orthodox view has it) entirely absent from Peel's 1829 parliamentary presentation (he raised it in debate, although not his introductory speech). The disorders associated with Chartism were certainly very much at the forefront of the 1838 debates. But even here there was a strong current of influential contemporary opinion agreeing with Disraeli that expanding the police throughout the provinces amounted to a declaration of civil war against the people and would be counter-productive. Social harmony could be restored only by the privileged part of the nation once more recognising their duties to the second nation (Watts-Miller, 1987, pp. 47–8).

Whatever fears for the survival of the social order there might have been, even at the height of Chartist agitation, these were not sufficient to overcome the traditional suspicion and miserliness of over half the counties of England and Wales, who refused to utilise the possibility of establishing a rural constabulary allowed by the 1839 Act. Nor was there any clear relationship discernible between counties which had experienced riots and those which had not in their readiness to institute a new police (Emsley, 1983, pp. 70–1).

Monkkonen has made similar points about the parallel thesis that the American city police were a straightforward response to rising crime or political and class conflict: 'If each city had adopted a uniformed police only after a riot, changing crime rate, or the need for a new kind of class-control agency, many places would not today have a uniformed police' (Monkkonen, 1981, p. 57). Rather, he argues 'growth of uniformed urban police forces should be seen simply as a part of the growth of urban service bureaucrats' (*ibid.*, p. 55). There is evidence that the establishment of the English provincial police was to some extent a product of a similar process of diffusion of models of rationalised urban administration (Emsley, 1983, pp. 78–81; D. Jones, 1983, pp. 157–9; Wells, 1991). A detailed study of the development of the Portsmouth police suggests, for example, that it was not the product of any pressure for reform arising out of crime or disorder, and the local elite were well satisfied with the old policing arrangements. The Portsmouth police were a part of the national process of spreading Whig conceptions of rationalised local government (embodied in the 1835 Municipal Corporations Act) which made all boroughs like Portsmouth establish a Watch Committee and 'new' police force (Field, 1981, pp. 42–8).

In short, the police reformers certainly perceived the threats of crime and disorder which both orthodox and revisionist historians pick out as the motives for police reform. But influential sections of the elite did not share this panic. The entrepreneurial activities of the reformers who became dominant in central government, and the diffusion of their model of rational local government administration, play a large part in explaining the setting-up of the new police throughout Britain. It was not an automatic reflex of urbanisation and industrial capitalism (Hart, 1978; Emsley, 1983, pp. 161–2, 1991; D. Jones, 1983, pp. 156–9).

(4) *Who opposed the new police?*

The revisionist critique of orthodoxy's dismissal of opposition to the police as misguided or malicious is confirmed by subsequent research. Weinberger has given the most thorough recent analysis of the varying currents of opposition to policing:

> In the 1830s and 1840s opposition to the new police was part of a 'rejectionist' front ranging from Tory to gentry to working-class radicals against an increasing number of government measures seeking to regulate and control more and more aspects of productive and social life. (Weinberger, 1981, p. 66)

The reasons for upper- and middle-class opposition encompassed fears for traditional civil liberties, apprehension about central government encroachment in local affairs, and resentment at the expense to rate-payers. Working-class hostility was roused by police intervention in recreational activities, and the use of the police to control industrial and political reform organisation.

Detailed analyses of the various parliamentary debates about the new police do suggest, however, that the complex and diverse currents of opinion among the propertied classes represented there do not fall neatly into any clear-cut politics of class interests. Whereas the manufacturers had perhaps more need for a new police than the gentry (as the revisionists argue) they were more influential in local borough government than at Westminster, so had an interest in resisting centralising measures like the 1856 Act (and *a fortiori* its two abortive predecessors). Above all, however, a close reading of the debates suggests the importance of varying political philosophies and principles which were not reducible neatly to sectional interest (Hart, 1978). Moreover, many contemporaries, lacking the benefits of hindsight (or perhaps even if they had them!), were genuinely unsure about the validity of conflicting arguments about the efficacy or counter-productiveness of new policing arrangements for crime control, social harmony and political order. Fears about threats to liberty, concern about fiscal prudence, anxieties about local democratic accountability of the police, were neither irrational nor readily correlated with identifiable sectional interest. But these partly independent conflicting ideological currents – misguided, laudable, or whatever – shaped not only the pace but the pattern of police reform.

(5) How long did opposition persist?

The evidence of sustained anti-police hostility and violence which the revisionists have accumulated is certainly sufficient to dispel the orthodox notion of easy and early acceptance of the new police by the mass of the population. But the revisionists err in the opposite way, neglecting the clear evidence of growing acquiescence and indeed support for the police amongst a broad section of the working class, as well as the middle class. In many places the police came to be accepted and used by sections of the working class quite soon after their inception. Nor can this be put down to their 'service' activities stitching a velvet glove of superficial acquiescence over the reality of the iron fist of repression (although the 'service' role of the police *was* significant – see Emsley, 1983, pp. 146–7, 158–9).

This is brought out clearly in Philips' (1977) study of the early years of the new police in the Black Country. Philips demonstrates that in many ways the police were resented by the working class. The incursion of the new police on working-class leisure activities through the enforcement of public order offences, or the use of the police by industrialists to control strikes and redefine traditional popular conceptions of the legitimacy of workers' 'perks' as pilfering, caused considerable disgruntlement. But it would be quite wrong to suggest that this amounted to a rejection of the legitimacy of the police. Analysis of the data on the social position of those victims who prosecuted offenders at quarter sessions in the 1830s and 1850s shows that although retail traders and industrial entrepreneurs were the most common prosecutors, a significant proportion of prosecutions (varying between 28 and 50 per cent) were brought by unskilled working-class people. Most assaults and property offences (then as now) were committed by working-class offenders against working-class victims. And although (for a variety of reasons) many victims did not prosecute, others did. There is certainly strong evidence here that many working-class people accepted the basic legitimacy of the laws protecting property, and the agents who enforced them, however much they may have resented certain specific aspects of property law (notably the Game Laws) which were clearly class-biased in intent and practice (Philips, 1977, pp. 123–9; Emsley, 1983, pp. 158–60; D. Jones, 1983, pp. 166–7). The working-class attitude to the law and its enforcement was clearly complex and ambivalent, and varied between different times and places. But there seems to have been in many areas as early as the 1850s a large measure of working-class assent to the basic legitimacy of the legal order, based not on ideological manipulation but on the use of its coercive aspects by working-class victims against offenders. Nor was the 'domestic missionary' role of the police uniformly resented by the working class. Some radical leaders, and the emerging 'respectable' working-class strata, saw control of 'the most dissolute and abandoned' habits of the rougher elements as not only an immediate menace in everyday life, but a threat to the political and social advance of the whole class (Emsley, 1983, pp. 157–8; Ignatieff, 1983, pp. 90–2; D. Jones, 1983, p. 166). By the 1870s it seems that the police had attained a large measure of legitimacy in the eyes of the working class, even though this could be readily disrupted by specific actions, such as stricter enforcement of the vagrancy or licensing laws (Weinberger, 1981, pp. 88–9). But the rhetoric of resentment against individual practices came to be couched in the terms of the system itself rather than a rejection of its legitimacy.

From opposing the very idea of a policed society, radical critics had
come to judge the police by those abstract standards laid down by the
system's pioneers; judicious discretion mixed with firm impartiality in
enforcing laws that were often blatantly biassed against working
people. (Field, 1981, p. 59)

(6) What was new about the new police?

Recent local research on several provincial forces suggests that
often the 'new' police were not very new. There were many
transitional policing innovations which paved the way.

In the provinces some towns and counties had small constabularies established by particular statutes in the 1820s, for
example under the Oldham Police Act 1826 and Cheshire Police
Act 1829. More generally, the Lighting and Watching Act 1833
enabled rate-payers to set up their own police forces independently of local justices and their old constables, and several small
town parishes utilised this Act. Davey's vivid account of the
Horncastle force shows that it was able to satisfy most of the
townspeople (who governed the force through an elected
Inspectorate) by successfully controlling the routine crime and
public disorder which worried respectable citizens (Davey, 1983).
By the time of the debates preceding the 1856 Act which did
away with these small independent forces, the argument was
about the distribution of costs and control of the professional
police, not the principle itself. The effectiveness of these local
forces has been minimised by orthodox historians, who see them
through the perspective which Chadwick foisted on the Parliamentary Commissioners in 1839 and 1853 with his creation of
the migrant criminal myth, implying the need for more
centralised policing.

In many provincial forces, despite the establishment of
nominally 'new' police as a result of the 1835 Municipal
Corporations Act, 'policing hardly changed . . . the paid watch
simply became the paid police' (Emsley, 1983, p. 68; see also
Field, 1981, pp. 43–7). Similar conclusions have been drawn
about the Rural Constabulary Act 1839. This left it to county
magistrates to determine whether or not to establish a force, and

if they decided to, who the Chief Constable would be, and the size of the force (up to a ratio of not more than 1 policeman per 1,000 population). Less than half of the counties of England and Wales took advantage of this permissive legislation, and even where they did, this did not usually signal a drastic change in either the style, personnel or intrusiveness of policing[11] (Philips, 1977, p. 64; Weinberger, 1981, pp. 78–9). Fiscal tightfistedness often vitiated the possibility that the police could be numerous enough to achieve close surveillance of any area (Emsley, 1983, pp. 73–4).

Nor does the evidence imply that the 'new' police represented a sharp break towards the establishment of a professional police with a significantly higher calibre of personal efficiency and virtue than the old constables. In many places they were, at least for a short time, largely the same men. The policy of not recruiting people with 'the rank, habits or station of gentlemen' (whether motivated by parsimony or political prudence) meant that the social status of the intake was similar to the old constabulary. Furthermore, all the studies document the very high turnover rates in the first decades of the new police, both as a result of dismissals for drunkenness or other peccadilloes, or through rapid resignation due to the discipline and demanding nature of the job (Philips, 1977, pp. 64–75; Field, 1981, p. 52; Weinberger, 1981, pp. 79–84; Emsley, 1983, pp. 71–3, 1991; Steedman, 1984, Chs 3, 4, 5). There was not as distinct a movement towards a powerful professional system of surveillance as suggested by both orthodoxy and revisionism, whether for protection or oppression of the population.

(7) What was the social impact of the new police?

The previous section implies that, for good or ill, the impact of the new police was not as considerable as either its defenders or detractors would claim. Their immediate effect was primarily the processing of more minor public order offences (Philips, 1977, pp. 84–7). In the longer term, however, the police force were undoubtedly connected with a general increase in the orderliness and pacification of Victorian society. Gatrell shows that from the 1850s until the pre-First World War years 'the war against criminal disorder was palpably being won by the State, and contemporaries knew it' (Gatrell, 1980, pp. 240–1; see also Radzinowicz and Hood, 1985, for contemporary views on the conquest of crime in this period).[12] The 'Watchman State' was not constructed at a stroke, but it did emerge eventually (Gatrell, 1988).

Other authors, while broadly concurring with Gatrell's picture of declining crime, are sceptical about the precise contribution of the police to this (Emsley, 1983, Ch. 7; D. Jones, 1983). However, it is arguable that the prime way in which the police affect law enforcement is not through their technical efficacy in apprehending criminals, which depends on many factors beyond their control, but by symbolising the existence of a functioning legal order. In this light the effectiveness of the police depends not so much on the *proportion* of offences they clear up, but on their showing the flag by clearing up a sufficiently high absolute number (Gatrell, 1980, pp. 242–3). As Emsley crisply puts it, 'while policemen were not the ultimate answer to theft and disorder which they and many reformers claimed (and continue to claim), they became the placebo of property' (Emsley, 1983, p. 162).

The police were also a factor in the declining extent of disorder, whether in the sense of riot or everyday standards of street conduct (Thurmond Smith, 1985). Obviously riot did not disappear, and in some periods political and industrial conflict intensified, as in the 1880s or the immediate pre-First World War period. On occasion the police were not only unsuccessful in controlling a crowd, but contributed to disorder by provocation or poor tactics (Bailey, 1981b, pp. 94–125; Emsley, 1983, pp. 143–6). But overall, the degree of collective violence tended to decline secularly, although as much because of changes in crowd behaviour as police effectiveness. The everyday orderliness of the streets increased, which evoked the approval of respectable citizens whatever the impact on those reliant on the street economy (Emsley, 1983, pp. 146–7; D. Jones, 1983, pp. 160–1).

In sum, while their initial impact on anything but the casual street economy and its marginal illegalities was small, eventually the police were implicated in a broader process of pacification or integration of Victorian society. Although the weight of their distinctive contribution to this is impossible to state precisely it was undoubtedly significant.

(8) Who gained from the new police?

The orthodox view has it that the police brought universal benefits, especially to the weaker sections of society. The revisionists argue the reverse. The police were an agent of oppression of the majority on behalf of the ruling class, with the middle class also deriving some gains from harassment of the street economy. The police institution also benefited police officers themselves, by providing a channel of social mobility to greater security, status and power.

The implications of recent research support both views partially. The working class did benefit from the police in so far as they resorted to the formal criminal justice machinery when victimised by assault or theft. It is by no means clear, though, that they had as much confidence in the new police as in the old parish constables (Philips, 1977, pp. 78–9, 124–5; Weinberger, 1981, pp. 71–2). Ultimately, however, they probably gained from the process whereby the police came to take over responsibility for most prosecutions.

But while gaining in their capacity as victims of routine offences of theft and assault and from some police services, in other respects the working class were at the sharp end of many police activities (Weinberger, 1981, pp. 73–6). This is especially true, of course, of the lower strata within the working class, those dependent on the street economy or irregular employment. They were the targets of the routine public order policing which the middle class supported enthusiastically. The regularly employed workers also suffered from police actions during periods of heightened industrial conflict. It is probable also that the quality of police respect would be inversely related to the social status of a person they were dealing with (Emsley, 1983, p. 152; Steedman, 1984, p. 6).

The middle and upper classes certainly gained a sense of security, which many contemporaries gratefully expressed. Others quickly began to take them for granted as the police became a socially invisible public servant (Steedman, 1984, pp. 6, 142–5). Some took this to the cynical conclusion that the police officer was a mere 'fool in blue' who did nothing but walk about, and they wondered if he was worth his weight in a higher rate (Steedman, 1984, p. 7).

At first it is clear that police officers did not gain from the job in terms of social mobility and a career. They merely took advantage of it for short spells while unable to obtain other work. Gradually, however, in the third quarter of the nineteenth century, the development of a notion of police work as a distinctive career, with a specific ideology of service, professional identity and craft skills, slowly emerged (Steedman, 1984, Ch. 8). Police work began to hold out an opportunity for social mobility to some working-class men.

(9) *Who controlled the police?*

The middle class and working class had a greater capacity to influence their parish constables, or local forces under such legislation as the 1833 Lighting and Watching Act, than they had after the creation of the new police. This was the basis of the working-class struggles over police control which have been documented for some northern towns (Foster, 1974). It was also the source of the objections of many towns to incorporation under the Municipal Corporations Act 1835, or the amalgamation with surrounding counties as proposed in 1856. On the other hand, it was one reason why Chadwick and other reformers wanted to have more centralised control. To them local control smacked of corruption and inefficiency. Their objections to local democratic control of parish forces echo precisely the arguments of contemporary Chief Constables about the supposed threat to their professional independence (Davey, 1983, p. 192).

The working class clearly had no possibility of influencing borough Watch Committees until the slow extension of the franchise to them. It was perhaps no coincidence that by that time Watch Committees had lost much of their power over the increasingly autonomous Chief Constables. The middle class had some degree of influence over Watch Committees, depending on the local political balance. They had less involvement in the gentry-dominated magistracy which completely controlled the county police until 1888.

Nominally, Chief Constables had the authority to control police policy and adminstration in the counties (Reiner, 1991, Ch. 2). However, as the magistracy chose men with a social background and standing which ensured a harmony of outlook, the gentry viewpoint dominated in county policing (Steedman, 1984, pp. 47–52). In the boroughs the powers in theory and practice of Watch Committee over Chief Constable remained paramount. Even the 1856 admixture of a measure of central control through the Home Office Inspectorate and Exchequer Grant did not change this pattern at first (Steedman, 1984, pp. 38–47). However, during the 1870s Chief Constables in both counties and boroughs began to assert and exercise a greater measure of professional independence. This was facilitated by a series of legislative changes conferring on the police more duties directly from national government, as well as more powers (*ibid.*, pp. 53–5, 62–3, Ch. 10).

In sum, the orthodox view has no foundation for the claim that the 'people' controlled the police, if by this is meant any concrete channel for the expression of this control. The new police signified a move away from a degree of popular control which had existed in some places over parish constables. They also emerged after the 1870s as increasingly autonomous of local government and magistracy. The police were on the route to becoming that autonomous body of professionals, the accountability of which has become a major source of controversy.

Conclusion: a neo-Reithian synthesis

All historians of the emergence of professional policing in Britain have shown that it was surrounded by acute political conflict. The orthodox historians are clearly wrong in their lack of appreciation of the rational basis of opposition to the police, rooted in different social interests and political philosophies. On the other hand, the revisionists over-emphasise the extent of continued working-class opposition, and the overt role of the police in class and political control. While not securing the quick and relatively painless passage into acceptance suggested by the Reithians, the police did gain increasing acquiescence from substantial sections of the working class, not only as a result of 'soft' service activities, but in their 'hard' law enforcement and order maintenance functions. This anchored consent in substantial benefits and cooperation, not mere ideological manipulation. The police succeeded in acquiring this degree of legitimacy, in which they were no longer widely seen as a politically oppressive force, by a combination of specific strategies which gave the British police a unique character, implanting them firmly in national mythology. I would claim that a *neo-Reithian* framework is the most appropriate for understanding this.[13] This is a perspective which would give due weight to the success of the police reformers and the tradition they created, but also recognises that policing is embedded in a social order riven by structured bases of conflict, not fundamental integration. The manner of policing such a divided social order may be more or less harmonious and consensual, or overtly oppressive, with important consequences. The precise processes by which the comparatively benign British policing tradition was constructed in the century after their controversial introduction, the manner of their legitimation and depoliticisation, will be the focus of the next chapter.

CHAPTER 2

THE RISE AND FALL OF POLICE LEGITIMACY, 1856–1992

From crushers to bobbies: the depoliticisation of the police, 1856–1959

The British police were established in the face of massive opposition from a wide range of political interests and philosophies. While middle- and upper-class suspicions were rapidly allayed, working-class resentment lived on, expressed in sporadic physical violence and symbolised by a stream of derogatory epithets for the new police: 'Crushers', 'Peel's Bloody Gang', 'Blue Locusts', 'Jenny Darbies', 'Raw Lobsters', 'Blue Drones'. Yet by the 1950s the police had become not merely accepted but lionised by the broad spectrum of opinion. In no other country has the police force been so much a symbol of national pride.[1]

Many contemporary statements testify to the almost universal accord which the police had attained. A 1955 Police Journal editorial claimed: 'The law-abiding sections of the community (and in this we include the larger majority of all classes, working, professional and leisured, alike) have come to accept the police more as guardians and less as oppressors. Time and experience have dispelled old fears' (28:4, October/December 1955, p. 245).

In the same year, Geoffrey Gorer claimed 'that the bulk of the population has . . . incorporated the police man or woman as an ideal and become progressively more "self-policing"' (Gorer, 1955, p. 311).[2] Michael Banton began his pioneering sociological study of the police with the 'idea that it can be instructive to analyze institutions that are working well in order to see if anything can be learned from their success' (Banton, 1964, p. vii). Above all, the fictional character PC George Dixon, who first appeared in the 1950 film *The Blue Lamp*, and was subsequently resurrected for a long-running TV series, embodied the quintessential beloved British bobby, and still stands as a regularly evoked ideal (Clarke, 1983).

By the end of the 1950s there were indications of increasing tension. Recorded crime was rising at a rate described by the Chief Inspector of Constabulary as an 'upsurge', 1958 saw race riots in Notting Hill and Nottingham, and there was growing police anxiety about their relations with the 'law-abiding', but increasingly car-owning, public. In the late 1950s a series of *causes célèbres* led to the November 1959 announcement by the Home Secretary of a Royal Commission 'to review the constitutional position of the police' (Bottoms and Stevenson, 1990). But it is significant that the Royal Commission's national opinion survey found 'an overwhelming vote of confidence in the police'. As far as police acceptance by the public is concerned, the 1950s seem a 'Golden Age' of tranquillity and accord, with only hesitant harbingers of coming crisis.

Policing by consent

The orthodox police historians see the police as having already overcome any serious opposition to their presence by the early years of this century. Critchley (1978), for instance, characterises the 1900s as 'the zenith' of police public relations in Britain (p. 326). He cites a 1908 *Times* editorial which claimed: 'The policeman in London is not merely guardian of the peace; he is the best friend of a mass of people who have no other counsellor or protector.' This rosy image has aroused the ire of the revisionists. Against its cosy complacency they pose a contrary picture. 'The "public" (meaning the middle and upper classes) . . . held their "bobby" in patronizing "affection and esteem" . . . but these sentiments were never shared by the undermass, nor in fact by the working class generally' (Roberts, 1973, p. 100). But there is no warrant for extrapolating this pattern of class conflict forward by half a century, as the revisionists are wont to do.

The Royal Commission on the Police Report (1962) has been criticised rightly for neglecting aspects of their own survey data which qualify the optimistic overall summary (Whitaker, 1964, pp. 15–17; Brogden, 1982, p. 205). However, an examination of the survey results suggests that there was no evidence of variation *by social class* in attitudes to the police. While 85.2 per cent of the professional and managerial classes had 'great respect' for the police, so too did 81.8 per cent of the skilled and 81.9 per cent of the semi- or unskilled working class; 24.3 per cent of the semi- and unskilled working-class and 29.8 per cent of the skilled working class respondents reported 'unsatisfactory experience' of police conduct, but even more (33.3 per cent) of the professional and managerial strata did. Whilst 12.1 per cent of the police sample thought the 'upper classes' were more resentful of the police than they had been ten years previously, only 10.5 per cent of them felt this about the 'working classes'. This confirms those contemporary opinions which stressed the widespread acceptance of the police *throughout the class structure*. There is copious recent evidence of hostility to the police among some sections of the population, especially young men and ethnic minorities (PSI, 1983). The revisionist view over-stresses, however, the scanty evidence of general working-class suspicion. The Shaw and Williamson (1972) survey of public attitudes to the police, one of the few to include a class dimension, is often cited as evidence of working-class reservations about policing (e.g. by Brogden, 1982, p. 204). But their data only show the tiniest of inter-class differences, and some results go in the opposite direction to the one predicted. For example, they find that 86 per cent of respondents in class III had 'respect' for the police, compared to only 81.7 per cent in class I.[3] To describe this as showing either special working-class consent to or conflict with the police is as meaningful as calling a half-drunk glass of water full rather than empty.

Apart from the empirical evidence, there are conceptual ambiguities in the much debated notion of policing by consent. Both the orthodox and the revisionist approaches operate with absurdly absolutist conceptions of what consensual policing could mean. Policing is an inherently conflict-ridden enterprise. The essential function and distinctive resource of the police is the potential use of legitimate force. Of course, the art and craft of successful police work is to minimise actual recourse to force. But a 'benign bobby . . . still brings to the situation a uniform, a truncheon, and a battery of resource charges . . . which can be employed when appeasement fails and fists start flying' (Punch, 1979b, p. 116).

If there was universal consensus about norms, values and appropriate modes of social behaviour there would be no need for a police force. In most situations there is somebody being policed against, whose assent to policing, at any rate there and then, is bound to be brittle. At best they may utter a grudging 'it's a fair cop, guv' in the time-honoured tradition of English gangster movies. But those who are frequently at the receiving end of police authority are unlikely to give it much consent other than a sullen acceptance of *de facto* power. Realistically, the most that 'policing by consent' can mean is not universal love of the police, but that those at the sharp end of police practices do not extend their resentment at specific actions into a generalised withdrawal of legitimacy from either individual officers or the institution of policing *per se*. 'Sheep never like their sheepdog', as one Chief Constable is reported as saying (Whitaker, 1964, p. 159).

By the 1950s 'policing by consent' *was* achieved in Britain to the maximal degree it is ever attainable – the wholehearted approval of the majority of the population who do not experience the coercive exercise of police powers to any significant extent, and *de facto* acceptance of the legitimacy of the institution by those who do. Police *power*, that is, the capacity to inflict legal sanctions including force, had been transmuted into *authority*, power which is accepted as at least minimally legitimate.[4] How did the police come to be accepted as legitimate authority figures rather than politically controversial bearers of power? How did their image change from 'crushers' to 'bobbies'?

The construction of consent

The achievement of consensus policing in Britain was partly the product of specific aspects of police organisational policy. It also was helped by (and helped) the process whereby the working class, the main source of initial hostility to the new police, came to be incorporated into the political and economic institutions of British society. Police acceptance was mutually interdependent with a wider process of pacification of social relations. Police policy was crucial to this. These policies were by no means absolutely determined by the political or social character of Britain. They were more or less conscious choices between options, and could have been different. At the same time they were not free-floating decisions, independent of the political balance and cultural traditions of British society. Many sociologists have argued that the distinctive character of English policing, its relative legality and eschewal of force, is a product of social homogeneity and tranquillity, especially as contrasted with the United States (Banton, 1964, Ch. 8; Manning, 1979, p. 43). But the opposite is the case. The architects of the benign and dignified English police image, Peel, Rowan and Mayne, adopted the policies they did because of the strength of opposition to the very existence of the police. They encouraged a low-profile, legalistic stance precisely in the teeth of the bitter political conflict and acute social divisions of English society in the first half of the nineteenth century, not as an expression of underlying harmony. In the United States by contrast, the more free-wheeling and aggressive style of policing evolved not as a consequence of social divisions, but of the political integration of American society as something approaching a property-owning democracy. Popular participation in government meant confidence that control of the police could be entrusted to the political process, rather than a tight framework of legal rules and regulations.[5]

The policy choices made by the creators of the English police were central to the way the force was accepted. But these policy-makers acted in conditions of class resistance and political conflict not of their own making, and were informed and limited by particular ideological traditions. There were eight specific policies laid down by Peel, Rowan and Mayne that were crucial for the engineering of consent in the face of initial opposition, which need to be explored before the process of legitimation down to 1959, and the subsequent repoliticisation, can be understood.[6]

Police policy and legitimation

(1) *Bureaucratic organisation*

The basis of the 'new' police idea was the establishment of a full-time force of professional police officers, organised into a bureaucratic hierarchy. This contrasted with the previous reliance on a motley assortment of part-timers, entrepreneurial thief-takers and amateur volunteers. Entry and promotion were meritocratic not partisan or nepotistic. Rowan and Mayne set initial entrance requirements that were quite demanding and stringently applied to applicants by the two Metropolitan Commissioners (Miller, 1977, pp. 26–7; Critchley, 1978, p. 52). We have seen in the last chapter that in many provincial forces established after the 1835 and 1839 Acts there was much more continuity between the 'old' and 'new' police. But in the provinces too, after 1856 and the introduction of a minimal element of standardisation through the Inspectorate of Constabulary, this began to change (Critchley, 1978, pp. 118–23). However, both private and amateur police remain part of the scene today, in the shape of the security industry and the Special Constabulary (see South, 1988; Johnston, 1991, 1992; Leon, 1991; Gill and Mawby, 1990).

Training was not taken very seriously in many forces until after the 1919–20 reports of the Desborough Committee, which introduced a much stronger element of standardisation and central direction into all aspects of administration and conditions of service. The Committee had been appointed following the 1918 and 1919 police strikes in London and Liverpool, and resulted in a major shift towards centralisation – Reynolds and Judge (1968), Critchley (1978, pp. 190–4) and Reiner (1978a, pp. 24–5). In the Metropolitan Police there had been some minimal training from the early days (Miller, 1977, p. 41).

Rowan and Mayne elaborated a strict set of rules and regulations governing not only the internal standards of dress, deportment and discipline, but the prescribed demeanour for dealing with the public (Miller, 1977, pp. 37–42; Critchley, 1978, pp. 52–5). These were inculcated during drill and training, and enforced by sanctions for disobedience. In the early years there was a high turnover due to dismissals, mainly for drunkenness.

A chain of command was constructed on quasi-military lines, and at first the policy was to appoint former non-commissioned military officers to the higher ranks, because of their experience as disciplinarians. This later changed in favour of internal promotion from the ranks (Wall, 1987, 1989; Reiner, 1991, Ch. 2). But the promotion system itself became an instrument of bureaucratic control. Only those who obeyed orders 'readily and punctually' could aspire to be promoted, for 'he who has been accustomed to submit to discipline will be considered best qualified to command' (Miller, 1977, p. 40).

The policy of bureaucratisation was partly contradicted by low pay. This, plus the irksome discipline itself, meant that all early police forces had a massive problem of rapid turnover. But during the 1870s the notion of policing as a career offering status and security, if not high short-term pay, began to emerge, and a more stable body of professional officers developed.

Although never realised completely, the image of policemen as disciplined members of a bureaucratic organisation of professionals was constructed by the 1850s in London. An 1856 article in the *London Quarterly Review* summed up the ever-uncertain process of conversion of human raw material into 'well-regulated machines', impersonal embodiments of bureaucratic authority: 'Amid the bustle of Piccadilly or the roar of Oxford Street, P.C.X. 59 stalks along, an institution rather than a man.'

(2)   The rule of law

The way in which the police maintained order and enforced the law was itself supposed to be governed by legalistic procedures and constraints. Adherence to the rule of law was a prime requirement of the Metropolitan Police. At first the London 'police courts' were generally unsympathetic to the force, and they remained fiercely concerned to maintain their role and image as independent regulators of the legality of police conduct (Davis, 1984, p. 332). On several occasions the magistrates laid down rulings which effectively halted particular law enforcement policies (*ibid.*, p. 328).

Although an impediment to the exercise of police power,

which the Commissioners resented, at a deeper level they were aware that subjection to legal regulation was a major factor in the legitimation of police authority. In any case the magistrates seemed to have become less wont to question police behaviour after mid-century, as indicated by a growing tendency to dismiss charges of assault brought against the police, and a greater readiness to convict on police evidence (*ibid.*, p. 329).

The Commissioners were well aware of the importance of the police maintaining an image of subjection to the rule of law as a way of alleviating opposition. They laid down strict regulations and sanctions governing the use of the wide discretionary powers conferred on constables by statutes such as the Vagrancy Act 1824 (source of the notorious 'sus' law), and the Metropolitan Police Act 1839, which conferred on the London police broad stop-and-search powers. While the Commissioners believed such powers were needed by constables, they exerted strict disciplinary sanctions over abuse, and encouraged 'all respectable persons' to bring complaints to them (Miller, 1977, pp. 4–12, 56–66). The Commissioners also laid down narrow rules on interrogation and treatment of suspects:

> It is clear that the Commissioners sought, on the whole successfully, to commit their men to the cautious exercise of their powers within the framework of legal protections of civil liberties. This principle was a . . . key element in securing public acceptance of the force. (Miller 1977, p. 94)

(3)   The strategy of minimal force

All police forces would claim to use as little force as necessary. The British tradition stands out, however, for its eschewal of arms. With characteristic forthrightness, Sir Robert Mark once articulated the crowd control strategy of the Metropolitan Police thus: 'The real art of policing a free society or a democracy is to win by appearing to lose.' Their secret weapon was not water cannon, tear gas or rubber bullets, but public sympathy. To this end, he claimed, the Metropolitan Police had trained an especially comely horse – the 'Brigitte Bardot' of police horses – to collapse, feigning death, at a word of command. This was guaranteed to win the support of the animal-loving British public. The British 'police advantage' of public support rather than lethal hardware as a means of crowd control was a deliberately chosen strategy (Bowden, 1978, p. 35, Ch. 9). It was a calculated response to the fears of an oppressive *gendarmerie* which had motivated so much resistance to the force.

Rowan and Mayne limited constables' weapons to the truncheon, carried concealed until 1863. The truncheon's use was intended to be a last resort. Complaints of police violence diminished after the early 1830s, implying that the Commissioner's regulations had some effect on behaviour (Miller, 1977, p. 49). On specific dangerous assignments or beats, specially selected officers might carry a pistol or a cutlass, but each occasion of use or even drawing of such a weapon was closely scrutinised, and if not justified as self-defence would probably result in dismissal.

Some post-1839 county police forces, notably Essex, did adopt a military model of policing (Steedman, 1984, pp. 21–5). But the strategy of policing which the Home Office encouraged after 1856 was prevention by 'a police force essentially civil, unarmed and acting without any assistance from a military force' (*ibid.*, pp. 32–8). The army was available as the ultimate back-up should preventive policing fail, and it was used on many occasions in the latter part of the nineteenth and early twentieth centuries. But gradually the non-lethally armed civilian police force became the sole means of riot control. Paradoxically, one of the last occasions troops acted in a public order role was in 1919 during the Liverpool police strike.

Although they have certainly never acted with kid gloves, there is no doubt that the British police developed a tradition of containing industrial disputes and political demonstrations with minimum force when contrasted with the experience of other countries. There have been particular periods of anxiety and controversy about intensified political and industrial conflict, with attendant complaints of police brutality and right-wing bias. The most notable have been the series of clashes between police and the organised unemployed of 'Outcast London' in the late 1880s, the bitter industrial disputes immediately before and after the First World War, and the conflicts between the police and the unemployed movement and anti-fascist demonstrators in the

1930s (J. Morgan, 1987; Weinberger, 1991). But research on the 1887 Trafalgar Square violence has shown clearly how the Home Office tried to ensure that police tactics were kept within legal limits (Bailey, 1981b, pp. 9–125). In the unprecedented economic and political crisis of the 1930s public order became an issue in a way it had not been since the middle of the nineteenth century. The violence surrounding fascist meetings was the stimulus for the Public Order Act 1936. Concern about the brutality used to suppress marches of the National Unemployed Workers' Movement, led to the growth of the National Council for Civil Liberties after 1934. A detailed consideration of 1930s' conflicts concludes however that despite considerable evidence of bias and brutality by police officers against the NUWM and anti-fascists, 'the police do seem to have reacted less in political terms than in response to the challenge to public order and to their own position as the custodians of law and order' (Stevenson and Cook, 1977, p. 243). Certainly, the level of violence or police repression was not comparable to that in most other industrial countries suffering from the depression. Geary (1985) documents the declining levels of violence between police and pickets in industrial conflicts between the 1890s and the 1970s, arguing that industrial conflict changed from something resembling a war to something more like a sporting contest. This pattern of non-violent and non-confrontational policing of the 'normal' industrial dispute was confirmed by Kahn et al (1983, Ch. 5). The policing of industrial disputes reverted to a higher level of violence in the mid-1980s, however, as we will see below.

As far as individual violence involving police is concerned, there is similar evidence of a sustained decline in the first century of policing. The revisionists have all taken assaults on the police as a sensitive index of working-class rejection (Storch, 1975; Cohen, 1979; Weinberger, 1981, pp. 67–71). Gatrell has shown that from the 1860s until the First World War there was a dramatic decline both in assaults in general, and specifically in assaults against the police. From a national annual average of 67.5 per 100,000 in 1857–60, the rate of assaults on the police had fallen to 24.1 per 100,000 in 1911–14, with consistent decline in between (Gatrell, 1980, pp. 286–93). Whatever the totality of reasons underlying this long-run decline in violence, it is clear that the police reflected and contributed to it.

(4) Non-partisanship

When the 'new' police force was established working-class leaders and Radicals saw it as a thoroughly political military and spy agency, 'the minion and paid servant of the Government' (*Poor Man's Guardian*, 11 October 1830, p. 3).

Peel, Rowan and Mayne recognised quite clearly that the key to legitimating the police was the presentation of an image of non-partisanship. Public acceptance depended upon the police not being seen as political. Rowan and Mayne declared that in the middle of acute social conflict they 'endeavoured to prevent the slightest practical feeling or bias, being shown or felt by the police . . . the force should not only be, in fact, but be believed to be impartial in action, and should act on principle' (cited in Miller, 1977, p. 12).

The police were insulated from direct political control, and police authorities (the Home Secretary, local Watch and Standing Joint Committees) tended to abstain from interventions in operational policy. It was not until the 1920s, though, that this discreet stance began to be transmuted explicitly into a notion of constabulary independence from policy guidance, which would have been considered 'so unconstitutional as to be absurd' in the nineteenth century (Marshall, 1965, p. 31).

Peel and the Metropolitan Commissioners did insist on strict exclusion of patronage in appointments and promotions at a time when this was normal civil service practice. Police officers were also denied the vote until 1887. This tradition dies hard. In an article celebrating the 150th anniversary of the Metropolitan Police, the then Commissioner Sir David McNee wrote: 'I no longer exercise my right to vote, nor have I since I was appointed a chief officer of police. Police officers must be men and women of the middle, bound only by the rule of law' (McNee, 1979, p. 25). Although enfranchised in 1887, police officers remain forbidden to join, or affiliate to (and until 1972 even to associate with) outside trade unions on the ground that this would impugn their political impartiality (Reiner, 1978a, pp. 111–12).

The insistence on suppressing indications of overt political control or partisanship softened the initial conception of the police as a tool of government oppression. As an 1864 article in *Chamber's Magazine* said of the police, 'they know nothing of politics; the man in blue preserves his neutral tint . . . the good old cause of order is the only side the policeman supports' (cited in Miller, 1977, p. 13).

(5) Accountability

Although the police were not formally controlled by any elected body, they were seen as accountable in two ways. First, the legality of police action was reviewable by the courts: they were held accountable to the rule of law (as seen in 2 above). Second, they were purported to be accountable through an almost mystical process of *identification* with the British people, not the state. Although lacking any tangible control by elected institutions, they were supposed to be in tune with the popular will because of their social representativeness and lack of special powers. The ideology developed of the constable as 'citizen in uniform', doing on a paid basis what all citizens had the power and social duty to do. This conception is most explicitly articulated by the 1929 *Royal Commission on Police Power and Procedure*, and repeated in the 1962 *Report of the Royal Commission on the Police* (Para. 30, pp. 10–11). As Reith summed it up, 'the police are the public and the public are the police' (Reith, 1956, p. 287). The recruitment policies of the police have always been attuned to this principle, drawing upon manual working-class backgrounds representative of the mass of the people. Since the First World War this principle has been supposed to govern even chief officer selection in all forces, and since the Second World War it has done, with all Chief Constables working their way up through the ranks and sharing working-class origins (Wall, 1987, 1989; Reiner, 1991). The principle of community identification with the police remains strong in Conservative rhetoric today, as in the official enthusiasm for various forms of citizen involvement (Mawby, 1991b; Gill and Mawby, 1990; Leon, 1989, 1990, 1991).

(6) The service role

The notion of the friendly bobby is summed up for modern ears by the cliché, 'If you want to know the time, ask a policeman.'

The meaning was rather different in the nineteenth century: 'The popular catch-phrase . . . reflected not so much the confidence of the Victorians in the reliability of the police, as their assumption that any policeman who did not quickly "win" a watch from the pockets of a drunken reveller was unnaturally honest or dull' (Rolph, 1962, p. 52).

The nineteenth-century police reformers quite deliberately cultivated the service role in order to secure legitimacy for more coercive policing functions. Chadwick was the most explicit about this. He urged that it would 'exercise a beneficial influence on the labouring classes . . . by showing them that they are cared for by the authorities, and are not, as they must but too commonly suppose, merely and exclusively the subjects of coercion' (Donajgrodski, 1977b, p. 67).[7]

Certainly in the nineteenth century the police carried out a number of tasks wider than law enforcement and order maintenance. Some were formal duties, such as inspecting weights and measures or inspecting bridges, others were informal, such as knocking people up early in the morning for work (Emsley, 1983, pp. 158–9). Then as now these were often regarded by the police themselves as unwelcome 'extraneous' duties (Steedman, 1984, pp. 53–4). Many of the service tasks benefited the middle class at the expense of the working class, such as the enforcement of nuisance laws. But others did benefit the working class too. How crucial the service role was in securing consent may be questioned, and to some it is mere ideological window-dressing (Brogden, 1982, pp. 208–19). Arguably, the criminal role of the police, in particular their taking over of most prosecutions, was a more valued and useful service to the mass of the population than the 'friendly' non-coercive 'services' to which the term is usually confined. But the 'service' role has played a part in securing police legitimation.

(7) Preventive policing

The primacy of prevention over detection is emphasised in the famous opening lines of Peel's celebrated instructions to the

Metropolitan Police. The practical implementation of this principle meant the concentration of the force's manpower on uniform patrol of regular beats in full and open public view. This was motivated not only by a belief in the efficacy of the police constable's 'scarecrow function'. It was also a response to that element in the anti-police opposition which invoked fears of the abominable French experience of undercover police spies.

This hostility to the idea of plain-clothes police delayed the formation of detective branches for many years. Mayne in particular was concerned to minimise use of detectives because of public fears about police spying (Miller, 1977, pp. 33–4). In 1842 Rowan was able to overcome partly Mayne's anxieties and they secured the Home Secretary's approval for a small detective branch of six men (Ascoli, 1979, pp. 118–20). When it was proposed to expand the number of detectives in 1845, *The Times* declared: 'If it be dangerous and perhaps unconstitutional, to maintain a few government spies, what will be the effect of impressing that character on the whole police force of this vast metropolis?' (cited in Baldwin and Kinsey, 1982, p. 11). By 1868 when Mayne died there were still only 15 detectives in a force of 8,000. Mayne's successor, Henderson, prompted partly by a moral panic about rising crime in the late 1860s, placed more emphasis on the detective branch, created permanent divisional detectives, and ended Mayne's policy of regularly rotating plain clothes officers back to uniform in order to reduce the risks of corruption. Mayne's fears were vindicated when, in 1877, the three top Scotland Yard detectives were involved in a major bribery scandal. Paradoxically, the response to this was the establishment of a separate Criminal Investigation Department. By the late 1870s the trend towards increasing specialisation and emphasis on detection was well entrenched, playing down the role of the general practice uniform constable.

In the 1880s the police had become sufficiently well entrenched in public confidence for the formation of a specifically political unit, the Special Irish Branch, initially to deal with Fenian terrorism (Porter, 1987). It subsequently acquired a wider remit than Irish terrorism, and became the Special Branch. But in the early years the primacy of the idea of prevention by uniformed patrol was a factor in the achievement of legitimation, quelling fears about armies of undercover spies.

(8)   Police effectiveness

The previous factors in the legitimation of the police all point to
ways in which strategy was more or less successfully directed to
allaying fears about the harmful consequences of the police. But
that the worse did not happen does not mean that anyone felt the
police had any positive value.

The final aspect of police policy contributing to their
legitimation was the cultivation of at least the appearance of
effectiveness, not just in terms of service tasks but the core
mandate of crime control and order maintenance. In the 1860s
there was a moral panic in the respectable classes about a new
'crime wave', and the police, especially the aged Mayne, were
blamed. Fear of crime was fuelled by anxiety about a supposed
epidemic of garottings (the Victorian equivalent of mugging) and
by rising official statistics of recorded indictable offences (Davis,
1980). Conservative critics bemoaned the pernicious consequences of soft-hearted penal policies and demanded stricter
control of ticket-of-leave men. They also campaigned for the
police to be 'armed with preventive powers similar to those
exercised by the Continental police'. This was precisely what
working-class spokesmen feared. As _Reynolds's_ newspaper
claimed: 'The Government proposes converting the English
Peeler into a species of continental policeman . . . the mouchard,
or spy, will become an established institution among us.'

These conflicting currents of debate brought renewed questioning of the basic structure of the police, in particular the
Metropolitan Police's tight centralisation which precluded local
accountability. This renewed politicisation of the police in the
late 1860s in the face of rising crime rates and a more general
sense of economic and political crisis anticipates uncannily events
a century later. However, neither the law-and-order panic nor
the revived political controversy about policing lasted more than
a few years, nor did a similar period of conflict in the late 1880s
(Bailey, 1981b).

As the bulk of the working class became reconciled to the
criminal justice system, they availed themselves of its services. A
sizeable proportion of the work of the police courts comprised
prosecutions and summonses for theft and assault brought by
working-class men and women. While most theft cases were

brought by the 'respectable' working class, 'more surprisingly it was members of the casual poor, sometimes convicted criminals themselves, who predominated in making assault charges' (Davis, 1984, p. 321). These prosecutions were usually a phase in the conduct of longer-running disputes between working-class people: 'a great many prosecutions brought by the working class did not so much replace informal sanctions as operate in addition to them' (*ibid.*, pp. 330–1). Slowly it seems, the new police and criminal justice system were inserting themselves into working-class life not only as an intrusive controlling apparatus but also at a potential means of redress. Historical understanding of this process is only now developing, but the growth of a sense of police effectiveness was probably at least as significant as the image-building aspects of legitimation. Police success 'in securing the cooperation of the public depended less on keeping a rosy image of impartiality than on securing a near-monopoly over the market in violence and redress. Street by street, the police negotiated a complex, shifting, largely unspoken "contract"' (Ignatieff, 1979, pp. 444–5). This was threatened by heavy-handed control of industrial or political conflict, or by over-zealous policing of working-class leisure pursuits. Recognising this the early Metropolitan Police Commissioners were discreet in their enforcement of laws which were unpopular with the working class, such as the Sabbath laws (Miller, 1977, pp. 129–38).

By the 1870s then, the police had come to be seen as offering an effective law enforcement service to the middle and upper classes, who complained when its quality seemed to decline. The working class too made use of it, but the less respectable sections of this class were predominantly at the receiving end of law and order campaigns. As long as the working class was and felt largely excluded from even minimal political and economic participation, so too would their acquiescence to policing be fragile and grudging.

The social context of police legitimation

The all-important final factor which facilitated the legitimation of the police was not an aspect of police policy, but the changing social, economic and political context. The working class, the main structurally rooted source of opposition to the police, gradually, unevenly and incompletely came to be incorporated into the political institutions of British society. (A succinct discussion is in Miliband, 1982.)

The process of incorporation has very clear limits. Although it enabled the bulk of the working class to share in the growth of the economy until the late 1970s, class inequality remains in proportionate terms virtually unaltered (Westergaard and Resler, 1975; Goldthorpe *et al.*, 1980). Nor have the universal franchise, the Labour Party or the trade union movement succeeded in making much of a dent in the monopolisation of powerful positions in society by a relatively small elite (Wakeford and Urry, 1973; Stanworth and Giddens, 1974; Stanworth, 1984).

None the less, the wide gulf between the 'two nations' which was sharply manifest to all in the mid-nineteenth century as the new police came into being, had become hedged around and blurred by the 1950s, the high point of police legitimation. In the 'affluent society' there was supposed to be an 'end of ideology' and this included controversy about the police. In the late 1950s this complacency was ending in many spheres of public life, and there was sufficient disquiet about policing to necessitate the announcement of the Royal Commission on the Police.

This should not detract from the accomplishment of the first century of policing. From a widely hated and feared institution, the police had come to be regarded as the embodiment of impersonal, rule-bound authority, enforcing democratically enacted legislation on behalf of the broad mass of society rather than any partisan interest, and constrained by tight legal requirements of due process. This was achieved by a variety of police organisational strategies, but these succeeded only because of the wider social context of working-class incorporation.

From plods to pigs: the politicisation of the police since 1959

From a position of almost complete invisibility as a political issue, policing has become a babble of scandalous revelation, controversy and competing agendas for reform. The police institution is beset by innovation and undergoing changes which seem the most momentous since the 1829 establishment of the Metropolitan Police. The tacit contract between police and public, so delicately drawn between the 1850s and 1950s, has begun to fray glaringly. The still open question is whether current efforts will suffice to repair it, but this is increasingly unlikely. At present there seems to be an increasing haemorrhage of public confidence (Jones et al., 1986; Crawford, et al., 1990; Skogan, 1990).

The 1960 Royal Commission on the Police was the outcome of a series of causes célèbres which seem in retrospect pretty small beer. In 1956 and 1957 disciplinary or legal proceedings involving alleged corruption were brought against the Chief Constables of Cardiganshire, Brighton and Worcester. Again in 1957, allegations were made in parliament that a policeman had beaten a boy in Thurso (a small Scottish town), and that this complaint had not been properly investigated. In 1959 a row in Nottingham raised the fundamental constitutional issue of the respective responsibilities for law enforcement of Chief Constable and Watch Committee. Captain Popkess, the Chief Constable, was suspended by the Watch Committee because he refused to give them a report of an investigation into criminal allegations involving councillors. The Home Secretary told the committee to reinstate Popkess, but the case illustrated the lack of clarity about the roles of Chief Constable, Watch Committee and Home Secretary (Marshall, 1965, pp. 13–14).

Other anxieties about policing mounted in the background. After 1954 the crime statistics began to rise inexorably each year, heralding 'a crime wave unparalleled in modern times' (Critchley, 1978, p. 254). The teddy-boys and beatniks of the mid-1950s created new 'folk devils' and presaged perennial moral panic about the threats to law and order posed by new and ever more bizarre styles of youth culture (Cohen, 1972; Pearson, 1983; Muncie, 1984; Davies, 1990). Future concerns about public order policing were signalled by the 1958 Notting Hill and Nottingham race riots, the 1956 anti-Suez demonstrations in Trafalgar Square, and the launching of CND and the Aldermaston marches in 1957. The immediate trigger for the Royal Commission was none of these grave matters, but a Whitehall farce. In December 1958 Brian Rix the comedy star was stopped for speeding by a PC Eastmond. An obscure argument developed between Eastmond and a civil servant who intervened in the incident, resulting in mutual assault allegations, which were settled out of court. This provoked a parliamentary debate which raised all the fundamental issues of police accountability. During the debate the Home Secretary indicated his intention to institute the Royal Commission. It considered the case for a national police force, the roles of Chief Constable, local police authorities and the Home Secretary, the relationship between police and public, the complaints system and police pay.

Despite rejecting the argument that a nationalised police would be a step towards a police state, the Commission did not propose nationalisation, although the case for it was effectively argued in a highly respected memorandum of dissent by Dr A.L. Goodhart. The majority report claimed that the advantages of rationalisation, coordination and efficiency could be achieved by a more limited programme of amalgamations and greater central control.

The Commission's proposals on accountability and complaints, and their implementation in the Police Act 1964, were widely seen as vague, confused and contradictory (Whitaker, 1964, Ch. 7; Marshall, 1965; this analysis is questioned by Jefferson and Grimshaw, 1984). The net effect of the act was clearly to strengthen the hands of the Home Office and of the Chief Constables at the expense of local police authorities (Marshall, 1973; Banton, 1974).

The continuing relevance of the problems which led to the Royal Commission were highlighted by some scandals that occurred before the passage of the Police Act 1964, and demonstrated the need for an effective system for complaints and accountability. One involved Challenor, a detective sergeant in the Met., who planted false evidence on at least two dozen suspects, apparently unnoticed by colleagues and supervisors (Grigg, 1965). The Sheffield Inquiry into allegations of brutality involving a 'rhino whip' underlined the reluctance of officers to 'hear, or speak, or see any evil' about their colleagues (Whitaker, 1964, pp. 136–7). There was also concern about rough police handling of the 1961 anti-nuclear protests.

Despite its inadequacies, the Police Act 1964 constituted a settlement which was generally accepted for a time. This was aided by the transformation of police organisation in the mid-1960s, centring on the new Unit Beat System of patrol. The emphasis was on technology, specialisation and managerial professionalism as the keys to winning 'the fight against crime'. 'The "British Bobby" was recast as the tough, dashing, formidable (but still brave and honest) "Crime-Buster"' (Chibnall, 1977, p. 71).

Given the now universal bad press accorded the 'fire brigade' policing style which the Unit Beat System brought into being, it is salutary to recall that its birth was greeted with general acclaim (Weatheritt, 1986). It was intended simultaneously to bolster efficiency, improve relations with the public, and advance the policeman's lot (*Police Federation Newsletter*, January 1967, p. 3; Martin and Wilson, 1969; Banton, 1973, pp. 102–4). As originally conceived, the area constables would have the function of preserving close relations with local communities, the Panda cars would provide a faster emergency service, the collator would analyse information provided by the patrol officers for use in detecting offences, and all policemen would gain enhanced status and job-interest. All birds were to be killed by the same stone. In practice, the system soon frustrated these hopes, partly because of shortage of manpower to implement it properly, but primarily because of the unintended consequences of the ability of rank-and-file culture to frustrate managerial purposes. The constables' action-centred perspective on policing was accentuated by the technology of fast cars, sirens and flashing blue lights. What was intended as professionalisation ended up as the politicisation of relations with the public (Holdaway, 1977, 1983; Reiner, 1978a, pp. 189–92). At first, however, the police image may have changed from Dixon to Barlow, but neither were politically controversial figures. The police were no longer plods, but not yet pigs.

By the end of the 1960s the growth of the counter-culture, and police clashes with anti-Vietnam war and anti-apartheid demonstrators in 1968–9, heralded a renewed politicisation of policing. In 1970, the Police Federation chairman announced to the annual conference: 'We have been eyeball to eyeball with the fanatics, the lunatics and the hooligans.' Later that year, the Federation magazine drew attention to the institution of a 'Pig of the Month' contest in *Frendz*, an underground newspaper.

> Should we be upset? Not at all. The pig has made a notable contribution to our national well-being over the centuries. As such, it has a great advantage over hippy squatters . . . whose concepts of sanitation are far more primitive than its own. . . . In America, they say P-I-G stands for Pride, Integrity and Guts. (*Police*, September 1970, p. 6)

What processes were transforming the police image from plod to pig? All the factors which produced the earlier depoliticisation of policing have had question-marks placed against them.

(1) Bureaucratic organisation?

Recruitment, training and discipline

The first element in the undermining of police legitimacy was the erosion of the image of an efficient, disciplined bureaucracy.[8] Partly this was a question of standards of entry and training which (though much higher than in the nineteenth century) had not kept up with general improvements. The generous pay award recommended by the 1960 Royal Commission had been intended to remedy this problem, but police earnings were rapidly outstripped by inflation. The poor educational standards of recruits – and in particular the shortage of graduates – which the Royal Commission had lamented, remained a concern (Martin and Wilson, 1969). Despite increasing attention to training which was straining the manpower capacities of forces (*ibid.*, p. 103), there were still many complaints that it was inadequate for the complex needs of modern society (Evans, 1974, p. 187; Whitaker, 1979, p. 215). The old emphasis on drill and discipline was also being eroded as a response to a growing ideology of 'man-management', and the need to match changing social fashions in order to attract recruits (Reiner, 1978a, pp. 186–94).

There have been many attempts in the last thirty years to raise educational and training standards. In the 1960s various schemes were introduced to attract graduates to the service, and encourage higher education for serving police officers (Rose, 1990b). These included the Graduate Entry Scheme, the Bramshill Scholarships, and the Special Course at Bramshill for potential high-flyers. (These have played an increasing part in the careers of senior officers, see Reiner, 1991). However, significant results have only been achieved during the 1980s, when as a result of the 1978 Edmund-Davies pay award (and unemployment outside the service) the intake of graduates has accelerated sharply to about 12 per cent of recruits per annum. There has also been increasing interest from serving officers in specialist criminal justice degrees (Brogden and Graham, 1988; Tierney, 1989). Significant changes have occurred in recruit training, as well, largely following from the 1982 Scarman Report (Fielding, 1988; Southgate, 1988; Bull and Horncastle, 1989). Despite the merit of these developments, they have not prevented an erosion of public confidence in police professional standards.

Corruption scandals

The main way that the image of the police force as a disciplined, impersonal bureaucracy came to be dented was by the series of Scotland Yard corruption scandals which rocked it after 1969 (Cox et al., 1977; Mark, 1978, Chs 7–10; Ball et al., 1979; McNee, 1983, Ch. 9; Alderson, 1984, Ch. 10; Punch, 1985). The establishment of the CID as a separate department in 1878 in the wake of a corruption scandal had only aggravated the problem. The Met.'s own historian concluded: 'it is beyond argument that by the summer of 1922 the CID had become a thoroughly venal private army' (Ascoli, 1979, p. 210). Allegations of malpractice by London detectives remained rife (Laurie, 1970, Ch. 10). None the less, the revelations published by *The Times* in November 1969 proved to be a bombshell that still reverberates. It was not simply that *The Times* had been able to tape-record discussions between detectives and a villain thus proving their allegations beyond the shadow of a doubt. Nor was it just that the corruption uncovered was very grave (involving deals to cover up serious crimes, setting up criminals as *agents provocateurs*, perjury and planting of evidence); what was most shocking was the revelation of the systematic, institutionalised and widespread network of corruption, the so-called 'firm within a firm'. The Yard's initial attempt at investigation only confirmed this, with a pattern of obstruction, leaks and disappearing documents. Eventually Frank Williamson, formerly a Manchester detective chief superintendent but in 1970 Her Majesty's Inspector of Constabulary (Crime), was brought in. But Williamson's investigation was also frustrated, and he resigned prematurely, in disgust at his experiences.

During the mid-1970s there were two more major corruption scandals at the Met., one involving the Drug Squad, the other the Obscene Publications Squad. Both revealed systematic malpractice, and led to the imprisonment of several senior detectives. The Drug Squad under Detective Chief Inspector Kelaher was implicated in unorthodox methods, including fabrication and manipulation of evidence in order to achieve major 'busts'. The 'Porn' Squad was riddled with graft on a grand scale. Relations between crooks and criminals were warm and intimate. On one occasion a pornography dealer went into Holborn Police Station wearing a CID tie to examine seized material for 'recycling'. Confiscated blue films were shown on the Squad's projector at regular Friday evening 'stag' parties (Cox *et al.*, 1977, p. 168).

The Home Secretary Reginald Maudling's answer was to appoint as Commissioner an 'outsider', Robert Mark, who had been Assistant Commissioner since 1967 but had previously served entirely in provincial forces. Mark's appointment was clearly seen as signalling a battle against corruption: 'He had the reputation of a "Mr. Clean", the "Manchester Martinet", the "Lone Ranger from Leicester"' (*ibid.*, p. 132).

Mark introduced a dramatic strategy of associated reforms, clearly seeing the excision of the 'cancer' at the Yard as the price of its continued independence. He established a new specialist elite department, A10, to investigate all complaints against police officers, put a uniformed officer in charge of the Yard CID and uniformed supervisors over all divisional detectives, abolished the specialist 'Porn' squad, moved many detectives back into uniform, rotated detectives frequently, and cultivated more open relations with the press. As a result of this new climate some 500 policemen left the force during Mark's period as Commissioner, many voluntarily in anticipation of being investigated.

The resilience of corruption at the Yard was shown by new revelations which emerged in 1978. These alleged involvement of detectives, including some in the Robbery Squad, in major armed robberies (Ball *et al.*, 1979). These allegations were an unwelcome by-product of the 1970s' strategy of developing 'supergrasses' – informants who are induced to reveal large numbers of names in return for immunity. (This tactic was subsequently transported to Northern Ireland, with equally dubious results; see Greer, 1987). The Commissioner, Sir David McNee, responded by setting up 'Operation Countryman' under the direction of the Dorset Chief Constable, Arthur Hambleton. A staff of 80 provincial detectives worked out of a building in Surrey (to avoid Met. interference) for 4 years, investigating more than 200 policemen. Hambleton and his team claimed on several occasions that their work was being sabotaged by corrupt Yard pressure, and by the time the operation was wound up only two convictions had been achieved. Yard officers in turn spread smears about the incompetence of the 'Swedey', as the provincial detectives came to be contemptuously called.

In his memoirs McNee denies there was a cover-up, and puts the blame on Hambleton, who he says allowed the inquiry to become swamped with too much dubious information. McNee claims that a higher proportion of accused Met. officers were criminally convicted while he was Commissioner than under Mark. McNee's personal integrity or dedication to rooting out corruption is not in question. But the 'Countryman' investigations (whatever the truth of the contradictory recriminations) cast doubt on any idea that the endemic corruption in the Yard detective squads had been finally eliminated. Evidence from research on contemporary professional criminals suggests a web of corrupt deals and malpractices (Taylor, 1984, Ch. 8; Hobbs, 1988). The picture given implies the verisimilitude of G.F. Newman's novels and plays about the pervasive corruption of detectives.

The 'Countryman' inquiry was especially disturbing because it did not involve specialist detectives in the vice area, which criminologists had long argued was a special breeding-ground for police corruption. The 250 years' experience of thief-taking suggests that the standard methods of plain-clothes criminal investigation, the cultivation of close relations with criminals as informants, operate perennially on the borderline of legality. No way has yet proven successful of promoting effective detection of serious crime without the dangers of corruption and other systematic illegalities and malpractices. As Tom Tullett, a former CID detective, and *Daily Mirror* chief crime reporter, put it in his eulogistic account of the 1960s Murder Squad investigation of gangland killings: 'In this kind of "war" the police had to think like villains themselves, using every ruse, trick and disguise' (Tullett, 1981, p. 243). The trouble is that rule-bending which may be justified initially by a sincere determination to 'crack down' on serious crime may serve as the 'invitational edge' of the kind of wholesale and predatory wrong-doing revealed in the 1970s (Manning and Redlinger, 1977). The explosion of corruption scandals was the product of the dangers inherent in traditional detective methods, coupled with the novel pressures of the 1960s and 1970s. These included the rise of large-scale organised crime, and growing toleration of some still illegal activities (like drug-taking or pornography) which increased their profitability and lessened the sense detectives had that conniving at them was harmful.

What is undoubtedly true is that the scandals dented the image of the police as impersonal and disciplined law enforcers, which the tradition built up by Rowan and Mayne had stressed. While in the 1960 Royal Commission survey 46.9 per cent of the public did not believe bribe-taking occurred, the 1981 Policy Studies Institute study of Londoners found that only 14 per cent believed the police 'hardly ever' took bribes (PSI 1983, vol. I, p. 249). During the 1980s there have been fewer scandals involving personal corruption, and attention has switched to abuses of police powers undermining the rule of law.

(2)   The rule of law?

The issue of police violations of legal procedures in the course of dealing with offences became acutely politicised in the 1970s. On the one hand, groups like the National Council for Civil Liberties publicised evidence of widespread police malpractice, while on the other the police began to lobby for greater powers to aid the 'war against crime'.

Civil libertarians had been arguing for years that the rights of suspects (encapsulated in the 'Judges' Rules', the non-statutory administrative directions laying down procedures for questioning and taking statements) were routinely violated (Whitaker, 1964, Ch. 7; Laurie, 1970, Ch. 10). Such claims were crystallised by the 1972 conviction, on charges arising out of the murder of Maxwell Confait, of three teenage boys, one of whom was mentally retarded (Baxter and Koffman, 1983). One boy's parents managed to get Christopher Price (then MP for Lewisham West) to take up the case, and after a three-year struggle the verdict was quashed by the Court of Appeal. (Evidence which emerged in 1979 completely exonerated the boys.) Concern about the case led to an official inquiry under Sir Henry Fisher, a High Court judge, which reported in 1977.

The Fisher Report found that the boys' rights had been violated in several ways, leading to their false confessions. They were interviewed without an independent adult being present; the boys were not informed of their rights to phone a solicitor or friend under the Judges' Rules; there were several improprieties in questioning and charging, amounting to unfairness and oppressiveness. Altogether, Fisher found 'some of the Rules and Directions do not seem to be known to police officers'. Fisher suggested that reform of the Rules should be conducted in the light of a broader inquiry – 'something like a Royal Commission'. The hint was taken up shortly afterwards when James Callaghan announced the Royal Commission on Criminal Procedure (RCCP), which reported in 1981.

Senior officers repeatedly claimed that police work could not be done effectively if legal procedures were properly adhered to (Mark, 1978, p. 58; McNee, 1983, p. 18(1–3)). The same opinion is common among the rank and file (Reiner, 1978a, pp. 77–81, 221–3). This view is translated into practice, according to observational studies. Holdaway describes a variety of tactics for controlling suspects which 'distance . . . officers from the constraints of legal rules and force directives' (Holdaway, 1983, p. 101), such as 'verballing' or 'working the oracle' (i.e.

fabricating statements) or physical force. The PSI study also found that while 'outright fabrication of evidence is probably rare . . . departure from rules and procedure affecting evidence are far more common . . . There will be no fundamental change as long as many police officers believe that the job cannot be done effectively within the rules' (PSI, 1983, vol. IV, pp. 228–30).

Apart from violations of rules concerning collection of evidence, there was also a mounting campaign in the late 1970s about police abuse of physical force, stimulated by a number of notorious cases (Box, 1983, p. 82; Ward, 1986). The refusal of the Director of Public Prosecutions to prosecute any police officers in connection with these only fuelled critics' suspicions. The Home Affairs Select Committee was induced in 1980 to examine the procedures for investigating deaths in police custody. This revealed a growing number of such deaths, from 8 in 1970 to 48 in 1978, with a total of 274 from 1971–9. The proportion of these officially categorised as due to 'misadventure' or 'accident' doubled. These figures underestimate the number of deaths connected with police custody, for they exclude those which closely follow release (like Liddle Towers) or from contact not leading to custody (like Blair Peach). On the other hand, there is no warrant for saying that anything like this number of cases involve police misconduct, let alone abuse or brutality (House of Commons Home Affairs Committee, 1980). Nevertheless, it was clearly an issue that provoked concern about police departure from the rule of law, and was an element in the politicisation process.

The RCCP Report was eventually transmuted into the Police and Criminal Evidence Act 1984 (PACE). This purported to provide a balanced codification of police powers and safeguards over their exercise, synthesising the concerns of the 'law and order' and the civil liberties lobbies. We will consider how far it succeeds in this in Chapter 6. What is certain is that the issue of police abuse of powers has increased rather than abated, especially in the late 1980s and early 1990s. Between 1989 and 1991 police confidence in the police was shaken by a series of scandals revealing serious malpractice. In October 1989 the Court of Appeal released the Guildford Four, the three men and a woman sentenced to life imprisonment in 1974 for the Guildford and Woolwich pub bombings. In the Lord Chief Justice, Lord

Lane's words, new evidence gathered by the Avon and Somerset Constabulary showed that some of the Surrey officers investigating the bombings 'must have lied' at the trial of the Four. *Police Review* commented that 'the service is facing the greatest attack on its creditability since the allegations in Operation Countryman'. The following year the Court of Appeal exonerated the Maguire Seven, who had also been jailed in connection with the bombings. A further blow to confidence in the police was the release in March 1991 of the Birmingham Six, who had been convicted in 1975 of the savage Birmingham pub bombings. In 1991 the case of Judith Ward (who had been convicted for a 1974 IRA coach bombing) was referred to the Court of Appeal, and a new inquiry set up into the conviction of four men for the 1978 murder of a newsboy, Carl Bridgewater. There was also continuing concern about a number of even older miscarriages of justice, such as the cases of Craig and Bentley, and Timothy Evans, in the early 1950s (Woffinden, 1989). Allegations of corrupt conspiracies to pervert the course of justice reached as high as the Cabinet in the Stalker case, arising out of the removal of John Stalker from his inquiry into fatal shootings by the RUC (Stalker, 1988). Possibly the most tragic case of all was Stefan Kiszko, who served sixteen years imprisonment for a murder which suppressed evidence showed he could not have done (*Sunday Times*, 23 February 1992, pp. 10–11).

Although these cases profoundly shook public opinion, police representatives often argued they had occurred before recent reforms, and could not happen under the procedures now in force. This argument was itself weakened by a number of *causes célèbres* involving more recent abuses. Some featured on the street violence not related to the bringing of a prosecution, and thus untouched by PACE, of which the most notorious was the 1986 attack on a group of black youths in Holloway (Holdaway, 1986). Directly calling into question police adherence to the rule of law was the scandal involving the West Midlands Serious Crimes Squad, which was disbanded in June 1989 by the then Chief Constable, Geoffrey Dear, after allegations of serious malpractice. (These led to a flurry of successful appeals by people convicted by the Squad.) Perhaps the most damaging blow of all was the Court of Appeal decision in November 1992 to uphold the appeals of the Tottenham Three, who had been convicted of the brutal murder of PC Blakelock during the 1986 Broadwater Farm riot, on the basis of forensic evidence that the accused's statements had not been recorded contemporaneously (as PACE requires). These investigations had supposedly taken place under PACE procedures.

The anxiety produced by these revelations of abuse was enough to make the Home Secretary announce in March 1991 (after the release of the Birmingham Six), the establishment of a Royal Commission on Criminal Justice, chaired by Lord Runciman, the first Royal Commission in twelve years. The change in public views of the police was encapsulated by a *Guardian* cartoon following the successful appeal by the Tottenham Three. A man, late for a date, offers his girlfriend the excuse: 'I asked a policeman the time, and he lied!'

(3) The strategy of minimal force?

Has the traditional policy of 'winning by appearing to lose' been abandoned, perhaps to be replaced by one of losing while appearing to win? This is the question raised by a clear trend to harder-line policing of political and industrial conflict. The preparedness of the police to cope with public order problems began to be expanded and refined during the 1970s (Bowden, 1978; Bunyan and Kettle, 1980; Ackroyd *et al.*, 1980; Reiner, 1980b; Manwaring-White, 1983; Gregory, 1985). The militarisation of policing has proceeded apace in the 1980s in the wake of yet more serious disorder (Brewer *et al.*, 1988; Northam, 1988; McCabe *et al.*, 1988; Jefferson, 1990; Waddington, 1991; Vogler, 1991).

Without much public debate *de facto* 'third forces' developed, specifically trained and readily mobilisable to cope with riots. The Metropolitan Police Special Patrol Group, originally formed in 1965 as a mobile reserve, clearly developed a paramilitary role in dealing with public order and terrorism. All forces now have similar units (under various names), specially trained in riot control, use of firearms and sometimes CS gas. Since 1974 all forces have also formed Police Support Units to help in controlling crowds, strikes and demonstrations. Each comprises twenty-three officers (an inspector, two sergeants and twenty constables). They are all specially trained for public order duties, including the use of shields, but they are normally engaged in ordinary policing at local level. However, they are readily mobilisable to deal with problems arising outside their own force under mutual aid arrangements.

The PSUs are coordinated in a crisis by the National Reporting Centre, established in 1972 and located at Scotland Yard. When in operation it is controlled by the current President of the Association of Chief Police Officers (ACPO). Its most controversial and prominent use was during the 1984–5 miners' strike.

All these mutual aid arrangements are the fruits of the establishment panic in 1972, after the Saltley coke depot had to be closed during picketing by miners after a six-day struggle. While Saltley was seen as an abject defeat by many Conservatives and police officers, it was regarded by others as an example of the traditional 'winning by appearing to lose' strategy. Reginald Maudling, the then Home Secretary, believed it would have been possible for sufficient force to be used to clear the gates, but the long-run consequences for social stability would be disastrous (Clutterbuck, 1980, p. 75; Jeffery and Hennessy, 1983, p. 236). After Saltley there was much debate about the need for a CRS-style 'third force'. The police succeeded in scotching the idea, but in effect created 'third forces' within their own organisations, as the 1984 miners' strike indicated. In this strike a massive, centrally coordinated police operation was directed by the National Reporting Centre, with much criticism of 'police-state' tactics (Coulter et al. 1984; Reiner, 1984, 1991, Ch. 8; Fine and Millar, 1985; Spencer, 1985; Percy-Smith and Hillyard, 1985; McCabe et al., 1988; Green, 1991). During the trial of miners on riot charges, it was revealed that in the early 1980s ACPO had produced a secret document, the Tactical Options Manual. This set out the blueprint for a finely graded response to public disorder, culminating in the militaristic tactics used at Orgreave and elsewhere during the strike (Northam, 1988; Waddington, 1991). Altogether the trauma of the miners' strike for policing has been rightly compared to the impact of Vietnam on the US military (Graef, 1989).

In addition to the SPGs and PSUs many other ordinary police officers now receive riot control training. The intensity of this is suggested by occasional pleas at Police Federation Annual Conferences that training be made less realistic because of an unacceptably high level of injuries on police courses. It is hard to remember the shock which greeted the bringing out of police riot shields at Lewisham and Notting Hill in 1977, replacing the traditional protection of dustbin lids. But shields, strengthened helmets and other protective equipment are now regular sights. After the police failure to contain the 1980 Bristol riots and their lack of success in preventing widespread damage and police injuries in the 1981 Brixton, Toxteth and other disorders, police preparation for riot control has redoubled, with Home Office support (Kettle and Hodges, 1982; Unsworth, 1982; Joshua *et al.*, 1983). During the riots themselves, of course, there was an evident intensification of police tactics, notably the first use of CS gas in riot control in mainland Britain, and high-speed driving of police vehicles to disperse crowds. Altogether in the 1981 riots levels of injury unknown for nearly fifty years in English disorders were inflicted on both police and civilians by boot, brick, fist, truncheon and petrol bomb.

The immediate response of Conservative politicians and police was to call for tougher tactics, equipment and legal powers for the police.[9] The government declared itself ready to meet these demands. Mrs Thatcher told parliament that the government agreed to the use of water cannon, CS gas and plastic bullets if Chief Constables wanted them. The army demonstrated the use of water cannon and armoured cars to a party of police chiefs, and offered riot helmets and sticks, armoured carriers and training in unarmed combat. A deputation of senior English police officers also visited Northern Ireland to discuss riot control with the RUC and see what lessons could be learned from their 'success'. The advice of the Hong Kong police was sought by ACPO (Northam, 1988).

The majority of Chief Constables initially expressed reservations about the rapid pace of change. A deputation from the ACPO met William Whitelaw, the then Home Secretary, on 15 July 1981 and voiced anxieties about the detrimental effects on the traditional police image of the introduction of too much offensive hardware. John Alderson, then Chief Constable of Devon and Cornwall, who represented the liberal pole of police opinion, expressed the gravest doubts:

> There has to be a better way than blind repression. . . . . We must
> not advance the police response too far ahead of the situation. It is
> even worth a few million pounds of destruction rather than get
> pushed too far down that road. (*Sunday Telegraph*, 12 July 1981; see
> also Alderson, 1984)

In the end it was this more balanced approach which prevailed
over Lord Scarman's Inquiry, which was set up by the
government in the wake of the Brixton riots (Scarman, 1981;
Benyon, 1984). Neither the tougher methods available after 1981,
nor the wider Scarman inspired reforms, were able to avert even
more serious urban riots in 1985, in West Midlands, Liverpool,
Brixton, and on the Broadwater Farm estate in Tottenham
(Gifford, 1986). The latter was the most disturbing outbreak of
all. Firearms were used against the police, and plastic bullets
deployed (but not used) by them. Most tragically there was the
savage hacking to death of PC Keith Blakelock, the first Met.
police officer to be murdered in a riot since PC Culley in the 1833
Coldbath Fields case. After the riots, the Met. Commissioner, Sir
Kenneth Newman, warned that he would use plastic bullets
should such violence occur again. His successor, Sir Peter Imbert,
argued at a Howard League lecture in 1987 that the 'winning by
appearing to lose' strategy had to be abandoned in the face of
regular disorder of such magnitude, or it would amount simply to
losing all the time.

Serious public disorder occurred again in an industrial context
at Wapping in 1986–7, during picketing outside the News
International plant. Many complaints of undue violence were
made against the police, and the Police Complaints Authority
upheld some of these after an investigation. However, although
charges were brought against several officers in 1989–91, these
were all dismissed as the passage of time was held to make
further proceedings unjust. Other apparently unjustified uses of
militaristic public order tactics occurred during the policing of
hippy convoys converging on Stonehenge (Vincent Jones, 1986).
During 1990 anti-poll demonstrations were the source of severe
public order clashes, especially following a march and rally in
Trafalgar Square on 31 March. In the worst rioting since 1985,
over 300 officers were injured, and 300 arrests made. Damage,
looting and violence fanned out from Trafalgar Square to
neighbouring areas in central London, with tourists, theatre-

goers and shoppers caught up in the mêlée. Despite the levels of violence and disorder, criticisms of police abuse and over-reaction surfaced quickly, and a Trafalgar Square Defendants' Committee was formed. In October 1990 a breakaway group from a south London anti-poll tax rally marched on Brixton prison to support those sentenced for the Trafalgar Square troubles. This led to serious disorder, with 45 police officers injured and 105 arrests. The Trafalgar Square Defendants' Committee blamed a 'pre-planned police attack'.

In recent years, the greatest public order concerns have not been industrial or political conflicts. A 'moral panic' has developed about disorder occurring in a variety of leisure contexts. In 1988 ACPO raised fears about growing disorder in rural areas cause by 'lager louts', with 'too much beer in their bellies and money in their pockets'. Subsequent Home Office research questioned the idea of disorder growing in *rural* areas (as distinct from towns in county force areas), and the alleged connection with affluence (Tuck, 1989). In 1989–90 there was great police concern about the spread of 'acid-house' parties, and the violence they stimulated, as several officers were seriously injured in raids. The most serious violence and disorder in a leisure context occurred, in September 1991, in riots on the Blackbird Leys estate, Oxford, and Meadow Well estate, Tyneside, after police attempts to curb joy-riding. The police were subject to criticism both for under-reacting to the joy-riding, and from other quarters for harassing teenagers suspected of joy-riding. Although the British police response to riots remained lower in profile than that of most foreign forces, there has undoubtedly been a stiffening of strategy, and more resort to technology, equipment and weaponry. Dixon is out and Darth Vader is in, as far as riot control goes. The changing image of the British bobby facing disorder was symbolised vividly by the new 'Robocop' body armour unveiled as the latest fashion in late 1991 (*Police Review*, 13 December 1991, pp. 2474–5).

Apart from the growing use of riot control hardware, there has been a rapid proliferation of firearms use by the police in Britain. Although still unarmed (apart from the traditional truncheon) on routine patrol, the number of occasions on which firearms are issued to the police has escalated inexorably. Many forces now deploy some cars carrying guns in their lockers, which can be used on orders from headquarters. The number of occasions when guns are fired by the police remains small, and the rules are tight (and were toughened following the Stephen Waldorf shooting in 1983, the most notorious 'cock-up' yet). Most police officers are adamant in wishing to remain unarmed for routine work, but there is a growth of support for being armed (as shown by a *Police Review* poll in 1990). This is related to a growth of recorded assaults on the police (Christopher, 1990). Whatever the justifications in terms of the growing violence faced by police in public order and routine patrol work, the traditional unarmed image of the British bobby has been undermined. Debate has raged about whether this has aggravated the violence which it is supposed to deal with (Jefferson, 1987, 1990; Waddington, 1987, 1991).

(4) *Accountability?*

Until relatively recently the independence of the British police force from control by any elected governmental institutions was often seen as a virtue, although there has also been a long-standing radical critique arguing that this was anomalous in a democracy (Lustgarten, 1986). However, in the United States, for example, several generations of police reformers regarded the British model of insulation from political control as a solution to problems of corruption and partisanship (Miller, 1977; Goldstein, 1977).

As policing has become more controversial in Britain in the last two decades, so the perception of the mechanisms of accountability has changed. The old mystical substitute of police identification with the public has come under strain as the police came to be seen increasingly as unrepresentative in terms of race, gender and culture, and alienated from the groups they typically dealt with as offenders and victims (PSI, 1983; Holdaway *et al.*, 1984; Bryant *et al.*, 1985; Jones, 1986, 1987; Hanmer *et al.*, 1989; Oakley, 1989; Young, 1991; Holdaway, 1991; Fielding and Fielding, 1992; Walklate, 1992). At the bottom of every specific conflict radical critics pin-pointed the police as being out of control by any outside bodies, the dark side of their vaunted independence, and hence unresponsive to the popular will. They sought to reform the structure of police governance so as to make police policy-making fully accountable to the electoral process. Sophisticated critiques by constitutional lawyers of the existing system appeared (Lustgarten, 1986; Lambert, 1986; Uglow, 1988), and the position came to be the orthodoxy of mainstream liberal as well as radical analyses of the police. While the police themselves have strongly resisted the full radical package, they have conceded increasingly the legitimacy of some aspects of the critique, especially about the complaints system (Goldsmith, 1991; Maguire and Corbett, 1991; Reiner, 1991, Ch. 11). For their part the Conservatives have wanted to maintain the constitutional status quo. They have, however, become increasingly concerned to render the police more accountable for their use of powers, and even more crucially, the effective use of resources (Morgan, 1987; Reiner, 1988b; Horton and Smith, 1988).

At the same time it was becoming increasingly evident that local accountability to police authorities had atrophied. It was being replaced by a degree of central control amounting to a *de facto* national force (Reiner, 1991). These issues will be fully explored in Chapter 6. What is clear is that the perceived lack of adequate accountability has been a major factor undermining their legitimacy in recent years.

(5) Non-partisanship?

The spectacle of James Anderton, Manchester's Chief Constable, or representatives of the Police Federation, preaching at the drop of a helmet about the sinking state of our national moral fibre became so familiar a sight in the 1970s that it is hard to appreciate quite how novel a departure from tradition it was (Reiner, 1978a, 1980a; Hall, 1979; Kettle, 1980; Taylor, 1980).

When, in 1965, the Police Federation, then a humble professional association rather than the media opinion leader it has become, launched at a press conference a pamphlet, *The*

Problem, which argued for police pay rises to help the fight against crime, the authorities were aghast. The official side of the Police Council hammered the Federation for its 'unprecedented breach of faith', while one member was quoted as saying, 'I never thought I would see the day when the representatives of law and order would be advocating anarchy.'

By 1980 the police, at all levels from Chief Constable down to the rank and file, seemed to set the terms of debate on law and order and social policy (Thompson, 1980). This change was heralded by the Marksist revolution at Scotland Yard, as Sir Robert Mark first began his career as pundit on all issues from crime and public order to the quality of car tyres, with a controversial Dimbleby lecture on BBC television in 1972.

In 1975, the Police Federation launched an unprecedented campaign for 'law and order'. It aimed 'to harness the public's growing concern about the state of crime and public order in Britain into a programme for positive action'. The Federation modelled itself on the liberal pressure groups of the 1960s which had successfully campaigned for reform of the law on capital punishment, homosexuality and abortion. The intention was to mobilise 'the silent majority', to influence politicians to support the 'rule of law', and to reverse the liberalising trend in penal and social policy. The campaign was condemned by many as a dangerous departure from the tradition of police non-involvement in politics. The Federation justified itself by asking 'What is "political" about crime?' It claimed the right to comment on legislation and policies which 'affected the working lives of police officers, who might have strong views on it'. In the event, the law and order campaign was shelved in 1976 as a bitter pay dispute developed which was to absorb Federation energies for nearly two years.

In 1978, the Federation relaunched the campaign specifically to influence the 1979 general election. Its Chairman Jim Jardine declared,

> We are anxious to make it a big election issue. We want the political parties to give serious and urgent thought to the problems of law and order and to say what they are going to do to stem the tide of lawlessness in their manifestos.

His promise that the Federation was 'strictly non-political and will not become involved in campaigning on behalf of any party' was belied by the close parallels between police statements and the Conservative Party's declarations on law and order during the campaign. Throughout 1978 and early 1979, a stream of strikingly similar and much publicised pronouncements appeared from police spokesmen and Tory politicians as part of what the media dubbed the 'great debate' on law and order. Two high points, which marked the increasingly explicit political involvement of the police, occurred near the election. A fortnight before polling day, Robert Mark hit the headlines with a broadside comparing the relationship between the Labour Party and the trade unions to 'the way the National Socialist German Workers' Party achieved unrestricted control of the German state'. The way that the media structured the debate in the terms set by what the *Daily Mail* called 'The gospel according to Sir Robert Mark' was neatly illustrated by the headline chosen by the *Evening News* to report James Callaghan's response: 'JIM PUTS IN THE JACKBOOT', which precisely echoed Mark's imagery. The day after Mark's intervention, the Police Federation placed a long advertisement in most national newspapers under the heading, LAW AND ORDER. In essence, it blamed government policies for rising crime and urged support for a set of proposals, ranging from higher police pay to stiffer penalties. The police–Tory symbiosis was underlined when, four days later, William Whitelaw gave a six-point pledge on law and order, which matched all the Federation's points. Despite this, Jim Jardine disingenuously claimed that the £21,000 series of advertisements had not been intended to sway voters. If not, it was a cavalier waste of his members' money.

In the event the advertisements proved to be an investment which reaped handsome dividends. On the first working day after the Conservative election victory, Federation leaders were summoned with urgency to Downing Street to be told that the new government would immediately implement in full the pay increase recommended by the Edmund–Davies committee. The result has been an increasing flood of police recruits. Symbolising the more open accord between the police and the new Conservative government, the Federation broke with past tradition (which had been that their parliamentary adviser was drawn from the opposition party) and reappointed Eldon

Griffiths, a Conservative MP noted for abrasive speeches on law and order. Some members were distressed that the Federation had 'nailed its flag for all to see to the Conservative Party mast', but the Federation justified the move by 'his commitment to the policies which the Police Federation had been putting forward on law and order'.

The 1979 election seemed to presage a situation comparable to the open politicisation of the American police. There so many candidates carry endorsements from rival police associations that even the voter concerned to support law and order might be confused about how to cast his vote. American police not only wield considerable political clout in determining who is elected, but have many times successfully lobbied to destroy liberal policies (Reiner, 1980a, pp. 379–90).

The climax of overt police involvement in political lobbying came in March 1982. This was a last-ditch backlash against a groundswell of establishment support for reforms in police policy and organisation: the 1980 triennial report of the Police Complaints Board (which suggested the need for an overhaul of the system for investigating serious complaints), the 1981 Royal Commission on Criminal Procedure, and above all the reverberating impact of the Scarman Report. In addition the Labour Party had become politicised over the issue of law and order. (The dying tradition of cross-party accord was well symbolised by a conference on community policing held at Exeter University in March 1982. Unable to address the audience in person, Merlyn Rees, the former Labour Home Secretary, sent along instead a speech by William Whitelaw, his Conservative opposite number, to be read out as it exactly expressed his views!)

In March 1982 when the Met. released its annual crime statistics, it analysed them by the race of robbers as identified by victims, highlighting the stereotype of the black mugger. This was an unprecedented use of official statistics in a manner that had clear political implications. It was widely interpreted at the time as an attempt to 'mug' Scarman (Sim, 1982).

Within the same week there was a blistering diatribe by James Anderton, in an hysterical speech condemning 'an enemy more dangerous, insidious and ruthless than any faced since world war two', and exposing an alleged 'long-term political strategy to destroy the proven structures of the police'. The Police

Federation fuelled the growing panic by an advertisement in most national newspapers arguing for the restoration of capital punishment. Police pressure on law and order was echoed by growing criticism from the Tory right of Whitelaw's supposedly 'soft' approach to crime. In the event the Conservatives did hold a vote on the restoration of capital punishment soon after their election victory in the summer of 1983, but it was defeated.

The March 1982 events were the high-water mark of overt police lobbying for law and order. McNee's successor as Metropolitan Commissioner from October 1982, Sir Kenneth Newman, has avoided the high-profile politicking of his predecessors, as has Sir Peter Imbert, the present incumbent, although both have been assiduous cultivators of the media. But far from 'mugging' Scarman, they introduced a profound redirection of policy in the Scarman spirit.

During the 1983 and 1987 general elections police interventions were about as vociferous as Sherlock Holmes' non-barking dog. In the late 1980s the police at chief officer level and Federation level were clearly trying to step back from the overtly politicised stance in favour of the Tories which reached its high point in the miners' strike of 1984–5.

The love affair between the Tories and the police cooled as public expenditure cuts began to bite on the police, and they feared a hidden agenda of incipient privatisation (Rawlings, 1991). For its part Labour has tried hard to repair broken bridges. Neil Kinnock was interviewed in *Police Review* in 1986 saying he had had a childhood ambition of becoming a policeman. Labour spokespersons have assiduously attended Police Federation conferences, and criticised the Tories for cutting police expenditure. In March 1990 during the critical Mid-Staffordshire by-election, Police Federation leaders appeared on a Labour platform. It would be exaggerating to claim that the police had switched partisan loyalties. Rather there was a return to cross-party consensus on law and order (accentuated in this and other areas by the replacement of Margaret Thatcher by John Major as Tory leader in late 1990). A minority of die-hards remained. One-fifth of chief constables stated in 1987–8 that they would resign if Labour came to power and implemented its proposals on police accountability (Reiner, 1991, p. 212). However, this stance is declining. The prototype of the outspoken Chief Constable, now Sir James Anderton, retired in 1991. He had become even more controversial in the late 1980s for his supposedly divinely inspired utterances on AIDS and other topics, as well as his involvement in the Stalker affair (Stalker, 1988). Despite this he retained the loyalty of his force throughout. A *Police Review* cartoon on his resignation well expressed their ambivalence. As Anderton is seen departing the station, one PC says to another: 'I'm sorry to see him go in a way. He was the only Chief Constable I've ever known who thought someone else was God!' By then most Chief Constables had come to believe overt police interventions in political and social debates were unwise (Reiner, 1991, pp. 210–19). None the less, the years of partisanship had tarnished, possibly irretrievably, the sacred aura hitherto enjoyed by the British police of being, like the Queen, above party politics.

(6)   *The service role?*

The service role continues to be paid lip-service by Chief Constables. Indeed, an influential current of police thinking stresses that contrary to the growing image of the police as primarily crime fighters, much if not most of uniformed police work (measured by time or number of incidents dealt with) consists of service calls for help. This message has been pushed by some police officers for two decades, notably those influenced by John Alderson, the former Chief Constable of Devon and Cornwall, with his philosophy of community policing, and by Bramshill Police Staff College (Brown and Howes, 1975; Alderson, 1979, 1984; Pope and Weiner, 1981). This school of thought urged that the large proportion of service tasks in the actual activity of the police ought to be more explicitly recognised and rewarded, and encouraged in training and force organisation. Community policing has now become an influential movement amongst progressive police chiefs in the United States and elsewhere (Skolnick and Bayley, 1986, 1988).

The very energy put into this campaign is an index of the degree to which the service aspects of policing were devalued and downgraded by the operative force status system. There is copious evidence that most rank-and-file policemen believe the service aspects of the work should have low or no priority. As one uniform constable summed it up: 'This idea of performing a public service is a load of cobswobble as far as I'm concerned' (Reiner, 1978a, pp. 213–17). Nor is there much evidence of the public seeing the police as a broad service agency (Brogden and Wright, 1979). In truth, the service work of the police is largely a by-product of their availability on a 24-hour basis, and their possession of coercive powers in order to perform their core mandate of order maintenance and law enforcement. When people call the police to a scene of trouble (even if there is no immediately obvious crime aspect) they do so not primarily because they require the services of an amateur priest, psychiatrist, nurse or marriage guidance counsellor, but because the problem needs authoritative resolution, by force if necessary (Bittner, 1974). To say that the police are a crypto-social work agency because so many of their calls involve this, is like saying sociologists are professional coffee drinkers because this is what they spend so much of their time doing (like I am now).

However, the encouragement of the service role was an effective device in police legitimation. (This is also true in other countries, cf. Weinberger and Reinke, 1991.) The devaluing of it by rank-and-file culture, as crime fighting became elevated to its glorified pedestal – a process encouraged unintentionally by Unit Beat reorganisation – was problematic for police legitimacy. The response of many Chief Constables was to set up specialist community relations units to provide an artificial surrogate for what tradition had held to be part of basic constabulary duty (Brogden, 1982, Ch. 8). Such specialist liaison units began to proliferate in the late 1960s as forces grew larger with the post-1964 wave of amalgamations, more distant from their communities, and specialisation of all kinds multiplied. Since the Scarman Report endorsed a kind of community policing philosophy this has become the orthodox analysis of the police role for all chief constables (Reiner, 1991, Ch. 6). The evidence of recent decline in public support has led to a redoubling of the effort to define policing in service terms, in the Met.'s Plus Programme and the ACPO Statement of Common Purpose and Values (Woodcock, 1991; Hirst, 1991). The success of these worthy attempts at relegitimation has yet to be seen.

(7)   Preventive policing?

Peel's original conception of policing emphasised patrol by uniformed constables as fundamental. This notion of the bobby on the beat as the essential bedrock of the force, to which all other specialisms are ancillary, remains a philosophy to which most Chief Constables pay constant homage. But in practice specialist departments have proliferated, and foot patrol has been downgraded. It is often treated as a reserve from which high-flying potential specialists can be drawn, and a Siberia to which failed specialists can be banished (Jones, 1980; Jones and Winkler, 1982). Whereas specialisms are always kept up to strength by temporary 'manning-up', or by replacing personnel who leave, the uniformed branch is often below its nominal complement of officers. Beat work is an apprenticeship through which all police officers must pass, but seldom wish to stay in or return to, and most patrolling constables are young and inexperienced. (It is not just a sign of hardening arteries to perceive policemen as getting younger all the time.) Uniformed patrol is also devalued in the rank-and-file sub-culture, looked down upon by the CID in particular (Reiner, 1978a, pp. 134–5; Graef, 1989).

The Unit Beat reorganisation represented a move towards specialisation within the patrol function itself. It encouraged the development of the hedonistic action perspective on police work, and glorification of the thrills of car chases, combat and capture (Holdaway, 1977, 1983). Relationships between Panda car drivers and the public were much more likely to be restricted to conflict situations than with old-style foot patrol. As a uniformed inspector put it to me: 'Before UBP you heard there was a fight round the corner, and by the time you got there, they were probably tucked up in bed together. Today the policeman is there in seconds, while it's still going on, and he has to sort it out.'

The abrasive quality which may have been unintentionally imparted to beat policing by reorganisation was augmented by the proliferation of mobile units, such as the Special Patrol Group. The SPG's role in public order has already been noted. It was also frequently used during the 1970s in anti-crime operations involving blitzes on designated high-crime areas, often ones with large ethnic minority populations (Rollo, 1980). Its contribution to the souring of police–black relations was noted by Lord Scarman.

During the 1960s and 1970s the meaning of crime prevention shifted. Originally it referred to the 'scarecrow' function of regular uniform patrol, augmented by the deterrent value of detection after the event. In the 1960s this was transmuted into a notion of prevention as pre-emption (as patrol became a 'fire brigade' emergency service). Pre-emption meant two things. First it meant the strategy, built into the Unit Beat System as its bedrock, of collecting and coordinating the low-level information provided by patrolling and area constables who were to be evaluated by the quality and quantity of information they accumulated (Baldwin and Kinsey, 1982). A central role in the system was given to the collator, the station-based officer whose task was to assemble and monitor the information provided from the streets. This largely consists of hunches based on the political and personal proclivities of individuals who arouse the idio-syncratic suspicions of local police. With the proliferation of computers in police forces (and the growth in capacity of the Police National Computer) this information has become more centralised and widely and readily available, as well as acquiring an insidious status as 'hard data'. As Duncan Campbell noted, this has fundamental implications for the character of policing: 'In this "pre-emptive" view, any citizen, certainly any socially uncharacteristic citizen, is a target for suspicion and observation. This quite explicit development in police planning has virtually put the whole of society under surveillance' (Campbell, 1980, p. 65).

The second meaning of pre-emption is the development of specialist crime prevention departments, whose function is the uncontroversial one of providing advice to citizens on methods of minimising the risk of victimisation, and alerting them to the dangers of some kinds of offences (Clarke and Mayhew, 1980). At first crime prevention departments were Cinderellas of the service, low status, low budget and low key. However, as crime prevention has become increasingly central to the government's law and order policy in the 1980s so they have blossomed into belles of the ball (Harvey *et al.*, 1989; Bottoms, 1990; Reiner and Cross, 1991, Ch. 1). The impact of such vaunted crime prevention efforts as Neighbourhood Watch is mixed however (Bennett, 1989, 1990; Forrester *et al.*, 1988).

In the view of some critics the community policing philosophy, emphasising both service and crime prevention work, is itself only a more covert (and therefore insidious) means of penetrating communities to acquire information (Bunyan, 1981; Christian, 1983, Ch. 17; Gordon, 1984). What seems clear is that the pursuit of greater effectiveness has meant a proliferation of specialist and plain-clothes units, reversing the original strategy of Peel, Rowan and Mayne. These policies are themselves a response to the undermining of the eighth ingredient of legitimation.

(8)   *Police effectiveness?*

Police effectiveness is a notoriously slippery concept to define or measure. But the official statistics routinely produced by police forces and published by the Home Office seem to record an inexorable rise in serious offences and decline in the clear-up rate since the mid-1950s. Whereas in the mid-1950s there were less than half a million indictable offences recorded as known to the police in most years, this rose above half a million for the first time in 1957. By 1977 it was over 2 million, 1982 more than $2\frac{1}{2}$ million and by 1991 it topped 4 million; 1990–1 has seen each quarter beating the previous record for the rate of increase of recorded crime (*Report of Her Majesty's Chief Inspector of Constabulary*, 1991). Before the war the percentage of crimes recorded as cleared up was always over 50 per cent. By the late 1950s it had dropped to about 45 per cent, and it is now around 38 per cent. The inadequacy of these figures is well known (Box, 1981, Chs 3 and 6; Bottomley and Coleman, 1981; Bottomley and Pease, 1986; Hough, 1987; Chatterton, 1987a; Reiner, 1988b; Audit Commission, 1990b; Walker, 1992). Many crimes are not reported to the police, so increases in the rate may mean a greater propensity to report rather than suffer victimisation. The clear-up rate is affected by many other determinants apart from detective effectiveness including massaging the figures (Young,

1991). None the less it is hard to argue that the recorded trends do not correspond to basic changes in the same direction, and they are certainly associated with a growing public fear of crime and a popular sense that police effectiveness is declining (Hough and Mayhew, 1983; PSI, vol. I, 1983; Lea and Young, 1984; Maxfield, 1984; Kinsey *et al.*, 1986; Mayhew *et al.*, 1989).

Police legitimacy has been undermined by their apparent inability to deal with crime in the suites as well as in the streets. As the salience of fraud problems has grown in the 1980s, so there has been increasing concern about police incompetence or partiality in this area (Levi, 1987).

The police themselves have until recently used the crime figures to bolster their law and order campaigns, lobbying for more resources and power. Paradoxically the very policies of increasing technology, centralisation, specialisation and professionalisation as a means of crime fighting may have aggravated the police ineffectiveness which motivated them.

In recent years the Home Office Research Unit has produced a growing volume of evidence (paralleling earlier American findings) indicating that current methods of patrol and detection are of dubious effectiveness (Clarke and Hough, 1984). Taking a lead from this (as well as the Scarman Report) several Chief Constables have attempted to redirect methods of policing towards a restoration of public confidence and cooperation – a new social contract as Sir Kenneth Newman called it (Reiner, 1991, Ch. 7).

There is some evidence that overall evaluations of the police by the public are not as dependent on technical effectiveness as on personal style (Jones and Levi, 1983; *Operational Policing Review*, 1990). None the less, the consequences of concerns about declining effectiveness leading to new tactics and provoking law and order campaigns was undoubtedly a factor in their politicisation in the 1960s and 1970s.

The social context of declining police legitimacy

Police activity has always borne most heavily on the economically marginal elements in society, the unemployed (especially if vagrant), and young men, whose lives are lived largely in the street and other public places (Stinchcombe, 1963; Cohen, 1979; Brogden, 1982; Jones, 1982, Ch. 7; Steedman, 1984, pp. 56–9). Such powerless groups have aptly been named 'police property' (Cray, 1972; Lee, 1981). Whereas the incorporation of the working class modified their systematic resentment at policing, police conflict with the residuum at the base of the social hierarchy remained. Studies of policing in all industrial societies shows this to be a constant (Brogden *et al.*, 1988, Ch. 6). The police themselves recognise this and their argot contains a variety of derogatory epithets for their regular clientele drawn from this stratum. In California they are 'assholes' (Van Maanen, 1978), in Canada 'pukes' (Ericson, 1982), in London 'slag' or 'scum' (PSI, vol. IV, 1983, pp. 164–5), and on Tyneside 'prigs' (Young, 1991). Drawn mostly from the respectable working class (Reiner, 1978a), the police are responsive to their moral values and adopt a disdainful scorn for those whose life-styles deviate from or challenge them. But however conflict-ridden, relations between the police and 'slag' are not usually politicised. Membership in the marginal strata is temporary (youths mature, the unemployed find jobs) and their internal social relations are atomised, so a sense of group identity is hard to develop. Moreover, police action against them has majority support, even (perhaps especially) from the respectable and stable adult working class (Johnson, 1976).

One crucial factor which politicised policing in the 1960s and 1970s was the development of social strata with a consciousness of antagonism towards (and from) the police. This owes something to the development of more self-conscious youth cultures, the return of long-term unemployment, and the increasing militancy of industrial conflict since the early 1970s.

A more crucial change, however, has been the catastrophic deterioration of relations with the black community. There is a long history of police prejudice against blacks and complaints of racial harassment. By the mid-1970s clear evidence mounts of blacks (especially black youths) being disproportionately involved in arrests for certain offences, partly (though not only) because of police discrimination. A vicious cycle of interaction developed between police stereotyping and black vulnerability to the situations that attract police attention (Stevens and Willis, 1979; Reiner, 1981b, 1985, 1989a; Lea and Young, 1984; Lea, 1986;

Jefferson, 1988). Unlike the traditional marginal strata, however, blacks have a consciousness of being discriminated against, and a 'lack of confidence in the police which can only be described as disastrous' developed (PSI, vol. IV, 1983, p. 326). Furthermore, the common experience of discrimination in other areas of social life means many 'respectable' adult blacks will share an identification and common cause with black youths in their struggles with the police, in a way that white adults from the respectable working class would not have done (Gilroy, 1987; Cashmore and McLaughlin, 1991).

The burden of recent research on police–public relations suggests clearly that while these remain harmonious with the majority of the population (including most of the working class) they are tense and conflict-ridden with the young, the unemployed, the economically marginal and blacks, especially if they also fit the other three categories – which they do disproportionately (PSI, vol. I, pp. 314–15, vol. IV, pp. 162–8, 1983; Jones and Levi, 1983; Southgate and Ekblom, 1984, pp. 28–30, 1986). What has happened to politicise policing since the 1970s is a growth in the size of these vulnerable groups, primarily due to the economic crisis, and a heightening of their self-consciousness as targets of policing.

This is due to long-term structural changes in the political economy of Western capitalism. Long-term structural unemployment (increasingly never-employment) has re-emerged, leading to the *deincorporation* of increasing sections of the young working class, especially amongst discriminated-against minorities, 'who are being defined out of the edifice of citizenship' (Dahrendorf, 1985, p. 98). A new underclass is forming not simply as a result of unemployment, but its seeming structural inevitability.

> The majority class does not need the unemployed to maintain and even increase its standard of living. . . . The main point about this category – for lack of a better word we shall call it 'underclass' – is that its destiny is perceived as hopeless. (*ibid.*, pp. 101–7)

There is much debate about the now popular concept of an underclass, and its conservative, culturalist version has unacceptable connotations of 'blaming the victim'. But the structurally generated formation of a completely marginalised segment of society is a major source of the huge growth recently of crime, disorder and tensions around policing. Unemployment is certainly not linked to crime or disorder in any straightforward, automatic way, as the Conservatives are ever ready to tell us. But there is now much evidence that in the present period at any rate it is a factor in the emergence of a young underclass which has the motive, the opportunity, and the lack of those social controls which are brought by social integration, to be a key part of the explanation of crime and disorder (Dahrendorf, 1985; Farrington *et al.*, 1986; Box, 1987; Field, 1990; Reiner, 1990). The conflicts between the socially marginal and the police are perennial, although they are now more extensive than during the postwar boom. However, the key to how this is translated into political debate is a long-term cultural change in the articulate opinion-forming middle class.

The police have lost the confidence of certain small but crucial sections of the influential and articulate 'talking classes', what may be described roughly as *The Guardian* or *The Independent* reading circles. This process of a developing gulf with some educated middle-class opinion has a variety of roots, stretching back to the invention of the car (Waddington, 1982a; Judge, 1983). But the most crucial are the growth of middle-class political protest since the early 1960s (CND, the anti-Vietnam War demonstrations, the 1960s' student movement and counter-culture) and the politicisation of forms of marginal deviance which involve some middle-class people, notably drug-taking and homosexuality.[10] This conflict with highly articulate and educated sections of the population has been of enormous significance in converting policing into an overt political issue.[11]

CONCLUSION

This chapter has charted the process of police legitimation in the century after 1856, and its reversal since the 1960s. Part II will consider the knowledge gained by studies of police culture and work. This historical and sociological understanding will be brought to bear on current developments and debates in Part III.

Sociology

CHAPTER 3

COP CULTURE

An understanding of how police officers see the social world and their role in it – 'cop culture' – is crucial to an analysis of what they do, and their broad political function. It is a commonplace of the now voluminous sociological literature on police operations and discretion that the rank-and-file officer is the primary determinant of policing where it really counts – on the street.[1] As James Q. Wilson puts it, 'the police department has the special property . . . that within it discretion increases as one moves down the hierarchy' (Wilson, 1968a, p. 7). It is often argued that legal rules and departmental regulations are marginal to an account of how police work operates. A central tenet of the highly practical culture of policing is that 'you can't play it by the book'. The core laws enforced by the police are the Ways and Means Act and 'contempt of cop', neither of which has as yet received any parliamentary or judicial imprimatur. The original impulse for much of the research on police discretion was a civil libertarian concern about the extent and sources of police deviation from due process of law through their espousal of a 'crime control' model (Packer, 1968).

In recent years this approach has come under fire from radicals, most notably and effectively Doreen McBarnet (1976, 1978a and b, 1979, 1981a, b and c).[2] She argues that the civil libertarian critique has failed to distinguish between abstract rhetoric about the general values underpinning the rule of law, and concrete legal rules: there is 'a distinct gap between the substance and the ideology of law' (McBarnet, 1981a, p. 155). The rights of suspects presumed by ideological rhetoric are not clearly encapsulated in statutory or common law rules giving them practical effect. The laws governing police practice are sufficiently permissive to give officers a wide range of discretion. The courts have often seemed ready to accommodate extensions of the rules to legitimate police practice. The assumption of writers like Skolnick that the police routinely violate the law makes the low-level operatives 'the "fall-guys" of the legal system taking the blame for any injustices' (*ibid.*, p. 156). But responsibility ought to be placed on 'the judicial and political elites' who make rules of sufficient elasticity to assimilate departures from idealised values of due process legality, which the law effectively condones or even demands. McBarnet's detailed examination of the content and operation of the rules of criminal procedure is of immense value. But it does not displace the need for analysis of the police sub-culture and the situational pressures on officers' discretion. To say that the laws governing police behaviour are 'permissive' is only to suggest that they do not even purport to determine practical policing (contrary to legal ideology). That leaves considerable leeway for police culture to shape police practice in accordance with situational exigencies.

Legal rules are neither irrelevant to nor completely determining of police practice. As the PSI study (1983) argues with impressive clarity, it is helpful to distinguish between three types of rules: 'working rules' are ones which police officers actually have internalised so that they become the effective principles which guide their actions; 'inhibiting rules' are external ones which have a deterrent effect – officers must take them into account in their conduct, because they are specific, thought likely to be enforced, and refer to visible behaviour; 'presentation rules' are used to impart an acceptable gloss to actions actually informed by different 'working rules'. The relationship between any of these sets of rules and the law is problematic. Legal rules may well be used presentationally, rather than being operational working rules or inhibitors. They then act as an ideological façade whereby the public at large can give the Nelson touch to the messy realities of policing. This all means that the standard legalistic response to revelations of police malpractice – slap on a new rule – may be irrelevant or even counter-productive (PSI, vol. IV, 1983, pp. 169–72).

The culture of the police – the values, norms, perspectives and craft rules – which inform their conduct is, of course, neither monolithic, universal nor unchanging. There are differences of outlook within police forces, according to such individual variables as personality, generation or career trajectory, and structured variations according to rank, assignment and specialisation. The organisational styles and cultures of police forces vary between different places and periods. Informal rules are not clear-cut and articulated, but embedded in specific practices and nuances according to particular concrete situations and the interactional processes of each encounter. None the less, certain commonalities of the police outlook can be discerned in the reports of many studies in different social contexts. This is because they are rooted in constant problems which officers face in carrying out the role they are mandated to perform, at any rate in industrial capitalist societies with a liberal-democratic political ethos. Cop culture has developed as a patterned set of understandings which help to cope with and adjust to the pressures and tensions which confront the police. Successive generations are socialised into it, but not as passive or manipulated learners. The culture survives because of its 'elective affinity', its psychological fit, with the demands of the rank-and-file cop condition.

Cop-culture: the core characteristics

The *locus classicus* for discussing police culture remains Skolnick's (1966) account of the policeman's 'working personality'.[3] What needs to be added to his analysis are the variations around his basic model, within and between police forces. Skolnick's portrait also fails to draw out the politically relevant dimensions of police culture. This culture both reflects and perpetuates the power differences within the social structure it polices. The police officer is a microcosmic mediator of the relations of power in a society – he is a 'street corner politician' (Muir, 1977). The values of the police culture act as 'subterranean processes in the maintenance of power' (Shearing, 1981a).

Skolnick synthesises all the earlier sociological research with his own findings to construct a sketch of the policeman's 'working personality' (Skolnick, 1966, Ch. 3). This is not an individual psychological phenomenon (as the term 'personality' misleadingly implies), but a socially generated culture. It is a response to a unique combination of facets of the police role: 'two principal variables, danger and authority, which should be interpreted in the light of a "constant" pressure to appear efficient' (*ibid.*, p. 44).

The 'danger' in the police milieu is not adequately represented by quantitative estimates of the risk of physical injury.[4] Other occupations – say steeplejack, miner, diver, anyone working with asbestos – may be exposed to higher risks of job-related disease or death. But the policeman is unique in regularly being required to face situations where the risk lies in the unpredictable outcome of encounters with other people. The police officer has to confront the threat of sudden attack from another person, not the more calculable risks of physical or environmental hazards. The extent of the seriousness of this obviously varies. It is undoubtedly less in Newbury than New York. But the police officer faces, behind every corner he turns or door-bell he rings, some danger, if not of firearms at least of fists.

The danger is linked to the next element which is integrally part of the police milieu, authority. It is because he represents authority, backed by the potential use of legitimate force, that the police officer faces danger from those who are recalcitrant to it. Traditional British police organisation and tactics have been directed towards minimising the use of force by converting power into authority, by making the individual constable a symbol of an impersonal and universally accepted law. But in each individual encounter this presentation is liable to be challenged when authority has to be exercised over someone. Danger and authority are thus interdependent elements in the police world, to which cop culture develops as a set of adaptive rules, recipes and rites.

Skolnick postulates a third environmental element producing cop culture: 'the pressure put upon individual policemen to "produce" – to be efficient rather than legal when the two norms are in conflict' (Skolnick, 1966; pp. 42, 231). Undoubtedly police officers experience external political pressure for 'results', more or less so at different times according to particular moral panics or trends in crime statistics. Under the pressure to get 'results' in the form of clear-ups, policemen may well feel impelled to stretch their powers and violate suspects' rights. (Notorious recent examples are the cases of the Guildford Four, the Birmingham Six, the Tottenham Three, and the West Midlands Serious Crimes Squad scandal.)

Skolnick over-emphasises the degree of external compulsion in this. Public expectations of the police are themselves inflated by police propaganda about their capacities as professional crime fighters, which they have elevated as their core mandate (Manning, 1977). Police officers are for the most part intrinsically dedicated to the goals of 'maintaining order' and 'fighting crime'.

Mission – action – cynicism – pessimism

A central feature of cop culture is a sense of *mission*.[5] This is the feeling that policing is not just a job but a way of life with a worthwhile purpose, at least in principle. 'It's a sect – it's like a religion, the police force' (constable, cited in Reiner, 1978a, p. 247). The purpose is not conceived of as a political enterprise, but as the preservation of a valued way of life and the protection of the weak against the predatory. The core justification of policing is a victim-centred perspective. As a constable put it to me: 'Speaking from a policeman's point of view it doesn't give a damn if we oppress law-breakers, because they're oppressors in their own right' (*ibid.*, p. 79).

The mission of policing is not regarded as irksome. It is fun, challenging, exciting, a game of wits and skill. Many commentators have stressed the hedonistic, action-centred aspects of cop culture (notably Holdaway, 1977, 1983; PSI, 1983, vol. IV, pp. 51–6). They are undoubtedly very strong and of central importance. The main substance to which the police are addicted is adrenalin (Graef, 1989). But the thrills of the chase, the fight, the capture, the 'machismo syndrome' (Reiner, 1978a, p. 161)

although rare highlights of the work, are not merely a sport.
They can be so uninhibitedly and delightedly engaged in because
they are seen also as worth while. In a policeman's own eyes he is
one of the 'good guys' and it is this which gives him the licence
for action. He is not just a racing driver or boxer in a blue
uniform.

This moralising of the police mandate is in many respects
misleading. It overlooks the mundane reality of everyday
policing, which is often boring, messy, petty, trivial and venal. It
permits the elision of the universally approved elements of the
police task (apprehending a murderer, say) and the political role
of policing in upholding a specific state and social order.
Certainly the 'sacred canopy' (Manning, 1977, p. 5) often drawn
over police work can be a tool of the organisation, protecting and
advancing its interest in gaining more resources, power and
autonomy from independent scrutiny. Nevertheless, it is important in understanding police work that it is seen as a mission, as a
worthwhile enterprise, not just another job. This makes its
established practices all the more recalcitrant to reform than if
they were merely self-serving.

The elements of mission in the police perspective are reflected
in their sense of themselves as 'the thin blue line', performing an
essential role in safeguarding social order, which would lead to
disastrous consequences if their authority was threatened. It
underlies their rejections of the right to strike. The removal of
their presence is typically seen as producing horrendous consequences:

> We're responsible people, who're not likely to turn around and jack
> the job in and leave the country open to anarchy. So that I'm not
> going to have to sit in the kitchen at night with a shotgun on my
> knees. (Reiner, 1978a, p. 110)

These views are of course partly presentational. Under the
Edmund–Davies pay formula, in operation since 1978, the police
receive an explicit monetary consideration for sacrificing the right
to strike. Nor does the evidence of police strikes elsewhere
confirm the popular view that they inevitably result in a
breakdown in social order, despite the well-known horror stories
of Boston 1919, Liverpool 1919 and Montreal 1969 (see Bopp,
1971; Ayres and Wheelen, 1977; and Reiner, 1978a, pp. 5–6).

But the sentiment is much more than a mere bargaining counter. The myth of police indispensability, of their essential mission 'to protect and serve', is central to the police world-view. Nevertheless, police officers rapidly acquire a set of views which have been rightly described as 'cynical', or 'police pessimism' (Niederhoffer, 1967; Vick, 1981). Policemen often develop a hard skin of bitterness, seeing all social trends in apocalyptic terms, with the police as a beleaguered minority about to be over-run by the forces of barbarism (Reiner, 1978a, Ch. 11). This pessimistic outlook is only cynical in a sense – in the despair felt that the morality which the police officer still adheres to is being eroded on all sides. It is not a Wildean cynicism which knows the price of everything and the value of nothing. Rather it resembles a Marxian account of commodity fetishism: price has sadly masked value. The very strength of the hard-boiled outlook of policemen derives from the resilience of their sense of mission. As Vick has put it, 'police pessimism can be taken seriously only if order and stability are excessively valued' (Vick, 1981, p. 121). Cynicism is the Janus face of commitment.

The salience of a sense of mission obviously varies between police officers. It was much more evident in the type I labelled the 'new centurions' (after the title of Joseph Wambaugh's seminal 1971 police novel) than those the argot calls 'uniform carriers', who shirk the work as much as possible (Reiner, 1978a, Ch. 12). But many (if not most) 'uniform-carriers', with their quintessentially cynical views ('It's the survival of the fittest. . . . You've got to look after No. 1. . . . The policeman should exploit his job to the full advantage') became that way precisely because of the effects of career disappointment destroying a prior sense of mission. Far from starting off as cynics, they joined with, if anything, excessively high ideals (*ibid.*, pp. 239–41 is a case study). As Sir David McNee once concluded, 'You have to be emotionally committed or you can't stand the life. . . . This isn't just a job, it's a cause' (quoted in Whitaker, 1979, p. 242).

Undoubtedly many policemen see their combat with 'villains' as a ritualised game, a fun challenge, with 'winning' by an arrest giving personal satisfaction rather than any sense of public service (Reiner, 1978a, pp. 215–16; PSI, 1983, vol. IV, pp. 61–6). But this cynical view may well function as a self-protecting shield to reduce the anxiety that the thief-taker's many failures would otherwise induce.[6] One constable advised me:

> All police work's a game. You get the people who do wrong and the people that try and catch them. Sometimes the wrong-doers get caught, sometimes they don't. If they get caught and copped, if they get nicked and weighed-off, fair enough. If they don't there's no point getting emotionally involved.

Cynicism about thief-taking as a game is thus functionally analogous to the role of humour as tension release, expressed in the motto, 'If you can't take a joke you shouldn't have joined this job' (Reiner, 1978a, pp. 216–17; Holdaway, 1983, pp. 138–54).

The core of the police outlook is this subtle and complex intermingling of the themes of mission, hedonistic love of action and pessimistic cynicism. Each feeds off and reinforces the other, even though they may appear superficially contradictory. They lead to a pressure for 'results' which may strain against legalistic principles of due process. *Pace* Skolnick's account, this pressure for 'efficiency' is not primarily derived externally but a basic motivating force within police culture. It does, however, relate to the other facets of cop culture – suspicion, isolation/solidarity, conservatism – in the way Skolnick suggests.

Suspicion

Most policemen are well aware that their job has bred in them an attitude of constant suspiciousness which cannot be readily switched off. As one detective put it to me:

> You drive along and you see things, or read things differently to your wife or friends. And invariably matchboxes and cheques are covered with car-numbers and this sort of thing. You go to the football, and you tend to be more aware, to keep your eye on the yobs. Or you notice odd things, like an old chap standing by a school. (Reiner, 1978a, p. 210)

Suspiciousness is a product of the need to keep a look-out for signs of trouble, potential danger and clues to offences. It is a response to the danger, authority and efficiency elements in the environment, as well as an outcome of the sense of mission.

Policemen need to develop finely grained cognitive maps of the social world, so that they can readily predict and handle the behaviour of a wide range of others in many different contexts without losing authority in any encounter (Rubinstein, 1973, Chs 4–6; Holdaway, 1983, Chs 6–7). Police stereotyping has been the subject of many critiques. These suggest that stereotypes of likely offenders become self-fulfilling prophecies as people with those characteristics are disproportionately questioned or arrested, leading to a vicious cycle of deviance amplification (Young, 1971). However, stereotyping is an inevitable tool of the suspiciousness endemic to police work. The crucial issue is not its existence, but the degree to which it is reality based and helpful, as opposed to categorically discriminatory in a prejudiced way – and thus not merely unjust but counter-productive for the police force's own purposes (Banton, 1983).

Suspiciousness does not only develop out of the intrinsic conditions of police work; it is deliberately encouraged by training. Skolnick cites an American manual giving detailed guidance for field interrogations which begins, 'Be suspicious. This is a healthy police attitude.' Among the Catch-22 tips for signs of the 'unusual' subject who should be stopped are: '7. Exaggerated unconcern over contact with the officer. 8. Visibly "rattled" when near the policemen' (Skolnick, 1966, pp. 45–6). A similar guide to the 'abnormal', embracing most of the population, is found in an English field manual by David Powis, a former Metropolitan Assistant Commissioner. Powis includes in his list of suspicious types, political radicals or intellectuals who 'spout extremist babble', or people in possession of a 'your rights' card, such as those provided by the NCCL (Powis, 1977).

While police suspiciousness and stereotyping are inescapable, the particular categories currently informing it are ones which reflect the structure of power in society. This serves to reproduce that structure through a pattern of implicit discrimination.

Isolation/solidarity

Skolnick and many other commentators have emphasised the marked internal solidarity, coupled with social isolation, of police officers (Clark, 1965; Westley, 1970, Ch. 3; Cain, 1973; Reiner, 1978a, pp. 208–13; Graef, 1989). They have been referred to as 'a race apart' (Banton, 1964), 'a man apart' (Judge, 1972), 'a beleaguered minority' (Alex, 1976).

Certainly, many police officers report difficulties in mixing with civilians in ordinary social life. These stem from shift work, erratic hours, difficulties in switching off from the tension engendered by the job, aspects of the discipline code, and the hostility or fear that citizens may exhibit to the police. Social isolation is the price to be paid for Peel, Rowan and Mayne's policy of elevating the British police as symbols of impersonal authority, and was to an extent a direct product of recruitment policies aimed at severing officers from their local communities (Miller, 1977, pp. 26–8). Internal solidarity is a product not only of isolation, but also of the need to be able to rely on colleagues in a tight spot, and a protective armour shielding the force as a whole from public knowledge of infractions. Many studies have stressed the powerful code which enjoins officers to back each other up in the face of external investigation (Stoddard, 1968; Westley, 1970, Ch. 4; Shearing, 1981b). The offences which colleagues shield are not necessarily major infractions to be protected from external eyes. Rank-and-file solidarity is often aimed at concealing minor violations (what Cain calls 'easing behaviour') from the attention of supervisory officers.

This points to a misleading aspect of Skolnick's emphasis on solidarity and isolation. First, it neglects the importance of conflicts inside the police organisation. Some of these are structured within the rank hierarchy and the force division of labour, say between uniform and detective branches. It is true that these internal conflicts may often be over ridden by the need to present a united front in the face of external attacks. But this is not always so. The fundamental division between 'street cops' and 'management cops' can be reinforced in the face of external investigation (Ianni and Ianni, 1983; Punch, 1983b). 'Management cops' are derided by the 'street-wise' operational officers. The depth of the gulf is due to the different, often contradictory, functions of the two levels. The 'management' have to project an acceptable, legalistic, rational face for policing to the public. This may mean complicity with misconduct in some circumstances, deliberately hearing, seeing and saying nothing. But when reform pressures become intense, the 'management' may be forced into confrontation with the street level. To an extent, however, the apparent gulf and conflict between 'street' and 'management' orientations is functional for the organisation itself (Grimshaw and Jefferson, 1987). It allows presentational strategies to be adopted by management levels in real ignorance of what these might cover up, while at the same time the sacrifice of some individuals as 'bent' ratifies the effectiveness of the disciplinary process as a whole (Shearing, 1981c).

The them and us outlook which is a characteristic of police culture makes clear distinctions between types of 'them' (as well as of 'us'). The police perspective on social divisions in the population clearly reflects the structure of power as filtered through the specific problems of police work (Reiner, 1978a, Ch. 11; Shearing, 1981a and c; Lee, 1981; Holdaway, 1983, Ch. 6; Young, 1991).

The social structure as perceived by the police is one in which the hard class distinctions of the past have been eroded. Many policemen subscribe to an ideal of egalitarianism (epitomised by remarks such as 'nothing would give me greater pleasure than being able to nick the Lord Mayor'). At the same time they are acutely aware of the status distinctions which exist (and their need to be finely tuned to them in giving and expecting the appropriate level of deference): 'You deal with everybody here. From the basic form of human life in the jungle conditions of the bad areas, to the elite of the town. The posh dinner parties that go on. You have to handle them all' (uniform constable). Society does not bestow fair and equal chances: as one constable remarked, 'It's hard for a kid if his mother's tomming it, and his dad's always in the boozer.' But between the limited extremes of the problem areas at the bottom of the scale, and the elite at the top, is the ordinary mass of the population and mobility here is possible, as reflected in many policemen's own lives, and dependent on merit and application.

The crucial divisions for the police do not readily fit a sociologist's categories of class or status. They are police-relevant categories, generated by their power to cause problems, and their congruency to the police value-system (Norris, 1989). The fundamental division is between rough and respectable elements, those who challenge or those who accept the middle-class values of decency which most police revere. But finer distinctions within these categories can be made which are generated by the police problematic. Seven important groups can be distinguished: 'good-class villains'; 'police property'; 'rubbish'; 'challengers' (Holdaway, 1983, p. 71); 'disarmers' (Holdaway, 1983, p. 77); 'do-gooders'; and 'politicians'.

(1) 'Good-class villains'

'Good-class villains' are professional (or at least experienced) criminals (PSI, 1983, vol. IV, pp. 61–4). Pursuing them is seen as worth while, challenging and rewarding, indeed the *raison d'être* of the policeman's life, however infrequently the ordinary officer might encounter such a case. Moreover, the villains are likely to play the game with the same understandings as the police. While obviously wishing to evade arrest, they do not normally challenge the basic legitimacy of the police. Relations with them may well be amicable – indeed, this may be cultivated by both sides for favours – the thin end of the corruption wedge.

(2) Police property

'A category becomes police property when the dominant powers of society (in the economy, polity, etc.) leave the problems of social control of that category to the police' (Lee, 1981, pp. 53–4). They are low-status, powerless groups whom the dominant majority see as problematic or distasteful. The majority are prepared to let the police deal with their 'property' and turn a blind eye to the manner in which this is done. Examples would be vagrants, skid-row alcoholics, the unemployed or casually employed residuum, youth adopting a deviant cultural style, ethnic minorities, gays, prostitutes and radical political organisations. The prime function of the police has always been to control and segregate such groups, and they are armed with a battery of permissive and discretionary laws for this purpose. The concern with 'police property' is not so much to enforce the law as to maintain order using the law as one resource among others. A major problem for the police is not to mistake a member of a higher-status group for police property. This danger is reinforced in policing ethnic minority groups where the police officer is not as attuned to the signals of respectability. It is also a problem which has become accentuated for the police with the growth of respectable middle-class involvement in 'deviant' activities. The demonstrator or pot-smoking hippy may be a university professor.

(3) 'Rubbish'

'Rubbish' are people who make calls on the police which are seen as messy, intractable, unworthy of attention, or the complainant's own fault (PSI, 1983 vol. IV, pp. 64–6). Domestic disputes are a common sort of call regarded as 'rubbish' by many police officers: 'With domestic disputes, the husband and wife going hammer and tongs, you've got to separate them, calm them down before you go. And you're not doing a policeman's job, you're doing a socialist's [sic]' (Reiner, 1978a, pp. 214–15, 244–5). 'Rubbish' are essentially people from the 'police property' groups presenting themselves as victims or clients for service, as they often do (PSI, 1983, vol. I, pp. 314–15). Indeed a major finding of crime surveys is the social isomorphism of victims and offenders (Hough and Mayhew, 1983; Jones *et al.*, 1986; Mayhew *et al.*, 1989).

(4) 'Challengers'

'Challengers' are defined by Holdaway (1983, pp. 71–7) as those whose job routinely allows them to penetrate the secrecy of police culture, and gives them power and information with which they might challenge police control of their 'property'. Doctors, lawyers, journalists and social workers are in this position (as are police researchers!). Efforts will be made to minimise their intrusion, and presentational skills used to colour what they see. The Scarman-inspired development of schemes for lay visitors to police stations is an attempt to ensure regular penetration of the backstage areas of the police milieu by organised 'challengers' (Kemp and Morgan, 1989). PACE attempts to facilitate access by relevant 'challengers' such as duty solicitors or 'appropriate adults' (Thomas, 1988; Sanders *et al.*, 1989).

(5) *'Disarmers'*

'"Disarmers" are members of groups who can weaken or neutralise police work' (Holdaway, 1983, pp. 77–81). They are groups who are hard to deal with either as suspects, victims, witnesses or in service work, because they are perceived as socially vulnerable and so allegations by them against the police may receive special sympathy. Holdaway specifies women, children and the elderly as the main disarmers.

Anyone may turn out to be an unexpected 'disarmer' because of the limitless naivety of the public, so the police officer has to be wary of every encounter. One constable told me of an incident where he let off with a warning a man doing 65 m.p.h. in the city, after he explained that his wife was in labour.

> A fortnight bloody later he writes to the chief constable. He explains all the circumstances and wants to thank me. I got dragged in there and given the thickest bollocking ever for condoning him going at 65 m.p.h. He dropped me right in it. (Reiner, 1978a, p. 246)

(6) *'Do-gooders'*

'Do-gooders' are principled anti-police activists who criticise the police and organise to limit their autonomy (Reiner, 1978a, pp. 221–3). The prime example is the 'National Council for the Prevention of Policemen Doing Their Duty' (the NCCL, now renamed Liberty). 'We're going through a spate of do-gooders who do no good! . . . They shout and shout to create problems or they'd be out of a job' (uniform constables, *ibid.*). A similar more recent development was the proliferation in the 1980s of police monitoring groups (Jefferson *et al.*, 1988).

(7) *Politicians*

Politicians are regarded suspiciously. They are remote and unrealistic ivory-tower idealists, corrupt self-seekers, secret subversives, or simply too weak to resist villainy (Reiner, 1978a, pp. 76–81):

> The trouble is the Government think they're legislating for educated men. . . . But the people here are animals, they're thick . . . MPs are out of context altogether. . . . They live in a different world. I mean, every meal these politicians have is a six-course one! (a uniform constable, *ibid.*)

Beset by all these threatening elements, the police become a solitary group: 'We're a tight-knit community. We've got to stand by each other because we're getting it from all angles. We get it from outside, the general public, we get it from solicitors, from QCs, we get it from our own bosses' (*ibid.*, p. 246). Running through the perception of the social structure is a distinction between the powerless groups at the bottom of the social hierarchy who provide the 'rubbish' and the 'police property', and the respectable strata, with distinct segments which in different ways threaten police interests. The police culture both reflects the wider power structure and reproduces it through its operations.

Police conservatism

The motto of the fabled Canadian Mounties is, 'Uphold the right', a quintessential statement of the police sense of mission. Critics have always charged that this really means, 'Uphold the Right', and undoubtedly the evidence we have of the political orientations of police officers suggests that they tend to be conservative, both politically and morally.

Partly this is a function of the nature of the job. The routine 'clients' of the police are drawn from the bottom layers of the social order. But control of the lumpen elements is not necessarily something which even politically conscious members of the working class would be averse to. However, in their public order role (and even more so in the work of the specifically political sections of the police, as Bunyan (1977) documents) the police are routinely pitted against organised labour and the Left. Furthermore, the force has from the start been constructed as a hierarchical, tightly disciplined organisation. Thus the police officer with a conservative outlook is more likely to fit in. Processes of selection and self-selection lead police officers to be conservative.

However, there are contradictory pressures at work. Fiscal and political prudence from the start dictated pay and recruitment policies which meant that the bulk of officers were drawn from the working class, and these processes still operate today. Even chief officers come predominantly from working-class origins (Reiner, 1991, Ch. 4). The police are an employee group whose grievances over pay and conditions of work has generated militancy and trade union organisation analogous to that of other workers (Levi, 1977; Reiner, 1978a; Bernstein *et al.*, 1982, Ch. 6). The 'deradicalisation' of the policeman is not automatic, but had to be constructed (and continuously reconstructed), as Robinson (1978) cogently argues. The tendency towards militancy and unionisation which develops in some police pay disputes has to be suppressed by appropriate carrot-and-stick strategies by the government (Reiner, 1978a). Usually, however, such policies are successfully accomplished, and the role of policing labour disputes inclines officers to anti-union views.

In the United States there is copious evidence of police political support for the Right and the far Right. Skolnick sums up his own interviews and observations by stating: 'A Goldwater-type of conservatism was the dominant political and emotional persuasion of police' (*ibid.*, p. 61). Further evidence of American police support for conservative politics, disproportionately great for their socio-economic position, is found in Bayley and Mendelsohn (1968, pp. 14–30), Lipset (1969) and Bent (1974, Ch. 5). These attitudes have been openly translated into political campaigning in the last twenty years. Police associations have on numerous occasions actively lobbied for reactionary political candidates, and in support of specific right-wing policies (Skolnick, 1969, Ch. 7; Bopp, 1971; Ruchelman, 1973, 1974; Halpern, 1974; Alex, 1976; Reiner, 1980a, pp. 379–90).

There is no comparable evidence of British police officers' political views. When I attempted to interview policemen about their political attitudes (as part of a wider study of police unionism) this was prohibited by the Home Office, as it was claimed that it would impugn the traditional notion of the police as outside any form of politics (Reiner, 1978a, pp. 11, 283). I have seen an unpublished 1977 dissertation by a police officer who interviewed a sample of colleagues in a northern city force, using the questions I had been prohibited from asking. He found that 80 per cent described themselves as Conservative – 18 per cent of whom were to the right of the party. The remainder were evenly divided between Labour, Liberal and 'don't know'. Of his sample, 80 per cent had voted in all recent elections. A slight rightward shift is indicated by the fact that 9 per cent had moved from Labour or Liberal to Conservative during 1974–7, with no movement in the opposite direction. Despite this, 64 per cent affirmed that the police should remain politically neutral at all times (reminiscent of the old saw about the superintendent stoutly declaring that his men took no interest in politics – they were all staunch Conservatives), 21 per cent wished for the right to join a political party without taking an active role, while 12 per cent wished to be able to take an active part in politics. The trend in the 1970s to more open involvement in political debate of Chief Constables and the Police Federation has already been described. It clearly expressed views which were symbiotically related to Conservative Party policies, and parallels (at a less explicit level) the American 'blue power' political campaigning of the 1960s and 1970s.

Apart from specific party politics, the police tend to hold views on moral and social issues which are conservative. 'Cops are conventional people. . . . All a cop can swing in a milieu of marijuana smokers, inter-racial dates, and homosexuals is the night stick' (Brooks, 1965; cited in Skolnick, 1966, p. 61). A 1960s' survey of New York police attitudes found that the two most disliked categories of people after 'cop-fighter' were the homosexual and the drug addict (Niederhoffer, 1967). Police hatred of homosexuals and hippies in California is well illustrated by Jacobs (1966, esp. pp. 13–17). I found similar support for a narrowly conventional morality in my interviews with British police (Reiner, 1978a, Ch. 11; see also Lee (1981) for Canadian evidence). The social philosophy of Chief Constables also tends to the conservative, although this is less stridently expressed (Reiner, 1991, Ch. 9).

Machismo

Despite this moral conservatism, in many respects police culture departs from puritanism. The police world is one of 'old-fashioned machismo'. Sexism in police culture is reinforced by discrimination in recruitment and promotion (Hanmer *et al.*, 1989). The contempt exhibited for such sexual deviance as homosexuality and paedophilia is accompanied by routinised 'sexual boasting and horseplay', often at the expense of women colleagues (PSI, 1983, vol. IV, pp. 91–7). Policemen are not notorious for their aversion to illicit heterosexual activities. As one constable told me, 'Policemen have one of the highest divorce rates in the country. There's always a bit of spare round the corner, because of the glamour of the job' (Reiner, 1978a, p. 212).[7] Nor are policemen notably abstemious from alcohol for all their contempt for users of other drugs. One hazard of police research is the taking of mental notes while sinking under a bar as the consumption of pints mounts. Police alcoholism has been a perennial problem from the early days of the force until the present (PSI, 1983, vol. IV, pp. 81–7). The alcoholic and sexual indulgences of police are a product both of the masculine ethos of the force, and the tension built up by the work. Their significance in this regard is brought out best by the novels of Joseph Wambaugh, in particular *The Choir-Boys* (1976), with their central theme of policing as a morally (even more than physically) dangerous occupation. The decidedly non-puritanical ethos about heterosexual behaviour, drinking and gambling can expose the police officer to strains, tensions and charges of hypocrisy when enforcing laws in these areas (Skolnick, 1966, pp. 56–7; PSI, 1983, vol. IV, pp. 92–3). This is a major factor explaining the greater propensity for police corruption in the specialist enforcement of vice laws.

It has always been tough for women police officers to gain acceptance. The establishment of employment for police women in the first place came only after a protracted campaign (Carrier, 1988). Despite formal integration today they continue to experience discrimination (Bryant *et al.*, 1985; Jones, 1986, 1987; Heidensohn, 1989, 1992). The difficulties they face in achieving higher rank are illustrated by the recent action claiming sex discrimination which has been brought by Alison Halford, Assistant Chief Constable in Merseyside (Grant, 1992).

Racial prejudice

A final most important aspect of police conservatism is racial prejudice. A large number of American studies demonstrate police suspiciousness, hostility and prejudice towards blacks, and vice versa. It is usually argued that this is a reflection of the racism of American culture generally, and especially the social groups from which most police are drawn (lower middle or working class with no more than high school education). Bayley and Mendelsohn (1968) sum up their own and many other studies: 'Are policemen prejudiced? The answer is yes, but only slightly more so than the community as a whole. Policemen reflect the dominant attitudes of the majority people towards minorities' (p. 144). (See also Westley, 1970, pp. 99–104; Skolnick, 1966, pp. 81–3; Reiss, 1971, p. 147; Rossi *et al.*, 1974, Chs 5–6.) American police have also been prominent in political opposition to the civil rights movement and in support for far-right political organisations with a racist character (Reiner, 1980a, pp. 383–8; Garrison, 1984).

There is similar evidence from many studies of British police racial prejudice. It is noteworthy that the earliest documentation of this prejudice pre-dates by many years official police allegations or statistical data claiming a problem of black over-involvement in crime. Cain's and Lambert's studies of city forces in the early and late 1960s show a clear pattern of rank-and-file police prejudice, perceiving blacks as especially prone to violence or crime, and generally incomprehensible, suspicious and hard to handle (Lambert, 1970; Cain, 1973, pp. 117–19). My own interviews in Bristol in 1973–4 found that hostile and suspicious views of blacks were frequently offered quite spontaneously in the context of interviews concerning police work in general (Reiner, 1978a, pp. 225–6). Of the sample, 25 per cent volunteered adverse comments, while 35 per cent in the central division (which included St Paul's) did so. One uniform constable summed up the pattern: 'The police are trying to appear unbiased in regard to race relations. But if you asked them you'd find 90 per cent of the force are against coloured immigrants. They'd never want you to do that research and come up with that sort of finding.' Other work from the mid-1970s to the early 1980s, conducted in a period in which black crime and especially mugging became heated political issues, confirms and amplifies the evidence of prejudice (Southgate, 1982, p. 11; Gordon, 1983, Ch. 4; Holdaway, 1983, pp. 66–71; PSI, 1983, vol. IV, Ch. 4; Reiner, 1985, 1989a; Lea, 1986; Jefferson, 1988).

However, it cannot be assumed that police prejudice is translated into behaviour expressing it. As the seminally important PSI study puts it:

> Our first impression after being attached to groups of police officers was that racialist language and racial prejudice were prominent and pervasive . . . on accompanying these officers as they went about their work we found that their relations with black and brown people were often relaxed or friendly. (PSI, 1983, vol. IV, p. 109)

American research suggests a similar pattern of disjunction between prejudice and discriminatory behaviour (Black, 1970, 1972; Friedrich, 1979). There are also hints in recent work that post-Scarman reforms may have reduced the overt expression of prejudice, or at any rate made it assume more subtle forms (Brown, 1988; Bull and Horncastle, 1989; Pearson *et al.*, 1989).

The other qualification that must be made to the recital of evidence of police racial prejudice is that it may be no more than a reflection of general societal prejudice. Until recently the consensus of social research (here and in the United States) suggested that, contrary to popular belief, police recruits did not have especially authoritarian or prejudiced personalities (Skolnick, 1969, p. 252; Reiner, 1978a, p. 157). Rather, they shared the values of the social groups from which they were drawn – the lower middle and respectable working classes, which constitute the bulk of society. This is, of course, a double-edged finding, for while police recruits may not be more authoritarian than the general population, the 'normal' degree of authoritarianism is disturbing in an occupation which wields considerable power over minorities. As Stuart Hall has commented trenchantly, Chief Constables would not state so cavalierly the equally true proposition that the police force must contain its fair share of criminals (Hall, 1979, p. 13). It must be noted too that prejudiced views are also common amongst Chief Constables themselves (Reiner, 1991, esp. pp. 204–10).

One much publicised article has challenged this orthodoxy (Colman and Gorman, 1982). The authors administered several psychological tests intended to assess dogmatism, conservatism and authoritarianism, as well as specific views on race relations, to three samples: a group of 48 police recruits at the beginning and end of basic training; 36 probationer constables with an average of 20 months' experience; and a control group of 30 civilians supposedly matched to the police groups in socio-economic status. They found that 'the police force attracts conservative and authoritarian personalities, that basic training has a temporarily liberalising effect, and that continued police service results in increasingly illiberal/intolerant attitudes towards coloured immigration.' Their results have been subject to severe criticism on methodological grounds, but they have defended themselves on most of the points of detail (Waddington, 1982b; Colman, 1983). Probably the most important criticism is that made by A.J.P. Butler who has conducted similar research of his own (Cochrane and Butler, 1980; Butler, 1982a). Butler stresses that the control groups had a higher average level of education, which could be at least part of the explanation for the more 'authoritarian' police recruit attitudes. Butler's sample of recruits did not suggest the police attract individuals with radically distinct value systems compared with a matched civilian control group. Nor does another more recent study of recruits (Brown and Willis, 1985). This shows up the importance of Colman and Gorman's own caveat about their data: 'Any attempt to generalise these results to other areas of the UK or to other countries is . . . unsafe' (Colman and Gorman, 1982,

p. 10). What Colman and Gorman's research does reveal is that (although not necessarily sharply distinctive from the population norm) the police recruits did manifest very hostile attitudes to ethnic minorities, as their quotes from open-ended responses clearly demonstrate.[8] On the question whether these views are indications of a distinctive authoritarianism, it is still best to be agnostic. It does seem, however, that such attitudes are accentuated with work experience, after a temporary liberalising effect during training (Fielding, 1988). Whether the profound changes in selection and training since Scarman will change this pattern remains largely untested, although there have been some promising early research results (Southgate, 1988; Bull and Horncastle, 1989).

Overall, it is both necessary and sufficient to explain the police outlook on ethnic minorities (and other issues) by the police function, and the circumstances of police work, rather than peculiarities of individual personality. Even if at some times and places distinctive personality types are attracted to policing, it would still be necessary to analyse the nature of police work as the determinant of the attraction. The crucial source of police prejudice is societal racism which places ethnic minorities disproportionately in those strata and situations from which the police derive their 'property'. This structural feature of police–ethnic minority relations bolsters any prior prejudice police officers have (Jefferson, 1988; Reiner, 1989a).

Pragmatism

The final element of police culture which it is important to stress is the very pragmatic, concrete, down-to-earth, anti-theoretical perspective which is typical of the rank and file, and indeed Chief Constables (with a growing number of exceptions). This is a kind of conceptual conservatism.

Police officers are concerned to get from here to tomorrow (or the next hour) safely and with the least fuss and paperwork. This makes them reluctant to contemplate innovation, experimentation or research, though this is changing with the impressive growth of a significant body of practice-oriented research through such bodies as the American and British Police Foundations – unrelated except in name – and the Home Office Research Unit. The limits of much in-house police research are, however, underlined by a study of it by the Deputy Director of the Police Foundation, which questions the tendency to find favourable 'foregone conclusions' (Weatheritt, 1986).

One review of the psychological literature on 'police personality' indicated that while the evidence on such overtly political issues as distinctive authoritarianism or racial prejudice among policemen was mixed, it did seem that police officers have a markedly 'empirical' cognitive structure (Adlam, 1981, p. 156). Recent training innovations have moved towards less didactic techniques to try and counter this (Adlam, 1987).

Variations in cop culture

The organisational division of labour is related but not reducible to a variation in distinct types of individual police perspective around the core elements of the culture. This has been noted by a variety of studies which have developed typologies of different police orientations and styles (Broderick, 1973; Muir, 1977; Walsh, 1977; Reiner, 1978a; Brown, 1981; Shearing, 1981c). What is remarkable is the degree of congruence between these typologies, independently constructed (at roughly the same time in terms of the date of the fieldwork) in three different countries.

Broderick (1973) suggests four 'ideal types' of police perspective: 'the enforcer' emphasises law enforcement at all costs, even if rules must be bent. He has an acute sense of the police as an isolated minority surrounded by a hostile public. 'The idealists' aspire to policing to be a profession, although they resent the public for failing to accord this status; they respect the values of due process, and see policing as having a wider function than crime control. 'The realist' sees both society and the police force cynically as a 'shambles'. 'The optimist' derives the greatest satisfaction from the non-crime tasks of helping ordinary people in trouble.

Walsh distinguishes 'street cops', attracted to police work because it is a secure job; 'action seekers', lured by the prospect of exciting work, especially crime fighting; and 'middle-class mobiles', attracted by the professional status of policing, and ambitious for career advancement. These styles are not fixed. An unsuccessful 'mobile' may eventually become a cynical 'street cop'.

Muir's (1977) study uses sensitive observations of twenty-eight police officers in an American city. It is unique in sociological studies of the police in centring on the question 'what makes a police officer good?', rather than the more common analysis of deviation. Muir approaches this by considering the way police officers deal with the problem of handling coercive power. The good cop has to develop two virtues: 'Intellectually, he has to grasp the nature of human suffering. Morally, he has to resolve the contradiction of achieving just ends with coercive means' (pp. 3–4). Intellectual vision can be 'cynical', i.e. based on a dualistic division of people into 'us' and 'them', fault-finding and individualistic; or 'tragic' seeing mankind as of one unitary substance and moral value, seeing action as complexly produced by chance, will and circumstance, and recognising the important but fragile nature of social interdependence. Moral understanding may be 'integrated', i.e. accommodating the exercise of coercion within an overall moral code; or 'conflictual' where it creates guilt because it is not related to basic moral principles. The two dimensions yield a fourfold typology of police officer: the 'avoider' (with cynical perspective and conflicted morality) shirks duties; the 'reciprocator' (tragic perspective and conflicted morality) hesitates to use coercive power even when appropriate; the 'enforcer' (cynical perspective and integrated morality) acts in the heat of conflicts and without understanding the need for restraint; the 'professional' (tragic perspective and integrated morality) is the 'good' cop. He is able to use violence where necessary in a principled way, but is adept at verbal and other skills which enable solutions to be resolved without coercive force wherever the opportunity for this exists.

My own study distinguished four main types of police orientation: the 'bobby', the ordinary copper applying the law with discretionary common sense, in a peace-keeping role; the 'uniform-carrier', the completely cynical and disillusioned time-server who'll 'never answer the phone if he can help it – it might be a job at the other end!'; the 'new centurion' (see Wambaugh,

1971), dedicated to a crusade against crime and disorder, seeing detective work as the central function, and emphasising the street cop as the repository of all truth, wisdom and virtue; the 'professional' policeman, ambitious and career conscious, with an appropriately balanced appreciation of the value of all aspects of policing from crime fighting to sweeping the station floors, equipping him for the largely public relations functions of senior rank[9] (Reiner, 1978a, Ch. 12).

Shearing's typology distinguished 'wise officers' who were morally committed to the police culture, but balanced the control and legitimation aspects of police work; 'real officers', the hard-nosed cops who saw the tasks of controlling the 'scum' as paramount, becoming the heroes of cop culture; 'good officers' who saw policing as a 'profession' and were committed to liberal-democratic values; 'cautious officers' who had 'dropped out', and were alienated from any of the purposes, policies or people involved in policing.

Brown's (1981) typology based on a study of three Californian police departments is somewhat different in that it primarily considers the crime-fighting styles of police officers. He develops a fourfold typology based on two variables: high/low aggressive-ness, and selective or non-selective enforcement (Ch. 8). His types are the 'old-style crime fighter' (high aggressiveness, selective concern with felonies only); 'clean beat crime fighter' (high aggressiveness, concerned with a broad range of police functions); and 'service-style', exhibiting low aggressiveness but sub-divided into those who avoid work where possible, and those seeing policing as a form of social service.

It is clear that these typologies, constructed for different purposes and with reference to different police forces, are remarkably similar. The basic types are as follows (translating the other author's labels into my terminology):

1. The 'bobby' (= Broderick's 'optimist' = Walsh's 'street-cop = Muir's 'professional' = Shearing's 'wise officer' = Brown's 'professional').
2. The 'new centurion' (= Broderick's 'enforcer' = Walsh's 'action-seeker' = Muir's 'enforcer' = Shearing's 'real officer' = Brown's 'crime fighters').
3. The 'uniform carrier' (= Broderick's 'realist' = Walsh's

cynical 'street cop' = Muir's 'avoider' = Shearing's 'cautious officer' = Brown's 'service type 1').
4. The 'professional' (= Broderick's 'idealist' = Walsh's 'middle-class mobile' = Muir's 'reciprocator' = Shearing's 'good officer').

The differences in nomenclature reflect differing purposes of particular studies, as well as conflicting conceptions of the 'good' police officer – is it possible to play it by the rules (Broderick), must we resign ourselves to the tragic inevitability of coercive power (Muir), or is the apparent conflict of roles ideologically functional for class control (Shearing)? This leads to explicitly opposed notions of the 'professional': the ideal embodiment of legalistic policing (Broderick), the wise, empathetic but un-tutored intuitions of Dixon-style beat work (Muir), a legitimating ideology for individual and collective social mobility (Reiner).

But the same underlying types are postulated: an alienated cynic, a managerial professional, a peace-keeper and a law-enforcer. These correspond with the basic organisational division of labour between management/rank and file, and CID/uniform patrol. But the differing orientations are already discernible in samples of uniform patrol officers, prefiguring future career developments.[10]

The culture of Chief Constables itself varies, with different perspectives typically related to the pattern of previous careers, the character of the force, and the experience of particular generations (Reiner, 1991, Ch. 12). Overall, British chief officers do not have fundamentally different cultural styles from the rank and file, having come from similar backgrounds and worked their way up the force hierarchy. However, they are more likely nowadays to espouse a community policing philosophy, and to see the value of all parts of the organisation, like the 'professional' described above. Their outlook is shaped by the need to accommodate to pressures from governmental and social elites.

The differing orientations do not seem related to demographic characteristics such as ethnic group and gender. No research on these issues exists in England as yet. But American work suggests there is no tendency for black officers to be different in work style from whites (Alex, 1969), or to be less punitive to other blacks (Black, 1972; Geller, 1983). It may be though that increasing the proportion of black officers changes the whole ethos of a department in ways which cannot be discerned in individual comparisons (Jacobs and Cohen, 1978; Sherman, 1983a). Nor is there evidence of significant differences in policing style between male and female officers (Bloch and Anderson, 1974; Sichel, 1978). Again, though, it is plausible that raising the proportion of women in the department might alter the masculine ethos. On the other hand, the whole burden of the argument of the chapter so far is that the culture of the police depends not on individual attributes but elements in the police function itself. Research on differing department styles implies that there is some scope for change, although this is constrained by the social and political context in which the department is embedded.

Variations in organisational culture

The *locus classicus* for considering differences in the styles of whole police organisations is Wilson's (1968a) study, *Varieties of Police Behavior*. Wilson suggested that three departmental styles could be distinguished. The 'watchman' style emphasised order maintenance and the patrolman perspective. Bureaucratisation, standardisation, professionalisation were barely developed, and political influence was rife. Patrol officers had much discretion in handling their beats. The 'legalistic' style operated with a law enforcement approach, attempting to impose universalistic standards impartially on all communities in the city. The organisation was bureaucratic and professionalised. The 'service' style emphasises helpful services. Where possible deviations are handled by cautions rather than prosecution (but they are dealt with formally, not ignored). There is much stress on public relations and community involvement. Although partly a product of departmental policy choices, the styles reflected social and political balances. 'Legalistic' departments replaced 'watchman' ones either after a corruption scandal bringing in a reform administration, or as a result of a slower process of change in the balance of power between class elements, elevating groups with an interest in rational and universalistic authority as a framework for long-run planning. It could run into paradoxical difficulties if introduced in an adverse social context. For example, while less racially discriminatory, the 'legalistic' style enjoined higher levels of law enforcement, and might thus adopt aggressive methods of patrol which blacks saw as harassment. The 'service' style was only developed in middle-class suburban communities with a value consensus.

Rossi examined the relationship between police practices, public opinion and police and political leaders' attitudes in seventeen cities in 1967–8 (Rossi *et al.*, 1974). Some cities seemed much more oriented to 'law and order' in their police practices, others more oriented to 'civil rights'. The different styles could not be accounted for by any characteristics of the individual police officers in the various cities (such as social background, age, education or race). The styles in departmental practices seemed to be features of the whole organisational culture. The degree to which police were acquainted with people in their local precincts and the perception of citizens as hostile accounted for some of the variance between cities, suggesting that controversial police practices were associated with the absence of close non-conflictual relations with the people in their patrol areas. But by far the largest factors associated with tougher policing were the attitudes towards black people and their aspirations held by the mayor and police chief. The more sympathetic the attitudes of these elites to blacks, the lower the frequency of controversial policing practices. The similarity of the mayors' and chiefs' attitudes were explicable by the fact that the police chief was usually hired and fired by the mayor. Altogether, variations in policing styles seemed closely associated with the views of the local political elite and police chief.

There is not much British evidence about differences in culture between police forces. Cain's (1973) study of a rural and a city force in the early 1960s indicated that the country police officers were more closely integrated into the communities they policed. The city officers were by contrast much more closely interdependent with their police colleagues, and alienated from the populations they policed, with more abrasive encounters. This was probably a consequence of the different conditions of policing in rural and urban areas rather than a function of organisational styles readily open to policy change. Urban/rural differences in style are a frequently recurring motif (Shapland and Vagg, 1988; Shapland and Hobbs, 1989).

Jones and Levi (1983) collected data on police and public attitudes in two forces whose Chief Constables stood at opposite poles in the spectrum of police debate. Devon and Cornwall Chief Constable John Alderson was the foremost exponent of the 'community policing' philosophy, emphasising the importance of a close and positive relationship between police and public as the essential precondition of effective policing, and seeing the police role as a broad one with a strong social service component. Manchester's James Anderton had the highest public profile of all Chief Constables, standing for a tough law and order approach.

Jones and Levi found that on a variety of indicators the public in Devon and Cornwall had more favourable judgements of their police than people in Manchester. Moreover, the police in Devon and Cornwall had a more accurate perception of their public standing than the Manchester police, suggesting a closer relationship. However, in both forces the police tended to over-estimate their public standing – a finding that contradicts the earlier 1960 Royal Commission survey which indicated that the police were too pessimistic about how the public saw them. One common criticism levied against the community policing policies of John Alderson was that while it might be appropriate for tranquil rural counties, it would be impracticable in a city. Jones and Levi found, however, that the contrast held true when Plymouth (the second largest city in the South West) was compared to Wigan (a relatively small northern country town), although Plymouth did have the lowest levels of expressed public satisfaction in the Devon and Cornwall force area. This suggests that while it is indeed harder to cultivate positive police–public relations in cities, organisational culture and style are also important variables. However, since the study was a one-off survey, it could not rule out the possibility that a different quality of police–public relations in the two areas pre-dated the introduction of the different force policies, and indeed partly accounts for them (Jones and Levi, 1983).

The clearest evidence of the possibility of introducing changes in police culture comes from an important recent ethnographic study comparing two inner-city London police stations (Foster, 1989). In one, substantial changes in policing style and practices were introduced successfully, altering the culture in the direction intended by the Scarman Report with its espousal of a community policing philosophy. The key ingredient of this achievement was the overall commitment and solid backing of the whole management hierarchy. Where this was lacking in the other station, traditional police culture remained resilient. A similar message of the possibilities of reform even in tough city areas is provided in a study of six innovative police chiefs in the United States, who set out to reorient their departments in a community policing direction (Skolnick and Bayley, 1986). However, it is left somewhat unclear how far this translated successfully into sustained change in practices on the ground.

Altogether it seems that there are significant differences in the culture of policing between different areas. What is less clear is the extent to which these are the products of policy choices which can effectively be made in areas with different social and political structures and cultural traditions.[11] Do societies get the policing they deserve, or can they do significantly better or worse? It is impossible to foreordain the degree of freedom facing reform strategies, although it is undoubtedly never very great. But the variations which have been found in departmental style do imply that the emphasis on the autonomy of rank-and-file culture in the interactionist research tradition may need some qualification. (The resilience of cop culture even in extreme situations is shown by Brewer and Magee's study of routine policing in Northern Ireland, see Brewer and Magee, 1990.) Further development of systematic comparative work would allow us to analyse just how much is constant in police work across a variety of contexts (Bayley, 1985; Mawby, 1991a).

Conclusion

There seem to be certain commonalities in cop culture as discovered by many studies in several different places and periods. These arise from similar elements in the police role in any advanced industrial liberal democracy, notably authority and danger.

Police culture and its variations are reflections of the power structures of the societies policed. The social map of the police is differentiated according to the power of particular groups to cause problems for the police, with the least powerful elements in society becoming police 'property'. The power structure of a community, and the views of its elites, are important sources of variation in policing styles (with 'divided' societies constituting an extreme case, see Brewer, 1991). The different orientations within the police reflect the two ways police organisations have to face in a class-divided hierarchical social order. Downwards by the rank and file, to the groups controlled with varying degrees of gusto or finesse; and upwards by the professional police chiefs, to the majority public and elite who want an acceptable face to be placed on what is done in their name.

CHAPTER 4

DEMYSTIFYING THE POLICE
Social research and police practice

There are two conflicting political mythologies about policing which have bedevilled debate. The law and order myth portrays the police as an effective force for the prevention and detection of crime, and advocates police power as the panacea for law enforcement and public order problems. It was the position espoused by the Conservatives and the police in the early 1980s. The repressive state apparatus myth depicts the police as an essentially oppressive political force creating crime and criminals through its labelling activities. In this view, community safety and harmony require the curbing of police power (e.g. Scraton, 1987).

Research evidence as opposed to presumption about what the police do (and especially the determinants of their actions) remains sketchy, despite a proliferation of studies in America and to a lesser extent Britain in the last three decades (Reiner, 1989b, 1992a). This is even more true when it comes to the question of assessing possible reforms and alternatives to current practice. But the evidence which exists indicates the falsity of both the law and order and repressive apparatus mythologies. Police work is more complex, contradictory, indeed confused, than either model allows. Both the above myths have lost force recently. They have largely been replaced by a consensual, community policing myth (Reiner, 1991, Ch. 6; Reiner and Cross, 1991, Ch. 1). This is equally based on untested and largely unexamined assumptions about the police role in practice. The research evidence will be considered in this chapter in relation to three specific questions:

(1) What is the police role? (2) How effectively is it performed? and (3) How fairly is it performed?

What is the police role?

A perennial chestnut of debate about the police role has been whether the police are best considered as a force, with the primary function of enforcing the criminal law, or as a service, providing balm for a sea of social troubles. The starting point for debate was the empirical 'discovery' that the police (contrary to popular mythology) do not mainly operate as crime fighters or law enforcers, but rather as providers of a range of services to members of the public, the variety of which beggars description.

Banton (1964), on the basis of an analysis of field diaries kept by a sample of Scottish policemen, and on observation and interviews (both in Britain and the United States) concluded:

> The policeman on patrol is primarily a 'peace officer' rather than a 'law officer'. Relatively little of his time is spent enforcing the law in the sense of arresting offenders; far more is spent 'keeping the peace' by supervising the beat and responding to requests for assistance. (p. 127)

Cumming *et al.* (1964) found in an analysis of phone calls by the public to an American force that over half involved demands for help or support in relation to personal and interpersonal problems, in which the police performed as 'philosopher, guide and friend'. This was replicated by Punch and Naylor (1973) in an analysis of the calls by the public to the police in three Essex towns in a two-week period. In a 'new town', 49 per cent were service calls, in an 'old town' 61 per cent; and in a 'country town' 73 per cent. Of the service calls, the largest categories were 'domestic occurrences' (e.g. family disputes or noisy parties) and 'highway accidents'. Martin and Wilson (1969) found that only 28 per cent of duty time in provincial forces (and 31 per cent in the Met.) was spent on crime-related work. Very similar results have been found in many other studies (McCabe and Sutcliffe, 1978; Hough, 1980; Antunes and Scott, 1981; Morris and Heal, 1981,

Ch. 3; Ekblom and Heal, 1982; Shearing, 1984; Smith and Klein, 1984).

The empirical findings about the nature of police activity stimulated two contradictory reactions. For the most part they were used to bolster a liberal argument which became the orthodoxy among progressive police administrators, chiefs and commentators between 1965 and 1975. This was that 'is' meant 'ought'. The police were *de facto* social workers, although not recognised as such. They were a 'secret social service' (Punch, 1979b). But because this was covert and seldom articulated, there was a need for the police to be better trained and organised to cope with the work that anyway accounted for most of their activity. If the law and order panacea for police problems was bigger guns, the liberal panacea was a sociology degree.

The 1974 conference at Cranfield, reported in Brown and Howes (1975), and the initiatives in community development in various police forces summarised in McDonald (1976), pioneered the view that the police role should be more broadly conceived. Not only should training adequately reflect the social service side of police work, but the police had a part to play in the formulation of social policies. The mandate of crime prevention should mean not only that the police engage in the traditional techniques of patrol and detection; they should collaborate with other social service agencies and government to tackle the underlying social causes of crime, as well as the symptoms. In British police circles this view has been most forcefully argued by John Alderson, former Chief Constable of Devon and Cornwall (Alderson, 1979, 1984; see also Moore and Brown, 1981). Altogether in the late 1970s there was an emerging consensus amongst some senior officers and academic commentators that the large elements of social service tasks in the actual activity of the police ought to be more explicitly recognised and encouraged in training and force organisation.

In recent years this has become the new post-Scarmanist orthodoxy of nearly all chief officers (Reiner, 1991, Ch. 6). The *Operational Policing Review* mounted in 1989 by all three staff associations seemed to indicate public preference for a more community-oriented style of policing. This has inspired the recent 'Statement of Common Purposes and Values' in which the police staff associations commit themselves to a mission based on the idea of service. Following the initiative of the Plus Programme in the Met., the HM Inspectorate and ACPO are now bent on the task of reconstructing police culture and practice around an ethic of service to the consumer (*Policing* Special Issue on 'The Way Ahead', Autumn, 1991).

Whilst this consensus was emerging at the top, there was a developing underswell of protest mainly rooted in the police rank and file. Several studies of lower-rank police views document the resentment of many at the extent to which 'service' calls detract from 'real' police work (e.g. Skolnick, 1966; Cain, 1973; Holdaway, 1977; Reiner, 1978a). The consensus of research has been that street-level police culture rests on an action and crime-fighting orientation. This was pithily summed up by one American patrolman: 'Every time you begin to do some real police work you get stuck with this stuff. I guess 90 per cent of all police work is bullshit' (Reiss, 1971, p. 42). The *Operational Policing Review* in 1991 confirmed by its survey of national samples of senior and rank-and-file police that this gulf still exists. While senior ranks increasingly favour community policing initiatives, the operational ranks remain wedded to a 'strong' crime fighting approach (Reiner, 1991, pp. 105–7).

The force/service debate rests on a false dichotomy. In so far as the two roles are distinguishable, they are interdependent, and derive from a more fundamental mandate of first-aid order maintenance. To clarify this, let me define the basic concepts. There are two dimensions underlying police work: (1) Is there consensus or conflict between the civilians and the police in an interaction? (2) Does the police action invoke the legal powers of arrest, prosecution, etc.? Putting the two dimensions together yields a typology of three possible types of police intervention (Table 4.1).

The first cell (the use of legal powers in a consensus situation)

Table 4.1 Dimensions of police work

	Police use legal powers ('law officer')	*Do not use legal powers* ('peace officer')
Consensus	—	'service'
Conflict	'law enforcement'	'order maintenance'

is blank. If there is no conflict about desired outcomes between civilian and police participants in an interaction, there is no need for the invocation of legal powers, which are inherently coercive.

The categories are all 'ideal types' and concrete incidents can only be classified into them after a contingent process of interaction in which different outcomes are possible. Take an incident I observed where police were called out because of incessant barking from a neighbour's dog. The police officer discovered that the owners were not in and climbed over the back garden fence to investigate because the dog sounded in distress. In the course of this the owners returned. The neighbours and the constable explained what had happened, and everyone was satisfied. The outcome was a good example of 'service' work. But it is possible that the neighbours would have got into an argument about the propriety of involving the police, and that an 'order maintenance' situation developed. Depending on many factors, but primarily the officer's orientation to his job, his assessment of the moral characters of the disputants, and his skills at defusing conflict, it is quite possible that the eventual outcome would have been an arrest for assault. (See Chatterton (1983) for a penetrating analysis of the contingent determinants of arrest decisions on assault charges.) Then the outcome would have been classifiable as 'law enforcement' work.[1] The nature of a police intervention is not totally foreordained by the 'call for service' made by a member of the public.

In terms of these more precisely defined types, most police work is neither social service nor law enforcement, but order maintenance – the settlement of conflicts by means other than formal law enforcement. Moreover, this is accomplished in the main by the distinctive police capacity, which is not possession of legal powers of arrest (though police powers do considerably exceed those of the ordinary citizen) nor social work skills, but 'the capacity for decisive action', as Bittner has put it: 'The policeman, and the policeman alone, is equipped, entitled and required to deal with every exigency in which force may have to be used' (Bittner, 1974, p. 35). The police mandate is the very diffuse notion of order maintenance, what Bittner has graphically called 'a solution to an unknown problem arrived at by unknown means'. But beneath the diversity of problems and means is the core capacity to use force if necessary. This does not mean that the police typically (or even often) use coercion or force to accomplish the resolution of the troubles they deal with. The craft of effective policing is to use the background possibility of legitimate coercion so skilfully that it never needs to be foregrounded. Several observational studies have given impressive accounts of how 'good' patrol officers can maintain peace in threatening situations, with their legal powers (including force) as a latent resource (Bittner, 1967a and b; Muir, 1977; Chatterton, 1983). The successful policeman draws on the authority of his office, as well as his personal and craft skills in handling people, rather than the core of coercive power – although sometimes this will not be possible. These skills are not adequately recognised, rewarded or understood, largely because popular and police preconceptions about the nature of the police task have precluded analysis of the craftsmanship involved in effective peace-keeping (Bittner, 1983).

However, order maintenance is just as problematic in terms of social and political justice as the higher profile issues of crime control. The observational studies which vividly depict many examples of good peace-keeping work fail to grapple with these problems adequately. For example, Chatterton gives a detailed account of the calming down of a domestic dispute without the arrest of the husband who had assaulted his wife (Chatterton, 1983, pp. 211–15). In Chatterton's analysis this was ultimately due to the officer exercising his sense of the justice of the man's position (and he gives a persuasive account of the details of the encounter which made this acceptable). In the case he describes an arrest accomplishing 'legal' justice would, from a wider moral or social perspective, have been both unjust and troublesome to all concerned.

This clearly raises the problem of whether we can rely on the personal sense of justice of patrol officers, and how its exercise can be made accountable. The typical handling of domestic 'disputes' as non-criminal, order-maintenance matters, rather than assaults, has been criticised effectively for many years by feminists, and has produced some change in forces around the world. One common reaction has been the encouragement of mandatory arrest policies, shifting this large category of calls unequivocally into 'law enforcement'. There has been much

debate about the effectiveness and desirability of such innovations (Sherman and Berk, 1984; Edwards, 1989; Hanmer *et al.*,
1989; Sheptycki, 1991). The issues of achieving and reconciling
fairness, effectiveness and accountability are just as acute for
order-maintenance work as for the areas of law enforcement
where they have been most widely discussed. This is brought out
clearly in recent American quantitative research on police
handling of inter-personal disputes, which shows evidence of
class, sex and race discrimination in the police reaction to such
incidents, analogous to similar evidence in crime work (Smith
and Klein, 1984). Even those commentators (among them some
eminent neo-conservatives) who have most passionately extolled
the virtues of beat policing and a renewed emphasis on order-
maintenance work have recognised the acute problems of equity
and accountability which are raised (Wilson and Kelling, 1982,
pp. 35–6).

That order maintenance is the core of the police mandate is
attested to in a variety of ways. It is reflected in the pattern of
specific demands placed upon the police by calls for service. Most
involve some element of conflict, not harmonious service requests
like fetching cats out of trees, but do not relate unequivocally to
a criminal offence. Second, it is a core mandate historically. The
main *raison d'être* for the 'new police' was crime prevention by
regular patrol (i.e. intervention in situations before crimes
occurred) as well as order maintenance in the sense of crowd
control. (For similar arguments in the American context, see
Manning (1977), Fogelson (1977), Walker (1977) and Moore and
Kelling (1983).) The unique character of British policing lies
partly in merging the tasks of law enforcement and order
maintenance (including crowd and riot control) into the same
organisation.

However, to say that the primary police role is order
maintenance is not to give the police responsibility for all
elements of social order. Their task is the emergency maintenance of order not the creation of its preconditions, as the
broadest philosophies of community policing seek (Alderson,
1979, 1984). As Waddington has put it: 'The police are the social
equivalent of the AA or RAC patrolmen, who intervene when
things go unpredictably wrong and secure a provisional solution'
(Waddington, 1983a, p. 34). In this analogy, they are neither

service station mechanics nor car makers. But, like the AA, they have a role in advising on policy relevant to their duties and cooperating with other agencies.

In recent years the influential 'new left-realist' school of criminologists in Britain have argued for a 'minimalist' policing approach (notably in Kinsey *et al.*, 1986; their views have also been supported by Uglow, 1988). The argument is that police intervention should be confined to cases where there is clear evidence of law-breaking, and then should take the form of the invocation of legal powers and criminal process. Only in this way, it is claimed, could it be ensured that police work is fully accountable to the law. This ignores, however, the large bulk of calls for service which are not unequivocally reports of crime. On a 'minimalist' strategy this would mean either not responding to such requests, or forcing the police response into a Procrustean bed of legalism untempered by discretion. Whilst the problem of ensuring equity and efficiency in order-maintenance or service work is daunting, the 'minimalist' approach would achieve the confinement of the police to a 'constitutional corral' (as Uglow puts it) only by excluding as illegitimate many problems for which people call the police.

What recent empirical work suggests is that a growing proportion of calls for police service, at least in urban areas, are reports of crime or 'potential crime' (Jones *et al.*, 1986; Shapland and Vagg, 1988, pp. 36–9; Shapland and Hobbs, 1989; this is also true in a number of other countries; see Bayley, 1985, pp. 120–7). This could partly be a result of reconceptualisation of some types of incident (e.g. domestic disputes) into the criminal category, by citizens, police and researchers. It is also plausible, however, that more criminal victimisation is occurring as well as more being reported by victims (Mayhew *et al.*, 1989). Certainly recorded crime rates have risen dramatically over the last decade and constitute a greater pressure on police forces, to which they have responded by increasing the number of specialists with law-enforcement functions (Dorn *et al.*, 1991a and b), even though uniform patrol still constitutes the bulk of personnel deployment (Tarling, 1988, p. 5). It is paradoxical that police strategic thinking has espoused a 'service' philosophy just as evidence is mounting of the increasing centrality of crime in police work. However, uniform patrol remains the bedrock of policing, and this will continue to be preoccupied with order-maintenance, rather than criminal investigation.

Order-maintenance is clearly a political enterprise, raising questions of definition, equity and accountability. The recognition that the distinctive police resource is the authority derived from the potential for the legitimate use of force places policing at the heart of the functioning of the state. However, it is a function which is both necessary and capable of fulfilment by the police. To regard the primary task of the police as crime control is dangerous for the police themselves, for there is now an impressive body of evidence which suggests not only that this is not being accomplished effectively, but that it could not be.

How effective are the police?

The police were part of a process which made cities less violent, crime ridden and disorderly during the course of the nineteenth century. The precise contribution of the police to this, compared with more general processes of social pacification, is hard to pin-point exactly, but it is probable that they were a significant factor. Even if they were no more successful in detecting crime than nowadays, the impact-effect of creating a regularly patrolling force which recorded, and where possible prosecuted, violations probably increased the risks facing offenders (Kelling, 1983, pp. 154–5). The nineteenth-century accomplishments of the police established a base line of order and crime control which the present-day police continue to maintain more or less successfully.

Since the Second World War in most industrial countries there has been a dramatic rise in recorded crime rates, public fear of crime, and anxiety about law and order as a public issue (Mayhew *et al.*, 1989). Until relatively recently discussions about criminal justice policy, and the police specifically, have been locked into the law and order myth that given adequate resources and powers the police could tackle the problem of rising crime. The only opposition to the law and order lobby was on the civil libertarian grounds that police effectiveness must not be bought at too high a price in the undermining of civil rights. However, a recent wave of (largely official and quasi-official) research in the United States and Britain has begun to question the assumption that increased police power and resources can control crime. (Useful surveys are Zander, 1979a; Clarke and Hough, 1980; Morris and Heal, 1981; Kelling, 1983; Clarke and Hough, 1984; Heal *et al.*, 1985.) This cautionary attitude to the effectiveness of increased police spending chimes a harmonious note with the fiscal parsimony of the conservative regimes now dominant in Britain and North America, if not with their traditional soft spot for the guardians of law and order (Reiner and Cross, 1991, Ch. 1).

Studies of patrol work

Since 1954 several studies have been carried out in the United States and Britain aimed at evaluating the effectiveness of foot and car patrol in crime-control work.[2] The initial American researches suggested that crime rates did decline if patrol strength was significantly increased. This early work was flawed methodologically and through data-rigging by the police (Morris and Heal, 1981, pp. 21–2). The English Home Office study conducted by Bright in the 1960s (which was too small scale to be regarded as anything but a tentative basis for conclusions) suggested that when an officer was introduced to patrol a hitherto uncovered beat recorded crime decreased, but that there was no significant further reduction from increasing the number of officers on the beat. This is in line with the general finding of patrol studies that increasing police coverage does not affect crime control beyond the base line achieved by having police at all (Wilson, 1975, Ch. 5; Kelling, 1983; Sherman, 1983a).

The most sophisticated of the studies of motorised patrol is the celebrated Kansas City preventive patrol experiment (Kelling *et al.*, 1974). This evaluated the effects of systematically varying patrol strengths between five sets of three beats, matched demographically, in crime rates, and in patterns of demand for police services. In each set one beat was chosen at random for 'normal' levels of patrol and acted as 'control' beat. Another set was designated for 'proactive' patrol, and patrolled two or three times as frequently as the 'controls'. In the third set 'reactive' patrol was carried out, with cars entering only in response to specific calls for service. The study found no significant differences between the areas in reported crime, rates of victimisation, levels of citizen fear, or satisfaction with the police. It was as if the level of preventive patrol made no difference to any policy goals at all. The experiment was subject to methodological criticism by Larson (1976) who claimed that the design of the study was not adhered to in practice, and visible police presence in the experimental and control areas was much the same. But the study (after some very hostile early responses from American police chiefs) has come to be generally accepted as establishing that increasing car patrol (at least within feasible limits) is not significantly related to crime levels. Nor is this surprising:

> Crimes are rare events and are committed stealthily – as often as not in places out of reach of patrols. The chances of patrols catching offenders red-handed are therefore small, and even if these are somewhat increased, law-breakers may not notice or may not care . . . a patrolling policeman in London could expect to pass within 100 yards of a burglary in progress roughly once every eight years – but not necessarily to catch the burglar or even realise that the crime was taking place. (Clarke and Hough, 1984, pp. 6–7)

If the preventive patrol car does not have much of a 'scarecrow' function and is unlikely to come across crimes in progress, might not the faster response to emergency calls which cars achieve increase the chances of apprehending criminals? After all, many of the technological developments in policing in the last twenty years – cars, radios, command and control computers – have been geared to this end. But again, British and American research concurs in the conclusion that few if any offenders are caught as a result of faster response by police. The main reason is that most offences (70–85 per cent) are discovered some time after the event, and most victims do not call the police immediately (Silberman, 1978, pp. 330–4; Clarke and Hough, 1984, pp. 8–9).

In recent years it has commonly been argued that car patrol may even be counter-productive with regard to crime control. It cuts the police off from non-adversarial contacts with the public, thus reducing cooperation and information flow (Sherman, 1983a). Cars may also accentuate the hedonistic action elements in police culture, producing a fruitless over-reaction to incidents (Holdaway, 1977, 1983).

The limited utility (and evident expense) of car patrol has stimulated a renewed enthusiasm for foot patrol in Britain and the United States. Early studies of foot patrol suggested it was no more effective than motorised patrol (Clarke and Hough, 1984, p. 6). But the 1981 Police Foundation study of foot patrol (based on surveys in twenty-eight cities and an experiment in Newark, New Jersey) had encouraging results. The Newark experiment was based on sets of matched beats of which some were randomly to discontinue foot patrol, some to continue it, and some to introduce it for the first time. Crime levels (measured by victimisation surveys and recorded crime rates) were not affected by the varied patrol methods. But in other respects the foot patrols had beneficial effects. Fear of crime declined, confidence in neighbourhood safety increased, and citizens evaluated police services more positively. Foot patrol officers were more satisfied with their work, had a more benign view of citizens, a more community-oriented conception of policing, and lower absenteeism rates. However, the study was not able to indicate whether these attitudes led to or resulted from these officers' assignment to foot patrol. Altogether, while confirming that policing has little impact on crime rates *per se*, the foot patrol experiment does imply that it can have a beneficial impact on the communal sense of security and order (Wilson and Kelling, 1982; Kelling, 1983; Moore and Kelling, 1983).

Although variations in the quantity of patrol do not seem to affect crime levels, it has been argued that qualitatively different styles or strategies of policing might do (Wilson, 1975, Ch. 5). We shall examine the evidence about this after considering research on the effectiveness of detective work.

Studies of detection

The lack of success of criminal investigation work is in one sense apparent from the low (and declining) proportion of crimes reported to the police which are cleared up. Before the Second World War the clear-up rate for indictable offences was usually over 50 per cent, but it is now down to 38 per cent. (The clear-up rate varies widely for different crimes. For violence against the person, sexual offences and fraud and forgery the clear-up rate is around 80 per cent. For theft and handling it is about 40 per cent, while for burglary, robbery and criminal damage it hovers around one-third: *Report of Her Majesty's Inspector of Constabulary* 1989, Table 4.3, p. 103.)

However, the clear-up rate is a notoriously inadequate measure of detective effectiveness (Audit Commission, 1990b; Walker, 1992). For one thing the denominator – crimes known to the police – can vary independently of offending behaviour if a higher proportion of victimisations are reported by the public (Sparks *et al.*, 1977; Hough and Mayhew, 1983; Mayhew *et al.*, 1989).

In the 1970s police manpower increased, but the absolute number of crimes cleared up increased even more, so that the proportion of crimes per officer which are cleared up has grown. This could even indicate an increase in detective efficiency, despite the fall in the proportion of recorded crimes which are cleared up. One English study has attempted to quantify the relationship between possible increases in manpower and likely improvements in clear-up rates. From a comparison of the clear-up rates of different forces in England and Wales, this concluded that a 10 per cent increase in overall manpower, directed entirely to the CID, would raise the clear-up rate by less than 1 per cent (Burrows and Tarling, 1982; Tarling and Burrows, 1985).

While the low clear-up rate has long been apparent, it is only relatively recently that studies of the detective function have been conducted which imply that even crimes which are cleared up are not usually detected as a result of investigative effort. This finding challenges the views of both the law and order lobby and radicals. Only a relatively small number of major incident enquiries fit the model of 'classical' detection, starting from the crime itself and systematically investigating those with motive and opportunity to commit it. But the radical view, elaborated most explicitly by Matza (1969), also attributed clear-ups to police investigative activity. This was supposed to follow one of two patterns, both with discriminatory and invidious social consequences of stigmatisation and criminalisation of vulnerable groups through a process of 'deviance amplification' (Young, 1971). The first method was what Matza called the 'bureaucratic' mode, which echoes the famous lines uttered at the end of *Casablanca* by police chief Claude Rains: 'Round up the usual suspects.' In this mode successful detection depends upon knowledge of the 'underworld'. Crimes are solved by culling the group of people 'known' to commit offences of a certain type, or by cultivation of informants. The second method is that of stereotyping and suspicion. People are apprehended because they fit the investigator's preconceived notion of particular kinds of offender. These methods undoubtedly play a part in crime work, but are mainly limited to specific types of offence, just as the 'classical' mode is. Vice work is more likely to rely on both the bureaucratic and suspicion methods, because the discovery and clear-up of vice offences relies entirely upon proactive policing as there are no cooperating 'victims'. Similarly, the more minor and vague 'public order' offences (and especially such amorphous categories as the notorious 'sus' law), which form a high proportion of patrol arrests, are heavily dependent on 'suspicion'. But the majority of the more serious 'notifiable' (before 1978 'indictable') offences are *not* cleared up by any of these modes of detection.

The major finding of studies of the process by which crimes are cleared up is that the prime determinant of success is information immediately provided by members of the public (usually the victim) to patrol officers or detectives when they arrive at the scene of a crime. If adequate information is provided to pin-point the culprit fairly accurately the crime will be resolved, if not it is almost certain not to be. This is the conclusion of all the relevant studies, whether conducted by observation (Reiss, 1971; Chatterton, 1976; Sanders, 1977; Ericson, 1981), analysis of records (Mawby, 1979; Zander, 1979b; Bottomley and Coleman, 1981; Burrows and Tarling, 1982; Brown, 1991), or a combination of both (Greenwood *et al.*, 1977; Steer, 1980). Not only does this pinpointing of the crucial importance of initial information emphasise the central role of the public in the clearing-up of offences, but also the important part played by the uniform branch. The proportions of crimes cleared up almost immediately (as a result of the offender still being at the scene when the police arrived, or being named or very precisely identified by victim or witnesses) was as high as 57 per cent in Steer's study and 62 per cent in Mawby's.[3] Of the rest, a high proportion were cleared up through questioning of offenders who admit other offences to be 'taken into consideration' (tic). Some studies suggest that as many as 40 per cent of property offences are cleared in this way (Lambert, 1970; Mawby, 1979) although Steer (1980) and Bottomley and Coleman (1981) found a lower proportion of tics (20 and 25 per cent, respectively). Nationally, around 26 per cent of clear-ups are by tic (Burrows and Tarling, 1982). A scandal about manipulation of the clear-ups attributed to tics and 'prison write-offs' (where detectives question convicted prisoners in order to get them to admit other offences) occurred in Kent in the late 1980s (*Observer*, 8 October 1989). Such dubious ways of clearing the books by massaging the statistics have apparently been rife for many years in other forces, too (Gill, 1987; Young, 1991). Indeed a police force which is assiduous in its crime recording may appear inefficient in comparison with less scrupulous neighbours (Farrington and Dowds, 1985).

Thus only a small proportion of crimes are cleared up by investigative techniques bearing any resemblance to either the 'classical' or 'bureaucratic' modes beloved by fiction. The cases involving anything approximating 'real detective work' are about 25 per cent of Steer's sample, 23 per cent of Mawby's and 13 per cent of Bottomley and Coleman's. This does not mean that detectives are useless or inefficient: 'The detective has a variety of skills. These include gathering information from the public; locating suspects; interviewing and, on the basis of information derived from both the public and suspects, of preparing cases for the prosecution' (Morris and Heal, 1981, p. 33). There is also of course the relatively small but significant category of offences for which the 'classical' and 'bureaucratic' modes are appropriate. But the studies do imply that there is probably scope for more effective management and coordination of the detective function, especially through 'case screening' to distinguish crimes according to 'solvability' (and whether they should be allocated to CID or uniform branches for investigation), and more effective proactive 'targeting' of some serious offences and offenders (PSI, 1983, vol. IV, pp. 343–4; Clarke and Hough, 1984, pp. 11, 14–15). However, when the Met. experimented with 'case screening' in 1987 the public outcry forced them to drop the system. There is in reality no alternative to case screening, however. Given the huge rise in reported crimes relative to police numbers, if no formal case-screening occurs cases just get added to CID loads. Detectives then informally screen them out by rationing their attention to a few cases. But if this is not done by formal policy criteria, there is neither knowledge nor accountability for the principles tacitly used by detectives.

Innovatory policing strategies

The idea that although more of the old police tactics do not work in reducing crime, other new strategies might, has stimulated two diametrically opposed suggestions: 'aggressive' patrol and crackdowns, and several variants of 'community policing'.

'Aggressive' patrol has been championed above all by James Q. Wilson in the United States. A cross-sectional study of twenty-three police departments purported to show that patrol aggressiveness produced a greater likelihood of arrests for robbery, and lower robbery rates as a result of a deterrent effect (Wilson and Boland, 1978). Their findings were criticised by a later study which showed that robbery rates increased (rather than declined) with greater police expenditure over time (Jacob and Rich, 1980). Wilson and Boland's (1981) reply argued that their thesis concerned the effects on crime of the structural characteristic of a departmental style of aggressive patrol, and was not refuted by longitudinal data about relatively small and short-term fluctuations in police expenditure. In my view this point is well taken, but as Jacob and Rich reply (1981), it limits the original claim. 'Aggressive' patrol is no longer presented as a readily adoptable tactic, but a structural element of departmental style which could be changed (if at all) only in line with more fundamental reforms of municipal government and wider socio-political change. A review of a variety of experiments in targeting 'hot spots' for aggressive crackdowns suggests occasional success, but on the whole mixed results (Sherman, 1992).

A further caveat about aggressive tactics arises in the San

Diego Field Interrogation study cited by Wilson and Boland in support of their thesis (Boydstun, 1975). This showed that heavy use of 'field interrogation' (i.e. stop-and-search) could reduce crime. However, the price was a considerable increase in public hostility. British research shows the same result. A substantial absolute number of mainly petty offences can be uncovered by stop-and-search methods, but as the 'hit' rate of successful searches is small (less than 1 in 10) the price in alienation of some sections of the public (primarily young males, especially blacks) is very high (Tuck and Southgate, 1981; Willis, 1983; PSI, 1983; Southgate and Ekblom, 1984). Since 1981 and the disastrous Operation Swamp which precipitated the Brixton riots, the British police have broadly accepted Lord Scarman's message. Any marginal gains in law enforcement due to aggressive tactics are not worth the cost in endangering public tranquillity.

The other type of innovative tactic starts from the central importance of public cooperation. These community-oriented strategies became the central post-Scarman orthodoxy in Britain. The somewhat similar team-policing schemes which flourished in the United States, especially in the early 1970s, have ambiguous messages. According to the evaluation of seven such projects by Sherman *et al.* (1973), the problem is that they were never really tried. Initial indications about crime rates, community cooperation and information flow were encouraging; but organisational problems, in particular middle-management hostility, frustrated full or sustained implementation.

Community policing schemes have proliferated in the 1980s in several American cities under a number of progressive police chiefs (Skolnick and Bayley, 1986, 1988). While there have been some notable success stories, the outcome is quite uncertain and variable (*ibid.*; Trojanowicz and Bucqueroux, 1990; Greene and Mastrofski, 1988).

The record of British initiatives in the community policing direction is similarly patchy. Many schemes have received positive in-house evaluations, but these are usually by partisans, and suffer from the 'foregone conclusions' syndrome of predictably happy endings (Weatheritt, 1986, pp. 18–19). Independent evaluations of policing innovations seems to have the opposite tendency: 'Nothing works.' This has been the 'bottom-line' of studies of community constables (Brown and Iles, 1985); directed patrol (Burrows and Lewis, 1988); crime prevention officers (Harvey *et al.*, 1989); focused patrol (Chatterton and Rogers, 1989); neighbourhood policing (Irving *et al.*, 1989); community policing (Fielding *et al.*, 1989); and neighbourhood watch (Bennett, 1989, 1990). In many if not most of these cases the problem lies in 'programme failure', difficulties in implementing the schemes as intended, and it is far from established that community-style strategies in general, or specific tactics like Neighbourhood Watch in particular, cannot work in principle. It is hard to measure the effect of innovations on broad outcomes like recorded crime or victimisation rates, which are affected by numerous other factors than the policing initiative, and truly experimental research designs which could overcome this problem in principle are almost impossible to arrange. This difficulty blights even the one celebrated case of a rigorously evaluated scheme with a positive result: the Kirkholt Burglary Prevention project which used 'cocoon neighbourhood watch' to concentrate on already victimised houses (Forrester *et al.*, 1988; Bottoms, 1990). One of the most methodologically self-conscious projects to evaluate policing initiatives (in the role of community constables, and domestic disputes) concluded that measures of good practice could be developed meaningfully only in relation to specific areas of police work, not globally, and were inescapably political (Horton and Smith, 1988; Horton, 1989). None the less in the 1980s the government's search for value for money in public services has led to the search for more adequate performance indicators in policing (Audit Commission, 1990a and b). The Inspectorate in particular are using an ever more elaborate matrix of indicators in their annual assessments of forces (Jones and Silverman, 1984; Sinclair and Miller, 1984; Butler, 1984, 1986; Waddington, 1986a and b; Bradley *et al.*, 1986, 1987; Hough, 1987; Chatterton, 1987a; Reiner, 1988b). It is unlikely that these have yet overcome the possibly intractable problems of measuring police effectiveness.

Altogether the research on crime control implies that the police more or less successfully maintain a bedrock of effectiveness. Neither more of the same (nor marginally different) tactics are likely to improve their capacity for detection or prevention to any substantial degree.[4] The final aspect of research on police practices which is of crucial importance to analysis of their political significance is the question of how fair the police are in their pursuit of effective law enforcement and order maintenance.

How fair are the police?

Since the 'discovery' by early research on the police that they routinely exercise a considerable amount of discretion in the way they enforce the law, there has been a plethora of work on the pattern and determinants of this (Goldstein, 1960; La Fave, 1962, 1965; Banton, 1964; Wilson, 1968a; Davis, 1969, 1975; Lambert, 1970; Reiss, 1971; Bottomley, 1973, Ch. 2 are some key examples of the early discussions). A central concern has been with the question whether discretion really meant discrimination, in particular against blacks.

The issue is more complex and harder to resolve than most polemics imply. Contrary to the implications of much radical criticism of the police, the evidence of a pattern of social differentiation in the use of police powers from which the young, the lower working class and blacks suffer most – although undeniable – does *not* in itself establish discrimination. The radical critique implies that the differential exercise of police powers against the socially disadvantaged and relatively powerless is the product of bias, stereotyping and the amplification of the apparent deviance of these groups (Chapman, 1968; Box, 1981; Young, 1971; Cashmore and McLaughlin, 1991). On the other hand, conservative writers would argue that this unjustly vilifies the police. The differential exercise of powers reflects not police discrimination, but the varying deviance of different social groups, as well as the police response to public demand and information which guides their essentially reactive interventions. If studies of police culture reveal hostile attitudes to minority groups, this is the product, not the determinant of police work (Waddington, 1983a, 1984a). Both positions embody an element of truth, but this has been clouded by abrasive either/or polemics. Some terminological issues must be resolved before the evidence can be reviewed. I shall adopt the following definitions:

1. 'Prejudice': the belief that all or most members of a particular group have certain negative attributes, a preconception which is carried into encounters with individuals in the category who may or may not actually have these traits. Examples are 'the people here are animals' (constable, quoted in Reiner, 1978a, p. 80), or 'all coppers are bastards'.
2. 'Bias': the view that some types of people should have preferential treatment regardless of their specific conduct on any particular occasion.
3. 'Differentiation': a pattern of exercise of police powers against particular social categories, which varies from their representation in the population (e.g. a disproportionate arrest-rate of young black males).
4. 'Discrimination': a pattern of exercise of police powers which results in some social categories being over-represented as targets of police action even when legally relevant variables (especially the pattern of offending) are held constant.

The attitudinal characteristics of prejudice and bias may, but need not, result in differentiation or discrimination. They may not be translated into action if legal, ethical, organisational or situational constraints preclude this. Nor does differentiation necessarily indicate discrimination. It could result from legally relevant differences between groups, for example, varying patterns of offending.

A somewhat more controversial, but important point is that even police discrimination may not be the product of prejudice, bias or unilateral police decision-making. It is necessary to distinguish five forms discrimination might take. Banton (1983) proposes a distinction between (1) 'categorical', and (2) 'statistical' discrimination. The former refers to invidious treatment of members of a group purely on account of their belonging to a certain social category, regardless of the relevance of this to any particular performance criteria. The latter refers to differentiated treatment of members of a group on the grounds of a belief that they are disproportionately likely to have certain characteristics, but without reference to specific behaviour of individuals. An obvious example is police stopping young blacks disproportionately because of the belief that they are more likely to get a 'result' (PSI, 1983, vol. IV, pp. 110, 230–1). This does not constitute a legally valid basis for 'reasonable suspicion', and is explicitly ruled out by the Code of Practice on stop-and-search powers under PACE. None the less, it is undoubtedly a factor in stop-and-search practices, but distinct from categorical discrimination against blacks *per se*.

To Banton's two types of discrimination I would add three further types: (3) 'transmitted' discrimination: where the police act as a passive conveyor-belt for community prejudices. For example, white citizens' racial prejudice may make victims label attackers disproportionately as black, leading the police to search for black suspects. As a senior policeman remarked during the Scarman Inquiry, if an offender is described as black the police do not look for a suspect who is white (Waddington, 1984a, p. 42). (4) 'Interactional' discrimination: where the process of interaction (say the rude demeanour of a suspect) produces a differential outcome which is dubiously justifiable legally. (5) 'Institutionalised' discrimination: where the consequences of universalistically framed enforcement policies or procedures work out in practice as discriminatory because of the structural bias of an unequal society. An example is the way that the institutions of privacy make certain actions (say drinking) actionable by the police only in public contexts to which the poorer classes are disproportionately restricted (Stinchcombe, 1963).

All these forms of discrimination may operate at either the policy level of senior echelons or rank-and-file discretionary decisions on the street. The two are interdependent. Rank-and-file discrimination, for example, may produce a higher recorded crime rate in areas with a high black population. If it is the (impartially framed) policy to respond in high-crime-rate areas with more aggressive patrol techniques (such as Swamp '81) then a vicious circle between rank-and-file 'statistical' and policy-level 'institutionalised' discrimination can ensue. (Blom-Cooper and Drabble (1982) suggest that this *did* happen in Brixton, but their statistics are criticised in Lea and Young (1984, pp. 163–4). See also Reiner, 1985, n. 103.).

The weight of the research evidence (although not absolutely unequivocal: see Waddington, 1983a, pp. 8–10) supports the following propositions:

1. There is a clear pattern of differentiation in police practice

with young males, especially if they are black and/or unemployed or economically marginal, being disproportionately subject to the exercise of police powers (as well as, on the other hand, being disproportionately victimised by violent offences).

2. Part of this can be explained by the disproportionate involvement in some offences (mainly minor and marginal ones) of these social groups as a result of their life circumstances. Even given this, however, there is evidence of police discrimination not explicable by differential offending.

3. Part of this police discrimination is 'transmitted', 'interactional' or 'institutionalised', that is, although not based on criteria which are sanctioned by law, it is compatible with the law given the discretion the police necessarily exercise. For example, if a person approached by the police for a minor offence where the officer would normally not proceed formally fails 'the attitude test' (i.e. is not sufficiently deferential) he might be sanctioned nominally for the offence, but really for 'contempt of cop'. (For examples, see Brown, 1981, pp. 194–201.)

4. However, there is also evidence of 'statistical' and 'categorical' discrimination. 'Statistical' discrimination, resulting from a prejudiced belief that certain kinds of people – say long-haired youths – are disproportionately likely to be offenders (which may or may not be correct), while usually at odds with legal specifications of adequate grounds for 'reasonable suspicion', arises out of a concern to police effectively. It is what Shearing calls 'organisational police deviance' in that it is 'designed to further organisational objectives rather than promote personal gains' (Shearing, 1981b, p. 2). 'Categorical' discrimination, the translation into practice of bias, is illicit from any point of view.

5. The evidence reviewed in Chapter 3 clearly documents police bias and prejudice. However, as argued there, the bulk of the research evidence (apart from the recent Colman–Gorman study) suggests these attitudes are not the product of prior peculiarities of the individual personalities of police officers, but a reflection of wider societal prejudice, accentuated by the characteristics of police work. I shall now examine some of the research which establishes the first four propositions.

Differentiation

The police stop and search, arrest, charge and use physical force against young, black, lower-status males disproportionately to their representation in the population. At the same time they also have disproportionate contact with them as victims or complainants for violent offences (PSI, 1983, vol. I, pp. 624, 124–6; Hough and Mayhew, 1983; Jones *et al.*, 1986; Crawford *et al.*, 1990; Skogan, 1990).

The US evidence is quite clearly in support of all these points.[5] The San Diego Field Interrogation study found that 100 per cent of people stopped were male, 66 per cent were black or Mexican–American, and two-thirds were juveniles (Boydstun, 1975, p. 61). A 1973 study of stops in Dallas found that young and/or black males were stopped more than proportionately to their representation in the population or in arrest statistics (Bogolmony, 1976). Young, black and/or lower-class suspects are more likely to be arrested according to all three of the large-scale systematic observational studies of police work carried out in the United States (the 1966 Black–Reiss research for the Presidential Commission on Law Enforcement, the 1970 Sykes–Clark–Lundman replication of it, and the 1977 Smith-Visher study; the first two are reported in Black, 1970, 1972; Sykes and Clark, 1975; Lundman *et al.*, 1978; Lundman, 1974, 1979 – all reprinted in Lundman, 1980; and usefully surveyed by Sherman, 1980; the latter study is reported in Smith and Visher, 1981; Smith and Klein, 1984). According to the Black–Reiss study, young or lower-class suspects are more likely to be treated harshly (Sherman, 1980, pp. 82–3). All those subject to excessive force were lower class. But this study found that a smaller proportion of black suspects were physically abused (although given their greater chance of being suspects the prospects of blacks or whites being at the receiving end of police force were the same. Reiss, 1968). However, blacks are far more likely to be killed by police than whites. The black death rate from police shootings is about nine times the white, while over half the victims of police shootings are black, although blacks are only 10 per cent of the US population (Takagi, 1974; Meyer, 1980; Fyfe, 1981; Binder and Scharf, 1982; Geller, 1983; Sherman, 1983b; Dunne, 1991). The evidence about the treatment of suspects after arrest is much more equivocal. Several studies of juveniles do not find that higher proportions of black or lower-class suspects are referred to court, although others do (Sherman, 1980, pp. 80–3).

The British evidence all points in the same direction. Being young, male, black, unemployed and economically disadvantaged are all associated with a higher probability of being stopped, searched, arrested, detained in custody, charged, making complaints against the police (especially of assault), and failing to have these complaints substantiated. Evidence showing disproportionate stops and searches of young males, especially if unemployed and/or black is presented by: Brogden (1981, pp. 44–52), Tuck and Southgate (1981, pp. 26–7), Field and Southgate (1982, pp. 50–3), Willis (1983, p. 14), McConville (1983, pp. 610–11), PSI (1983, vol. I, pp. 95–102, vol. III, pp. 96–7) and Southgate and Ekblom (1984, pp. 15–19). (Lidstone (1984, p. 454) gives evidence of discrimination in the use of powers of search of premises without a warrant.)

Differential arrest rates of the young, male, black and economically marginal are found by several studies. The most systematic evidence is the Home Office analysis of the 1975 Metropolitan Police statistics (Stevens and Willis, 1979). This showed higher black than white arrest rates in all offence categories, but especially for assault, robbery, 'other violent theft', and 'other indictable offences'. Asians were underrepresented in all offence categories except assault. (On low Asian involvement as suspects with the police, see Mawby and Batta (1980).) Other evidence for disproportionate arrests of blacks, young males and the unemployed is found in Field and Southgate (1982, pp. 50–3), PSI (1983, vol. I, pp. 118–26, vol. III, pp. 88–91) and Cain and Sadigh (1982). Once arrested, juveniles who are working class (Bennett, 1979; Fisher and Mawby, 1982) or black (Landau, 1981; Landau and Nathan, 1983) are less likely to be cautioned as opposed to charged and prosecuted. Unemployed or unskilled working-class young men, especially if they are also black, are also much more likely to be detained in police custody after arrest and before being charged (Morgan *et al.*, 1990).

Blacks are more likely than whites to say they have wanted to make a complaint against the police (Tuck and Southgate, 1981, pp. 38–9). Blacks, especially young ones, and older Asians are more likely to bring complaints than whites, and this proportion is increasing. Blacks are more likely to make serious complaints, especially of assault (Stevens and Willis, 1981; Maguire and Corbett, 1989, 1991). Nearly a quarter of all complaints alleging brutality are made by blacks or Asians (who constitute about 6 per cent of the population). On the other hand, ethnic minorities and the unemployed or economically marginal are less likely to have their complaints substantiated (Box and Russell, 1975; Stevens and Willis, 1981; Box, 1983, pp. 82–91). Correspondingly with this, blacks are more likely to claim knowledge of police use of excessive force on the basis of personal experience (PSI, 1983, vol. I, pp. 265–7).

Altogether the evidence supports the PSI's view that 'the weight of police activity bears much more heavily on sections of the lower working class and others whom the police tend to lump in with them' (PSI, 1983, vol. IV, p. 166).[6] Those upon whom the differential exercise of police powers falls disproportionately are the same groups as were characterised as 'police property' in the exploration of 'cop culture' in Chapter 3 (Brogden *et al.*, 1988, Ch. 6). It remains to be seen, however, to what extent the clear pattern of police differentiation involves discrimination, i.e. use of police powers unjustified by legally relevant factors, and further what kind of discrimination is involved.

Discrimination

To a large extent the pattern of differentiation described so far can be accounted for by differential rates of offending. The degree of police discrimination is less than would be implied by a superficial reading of the social distribution of stops, arrests and other exercises of police power.

This is least true, however, of the lower-level occasions of police intervention, especially street stops. Black youths constitute a much higher proportion of stops of 'innocent' than of 'guilty' suspects (Piliavin and Briar, 1964, p. 212). In the American research, the likelihood of police stopping black males is disproportionate not only to their representation in the population, but also in arrest statistics (Bogolmony, 1976,

p. 571). The British data do not replicate this pattern. An equal proportion of stops of whites and blacks produces a 'result' in the sense of the recording or prosecution of an offence (Willis, 1983, p. 1; McConville, 1983, p. 612; PSI, 1983, vol. I, p. 116), although it must be stressed that the 'hit' rate for all stops is very small (around 10 per cent) – i.e. most people stopped are innocent of an offence.

The American studies of arrest patterns all show that much, but not all, of the disproportionate arrest rate of blacks, youths and the lower class can be accounted for by differences in the seriousness of offences which are alleged (i.e. a legally relevant criterion. Black and Reiss, 1970; Black, 1972; Lundman *et al.*, 1978; Smith and Visher, 1981). With regard to the question of physical abuse of suspects, and especially the most controversial issue of police shootings, the American evidence is mixed. While some studies find that most of the disproportionate shooting rate of blacks is accounted for by varying arrest patterns, the weight of the evidence suggests that blacks and lower-class suspects are victims of police force more often than could be expected on the basis of arrest or other legally relevant differences (Meyer, 1980; Sherman, 1980, pp. 81–3; Geller, 1983).

In England too, the most rigorous evidence on these issues suggests that the disproportionate arrest rate of young black males is partly the product of police discrimination, but partly of differential rates of offending – which can be accounted for by the age profile and socio-economic deprivation (as measured by such indices as unemployment or home-ownership rates) of the black population (Stevens and Willis, 1979; PSI, 1983, vol. I, pp. 121, 71–5; vol. III, pp. 96–7). The precise balance of these two factors is hard to ascertain. But evidence of police discrimination can be adduced from the fact that blacks were most heavily arrested for two offences which allow the greatest scope for selective perception by police officers: 'other violent theft' and 'sus' – for which the black arrest rate was fourteen or fifteen times the white (Stevens and Willis, 1979). Cain and Sadigh's (1982) study also shows disproportionate black prosecutions for 'victimless' crimes dependent upon police initiative. (But their data further show disproportionate charging of blacks for offences not dependent upon proactive policing, such as offences against the person, a point ignored by their own interpretation of their data.) Both the Home Office and PSI studies point to victim identifications of the race of offenders as supporting the claim that the disproportionate black arrest rate reflects varying involvement in offences, as well as police stereotyping (although victim identifications may themselves be, at least in part, a consequence of public stereotypes). But as Stevens and Willis argue, the extent of the black:white arrest differential is so great that it would be implausible to attribute it all to police discrimination. They calculate that, on the hypothesis that black and white crime rates were identical, and the arrest imbalance was entirely due to 'mistaken' arrests of blacks, then 76 per cent of all black arrests would have to be 'mistaken' (Stevens and Willis, 1979, pp. 28–34).

Lea and Young, in an important book aimed at developing a new 'socialist–realist' analysis of crime, have accepted the validity of the Home Office and PSI analyses (Lea and Young, 1984). They explain the disproportionate black arrest rate as the consequence of two mutually reinforcing processes: 'increased . . . black crime and police predisposition to associate blacks with crime become part of a vicious circle' (Lea and Young, 1984, p. 167; see also Lea, 1986).

Lea and Young have been subject to a torrent of criticism, accusing them of capitulating to 'the weight of racist logic' and of lending 'sociological credibility to police racism' (Gilroy, 1982, 1983; Bridges, 1983a and b; Gutzmore, 1983; Scraton, 1985, 1987). In this plethora of vituperative criticism there is no serious attempt at a rebuttal of Lea and Young's argument. Any such engagement with the issue of explaining the black arrest rate as the outcome of anything but a protean and all-pervasive racism is dismissed as 'empiricist haggling over official crime statistics' (Gilroy, 1983, p. 146). But this sort of characterisation of all police and all aspects of policing as equally and undistinguishably racist precludes any serious analysis of how and why policing changes, and of separating out potentially positive developments within police strategy and thinking. The state, and its coercive apparatus the police, are blanketed together as a monolithic reflex of the racist logic of capital.

Against this position Lea and Young mount several powerful arguments. First, for many years during which there was clear evidence of widespread prejudice in the police force, official arrest statistics (which probably exaggerate black involvement in crime) did *not* depict blacks as arrested disproportionately. This was the clear conclusion of Lambert's study of Birmingham crime statistics in the late 1960s, and of the police evidence to the House of Commons Select Committee on Race Relations in 1971–2 (Lambert, 1970). But by the time of the 1976–7 Commons Select Committee on Race Relations and Immigration the police were claiming that the position had changed, and there was a disproportionately high rate of young black crime.

Apart from the implausibility of the changing black arrest pattern in the 1970s being the result of a sudden shift in police thinking, Lea and Young stress that it would be strange if the life circumstances of young blacks did not produce some increase in offences. 'The notion that increasing youth unemployment . . . a high young population in the black community . . . racial discrimination and the denial of legitimate opportunity, did not result in a rising rate of real offences is hardly credible' (Lea and Young, 1984, pp. 167–8).

All this is not to deny that 'moral panics' may be created by the practices of the police, the judicial apparatus and the media, as shown, for example, by the Centre for Contemporary Cultural Studies. Their book, *Policing the Crisis*, gives a detailed account of the 'mugging' scare of 1972–3, and how it was constructed by police, judiciary and media (Hall *et al.*, 1978). However, there can be little doubt that during the 1970s 'mugging' (i.e. robberies involving street attacks on strangers) became more prevalent and a not insignificant risk for vulnerable categories of people in some areas (although not for the population overall), and that black over-representation in arrests for this cannot be the product exclusively of police policy or prejudice (Pratt, 1980). *Policing the Crisis*, for all its emphasis on the moral panic associated with mugging as symbol of increasing state and societal authoritarianism, did not deny its reality (Hall *et al.*, 1978, p. 390).

It seems clear that the disproportionate black arrest rate is the product of black deprivation, police stereotyping and the process by which each of these factors amplifies the other. To recognise that the police statistics have some basis in a reality of black crime is important because it underlines the point that more needs to change than just setting straight mistaken police stereotypes or prejudices.

The most systematic evidence of pure police discrimination comes from Landau's two studies (1981; Landau and Nathan, 1983) of the processing of juvenile offenders by the Metropolitan Police. The first concentrated on decisions by station officers about whether to charge offenders immediately or refer them to the juvenile bureau. Holding constant the legally relevant variables of offence type and previous criminal record, blacks were more likely to be charged immediately rather than being referred to the juvenile bureau (Landau, 1981).

Landau's later study examined the decisions of the juvenile bureau itself about whether to charge or caution those referred to it. He notes that given the assumption that the earlier police decision would have screened out the 'worst' cases, it could be expected a priori that more people would be cautioned in those categories which are treated more harshly at the earlier stage. But in fact for 'crimes of violence' and 'public order' offences blacks are more likely to be treated harshly at both stages: they are less likely to be referred to the bureau, and less likely to be cautioned by it, holding constant the nature of the offence and past record. This could partly be accounted for by a lesser likelihood that cases involving blacks satisfied the legal preconditions for the cautioning process: an admission of guilt, and the consent of the victim. But part of the difference is 'pure' discrimination not explicable by 'legal' factors (Landau and Nathan, 1983).

A similar conclusion emerges from the data about complaints. Some, but not all, of the class and ethnic differences can be accounted for by legally relevant factors. Black complainants are disproportionately involved in trouble with the police at the time of the complaint. A higher proportion of them were under arrest or had previous records. Police were more likely to allege suspect's provocation as a justification (i.e. assault or violent struggling) in the cases of black complaints of assault by the police (Stevens and Willis, 1981). In other words blacks (and other vulnerable groups like young unemployed men) are more likely to have the characteristics of 'discreditability' which make it improbable that their complaints will be substantiated.

The evidence clearly suggests that part but not all of the social differentiation apparent in the exercise of police discretion is accounted for by legally relevant factors like offence patterns.

But there is a further element of class, age and race discrimination, encompassing 'transmitted', 'interactional', 'institutional', 'statistical' as well as pure 'categorical' discrimination.

Transmitted discrimination

The role of 'transmitted' discrimination (i.e. where the police act as transmitters of public discrimination) is indicated in several ways in the research. It is implied in the key role of victim and witness information and identification in the clear-up of crime, which was emphasised earlier in this chapter. It is also indicated in the significance attached by police to victim specifications of the race of their assailants. The American research underlines the central importance of complainants' wishes as a determinant of arrest decisions, after controlling for legal variables like offence seriousness (Black and Reiss, 1970, pp. 70–1; Lundman *et al.*, 1978, p. 84; Smith and Visher, 1981, p. 173).

Interactional discrimination

Many researchers have stressed the context and process of interaction itself (especially the respect accorded by a suspect, which may itself depend upon the officer's approach) as a crucial determinant of whether arrest or charging takes place (Piliavin and Briar, 1964, p. 206; Ferdinand and Luchterhand, 1970, p. 510; Black, 1972, p. 1103; Sykes *et al.*, 1976, pp. 177–8; Brown, 1981, pp. 194–201; Landau, 1981, pp. 42–3; Smith and Visher, 1981, pp. 172–4; Southgate, 1982, pp. 4–9). Such penalising of 'contempt of cop' is, of course, not a valid legal basis for arrest. But many quite proper arrests may result from the suspect's failing the 'attitude test' and thus incurring sanctions for an offence which might otherwise be overlooked. Nor is this necessarily wrong in view of the imperative of the police officer appearing to maintain control, especially in public situations – which is why the presence of bystanders increases the probability of arrest (Smith and Visher, 1981, pp. 172–3).

Institutionalised discrimination

A key example of institutionalised discrimination is the directing of extra police resources or more aggressive tactics to 'high-crime' areas suffering from social deprivation. The result will be a greater probability of stop and search, arrest, etc., for those people living there who are vulnerable to police attention, i.e. young black and/or unemployed men (Blom-Cooper and Drabble, 1982).

Another example is the use of indices of the probability of reoffending (which themselves are an example of 'statistical' discrimination) in a routine way to determine decisions such as cautioning or charging. These indices of 'problem family' backgrounds and the like, even if used universalistically by the police bureaucracy, will result in discriminatory decisions (Landau and Nathan, 1983, pp. 143–5).

Finally the poignant complaints about police inattention to racial attacks may indicate not so much lack of concern as unthinking application of standard preconceptions and procedures which assume individual motivations for offences. The 'normal' procedures of the police institution may indirectly disadvantage ethnic minority victims (Klug, 1982; Gordon, 1983, pp. 48–59; Bowling and Saulsbury, 1991).

Statistical discrimination

This is pinpointed in several studies as the main cause of discrimination in stop-and-search exercises, due to the police presupposition that particular groups – say, young people dressed in certain styles – are more likely to carry evidence of some offences – say, drugs (Stevens and Willis, 1979, pp. 31–3; Willis, 1983, p. 25; PSI, 1983, vol. IV, pp. 230–9). It is clear that this is not a legally acceptable basis for 'reasonable suspicion'. But it results from a concern with effective policing, however misguided this might be in that frequent stops and searches of 'innocent' people magnify hostility to the police in vulnerable groups, and in the end undermine law enforcement (PSI, 1983, vol. IV, pp. 322–3).

Categorical discrimination

Undoubtedly some discriminatory use of police powers is a reflection of categorical bias of the kind found in police culture. However, it is hard to pinpoint it as a separate factor from the overall context of encounters, which is why observational studies of policing tend to emphasise the absence of pure discrimination which cannot be justified or at least explained in some sense by the process and context of encounters. At the same time observational studies do portray a prevalence of prejudiced opinions, not directly translated into police practice (Black, 1972; Holdaway, 1983; PSI, 1983, vol. IV, Ch. IV). But it is likely that prejudices do also over-determine the conflict-ridden character of many police encounters with black people.

Conclusion

The pattern of discrimination and the map of the population found in police culture are isomorphic. They are both interdependent and bound within the wider structure of racial and class disadvantage (Brogden *et al.*, 1988, Ch. 6; Jefferson, 1988; Reiner, 1989a). Although it may sometimes be that discrimination is associated with prior individual police attitudes of a prejudiced kind, the fundamental processes are structural. Even if recruits were not especially prejudiced at the outset, the evidence on the impact of the experience of policing suggests they tend to become so.

The young 'street' population has always been the prime focus of police order maintenance and law enforcement work (Brogden, 1983b). The processes of racial disadvantage in housing, employment and education lead young blacks to be disproportionately involved in street culture. They may also become engaged in specific kinds of street crime, for reasons which have already been indicated. At the same time, the relative powerlessness of ethnic minorities and lower-working-class youth mean that the police may be less constrained and inhibited in dealing with them. In times of economic crisis and competition for jobs and other resources, the majority group (especially the white working class) might indeed benefit from the effects of over-policing of blacks, because black stigmatisation as criminal, the acquisition of criminal records, reduces their competitiveness (Johnson, 1976, p. 108). For all these reasons, the economically marginal ethnic minorities, and especially their youth, are prone to become 'police property' (Lee, 1981). These structural aspects are the hard core of police conflict with the under-class who constitute their main clientele. But they are exacerbated by cultural factors such as police prejudice, which, if reflected in verbal and other abuse, can make even normally uncontroversial service work fraught with tension. Finally, once conflicts become common a vicious cycle develops whereby police officers and their 'property' approach encounters warily with pre-existing hostility and suspiciousness, and interact in ways which only exacerbate the tension.

Overall, this chapter has argued that the primary mandate of the police is emergency order-maintenance, for which they are entrusted as specialists in (if not monopolists of) the use of legitimate force on behalf of the state. At certain times and places much if not most of their role will be service work, but at present the crime element is increasing. Their present effectiveness in law enforcement is apparently small and declining, but this is largely because of pressures arising from wider social and cultural processes. Attempts to measure police effectiveness are bedevilled by the absence of adequate performance indicators even in relation to crime work, and certainly for the broader aspects of policing. The exercise of police powers historically and now bears down most on the economically and social marginal, especially from ethnic minorities. The growth in the size of these 'police property' groups which has resulted from government economic and social policy in the 1980s has been the major factor undermining police effectiveness and legitimacy, and the apparently discriminatory use (or misuse) of powers.

CHAPTER 5

MYSTIFYING THE POLICE
The media presentation of policing

Mass-media images of the police are of central importance in understanding the political significance and role of policing. We have seen that neither uniform patrol nor plain clothes investigation work is very successful in crime control. However, it should not be concluded from this that the police are not an effective and important part of the processes of order-maintenance. The police are an integral aspect of the presentation of society as governed by the rule of law. They signify that there exists an agency charged with the mandate of apprehending offenders, so that there is always some prospect (however small statistically) of penal sanctions – a deterrent function. Moreover, the processes of detection, apprehension and punishment are supposedly bound by fair, legalistic constraints of due process – they represent deterrence as justice not brute force. In Chapter 2 we saw that the architects of the British police tradition were concerned to construct an image of the bobby as both effective and the embodiment of impersonal rational–legal authority. In large-scale, complex and class-divided societies, however, the practical experience of different segments of the population with the police is very uneven. Police activity bears most heavily upon a relatively restricted group of people at the base of the social hierarchy, who are disproportionately the complainants, victims or offenders processed by the police. Politically, though, the most crucial sectors for determining police prestige, power and resources are the majority higher up the social scale, whose contacts with the police (and certainly any adversarial encounters) are confined mainly to their traffic control functions.

171

For these strata the mass media are the main source of perceptions and preferences about policing. Moreover, even in the lower-status groups where police contacts are more frequent, they are largely restricted to a distinct segment: young males. The attitude to the police of the women and older men in these groups is crucial, in particular for the flow of information, and the probability that routine encounters can be conducted relatively peaceably, without the ever-present potential of explosion into collective confrontations. The media-constructed image of policing is thus vital for the attainment of that minimum of 'consent' which is essential for the preservation of police authority. This image does not float free of the actualities of policing, but it is not a mirror reflection of them either. It is a refraction of the reality, constructed from it in accordance with the organisational imperatives of the media industries, the ideological frames of creative personnel and audiences, and the changing balance of political and economic forces affecting both the reality and image of policing.

The crucial political significance of media presentations of policing has long been recognised by police officers themselves. There are many examples of use of the media by the police to construct 'crime waves' as devices for accruing organisational prestige and resources (Hall *et al.*, 1978; Christensen *et al.*, 1982). The long tradition of respectable anxiety about subversive media effects is embodied in continuous demands for more censorship and control. What is relatively recent, and much harder to come by, is any systematic attempt to assess or analyse content and meaning. Conceptions of the political and social implications of media presentations of crime and law enforcement can be broadly divided into two opposing perspectives.[1] The first view holds that the media ought responsibly to inculcate respect for legal and moral norms and their appointed guardians. Commercial exigencies, however, exert constant pressure to pander to base appetites and emotions, leading all too often to sensationalist and exploitative glorification of the criminal and denigration of the police. The opposing view regards the media as propagators of a dominant ideology sanctifying the existing institutions of the social order, the laws by which their operations are expressed, and the repressive apparatuses which maintain them. Struggles for or against dominant values and rules are transformed by the media into metaphysical confrontations of universal good and evil. They are thus depoliticised, as is the role of the police as an arm of the state.

I would argue that both the 'subversive' and 'hegemonic' views of the role of media images of law and order are too simple. In an unequal and hierarchical society competition in presenting ideas is as structurally loaded as all conflicts. Very broadly the weight of images portrayed by the mass media will be supportive of the existing social order in any relatively stable society. These images reflect and reinforce the views and self-perceived interests of the majority, not just an elite. On the other hand, demands of credibility and comprehension produce a reflection in media presentations of changing patterns of conflict. Images across the range of media may be contradictory, or even present a consensus for reform at particular times. The key to understanding the content of the media is knowledge of the organisational dynamics, ideology and professional imperatives of the productive personnel and institutions (Ericson *et al.*, 1987, 1989, 1991; Murdock *et al.*, 1989; Ericson, 1991; Sparks, 1992).

This chapter will examine the pattern and implications of media presentations of the police, in both purportedly 'factual' and 'fictional' products.[2]

'Factual' images

Sir Robert Mark, who encouraged a policy of unprecedented openness between the Metropolitan Police and the news media, well described the relations between police and journalists as 'an enduring, if not ecstatically happy, marriage' (Speech to the Institute of Journalists, 30 November 1971). Overall the treatment of the police by the news media has been such as to legitimate their role and activities. But this outcome has been neither smooth nor unruffled. Conflict has frequently arisen between police and journalists over specific issues, and many police officers have a genuine sense of the media as biased against them. These perceptions are not unfounded. The media, even while reproducing perspectives fundamentally legitimating the police role, none the less criticise and question many particular police actions and individual officers. As long as this is not carried too far, the existence of the media as apparently independent, impartial and ever-vigilant watchdogs over state agencies on behalf of the public interest is conducive to the legitimation of these apparatuses (but not individuals working within them). This process of legitimation could never be effective if the media were seen as mere propaganda factories.

Law and order themes are a basic staple of news reporting. The American research has been summarised by Dominick (1978), who found that 'a typical metropolitan paper probably devotes around 5–10 per cent of its available space to crime news' (p. 108). This overall proportion masks the special prominence given many crime reports, in terms of placement, story length and headlining (Garofalo, 1981, p. 332). The amount of attention given to crime news is much greater in popular than 'quality' papers (Dominick, 1978, p. 109). A later study, that adopted a broader definition of crime news, found 22–8 per cent of topics mentioned in newspapers were crime related (Graber, 1980). British research indicates similar prominence is given to law and order news, especially by the more popular newspapers (Roshier, 1973; Ditton and Duffy, 1983).

Both American and British research finds an emphasis on reports of specific crimes, rather than analyses of trends, causes or remedies (Roshier, 1973; Dominick, 1978, p. 108). The amount of attention given crime bears no relationship to trends in official crime statistics (Roshier, 1973; Graber, 1980, p. 24; Garofalo, 1981, pp. 322–3).

There are structured differences between the characteristics of crime and criminals which are reported by the media, and the picture conveyed by official statistics, victimisation or self-report studies (Mayhew *et al.*, 1989). The following divergences have been found by all the British and American research:

1. The media over-report serious crimes, especially murder, crimes against the person, or ones with a sexual element. This may not be surprising, although Hauge's (1965) Norwegian study shows it is not a universal phenomenon. But it has ideological consequences for perceptions of the police role.
2. The media concentrate on crimes which are solved. Offences which are reported by the media at the time of their

occurrence are disproportionately the serious offences of inter-personal violence which have the highest clear-up rates. Most other offences are only reported after an arrest. Indeed, reports are frequently based on trials, especially the opening prosecution stage and the judge's summing-up and sentencing.

3. Offenders reported in the media are disproportionately older adults, and from a higher social class than their counterparts in reality. (The same is true of victims.)

In short, the news media present a picture of crime which is misleading in its focus on the serious and violent, and the emphasis on older, higher-status offenders and victims. Reporting also exaggerates police success in detection.

The corollary of this is a presentation of the police which is without doubt generally favourable. The police are cast in the role they would want to see themselves in – as the 'thin blue line' between order and chaos, the protectors of the victimised weak from the depredations of the criminally vicious. The media (with particular inflections ranging from the more liberal 'quality' organs like *The Guardian* or *The Times*, to the more overt vigilantism of the popular tabloids) generally support the police role and even the extension of police powers. Chibnall's study (1979) of Fleet Street crime reporters found that they explicitly saw it as their responsibility to present the police in a favourable light. A typical quote said: 'If I've got to come down on one side or the other, either the goodies or the baddies, then obviously I'd come down on the side of the goodies, in the interests of law and order' (Chibnall, 1977, p. 145).

At the same time, belief in their watchdog role has led reporters assiduously to pursue stories of police wrong-doing. The most notable example is *The Times* (1969) revelation of widespread corruption in the Metropolitan Police, which sparked off Mark's shake-up in the 1970s. But police corruption stories are usually located within a 'one bad apple' framework, implying that the discovery and punishment of the rare evil individual is proof that the police *institution* remains wonderful.

The sources of this basically favourable framework of news about the police are threefold:

1. A variety of concrete organisational pressures underlying

news production have unintended pro-police ideological consequences. The tendency to report cases at the stage of the trial derives partly from the economy of concentrating reporters at institutional settings like courts where newsworthy events can be expected to occur regularly, but it results in exaggerating police success. The police control much of the information on which crime reporters rely, and this gives them a degree of power as essential accredited sources. The institutionalisation of crime reporters itself became a self-generating cause of regular crime news, and over time they can be expected to develop a symbiotic relationship with their reliable contacts, notably the police (Chibnall, 1977, Chs 3 and 6). The need to write reports to fit the time schedules of news production contributes to their event orientation, the concentration on specific crimes at the expense of analysis of causal processes or policies (Rock, 1973, pp. 76–9). Considerations of personal safety and convenience lead cameramen covering riots typically to film from behind police lines, which structures the image of the police as vulnerable 'us' confronting menacing 'them' (Murdock, 1982, pp. 108–9). These and other production pressures lead to a pro-police stance quite independently of any conscious bias (Ericson *et al.*, 1987, 1989, 1991; Ericson, 1991).

2. The professional ideology of reporters, their intuitive sense of newsworthiness, what makes a 'good story', can be analysed as a system of values which both emphasises crime incidents, and underlies their particular representation (Hall *et al.*, 1978; Ericson *et al.*, 1989). Such elements of perceived newsworthiness as immediacy, dramatisation, personalisation, titillation and novelty are conducive to an emphasis on violent and sensational offences (Chibnall, 1977, pp. 22–45).

These processes become most apparent in the handling of explicitly political issues with law and order dimensions, such as coverage of Northern Ireland (Hillyard, 1982). This was shown in a detailed behind–the–scenes study of the production process of news reports about the 27 October 1968 anti-Vietnam War demonstration in Grosvenor Square (Halloran *et al.*, 1970). The media constructed their reporting around the issue of violence, crystallised in the famous 'kick photo', showing a policeman being held and kicked by two demonstrators, which appeared prominently on most front pages the day after the event (Hall, 1973). This aided the subordination of the wider political questions involved in the demonstration to one dramatic incident of anti-police brutality. A similar role was played in reporting of the Grunwick strike by a photo published on all front pages on 24 June 1977, showing a bleeding, silver-haired, unconscious policeman lying in the road. (It was used by the Police Federation to back their pay campaign that year.) The professional values of newsworthiness are a crucial determinant of the character of crime and police reporting, quite independently of any overtly political considerations.

3. The nature of law and order coverage is also, of course, profoundly affected by the explicit political ideology of the press, which is predominantly conservative. The broadcasting media are dominated by a viewpoint representing the 'moderate middle', taking for granted certain broad beliefs and values – what Stuart Hall has succinctly called 'a world at one with itself'. The master concepts of news ideology include such notions as the 'national interest', the 'British way of life' and the 'democratic process', seen as threatened by mindless militants manipulated by a minority of extremists representing anarchy and subversion, with only the 'thin blue line' to save the day for law and order (Chibnall, 1977, p. 21). Both straightforward crime and political conflict are presented as the same pathology, with the police celebrated as guardians of the normal (Ericson *et al.*, 1991).

The police, however, often see themselves as denigrated and under attack in the news media. Criticisms of the press are frequently made by police spokesmen, summed up by Robert Mark's complaint in a speech to the London Press Club in 1974 that 'Without doubt the most abused, the most unfairly criticised and the most silent minority in this country' were the police.

Part of the explanation of this discrepancy between police views and content analyses of media presentations lies in the anxiety of police officers about the headline revelations of police malpractice, which is not assuaged by 'one bad apple' editorialising.[3] Criticisms are perceived bitterly, while favourable comments seem less salient. Another factor is the police sense that they are inhibited from giving their side of many stories which may be *sub judice* or subject to official inquiries (Tumber, 1982, pp. 14–21). Because of anxieties about their reporting, and realisation of its importance, the police have tried to handle their relations with the media carefully (Chibnall, 1977, 1979). Scotland Yard opened a press office in 1919, largely because of fears about unauthorised leaks produced by reporters bribing officers.

Since then relations between the press and the police have fluctuated. In the 1920s and 1930s Yard cooperation with the press remained relatively cool, and reporters gained their information largely by *sub rosa* tactics. The advent of Sir Harold Scott as Commissioner in 1945 marked a high spot in police–press cordiality, the dawn of the 'Golden Age' of crime reporting (coinciding with the 'Golden Age' of public confidence in the police), when a few detectives, notably Robert Fabian, achieved superstar status. Scott anticipated Mark in his appreciation of the value of good relations with the media. The late 1950s *causes célèbres* which heralded the Royal Commission on the Police marked a new strain on police–press cordiality, as the police became concerned about media highlighting of their peccadilloes. However, the mid-1960s were glowing ones for press treatment of the police. The reorganisation of the police was welcomed as a modernising breakthrough, and their gang-busting successes against the Krays and Richardsons duly celebrated. The high point in press eulogising of British police virtue was the laudatory way their handling of the counter-cultural manifestations of the spirit of 1968 (notably Grosvenor Square) were contrasted with repressive foreign heavy-handedness.

The police–press accord was threatened by the 1969 and later corruption scandals, but Mark dealt with these not by shutting out the media, but manipulating them skilfully through a policy of openness, enunciated in a memorandum of 24 May 1973. This was part of a coherent strategy of reform intended to fend off threats to police independence (Chibnall, 1979). Mark's manipulation of the media was admitted by him in a BBC TV interview on 12 July 1977, following his retirement. Referring to his denial (during the 1972 Dimbleby Lecture) of any connection between pornography and police corruption, he claimed this had been tactical.

I was like a surgeon who had to cut out a major cancer without killing the patient, in other words I had to do great execution among the CID while at the same time maintaining their morale and to some extent maintaining public belief in them. Well, this isn't a simple operation, you know, you've got to . . . mask your real intentions behind your words occasionally.

Following Mark's replacement by McNee as Commissioner in 1977, relations with the media seemed to become more abrasive. A number of incidents led to harsh police criticism of the media, especially the BBC (*Police*, October 1979, pp. 4–6). The most prominent *cause célèbre* was the virulent police reaction to the *Law and Order* series of plays, broadcast in April 1978. The Prison Officers' Association and the Metropolitan Police for a time withdrew facilities from the BBC in protest.

The abrasiveness in police–press relations in this period was not so much a consequence of personalities, of McNee being a less adroit media manipulator than Mark. It was a symptom of the politicised state of policing. Media coverage of Southall and other conflicts was seen by the Left as generally loaded in favour of the police, whatever the Federation may have thought (Wren-Lewis, 1981–2). The 1979 general election was the culmination of the process of more partisan police interventions in politics (Clarke and Taylor, 1980; Reiner, 1980a; Taylor, 1980). The media were used by the law and order lobby to build up a climate conducive to their demands, but at the same time there was an undercurrent of questioning of police practices, perceived most clearly by the police themselves.

These contradictory currents became especially acute and apparent in media coverage of the 1981 riots and their aftermath. Some radical analyses of this coverage saw it as almost uniformly condemnatory of the rioters, supportive of the police and the government's immediate response of tooling up the coercive capacity of the force (Sumner, 1982b). Later, more complex radical analyses portray the media accounts as incorporating a degree of criticism of police practices as a possible contributory cause of the riots, although downplaying participants' perceptions. Highlighted instead was the copycat theory, which stripped the riots of any meaning (Tumber, 1982).

The most complex analysis is Wren-Lewis's (1981–2) which

distinguishes three different discourses which were present in media coverage. The 'law and order discourse' portrayed the clashes as an inexplicable eruption of sheer hooliganism requiring firm repression by an adequately equipped police force. The 'contra-discourse' was a radical one standing the first on its head. The riots were seen specifically as anti-police demonstrations provoked by heavy-handed police harassment. The 'social causality discourse' (favoured by the Labour Party's leaders) emphasised the importance of the failure of government economic policy as the root cause of discontent, but accepted the need for effective policing to suppress the unacceptable symptoms of this, the street disorders. Wren-Lewis emphasises the novelty of presentation of the contra-discourse during media analyses of Brixton. In 1981 the contra-discourse was given some prominence in the 'interpretive' stage after the riots died down. The initial 'revelation' stage of reporting Brixton was heavily loaded by the law and order discourse, carried above all by the vivid pictures of violent clashes in the early newscasts. However, after the establishment of the Scarman Inquiry into the April disorders, the media discussions moved into a stage of closure, attempting to play down the contra-discourse and re-emphasise the law and order discourse. When the July 1981 disorders erupted in Brixton, Toxteth, Moss Side and elsewhere far less attention was allowed to the contra-discourse, and reportage was heavily weighted to the law and order frame. Wren-Lewis thus points to the novel appearance in media discussions of Brixton in April 1981 of some critical views on policing. But he finds a strong move to displacement of this by a pure law and order discourse following the appointment of Scarman, and the July riots.

A close reading of Wren-Lewis and the other early radical analyses of the 1981 riots suggests that they simply invert the law and order frame and accept the contra-discourse. Any diversions from this are seen as disingenuous, or the product of the temporary early shock of the riots disrupting existing conventional views. For example, Wren-Lewis sees the reluctance of police chiefs to contemplate use of the CS gas and bullets offered by the government after the July riots as merely a device to enhance the image of 'responsibility and sincerity of police chiefs . . . as the narrative reaches its coercive closure' (p. 32). It is unthinkable within the contra-discourse that there should be genuine disagreement within the state apparatuses, with police chiefs at the liberal pole on this occasion.

But the early analyses stop the story too short. Closure is supposed to have been reached by the *establishment* of the Scarman Inquiry. In fact, the Report itself heavily incorporated the contra-discourse, seeing policing mistakes as a core factor sparking the disorders. Indeed the Report united the contra and social causation discourses, largely rejecting the law and order one. It was lapped up by the media, which gave much attention not only to Scarman's criticisms of police tactics, but also to John Alderson's more critical evidence to Scarman on 2 September 1981. Later documentaries on the issues raised by the riots allowed more weight to criticisms of the police and government, and accorded a measure of meaning and legitimacy to the rioters themselves, notably Simon Winchester's *Chronicle* programme 'Riot: An Investigation' (24 February 1982, BBC2). Thus media coverage of the long-term impact of the riots and the Scarman Inquiry allowed considerable scope to critical discourses, and on the whole rejected the law and order framework (Murdock, 1982, pp. 110–15). This was undoubtedly a major factor allowing the riots and the Scarman Report to presage a move to a new climate of reform within the police.

Both Metropolitan Commissioners in the 1980s, Sir Kenneth Newman and Sir Peter Imbert, have been at least as adroit media spokesmen as Mark. But whereas Mark manipulated the media to politicise law and order issues, Newman and Imbert used them to try to cultivate legitimacy. Newman's stock with the media declined after the Broadwater Farm riot of 1985, which indicated the failure of his attempts to construct a 'new social contract'. Imbert has enjoyed a good press for most of his period of office, and the Plus programme he initiated has won plaudits as heralding 'Glasnost at the Yard', even from erstwhile critics. Imbert has been a propagator of openness in police–media relations since his days as Chief Constable of Thames Valley in the late 1970s, when he made the courageous decision (controversial with many colleagues) to allow facilities for Roger Graef's celebrated fly-on-the-wall TV series, *Police–Thames Valley* and its successor *Operation Carter*.

Despite this, the general coverage of police matters since the mid-1980s has become increasingly critical, with much news footage revealing apparent abuses during key public order clashes (notably the miners' strike, Wapping, and the 'Battle of the Bean Field' in 1986 when hippies travelling to Stonehenge were shown being violently handled by police officers). Even such events as the 1990 Trafalgar Square poll-tax demonstration, which initially seemed to portray the police favourably, subsequently were subject to media analyses probing allegations of mishandling and malpractice. Above all the media have been prominent in the process by which the major *causes célèbres* of police abuses leading to miscarriages of justice have been revealed, notably the Guildford Four, the Birmingham Six and the Tottenham Three. In each case individual investigative journalists and documentaries have been pivotal factors in discrediting the police evidence (Mullin, 1989; Woffinden, 1989). Media coverage of the apparent police failure to cope adequately with rising crime has also become increasingly critical. The emerging critical consensus is best encapsulated in a celebrated editorial in *The Independent* (26 January 1990) which spoke of 'institutional rot' in the police.

Whilst the media have played their part in the development of a crisis of confidence in policing in the early 1990s, they have reflected rather than created this conjuncture. There are deeper sources of loss of faith in the police by government and opinion-formers, as well as the general public, not least the convenience of the police as a scapegoat for more fundamental failures of the criminal justice system and law and order policy. However, the police contributed to their own problems by the way their own 'law and order' campaigns of the late 1970s and early 1980s used the media to create unrealistic expectations of what more police powers and resources could achieve. What is clear is that media presentation of police issues is now much more complex than either the 'hegemonic' or 'subversive' perspectives implies.

'Fictional' images

Crime and law enforcement have always been staple parts of the mass entertainment media. Historians of detective fiction are fond of tracing roots back to the Bible and Greek mythology, seeing Cain and Abel or the Oedipus myth as crypto-crime stories (Sayers, 1928). In the eighteenth century there was a flourishing trade in broadsheets, ballads, 'memoirs' and novels about the exploits of highwaymen like Dick Turpin or Jack Sheppard, and thief-takers like Jonathan Wild. But the real take-off in crime and detective fiction occurs with the formation of modern police forces in Europe in the early nineteenth century. There was a mushrooming output of fictionalised memoirs of ex-detectives from the Sûreté or the Bow Street Runners. The prototype was the publication in 1828–9 of the *Memoirs* of Vidocq, a thief turned thief-taker who ran the Paris police detective bureau after 1817. Modern detective fiction is usually traced back to Edgar Allan Poe's trilogy of short stories about C. Auguste Dupin, the archetypal ratiocinative sleuth, starting with *The Murders in the Rue Morgue* (1841). The birth of detective fiction coincides with the development of modern police forces. Both can be traced to anxieties of similar kinds among the respectable literate strata, fears about the threat to social order represented by the 'dangerous classes' (Palmer, 1978; Knight, 1980; Porter, 1981). They embody similar models of the solution to these concerns about conspiracy and subversion: the rational and unfailingly resourceful individual symbolising a superior ideal of self-disciplined initiative, who is symbiotically related to a well-ordered social organisation.

Since the mid-nineteenth century crime and detective fiction has been a prominent part of the output of all the dominant mass media. Popular heroes, including Sherlock Holmes, Charlie Chan, The Saint, Dick Tracy, Sam Spade, whatever medium they originated in, remain perennial favourites in all entertainment forms: novels, pulp magazines, comics, theatre, cinema, radio, television. About a quarter of all fictional works sold in Britain and America are crime stories. Between 1958 and 1977 the proportion of prime-time TV shows in America featuring crime and law enforcement averaged between a quarter and a third (Dominick, 1978, p. 114).

Crimes and police officers are even more ubiquitous than that, appearing in almost all fiction, from Punch and Judy through Dostoevsky to *Singin' in the Rain* (with Gene Kelly dancing around a bewildered cop). None of these is without some significance for images of the police, but I shall concentrate on the crime genre specifically as the richest source of such conceptions.[4] Within this genre (i.e. fictions with crime and law enforcement as the central thematic elements) a broad division can be drawn between *criminal* tales (where the central character is a person or persons – professional or amateur – engaged in criminal activity) and *law enforcement* stories (where the central character is a crime fighter, whether amateur or professional).

Some interesting work has analysed quantitatively the content of prime-time crime shows in American TV (Dominick, 1978; Pandiani, 1978; Garofalo, 1981, pp. 325–7). The most striking finding is the remarkably similar pattern of representation of crime, criminals and law enforcers between news coverage and fiction (and consequently a similar pattern of divergence from official statistics). Four important structural characteristics are found in TV crime shows:

1. Most crimes depicted are serious, involving considerable violence, large-scale theft or extensive damage to property. Murder, assault and armed robbery constitute about 60 per cent of all TV fiction offences.
2. Criminals are rational and purposive, not impulsive, confused, drifting or driven. They are high-status, middle-aged, white men. Their main motive is greed, although they usually have to engage in violence to achieve their ends.
3. Law enforcers are more likely to be amateur than professional. If professional police, they are usually detectives. They are predominantly unattached, economically comfortable, white males in middle adulthood.
4. The law enforcers almost invariably solve or foil the crime(s), usually through the exercise of remarkable personal skill and daring.

All these elements are the precise opposite of the pattern of real offending and policing. On the other hand, the characters, themes and milieux have similar features to most other prime-time TV entertainments, which portray predominantly comfortable-to-affluent middle-class, middle-aged life-styles (Pandiani, 1978).

These are the basic features of the crime genre which seem to transcend the particular inflections of specific sub-types which vary between times and cultures. They constitute the core myth of law and order around which numerous variants can be constructed. Crime is portrayed as a serious threat, certainly to the property and person of individual victims, but often extending to the social order *per se*. Even if any single crime does not endanger civilisation itself (although in fiction it often does), the volume of criminal activity shown in crime entertainments amounts to such a threat. However, the forces of law and order can and do regularly contain it. They are thus portrayed as essential and valuable, even pivotal, institutions in our society. Furthermore, although crime seldom prevails, criminals are formidable and worthy foes of the law enforcers. They are not defeated because they are unintelligent, resourceless or puny, but because of the superlative prowess and dedication of the law enforcers. Around this core myth, however, there can be quite varied permutations, with radically conflicting perspectives on the virtue, justice, likeability and sympathy accorded to law enforcers, the criminal justice system and offenders.

There have been numerous more or less scholarly analyses of crime films (McCarthur, 1972; Shadoian, 1977; Rosow, 1978; Clarens, 1980), detective fiction (Haycraft, 1941, 1946; Watson, 1971; Symons, 1972; Cawelti, 1976; Palmer, 1978; Knight, 1980; Porter, 1981; Benstock, 1983; Most and Stowe, 1983; Mandel, 1984), detective films (Everson, 1972; Tuska, 1978; Parrish and Pitts, 1990a), detective TV shows (Meyers, 1981, 1989), and fictional images of specific, highly prestigious elite police forces (Walden, 1982; Powers, 1983). The fictional treatment of the *police* has only been the subject of a handful of studies, examining police novels (Dove, 1982; Dove and Bargainnier, 1986), police films (Reiner, 1978b, 1981c; Park, 1978; Inciardi and Dee, 1987; Parrish and Pitts, 1990b) and, most commonly, TV cop shows (Weiner, 1973; Fiske and Hartley, 1978, Ch. 12; Hurd, 1979; Kerr, 1981; Clarke, 1982, 1983; Carter, 1982; Sparks, 1992). The paucity of studies of police fictions reflects the fairly recent emergence of the cop to hero status, coinciding with the advent of TV as the primary mass entertainment medium in the early 1950s. Novels and films with police heroes (the 'police procedurals') did not really emerge as a distinctive sub-genre until the late 1940s, so that television is the only medium where the professional police officer has always featured as an heroic figure.

To facilitate discussion of the varying kinds of law enforcement story (whether in literary, film or television form), their fluctuating dominance and social meanings, I have classified them into twelve ideal-type models, shown in Table 5.1. These are distinguished by their treatment of seven elements: the hero, crime, villain, victim, social setting, the police organisation and narrative sequence.

Law enforcement narratives are connected to some other closely related genres, such as the espionage, investigative reporter or lawyer/district attorney/court-room stories (Harris, 1987). They also have been subject to many comic or parodic treatments. The criminal protagonist side of the crime genre could similarly be analysed into different recurring patterns, although none of these leads will by pursued here.

I shall now give a brief account of the image of the police in each type.

The 'classic sleuth'

The majority of detective stories between the heyday of Sherlock Holmes at the turn of this century and the 1930s were classic sleuth mysteries. This sort of story remains popular in the form of the lavish screen versions of Agatha Christie novels which have been big commercial successes for the British cinema since *Murder on the Orient Express* (1976) (Reiner, 1981d). The story revolves around a puzzling crime by an unknown offender – often one that was seemingly impossible to commit. There are a variety of possible culprits, but by the use of what Agatha Christie's Hercule Poirot called his 'little grey cells', the eccentric hero with supercharged neurons eliminates all the red herrings and points the finger at an unlikely culprit. The police are usually portrayed as bumbling buffoons or at best unimaginative bureaucrats, capable of handling routine offences but quite out of their depth with a case of any complexity. Their lack of perceptiveness (as well as that of the hero's companion and chronicler, the Dr

Watson figure) operate as devices to show up the hero's genius. The sleuth is usually an amateur or a consulting detective. Occasionally, however, he may be a professional policeman, as with Freeman Wills Crofts' Inspector French, Ngaio Marsh's Roderick Alleyn, Michael Innes' Inspector Appleby, Earl Der Biggers' Charlie Chan and, more recently, P.D. James' Adam Dalgleish. But these are mostly quite unusual and exceptional police officers, of independent means and elite education, spouting poetry, esoteric allusions and classical quotes with the snootiest amateur sleuth in the Philo Vance mould. Charlie Chan is never portrayed working out of his Honolulu office, but is forever globe trotting and treated like a visiting dignitary. These men clearly never joined police departments for anything as vulgar as a modest but secure pay cheque. Rather, the job provides them with a more predictable and plausible supply of mysterious corpses than their amateur counterparts' reliance on invitations to spend weekends at creepy country mansions. Unlike later models of fictional police, these super-sleuths are in the great detective tradition, relying on brainpower not police power or firepower (Dove, 1982, Ch. 2).

Contrary to the theory expressed by Rex Stout (creator of Nero Wolfe and a master of the classic tradition) 'that people who don't like mystery stories are anarchists', the classical sleuth story is not really a law and order fable. The generally dim picture of the regular police militates against this. So does the image of a society with so ordered, predictable and regular a daily round that the minutest deviation from routine constitutes a clue to the eagle-eyed sleuth. But above all it is a structural probability built into the plot requirements that the victim had it coming and merits no sympathy. He must be an 'exceptionally murderable' person, so odious a bundle of unpleasant qualities that all the other characters have ample motive for murder, supplying an abundance of red herrings (Grella, 1970, p. 42). Furthermore, the sleuth does not want to be burdened with anything as mundane as legal requirements of proof. A good way out of this is for the murderer to be so sympathetically motivated that the sleuth, having demonstrated his prowess by discovering the culprit's identity, does not turn him over to the police. The detective in effect acts as a vigilante, invoking his private sense of justice not due process of law (Ruehlman, 1974).

Table 5.1 Law Enforcement Stories

Type	Hero	Crime	Villain	Victim	Setting	Police organisation	Plot structure
Classic sleuth	Grey-celled wizard (usually amateur).	Murder by person(s)/ method unknown.	Personal motive – outwardly respectable.	Exceptionally murderable.	Respectable upper-class, often rural.	Honest, well-meaning, rule-bound plods.	Order – crime – red herrings – deduction – order restored.
Private eye	Self-employed. Motive: honour. Skill: dedication, moral intuition.	Greed and/or passion murder. Mystery not crucial.	Apparently respectable and/or professionals. Several cross-plotting.	Not always clear. Client (i.e. apparent victim) often morally dubious.	Respectable upper-class façade masking corruption, and underworld.	Brutal, corrupt, but may be tough and efficient.	Moral disorder – private eye hired – blows, brawls, bullets, broads and booze – use of moral sense – 'solution' – moral disorder continues normally.
Police procedural	Routine cops, using footwear, finger-prints and forensic labs.	Murder, usually for gain. Who-dunit less important than how ap-prehended.	Usually professional, and not sympathetic.	Ordinary, respectable folk. Weak, guileless innocents.	Cross-section of urban life, including cops' home.	Team of dedicated professionals. Hierarchical but organic division of labour.	Order – crime(s) – one damn thing after another – use of police procedures – order restored.
Vigilante	Lone-wolf cop or amateur. Skill: ruthless fanaticism.	Bestial behaviour by habitual, not necessarily	Psycho-pathic. Unsym-pathetic even if 'analysed'.	Tortured innocents, though gullible.	Urban jungle, ruled by naive, incompetent elite.	Rule bound bureaucrats vs. wise street cops.	Rampage in urban jungle – ruthless chase – elites try to

	economic, criminal.						
Civil rights	Professional, dedicated, legalistic cop.	Mystery to allow hero to exhibit professionalism.	Usually personal motive, with modicum of sympathy to justify concern for rights.	Respectable/ influential: strong pressure for 'results'.	Unequal society. Money and status 'talk'.	Servants of power.	Unfair order – crime – innocent accused – professionalism – solution – fairer order.
Undercover cop	Skill is courage + symbiosis with underworld: ability to 'pass'.	Organised racket.	Professional organised structure. Leader unknown (or proof required).	Ordinary citizens.	Underworld.	Team of professionals to give hero back-up.	Order – crime – infiltration – hero's rise in racket – solution – combat – order.
Police deviance	Honest 'loner' cop.	Police brutality or corruption.	Other law-breaking cops.	Suspects or ordinary citizens.	Police station + underworld.	Rotten basket, or bad apples.	Police deviance – investigation – control of deviance or of investigator.
Deviant police	Rogue cop or Freudian fuzz.	Police protagonist's brutality or corruption.	Professional crooks who 'invite' his brutality or corruption.	Suspects, processed by protagonist, or general public.	Police station + underworld.	Generally honest but bad apple(s).	Temptation – fall of protagonist – chance of redemption – redemption/ death.

Type	Hero	Crime	Villain	Victim	Setting	Police organisation	Plot structure
Let 'em have it	Elite gang-busters.	Organised racket.	Known gang (maybe unknown leader).	Ordinary folk.	Underworld vs. overworld.	Tough combat unit.	Order – rackets – battle – victory – order.
Fort Apache	Team of routine cops.	'Raids', skirmishes with ethnic minority enemy.	Ghetto toughs, and renegade or foolish whites.	Police outpost in hostile enemy territory.	Beleaguered minority. Camaraderie broken by discipline and deviants.	Cold war – incident – threat of all-out war – trouble-makers neutralised – cold war.	
Police community	Routine patrol cops: very human.	Many petty mis-demeanours. Tempt cops to cynicism.	No specific person. Real villain is despairing cynicism.	Ordinary citizens. Many are unsavoury 'assholes'.	Police station/ car, contrasted with city jungle and domestic tensions.	Brotherhood, 'family' of disparate types.	Picaresque. Will cop save or lose his soul?
Community police	Routine patrol bobby: very human.	Petty, if any.	Prodigal son, if any.	Ordinary folk. Salt-of-the-earth types.	Organic, integrated community.	Microcosm of larger community. Non-divisive hierarchy and specialisation.	Order – everyday human problem – police use moral wisdom + social bonds – order restored.

The 'private eye'

The novels and stories of Dashiell Hammett in the late 1920s and early 1930s, heralded a new kind of detective mystery: the tough, hard-boiled private eye story. In the hands of his successors, notably Raymond Chandler, Ross MacDonald and Mickey Spillane, the private eye became the dominant model of the law enforcer during the 1940s, on screen as well as in literature. In Chandler's famous puff for the superiority of the private eye over the classic mystery, its virtue is said to lie in its greater realism (Chandler, 1944). This doesn't really hold any water. The milieux and characters of the private eye may be more sordid and seedy, but the hero is a far more romantic figure than the sleuth, and especially in Chandler's hands becomes that modern knight errant, the lone man of the mean streets. Furthermore there is a strong vein of social criticism and political commitment, usually of a radical or at least populist kind. (Spillane is an exception only in the sense that his politics are of the radical Right.) The private eye is plunged into a quixotic quest through the murky corruption of a modern metropolis, by a client who more often than not is as treacherous as the initial suspects. A particular mystery may eventually be solved (although the puzzle element is never of any real importance), but society itself can never be set to rights by such individual action as the hero is capable of. The police are often a part of the network of corruption, on the take and/or brutal. But they are not stupid or weak. Some may even be effective law enforcers in a bureaucratic way. The private eye's superiority is not his special skill, but his moral integrity and dedication compared with the corrupt run-of-the-mill cops, and his ability to violate bureaucratic procedure and cut corners.

The police procedural

The police procedural story emerged in the late 1940s as an apparently more realistic successor to the private detective (Dove, 1982, Ch. 2). It appeared more or less simultaneously in all media: novels, in the hands of such pioneers as Hilary Waugh in the United States, and John Creasey in England (especially his *Gideon of the Yard* series, written under the pseudonym J.J. Marric); the cinema, spearheaded by *Naked City* in 1947 (later a long-running TV series); radio and TV, with Jack Webb's *Dragnet* – the quintessential police procedural. Webb's famous catch-phrase, 'Just give us the facts, ma'am', sums up the procedural's distinctiveness. The heroes are ordinary, un-glamorous, routine cops, with more or less happy domestic lives (which are often depicted), doing a job with professional skill and dedication, but no exceptional talent. They solve cases success-fully because they have the back-up of an efficient organisation, technological aids and legal powers. Often they are harassed and must work on several cases simultaneously, an early device to lend an aura of verisimilitude that rapidly became a cliché. The organisation is an integrated one, with differences of rank or function not leading to conflict. Authority is accepted without undue deference or resentment. At the same time professional pride and camaraderie do not lead to alienation from the public. The cop has a private life which is meaningful and humanising. At the level of physical detail and iconography the procedural is clearly more 'realistic' than the earlier kinds of mystery. But they really give scarcely more accurate an account of police work in general.

The vigilante

The vigilante is either a lone wolf cop or an aggrieved private citizen. The prototype of the former is Clint Eastwood's *Dirty Harry*, and of the latter the Charles Bronson character in *Death Wish* (1974), based on a Brian Garfield novel.

The vigilante story is an implicit denial of the procedural's values. Police procedure is impotent in the face of crime. Only the street-wise cop, understanding the vicious nature of criminals, can deal effectively with them, defying any restraints posed by legal or departmental rules and regulations. The vigilante tale is a quite explicit law and order fable, proposing police power as the only solution to the major menace of crime. The obvious plot device for achieving this end is the representation of ordinary city life as an urban jungle, and the specific crime/criminals focused on as especially bestial. The department is not the integrated organisation depicted in the procedural. Above all it is divided by the absolute gulf and conflict between street cops and the management cops who restrain them for 'political' reasons. The citizenry, although nominally the justification for the vigilante's battle, do not adequately appreciate or support his actions, preferring to know as little as possible about the men who remove their moral garbage.

The vigilante story is a clear reflection of the law and order politics which Richard Nixon used to secure his 1968 presidential victory. From early 1968 until the mid-1970s – the heyday of the vigilante story – law and order was regularly named as the main domestic problem by opinion polls in America. The cop became the rallying symbol for white 'backlash' and middle-aged 'kidlash', with 'support your local police' as the effective code word. The vigilante films are peppered with specific references to the contemporary law and order debate, as in Dirty Harry's attack on the controversial Supreme Court decisions of the early 1960s (such as *Miranda* and *Escobedo*) which strengthened suspects' rights.

The vigilante cop model was translated for English audiences by the exceptionally popular *The Sweeney*, and its derivatives like *Target*. Despite some softening (and new models) in recent years, the vigilante cop story remains the most common type, witness the recent success of the later Dirty Harry films and derivatives like Bronson's 1983 *10 to Midnight* (in which he voiced the credo of all vigilante cops, 'Forget what's legal, do what's right!' or the 1986 *Cobra* in which Sylvester Stallone gives a suspect his 'right to silence' by shooting him). The main recent modification is a greater attempt explicitly to justify the vigilante's actions, as in T.J. Hooker's remorseless philosophising along the lines of, 'You know the difference between a conservative and a liberal? A conservative is a liberal who's been mugged.'[5]

So successfully did the vigilante story articulate widely shared sentiments, not only about law and order but also the counter-cultural and radical (as well as conservative) disenchantment with bureaucracy, that it has come to seem *the* archetype of cop fiction. It is why police stories are widely regarded as law and order mythology, although there have been radically different fictional models of policing which have been popular at different times.

The civil rights story

The civil rights cop story is the vigilante narrative stood on its head. The police organisation (and its political masters) are so concerned with 'results' that they trample over due process and legal procedures. The hero is a cop in the procedural mould (who would have been happy in Jack Webb's team) but confronts an unprofessional organisation. The plot allows him to prove that cops can have their cake and eat it. Only by following due process can they avoid fitting up the wrong suspect, thereby allowing the guilty (and dangerous) men to go free.

The quintessential example of this narrative is John Ball's 1965 novel *In the Heat of the Night*, which was made into an enormously successful, Oscar-winning 1967 film. Virgil Tibbs (Sidney Poitier), a black, big-city detective, is arrested as a murder suspect merely because he is a black stranger passing through the small Georgia town of Sparta. Tibbs is able to use his professional skills coolly and calmly to find the real culprit, teaching the sloppy and bigoted local police chief (played by Rod Steiger) that the college degree is a more effective tool of detection than the third degree.

Another novel in the same spirit was Roderick Thorpe's *The Detective*, and especially the very successful (commercially and critically) 1968 film derived from it, starring Frank Sinatra. Joe Leland, the eponymous hero, is once again the classic Joe Friday type in a department riddled with brutality, corruption and 'politics', which he tries to resist. The moral of the superiority of due process is learned when Leland uncharacteristically uses psychological pressure to get a confession from a murder suspect (to stop his colleagues beating him up), but discovers after the man has gone to the chair that he was innocent (Wilson, 1968b; Reiner, 1981c, pp. 209–10).

The civil rights phase in cop stories only lasted a few years – from about 1965 to 1968. Although in general it would be misleading to see fiction as directly reflecting political events, in this case the connection is quite plain. Throughout the 1960s until 1968 the major domestic problems (as indicated by opinion polls) were seen as 'racial problems' or 'civil rights'. As we have seen, the emergence in 1968 of law and order as the prime domestic political issue coincides with the displacement of the civil rights by the vigilante cop story.

The 'undercover cop'

Although the 'undercover cop' tactic may be used by any style of policing, there is a special symbiosis between it and vigilantism. This is partly because it involves the hero in morally dubious practices of deception and conniving at crime (if not being an *agent provocateur*). It is also because, in order for it to be plausible that the hoods accept the hero as one of them, he has to have the image of a deviant. When clean-cut procedural cops like Mark Stevens in the 1948 film *Street With No Name*, or Edmond O'Brien in the 1949 *White Heat* infiltrate gangs it is hard to credit the crooks' gullibility. It is much more plausible when James Cagney, with his established gangster persona, does undercover work in the 1935 *G-Men*. Indeed, what needs heavy work explaining is his employment as an FBI agent! The same is true of Edward G. Robinson's similar role in the 1936 *Bullets or Ballots* (Reiner, 1981c, pp. 200–3).

Police deviance (good apple in rotten barrel)

The police deviance story has affinities with the civil rights stories. It portrays the struggle of a single honest cop against a corrupt organisation. The difference is that the civil rights narrative concerns the violation of rights to achieve convictions, rather than exploitation of the job for personal financial reward.

The police deviance story is very much a development of the 1970s following the Knapp Committee investigations revealing the pervasive corruption of the New York Police Department.

The quintessential example is the book and film based on the experiences of *Serpico*, the honest cop whose revelations stimulated the Knapp Commission. Many other individuals involved in these events have produced memoirs or fictionalised accounts (e.g. *Prince of the City*, 1982), and police deviance stories continue to be a vigorous sub-genre (*Year of the Dragon*, 1985; *The Untouchables*, 1987; *Q. and A.*, 1990; *Internal Affairs*, 1990).

In Britain too the Scotland Yard scandals stimulated several novels and plays focusing on the issue of police corruption. Bernard Toms' *The Strange Affair* (1968 – also filmed, starring Michael York) focused, like *Serpico*, on the (unsuccessful) struggles of a lone honest policeman. G.F. Newman's later *Bastard* series of novels, the even better-known *Law and Order* novels and play trilogy, and the *Operation Bad-Apple* play, all explore the world of policing in a critical light reflecting the impact of the 1970s' corruption scandals. (*Operation Bad-Apple* is clearly a *roman-à-clef* deriving from the Countryman investigations.) Newman's work is really on the margins of the police deviance/deviant police categories, as not only the organisation but even the main police protagonist are portrayed as corrupt.

Deviant police (bad apple in clean barrel)

There are two sub-variants of this category. In the 'Freudian fuzz' stories the central character is a cop who is driven into vigilante style brutalities, which (unlike in the vigilante narrative) are not approved of. His rule breaking is the product of the combined pressure of the general cynicism induced by police work and some special psychological weakness of the hero, which although 'analysed' by the narrative does not morally justify his actions. The quintessential example is Sidney Kingsley's play *Detective Story* and the 1951 movie version of it. (For other examples, see Reiner, 1981c, pp. 205–7.) The 'Freudian fuzz' is not a bad man, so he is allowed some chance to redeem himself, even though it usually costs him his life.

The other variant is the 'rogue cop' story, where the

protagonist is led into deviance at least partly for personal gain, although the 'invitational edge' of temptation will be stressed so that his actions are seen as comprehensible if not condonable. Good examples are the 1950 Joseph Losey film *The Prowler*, and the 1954 *Rogue Cop*. Because the protagonist is not thoroughly evil, he is also usually allowed redemption through self-sacrificing death.

Where the police deviance/deviant police narratives are combined (bad apple in rotten barrel), as in G.F. Newman's works, the bleakest image of the police in popular fiction is achieved. Recent American police deviance stories have also tended to increasing pessimism, with corruption seen as endemic rather than episodic (e.g. *Internal Affairs*).

'Let 'em have it'

Unlike the other categories there are no examples of this type with any pretensions to seriousness. It is the province of the 'B' movie, the pulp magazine or novel, the Saturday morning serial, and the comic-strip. None of the moral, political, or even practical problems or dilemmas of policing is touched upon, as they are in some way by all the other categories. Rather, this type forms the bed-rock imagery of 'cops versus robbers' stories from which the others construct more complicated permutations. The stories are simple sequences of planning and executing skirmishes, raids and battles in the 'war against crime' between police and hoodlum organisations. Examples are such G-men films of the 1930s as *Let 'Em Have It, Muss 'Em Up, Don't Turn 'Em Loose* and *Show 'Em No Mercy* (vigilante stories without this being seen as a controversial stance), or the perennially popular Dick Tracy character (originating in a 1930s comic-strip, but graduating to 'B' feature and serial films and radio, and recently revived in Warren Beatty's 1990 blockbuster). With the growing sophistication of post-1950s cinema, this type disappeared from the large screen. But it continued in such popular TV series as *The Untouchables* or *Starsky and Hutch*, although with inflections reflecting the fashions of the day (the procedural in the former, the vigilante in the latter). In recent years there has been something of a big screen comeback, in *Dick Tracy* and lesser offspins, part of a Hollywood return to nostalgic escapist adventures which began with *Star Wars* and *Superman* in the late 1970s and continues with *Batman* in the law enforcement genre.

'Fort Apache'

The 'Fort Apache' story is distinguishable more by its setting than narrative structure. The quintessential example is Heywood Gould's novel *Fort Apache–the Bronx*, and the 1981 Paul Newman film it inspired. This is partly a picaresque account of the police community, partly (unsolved by the cops) murder mystery, partly a 'civil rights' story. The distinctive feature is embodied in the title. The police are portrayed as the old US cavalry, a beleaguered garrison in hostile territory. The military metaphor invites comparison with the 'Let 'em have it' sagas, but the depiction of the 'enemy' is crucially different. In the G-Men or Dick Tracy stories the hoods are unequivocally evil. In the Fort Apache theme the police are opposed by people of a different race. Not only do distinctions have to be made between the 'good' and 'bad' members of it (the hero of *Assault on Precinct 13* is a black cop), but even the hostiles who attack the police are reacting to oppression (in the liberal variants like *Fort Apache-the Bronx*, or Tony Richardson's 1982 *The Border*), or at least represent a distinct if alien culture. (Even the savage gangs who callously murder a little girl in *Assault on Precinct 13* are shown as having a code and rituals, and have taken to the warpath because of police harassment.) Implicitly the tense relations between the police and the ghetto residents whose borders they patrol are the products of the racism and uneven economic development of white America, although the prime focus of sympathy is the cop who has to carry the can for the sins of the majority. In all these films the evil action of renegades on both sides threaten (or produce) all-out war, although the hero struggles to contain it. Ultimately, however, the police can at best lower the temperature of the cold war between ghetto and suburb, not remove the sources of conflict. The Fort Apache stories reflect the civil rights *vs.* law and order debates some years on, with a pessimistic, albeit liberal slant. There is little faith in the efficacy of either civil rights or repressive policies to do more than contain a 'dreadful enclosure'. This is clear in the most recent example Dennis Hopper's controversial *Colours* (1988).

Police community

The police community stories are everyday tales of ordinary cop folk. They are best illustrated by the novels of former Los Angeles police sergeant Joseph Wambaugh (1971, 1973, 1976), and their film derivatives, especially *The New Centurions*, *The Blue Knight*, *The Choirboys*, and the TV series *The Blue Knight* and *Police Story* (Reiner, 1978b). The more recent and very successful *Hill Street Blues* continues some of the same themes, with much less reverence for the police force.

Although crimes feature in these stories, they are not central to the narrative, and are mainly petty misdemeanours rather than serious offences. The true theme of the stories is the moral development of the police officer, and the internal relations of the police community. The narratives are a picaresque portrayal of the bewildering array of incidents the patrolling cop encounters. The linking question giving these episodes coherence is whether the cop will safeguard his soul, or surrender to the besetting sin of cynicism, and take refuge in alcohol, suicide or brutalisation. While the police form an internal community of sorts, they are divided from ordinary citizens, who if not themselves corrupt are unappreciative 'ass-holes' who don't back up the police. Whereas the domestic life of the procedural policeman was happy (with the occasional trivial tiff over missed Christmas dinners and the like just adding a touch of verisimilitude), and the vigilante's home life non-existent apart from casual sexual encounters, the 'blue knight' reluctantly and sadly sees his marriage and family fall apart as a necessary consequence of his higher calling. The police community stories embody the cop culture portrayed by American sociological studies, emphasising the social isolation and internal solidarity of the police fraternity.

Community police

The community police stories are the English equivalent of the American police community narrative, the differences reflecting the divergent images and predicaments of the bobby and the cop. The quintessential exemplar is the *Dixon of Dock Green* television series (although *The Blue Lamp*, the 1950 film which introduced the PC George Dixon character – and killed him off within the first hour – was much more of a straightforward crime-fighting procedural than the television series which resurrected Dixon). Although displaced by the harsher *Z Cars* and the later vigilante style of *The Sweeney*, the community police narrative has recently staged a remarkable comeback in the successful *Juliet Bravo* and *The Bill* series (and other spinoffs like *Rockcliffe's Babies* or *Specials*), reflecting the new fashion for 'community policing' in the political debates about law and order (Clarke, 1982, 1983; Murdock, 1982, pp. 115–20; Willis, 1983).[6]

The keynotes of the community police story are an emphasis on the harmonious relations within the police force, and between it and the wider society. This perspective is shared with the procedural, which originates in the same period. But unlike the procedural the emphasis is on the non-crime-related tasks of the police, and even when crime fighting, the human rather than organisational or technological resources of the police are stressed. Like the procedural policeman (but contrary to the vigilantes or police deviants), the community police not only stick to the rules but are more effective as a result.

A more recent variant in some British TV series is the *bureaucratic* police story. These focus on senior management levels of the police (e.g. *Waterfront Beat* and *The Chief*). They are a variant of the police community/community policing stories in that they portray the whole gamut of police work, not just crime, and are primarily concerned with the internal politics of the police bureaucracy rather than any mystery plot. Unlike earlier versions, however, the story is told from the management not street cop perspective. The emergence of this variant is clearly a response to the politicisation of policing, and the comparatively greater salience in public debates of policing policy issues as opposed to individual cases. None of these examples have been particularly successful, however, and the more immediately crime-oriented work of street level police, especially detectives, is likely to retain its fictional centrality.

The changing image of the police

The crucial break in the fictional image of the police is the late 1940s when for the first time routine police officers (rather than G-men and the like) begin to appear as hero figures, in the American and British procedurals, and the British community police stories. Before then the ordinary copper was a background not a leading character. He was a servant figure, and like other servants, public or private, socially invisible. This was illustrated well by Thomas Burke's classic 1912 short story, *The Hands of Mr Ottermole*, later filmed as an episode of Hitchcock's 1950 television series. In this the mysterious mass murderer whom nobody observes is in fact a patrolling bobby, seen by everyone but noticed by none.[7]

The precondition for the emergence of the policeman as a credible hero figure was the professionalisation of the police and their espousal of the important social mandate of crime control (Fogelson, 1977; Walker, 1977). Jack Webb received unprecedented facilities for making *Dragnet* from William Parker, then chief of the Los Angeles police department, and a leader of the professionalisation movement. Webb responded by writing a eulogistic account of the LAPD 'from the inside' (Webb, 1959). *The Blue Lamp* also began with introductory shots and voice-over emphasising the importance of both the uniformed bobby and technological professionalism in the battle against 'the crime wave'.

If the precondition for police heroes is professionalisation, the demand for them (and for professionalisation) comes from the notion that other informal and amateur means of peace-keeping are no longer adequate. The procedural and the community police story imply a society where order maintenance requires a professional organisation, but this can and does operate democratically, with community consent and according to the rule of law.

The deviant police and civil rights stories, which emerge in the later phases of the procedural cycle but before the vigilante boom, imply that legalistic policing is breaking down, at least for some cops in some forces. But it is still maintained as an ideal. The 1970s' vigilante stories (apart from the procedurals, the most popular and influential cycle) reject the model of liberal policing altogether as naïve wishful thinking. They imply a society so deeply threatened by extremes of evil that only the most drastic and unrestrained forceful measures can save it. Although the heyday of vigilantism suppressed any civil rights stories, the police deviance mini-cycle of the 1970s flourished simultaneously, emphasising the unacceptable face of the law and order policies which vigilantism encouraged. The police community stories of that period also pointed to the dangers for the police themselves of the law and order mentality.

The overall trend throughout these developments is clearly towards increasing bleakness, and the culmination of this for the US cop fictions was the Fort Apache story. Although portrayed as a gallant band patrolling the borders between civilisation and the chaos that the racism and ruthless economic advance of that 'civilisation' has engendered in its ghetto areas, there is little faith in the prospect of any final solution, either liberal reforms or total repression. In British police fiction a similar bleak conclusion is proposed by G.F. Newman's combination of the police deviance/deviant police models in a portrait of endemic corruption and rule breaking. The only alternatives in his world are to let the villains carry on absolutely without regulation, or to attempt control with the inevitable consequence of the corruption of the controllers, even as they do the job as well as possible within their lights. Crime control conforming to a legalistic conception is unattainable. The ultimate in hostile fictions was Jim Allen's play *United Kingdom* shown on BBC TV in 1981 and portraying the police as an oppressive political force.[8] The deepening darkness of the mood of police fictions matched the politicisation of law and order issues in the late 1960s and 1970s, as well as a growing undercurrent of realisation by conservatives and liberals alike (fed by criminological and penological research) that 'nothing works'.

In Britain at any rate this log-jam was partially broken by the 1981 riots, the Scarman Report, and the flurry of 'community policing' initiatives in many guises. This cautious optimism is reflected in the renewed fictional enthusiasm for community police stories like *The Bill*. In the United States too, there has been some softening of the police image on television since the peak of vigilantism as such offerings as *Hill Street Blues*, *Cagney and Lacey* and *T.J. Hooker* imply in different ways. However, there is no return to *Dixon* style harmony. The police community is shown with its own internal conflicts based on gender, race, age, rank and specialism, and as dealing with a much more fragmented outside world.

Conclusion

Both the 'factual' and 'fictional' presentations of the police broadly legitimate the police role in presenting them as necessary and for the most part effective. But critical analyses of the media treatment of law and order issues over-emphasise this legitimising function. It coexists not only with media criticism of specific police actions and individuals, but even of the whole direction of police policy, at times building up to a consensus for reform. Moreover, the media image of the reality or ideal of policing is not monolithic, either in any one period or between different times. Nevertheless, a broad threefold pattern of change can be discerned corresponding to the trends in police politicisation. The culmination of the long process of police legitimation leads to the 'Golden Age' of crime reporting as well as consensual police fictions (procedurals and community police stories). The unintended outcome of professionalism becomes in the late 1960s a renewed politicisation. Law and order becomes a major political issue, reflected in (and stimulated by) news and fictional media presentations. In the early 1980s, however, there is a struggle to restore legitimacy manifested both in police policy and debate, and in media accounts, both 'factual' and 'fictional'.[9] Any new legitimating myth must, however, take account of the much more sophisticated public awareness of conflict, inside and outside the police organisation.

PART III

Law and politics

CHAPTER 6

POLICE POWERS AND ACCOUNTABILITY

The 1980s have seen profound changes in the legal and constitutional status and powers of the police. Their powers and accountability have been transformed by a set of overt changes in statute and case-law, and by covert changes in policy and practice. On the one hand, the Police and Criminal Evidence Act 1984 (PACE) attempted a codification of the powers of the police to investigate crime, and the safeguards over their exercise, whilst the Public Order Act 1986 clarified their powers in this significant area. Also in 1985 the Prosecution of Offences Act created the Crown Prosecution Service, removing this major law enforcement responsibility from the police and introducing an extra element of accountability in the processing of cases. On the other hand, legal change and political practice have eroded to virtual impotence the local police authorities who are supposed to be the crucial local leg of the tripartite system for police governance instituted by the Police Act 1964. At local level Chief Constables have become less accountable, whilst at the same time their accountability to central government has grown apace, with some commentators claiming we now have a *de facto* national police force. The riots of 1981 and the Scarman Report were one crucial source of these developments.

The year 1981 was a climacteric for the politicisation of policing in other ways, too. The debate about police powers and accountability which had been joined with vigour and increasing venom came to a head. The Royal Commission on Criminal Procedure, announced to parliament by James Callaghan on

23 June 1977, was established as a response to opposing pressures. On the one hand, there was growing evidence and complaint about police abuse of powers (crystallised by the Fisher Report on the Confait case). On the other hand was the law and order lobby's lament that the extent of suspects' rights made the police operate with 'one hand tied behind their back' (as the Police Federation chairman put it). The RCCP mounted an extensive programme of research to provide a baseline of knowledge about the working of criminal procedure. It was also inundated by evidence from the opposing lobbies, with the police organisations presenting a 'shopping-list' of demands for new or enhanced powers, and the civil liberties groups arguing for tighter control over police powers.

When the RCCP Report was published in January 1981 it was greeted with almost universal condemnation by the Left and civil liberties groups. Indeed, the tone had been set a week before publication in an article by Harriet Harman of the NCCL, based upon a leaked copy (*New Statesman*, 2 January 1981, pp. 6–7). Harman concluded that the RCCP Report constituted a 'triumph of the "law and order" lobby', and she supported the views of two members of the Commission (known to be Jack Jones and Rev. Wilfred Woods) who are referred to several times as dissenting from proposals that widened police powers. The essence of Harman's criticism was that 'while the new powers which the police are to receive are spelt out in uncompromising detail, the nature of any compensating obligations remains extremely vague'. This line was echoed by Labour, the Liberals and all the civil liberties groups. This root-and-branch rejection of the Report by most Left and liberal opinion was continued in more considered academic contributions (Hillyard, 1981; McBarnet, 1981a, b and c, 1982; Baldwin and Kinsey, 1982, Chs 5–7; Hewitt, 1982; Ch. 1; Kinsey and Baldwin, 1982). However, the mainstream legal organisations (the Bar and the Law Society) responded with broad approval coupled with detailed reservations. This was also the stance adopted by a minority of Left and liberal commentators and academics (Dean, 1982; Jones, 1981; Kettle, 1981a and b; Leigh, 1981; Merricks, 1981; Reiner, 1981a; Zander, 1981, 1982). The police had regarded the establishment of the RCCP, in the words of the Superintendents' Association with 'almost universal pessimism', fearing that against 'law and order . . . will be ranged the big guns of every minority group and sociological agency'. But when the report was published the police reception was very favourable. The Police Federation magazine, for example, headlined its article on the Report 'Nice One, Cyril!', praising the efforts of chairman Sir Cyril Philips and his team as providing 'a few fillips for justice' (*Police*, February 1981, pp. 3, 14–22).

In October 1982 the then Home Secretary William Whitelaw published the first version of the Police and Criminal Evidence Bill (henceforth to be called 'Mark I'). It was claimed that this was based largely on the RCCP Report, and undoubtedly it did adopt many of its suggestions. However, it did so in a one-sided way. The RCCP proposals for greater police powers were incorporated or extended, but many of the safeguards were omitted or weakened. The RCCP had placed great weight on the concept of 'a fundamental balance' between suspects' rights and the powers of the police, seeing the proposals it made as an integral whole. Walter Merricks, the leading light of the 'liberal' wing of the Commission, complained that the government had 'pulled apart a package we had fully stitched together' (*The Times*, 19 November 1982). On the other hand, police opinion continued to be delighted. Les Curtis, the Police Federation Chairman, claimed the Bill 'provides for the first time a framework which will make it possible for the police to make a real impact on the fight against crime' (*The Guardian*, 25 March 1982).

Mark I aroused a storm of controversy which united the Left and the civil liberties groups with a broad spectrum of middle-of-the-road and even conservative opinion. In particular, the proposals to empower the police in some circumstances to obtain search warrants from a circuit judge for material held on a confidential basis by professional advisors met a furore of criticism. An attack was launched against these clauses by a solid phalanx of august bodies representing the legal and medical professions, the church, journalists and social workers. The government was so out-gunned that it had to modify the clauses considerably. Altogether Mark I had a very rough parliamentary ride before it fell automatically with the May announcement of the June 1983 general election.

A revised Bill (Mark II) was introduced in the Commons in

October 1983, with a number of new features. These were a response to some of the criticisms and amendments of Mark I. Mark II regained the 'support with reservations' accorded the RCCP by the mainstream professional law bodies and had a much better press reception. The Left, civil liberties groups and some academics continued to oppose it (Bridges and Bunyan, 1983; Christian, 1983; *Policing London*, December 1983; *Rights*, Winter 1983, p. 9; Baldwin and Leng, 1984; Freeman 1984). The police reception to Mark II was distinctly cooler. The Police Federation lamented, 'It's not the Bill it was! . . . the Government appears to have capitulated all along the line . . . in its anxiety to placate the legal lobby (the most powerful cross-party alliance in British politics)' (*Police*, January 1984, p. 4). The final product of the long debate about police powers, was a package which, as it accommodated itself to the twists and turns of contradictory pressures, seemed to end up really pleasing no one (Leigh, 1986).

The year 1981 was a climacteric not only in the debate on criminal procedure. The riots of the spring and summer of that year, and the Scarman Report on the Brixton disorders, were a turning-point in the increasingly politicised debate about police organisation and strategy, and the accountability and constitutional position of the police. None of these issues is separable, of course, except for expository convenience. One weakness of the RCCP was undoubtedly that the broader issues of complaints procedures and accountability were seen as beyond its terms of reference, and were only touched upon. But the riots and Scarman forced them back into the package, so that PACE does now contain reforms of the complaints system, as well as proposals for community consultative arrangements, and was rapidly followed by the creation of an independent prosecution service.

The issues of police powers and accountability are of course interdependent and intimately related. The fundamental problem raised by both debates is how to control police actions, especially in the light of their considerable discretion (Freeman, 1981). The police inevitably have discretion in the enforcement of laws, for at least two reasons. One is that they do not, and never could, have adequate resources for full enforcement of every law. There is thus an inescapable necessity for choice about priorities.

Second, even the most precisely worded rule of law requires interpretation in concrete situations. The logically open texture of rules in application makes an element of at least implicit discretion inevitable. In addition to these considerations which render discretion unavoidable, it is also desirable. Full enforcement would violate generally accepted criteria of justice, as recognised in those cases where it is quite uncontentious that prosecutions should not occur: very old or young offenders, 'stale' offences which are not serious, the policy of not prosecuting drivers when injuries have been inflicted on their 'nearest and dearest', etc. In addition, with the more amorphously defined 'public order' offences, criteria of what constitutes a disturbance are situationally variable. What is accepted in Soho would scandalise in Suffolk (Smith, 1987; Sherr, 1989).

The problem of how the inescapable and justifiable discretion enjoyed by the police can be controlled exists at two levels: the level of policy-making for the force as a whole – the assessment of priorities in resource allocation and broad overall strategy and style – and the street-level actions of rank-and-file officers. In addition there is the task of providing channels of complaint about abuse and dissatisfaction. At present mechanisms only exist for complaints about individual officers and their specific actions. But it would be desirable to have means for citizens to raise complaints about policy and tactics. Before examining the recent changes in each of these areas, some fundamental principles for assessing police powers and accountability must be considered.

First principles: the significance of formal powers and accountability

There are two related and fallacious assumptions common to the law and order and civil liberties lobbies. Both emphasise law enforcement as the central police function, and adopt the rational deterrence model of classical criminology, albeit at different stages of the argument. In this sense both sides have failed to take on board the implications of social research on the police. Neither has adequately considered or explained the fundamental question, 'What are police powers for?', an issue which must be addressed before it can be decided what powers are necessary and how they can be regulated.

If pushed on this issue both camps would say the police are primarily concerned with preventing and detecting crime. Civil libertarians might be more cautious in their statement of this but it is implicit in many denunciations of present police initiatives (e.g. Christian, 1983, pp. 12–13; Gordon, 1984; Kinsey *et al.*, 1986). The historical and sociological evidence should have made clear that crime fighting has never been, is not, and could not be the prime activity of the police, although it is a part of the mythology of media images and cop culture. The core mandate of policing, historically and in terms of concrete demands placed upon the police, is the more diffuse one of order maintenance. Only if this is recognised can the problems of police powers and accountability really be confronted in all their complexity, and perhaps intractability. The vaguely defined 'public order' offences like breach of the peace or the vagrancy acts (which are such a scandalous embarrassment from either a crime control or due process approach) speak to the very heart of the police function.

Given this, the implicit goal of many civil libertarian critiques – a precisely and unambiguously defined set of criminal offences and police powers to deal with them – becomes an unattainable chimera. Moreover, it is a dangerous rather than merely confusing chimera. For it makes conduct that should really be approached as a low-level nuisance come to be assimilated to an all-encompassing omnibus category of 'crime'. Given that people will frequently place demands upon the police for control of low-level disorderly conduct, such as rowdyism, there are only two possibilities. Either the police are restricted absolutely to consensual methods, or they are given some sort of graduated powers to deal with people coercively in the (not unlikely) event that they do not respond to firm but mere exhortation. Giving the police powers may reduce the incentive to develop tactics for a consensual resolution. But this problem has to be dealt with by some other means (the task of 'safeguards'), not by denying powers to cope with the most common kind of request for police action. This is what the Public Order Act 1986 sets out to do, albeit with very uneven success (Smith, 1987; Sherr, 1989; Lacey *et al.*, 1990; Newburn *et al.*, 1991).

One crucial barrier to the development of a rational approach to police powers is the failure adequately to distinguish grades of offences. Civil libertarians are rightly unenthusiastic about the requirements of police effectiveness, especially in the area of 'peace keeping', if the usual consequence of improved efficiency is the unwarranted and counter-productive punitive sanction of imprisonment. An axiom of the associated reforms of police, criminal procedure and punishment in the early nineteenth century was that disproportionately harsh penalties actually impeded effective sanctioning by discouraging public support for prosecution and convictions. This lesson needs to be learnt again. The precondition for a consensus on police powers is that their exercise should not be seen as condemning those who are convicted to unjustifiably harsh, fruitless punishment. Policing does require some broadly defined powers for order maintenance, the formulation and use of which cannot fully satisfy due process criteria. But this can only be accepted if it is not associated with the imprisonment and criminalisation of petty offenders. A more differentiated, finely tuned and targeted discrimination between offenders is necessary, as well as a more just regime for those who are imprisoned (Woolf, 1991).

It is not just civil libertarians, of course, who tend to discuss police powers as if the only function of policing was crime detection. In the 1984 Home Office Working Paper *Criminal Justice*, the Police Bill was described as 'The main current policy initiative in the field of police powers to combat crime.' When Leon Brittan launched Mark II in the Commons he justified it as providing 'adequate and clear powers to conduct the fight against crime'. Now the reformulation of police powers (although arguably justifiable for other reasons) cannot be regarded as crucial for combatting crime. In Chapter 5 it was shown that the clear-up of crimes is only marginally dependent on police initiative, and largely results from information provided by the public. It is not plausible that changes in police powers would significantly increase police effectiveness in crime control. For one thing, most suspects do not assert their rights (e.g. of silence) even if cautioned (Zander, 1979a and b; Sanders *et al.*, 1989; Greer and Morgan, 1990). There is no evidence that rules of criminal procedure allow a significant proportion of suspects to avoid conviction, *pace* the 1979 claim of the Police Federation

Chairman that if these rules were suggested as a new board game, 'Waddingtons would have turned it down because one player, the criminal, was bound to win every time.' About 80 per cent of crown court and 90 per cent of magistrates' court trials result in a conviction, mainly because of guilty pleas (Baldwin and McConville, 1977, 1979; McBarnet, 1981a; McConville *et al.*, 1991). Despite some conflict on the point the weight of the evidence does not suggest any greater likelihood of professional criminals exploiting their rights than 'small fry' (Zander, 1974; Baldwin and McConville, 1977, 1979; the contrary view is implied by Mack, 1976; Williamson and Moston, 1990). The Royal Commission's own research concluded that 'There are no obvious powers which police might be given that would greatly enhance their effectiveness in the detection of crime' (Steer, 1980, p. 125). This view has now come to be the consensus of Chief Constables, although their predecessors were central to the pressures leading to the expansion of powers under PACE (Reiner, 1991, pp. 144–60).

If the law and order lobby errs in postulating the rational deterrent model with regard to policing crime (more police power + greater deterrence = less crime), the civil liberties lobby adopt the same model for policing the police. It is amazing that all the insights of the new radical criminology drop by the wayside when it comes to considering police wrong-doing. But sauce for the crook should be sauce for the constable.

For years it has been the refrain of radical and liberal criminologists when arguing against the 'hang 'em, flog 'em' brigade that policing and penal policy have a limited and primarily symbolic role in restraining deviance. This analysis should be extended to police deviance. The main way that the sanctions and enforcement machinery proposed by a rational deterrence model can be effective is by the impact they may have on the cultural controls in a community, including the police. It is these cultural understandings which are the immediate determinants of law-abidingness or deviation. What needs to be more precisely explored is the relationship between formal rules of law and procedure and the sub-cultural rules which are the guiding principles of police conduct.

There are two competing views on this in the research literature. In the interactionist tradition it has largely been assumed that formal rules are primarily presentational (Manning, 1977, 1979; Holdaway, 1979, 1983; Chatterton, 1979; Punch, 1979a; Fielding, 1984). They are the terms in which conduct has to be justified, but do not really affect practice. It is the police sub-culture which is the key to understanding police actions. This sometimes amounts to an extreme rule scepticism. As McBarnet has put it, 'Sociologists of the police have tended to treat the notion of legality as unproblematic, not because they assume the police operate according to these principles, but rather because they assume the opposite, that they are largely irrelevant in practice' (McBarnet, 1979, p. 25).

But what is the relationship of sub-cultural norms to the formal rules? First, the interactionist studies themselves point to some impact of formal rules, for example in the emphasis on rank-and-file solidarity aimed at shielding deviant practices from the senior ranks, and the need always to have a good story to 'cover your ass'. Rank-and-file sub-cultural autonomy is thus limited to a degree by formal controls, but how much, when and in what way has not been adequately explored as yet. Second, the police sub-culture is by no means radically distinct or deviant in its values from either legal or popular morality. As Jack Webb used to say on his television show *Dragnet*, 'The problem with the police is that they have to recruit from the human race.' The police are broadly representative of the population.

While there is some tolerance for rule-bending in police sub-culture, that does not mean there is *carte blanche* for gross abuse. All studies of the informal understandings of police culture (even quite critical ones) imply that there are moral norms which, while tolerating malpractices like 'verballing' or even physical force in some circumstances, and certainly permitting non-legally justified exercises of discretion, proportion these to moral judgements of desert and necessity (Klockars, 1980; Baldwin and Kinsey, 1982, pp. 49–50; Chatterton, 1983, pp. 210–15; Holdaway, 1983, Chs 8 and 9; PSI, 1983, vol. IV, Ch. 5). The police sense of justice as revealed in these studies, while often deviant from the formal rules, is bound by constraints which probably reflect widely shared sentiments in the community, and are not absolutely autonomous.

The danger with relying on the police sub-culture's sense of justice becomes acute, however, when there is moral conflict, confusion or change in a society, and police ethics are at odds with those of their 'clients'. When the police deal with those who are regarded as 'alien', disreputable and 'police property' the constraints of traditional communal morality are not an adequate protective guide or check. But contrary to the implications of many radical critiques the problem in contemporary liberal democracies is not how to protect the majority, the 'public', from police oppression, but vulnerable minorities.[1] This limits the potential of 'democratic accountability' as a panacea against abuse. While arguing the case for accountability of the police to the electoral process, Lea and Young frankly admit that 'One of our constant nightmares is that if there was a completely democratic control of police in areas such as Hackney, the resulting police force would look exactly the same as the present' (Lea and Young, 1984, p. 270). Unfortunately, their attempts to dispel this are rather unpersuasive. A crucial issue in the police accountability area is the 'tyranny of the majority' problem (Day and Klein, 1987). As many studies argue, the main occasion when the rules of criminal procedure are dangerously stretched is in relation to 'the lesser offender, who is often intellectually and economically impoverished' (Lidstone, 1981, p. 465) or drawn from a vulnerable and powerless social group. 'Democratic controls' through the electoral process are not much help here. What has to be achieved is the incorporation within the operative police sub-culture of working procedures and norms which embody the universalistic respect for the rights even of weak or unpopular minorities which the rhetoric of legality purports to represent (Goldsmith, 1990). The task of reform is neither just laying down the law, nor achieving majority control. It is knowing what policy changes could achieve their desired objectives, bearing in mind the refracting effects of the rank-and-file sub-culture (Johnston, 1987, 1988).

The second, more recent strand in research literature on the police is a structuralist one. This argues that the source of deviance is not rank-and-file sub-cultural autonomy but the encouragement by senior officers, judges and the state elite of deviations from the ideal of legality through a permissive structure of vaguely stated legal rules, and the accommodation of case law to police practices (McBarnet, 1979, 1981a and b; Brogden, 1982; Jefferson and Grimshaw, 1984a and b; Grimshaw and Jefferson, 1987; McConville *et al.*, 1991). But the interactionist emphasis on police fears about the need to 'cover your ass', while questioning their overall claims of sub-cultural autonomy, also imply that senior officers are not content to connive at every type of malpractice (Fielding, 1981). The structuralist case needs qualification in terms of specifying which rules, in which circumstances, may be bent, and in what ways. The fact that police work is dispersed and of low visibility, and that judges may accommodate police practices in many judgments so that sanctions are often effectively weak, does not mean that the formal rules have no impact or that anything goes (McConville and Baldwin, 1981, Ch. 10).

The prime problem in controlling police deviations from legality is not the permissiveness of law but conflicts of evidence about whether malpractices have occurred in fact. In such arguments the suspect is usually at a structural disadvantage, which is why complaints are so seldom upheld (Box and Russell, 1975; Maguire and Corbett, 1991). When tape-recording of interviews was introduced in Scotland many more suspects seem to have taken the 'scenic route' to the police station (McConville and Morrell, 1983), which suggests that the law is less permissive than the structuralists claim. A similar implication can be drawn from the high proportion of exercises of power which are by 'consent' (Lidstone, 1984; Dixon, 1990), although this raises the factual problem of knowing how full, voluntary and informed citizen agreement is. The rules *do* prohibit many forms of police conduct, which can none the less be engaged in because of the problems of enforceability due to the low visibility of police work (Reiner and Leigh, 1992).

Much of the criticism of the Police Act rests upon what I have called 'a law of inevitable increment: whatever powers the police have they will exceed by a given margin' (Reiner, 1981a, p. 38). As Ole Hansen of the Legal Action Group put it: 'If they exceed their present powers why should they not exceed wider powers?' (Letter to *New Society*, 22 January 1981, p. 161). But police abuse is not the product of some overweening constabulary malevolence constantly bursting the seams of whatever rules for regulating conduct are laid down. It is based on pressure to achieve specific results, using traditional techniques which may often be inadequate. This pressure is derived partly from public expectations as mediated by the police organisation and sub-culture. If the police can achieve their proper objects within the law then one strain making for deviation disappears. This does not mean that unacceptable practices should be legitimated. But it does suggest that the police must have adequate powers to perform the core tasks which are expected of them. If they do not, then the police culture may develop a disdain for legality which will multiply abuses. It is a commonplace of liberal criminology that it is counter-productive to pass unenforceable laws because this breeds more general contempt for the law. The same is true of rules of criminal procedure which are so narrow that the police regularly violate them in pursuit of objectives which would probably have wide approval.

Effective regulation of police powers and accountability requires that the rules of criminal procedure should be enforceable in the sense that they are broadly acceptable to and respected by the police. Internal disciplinary procedures must mesh with the external structure, in the way that the RCCP suggested (Reiner, 1981a, pp. 39–40). If external controls are forced on a hostile police they are likely to prove empty or even counter-productive gestures.

> The art of achieving accountability . . . is to enlist the support of the police in disciplinary activities. . . . For processes of external regulation . . . to be more than a highly publicised morality play, the police must become convinced that they will be trusted to bear . . . the active responsibility for ensuring correct performance. (Bayley, 1983, p. 158)

Accountability institutions will only be truly efficacious in affecting police practices if they win over and work in conjunction with internal disciplinary and self-controlling processes. They cannot be forced by a heavy hand.[2]

An obvious objection that could be levelled against the above argument is that the whole nature of police policy and organisation has changed so fundamentally in recent years that there can be no prospect of internal reform. As a response to the control requirements of a capitalist social order in deepening crisis, policing has moved away from a supposed 'consensus' style bound by the rule of law to a fundamentally different approach, variously called a 'militaristic' (Lea and Young, 1984; Kinsey *et al.*, 1986; Jefferson, 1987, 1990; Northam, 1988), 'pre-emptive' and 'fire brigade' (Baldwin and Kinsey, 1982), 'technocop' (Manwaring-White, 1983), 'coercive' (Christian, 1983), 'authoritarian' or 'law and order' (Hall *et al.*, 1978) style.[3]

To some extent this picture of a drift to a more coercive and lawless police is a kind of liberal 'moral panic'. Radical criminology has tended to debunk popular concern about 'crime waves' by emphasising the patchy data on which these are based, the role of the media and moral entrepreneurs in highlighting sensational but unrepresentative cases, the mythical construction of a 'Golden Age' of tranquil law-abidingness, and the counter-productive consequence of 'deviance amplification'. All these accusations could be levelled at the recent growth of liberal and radical concern about police power.

There is no adequate basis for the view that police abuse or disregard of legality is increasingly prevalent, although there is, of course, a plentiful number of highly disturbing *causes célèbres*. But police lawlessness was rife in the past too. A fascinating illustration is Sir Robert Mark's autobiographical account of his youthful indiscretions as a pre-war Manchester constable, such as breaking a drunken navvy's leg with an illegal truncheon (Mark, 1978, pp. 28–9). He also documents the prevalence in the late 1940s of interrogation by physical force (such as holding suspects heads down lavatories) and the meting out of brutal summary justice to those who assaulted the police. There is similar evidence in Brogden's oral history of inter-war Liverpool policing (Brogden, 1991). I am not suggesting that police practices are now more law-abiding, rather that we don't really know what the trend is. The extent of police deviance at any time is an unknown 'dark figure'. Increasing concern is as likely to be due to changing public sensitivity and values as to a growth of real police misconduct. Public perceptions of what constitutes intolerable police behaviour are likely to have changed of late. This is a result of rising educational levels, the growth of adversarial contact between police and the middle class (due to the motor car and the 1960s rise of middle-class political dissent and involvement in deviant activities like drug-taking), and the self-consciousness of the black community about racist abuse.

At the same time there have been profound changes in police organisation and tactics: more centralisation, specialisation and utilisation of technology, and an increased mobilisation of coercive capacity to deal with public disorder. But the critics over-emphasise the degree of conscious rationality, consistency and intent in the changes they document. The representation of the drift to 'militaristic' or 'fire brigade' policing as the outcome of coherent, planned policy misleadingly implies that what is needed is primarily a reversal of these policy decisions. But the development of 'militaristic' and 'fire brigade' tactics was largely the *unintended* consequence of strategies aimed at enhancing professionalisation and efficiency while retaining or even improving a cooperative public relationship. The Unit Beat reorganisation was intended to improve community relations along with efficiency (Weatheritt, 1983, 1986). That this is not how it worked out is due to the resilience of rank-and-file sub-culture, the growth of concern with crime and disorder, and lack of resources for adequate implementation (Holdaway, 1977, 1983). The episode constitutes an important warning about the prospects of achieving rational and purposive change.[4] This will have to involve far more profound reorganisation than a mere alteration of formal policy. But the importance of police cooperation at all levels in any potentially successful change means that formal accountability is not the crucial issue, and struggles over nominal policy control which alienate the police may well be counter-productive (Butler, 1982b).

Police management theory (Bunyard, 1978; Butler, 1984) tends to assume a mechanistic model of police organisation, whereby police behaviour is a practical enactment of rules and directives, a chimerical and unrealistic notion (Bradley *et al.*, 1986; Grimshaw and Jefferson, 1987). Textbook expositions of legal powers usually imply the same mechanistic relation between rules, policy and practice. Civil libertarian critics emphasise the extent of present departure of practice from legal requirements. However, they imply that this gap, whether inadvertent or intentional, can be narrowed if not closed. They argue that making the formal rules tighter, and enhancing external accountability are desirable and feasible ways of controlling police practice. The arguments of observational research imply that there are structural and cultural impediments in the way of this. The low visibility of police work, and the low status and hence political credibility of the typical recipients of police power make this unlikely as a straightforward strategy of reform. The function of formal rules and accountability mechanisms in the regulation of police work is more indirect and subtle. We can distinguish three such functions:

1. *The constitutional function.* Rules and accountability structures have a symbolic function in asserting the ideal of police subordination to democracy and the rule of law. They must express values and norms which are defensible with respect to the principles of due process legality.
2. *The cooptive function.* They will only become effective if they transform and coopt the informal values of police sub-culture. Because of this they should not be expressed in so purist or hostile a fashion that they result in a defensive closing of police ranks.[5]
3. *The communicative function.* Some signalling mechanism registering the need for change is necessary to spark off internal reforms, a task often performed by 'scandals' in the absence of adequate channels for the routine communication of grievance and complaint (Sherman, 1978a, 1983a and b).

All of these three essential functions of institutions of accountability can be achieved without formally complete subordination of police decision-making to the control of democratically elected bodies. This is usually denied by critics who argue emphatically that anything short of complete and explicit control of police policy-making by elected politicians is an inadequate sham (Baldwin and Kinsey, 1982; Dean, 1982; Lustgarten, 1982, 1986; Christian, 1983; Lea and Young, 1984; Kinsey *et al.*, 1986; Downes and Ward, 1986; Baldwin, 1987, 1989; Brogden *et al.*, 1988; Uglow, 1988; Stephens, 1988, are some examples).[6] I would contend that elected control of police policy-making is neither necessary nor sufficient for accomplishing the goal of a police force whose operations are 'democratic'. (By this I mean that they respect due process rights, do not discriminate unjustifiably in enforcement practices, and follow priorities which are in line with popular sentiment where this is clear, or which discreetly balance contending priorities in a divided community.)

There are no valid constitutional or historical grounds *in principle* for exempting the police from control by democratically elected policy-making authorities. Such claims have long been definitively demolished (Marshall, 1965; Lustgarten, 1986). But this does not entail that it is the most sensible goal to strive for in the present context, from the point of view of achieving a police force which is 'democratic' in the sense defined above (as Marshall has argued in a reconsideration of the issue: Marshall, 1978).

The dangers of a 'tyranny of the majority' are accentuated in so politicised a context as that in which policing operated during the 1980s. The rights of minorities cannot be guaranteed by majoritarian forms of democracy alone. They must be bolstered by a degree of professional independence and legal accountability, as well as at least what Marshall calls an 'explanatory and cooperative' mode of accountability to elected representatives. Scarman recommended, and PACE implements, a form of this lower-level accountability in the shape of local consultative committees. This 'softly, softly' approach was widely condemned as a sop by advocates of the notion that nothing short of unequivocal control by elected authorities will do. It has been cogently argued that they could be *more* effective in making the police responsive to outside, 'community' views (Savage, 1984). Experience so far suggests, however, that they are better at communicating police views to atypical 'representatives' of the public than vice versa, and function essentially to legitimate the status quo (Savage and Wilson, 1987; R. Morgan, 1987, 1989).

There has also been much discussion, stretching back to the 1962 Royal Commission Report, of the desirable balance between local and central accountability. It has been assumed (for example, by criticisms of the role of the National Reporting Centre in the 1984 miners' strike) that any move towards centralisation, and *a fortiori* a national police force, is an abrogation of democratic policing and a step in the direction of a 'police state' (Reiner, 1984). The 1962 Report of the Royal Commission on the Police argued cogently that centralisation of police forces was neither sufficient nor necessary for a 'police state'. '[I]f that were the test, Belgium, Denmark and Sweden should be described as police states. The proper criterion is whether the police are answerable to the law and, ultimately, to a democratically elected Parliament' (pp. 45–6). None the less, the

Royal Commission (with a spirited dissent from Dr A.L. Goodhart) rejected the idea of a national force because of the value of 'partnership between central and local government'. The best of both worlds could be attained, it hoped, by a combination of beefing-up the Home Secretary's responsibility for provincial police efficiency, while retaining local police authorities with somewhat amorphously conceived duties to provide for 'adequate' forces. The arrangements enacted by the ensuing 1964 Police Act will be evaluated presently. The trenchant arguments of the Royal Commission do, however, refute the notion that a more centralised police force is *ipso facto* alien to democracy. However, it is clear that present trends are enhancing the power of central bodies over police policy, and these are not accountable in any serious way at all (Reiner, 1991).

Police powers: recent trends and developments

The culmination of recent debates in this area was Mark II of the Police and Criminal Evidence Bill, which was enacted at the end of October 1984. PACE embodies a set of changes in police powers, procedures and processes of accountability of considerable scope and importance.[7] PACE is the single most significant landmark in the modern development of police powers. This is despite the fact that much of its content had already been prefigured by piecemeal changes in statute and case-law (not to mention *sub rosa* police practice) in the years leading up to it (for detailed reviews see Leigh, 1985; Reiner and Leigh, 1992). As a statutory codification and rationalisation of police powers and the safeguards over their exercise it has a symbolic and a practical importance which is hard to exaggerate and it has always attracted much controversy. The Act's many critics saw it as signifying a lurch towards 'policing by coercion' (Christian, 1983). The official claim was that it balanced powers and safeguards, with the 'objective of encouraging effective policing with the consent and co-operation of society at large' (Home Office *Working Paper on Criminal Justice*, 1984, p. 15).

It is my contention that neither viewpoint is defensible. On the one hand, there is no warrant for the government's claim that the Act helps the 'fight against crime'. This is because, as the Home Office's own researches have argued: 'the evidence is strong that the capability of the police to affect levels of crime through deterrent strategies is limited' (Clarke and Hough, 1980, p. 8). On the other hand, most of the criticism of the Police Act has given a completely misleading impression of it. Many discussions represent it as involving 'a draconian increase in police powers' (Lea and Young, 1984, p. 254).

PACE purports to implement the RCCP's principle that 'a fundamental balance' had to be struck between 'the rights of the individual in relation to the security of the community'. This notion was in fact built into its terms of reference, which instructed the Commission to have regard 'both to the interests of the community in bringing offenders to justice and to the rights and liberties of persons suspected or accused of crime'. As many critics correctly pointed out, the sharp dichotomy implied between 'individual' and 'communal' interest is untenable. The 'communal' interest is ill served by abrogation of 'individual' suspects' rights which lead to wrongful convictions and the continued freedom of the truly guilty. An adequate framework of civil liberties is as much the interest of any civilised community as is security from crime. Nor was there any reason to think that the extent to which suspects' rights were protected by the rules of criminal procedure constituted a significant stumbling-block to 'bringing offenders to justice' (Zander, 1979a and b).

But if the contrast between 'communal' and 'individual' interest as presented by the RCCP is flawed, it none the less bears a kernel of truth. In relation to any specific investigation the tighter the protections afforded individual suspects the greater the difficulties of securing a conviction. From the point of view of both the legislature and the police officer this gives rise to what has aptly been called 'the Dirty Harry dilemma' (Klockars, 1980).[8] Rules constructed too loosely undermine the pretensions of the system of criminal procedure to sift out offenders accurately and fairly from innocents. If they are pitched too restrictively not only do obviously guilty offenders escape justice, but police respect for the rule of law is undermined, with the counter-productive consequence that violations of due process may increase. Wherever the balance is drawn, the individual officer in some cases will confront the Dirty Harry dilemma of either violating the rules or allowing offenders of whose guilt he is convinced to go free.[9] The problem is to place the balance so that there is neither an abandonment by the legal system of its role of enunciating and protecting just procedures, nor demoralisation of the police through too frequent exposure to Dirty Harry situations. PACE is attacked by both the police and civil liberties lobbies as drawing the balance too much on the other side. This itself might be taken as indicative of it having at last got the mixture right, but the matter needs closer consideration.

The content of PACE

PACE purports to be based on the RCCP's principle of 'a fundamental balance' between adequate police powers and safeguards over their exercise. How adequately it realises this aspiration is highly debatable.

On the one hand, the Act gives the police a plethora of powers which they did not possess on a statutory basis before. To a degree this extension of powers is nominal rather than real, for much is a rationalisation and codification of hitherto haphazard statute and common law, or a legitimation of what was already police practice.

On the other hand, the exercise of statutory powers is governed by requirements which are set out partly in the Act itself, partly in the accompanying Codes of Practice. These codes provide detailed procedures regulating stop and search; search and seizure; detention and questioning of suspects; identification parades; and tape-recording of interviews. A revised set of codes, incorporating some of the lessons of the first five years of PACE, came into effect on 1 April 1991 (Zander, 1991, p. 60).

These codes are underpinned by s.67 of PACE, which makes failure to comply with them a disciplinary offence, and makes a breach admissible as evidence in any criminal or civil proceedings, if thought relevant by the judge(s). The Act also implements the RCCP's solution to the difficulties of reviewing police actions posed by the low visibility of routine police work.

This is to establish a variety of recording requirements for each exercise of a police power, giving reasons for what is done. There is also a requirement that interviews be contemporaneously recorded. Backing up particular safeguards for specific powers the Act also includes sections purporting to enhance police accountability more generally. There is an obligation imposed on police authorities to make arrangements for consulting the views of the local community (s.106), and Part IX establishes the Police Complaints Authority which enhances the independent element in the complaints system.

This basic scheme, combining extension and rationalisation of powers with procedural safeguards resting fundamentally on reporting requirements, runs through all the major provisions of PACE. A clear illustration is the issue of stop-and-search powers. These are clearly boosted by s.1, which extends nationally the power to search for stolen goods previously only granted by local legislation to some metropolitan areas. New powers are given to stop and search for articles made or adapted for use or intended to be used for burglary, theft, obtaining property by deception, or taking a motor vehicle without authority. Finally a power to stop and search for offensive weapons is provided (defined as weapons made or adapted for use to cause injury, or intended by the person carrying them to be so used).

Altogether, stop-and-search powers are clearly extended by PACE. There are two main safeguards over them. First, record-keeping: constables must make detailed records of each search, and of the reasons for it, and tell the suspect he has a right to request a copy within twelve months. Second, Code of Practice A specifies that stops and searches must be justified by 'reasonable suspicion' for which there must be an objective basis, connected to the individual searched. It cannot arise only from an individual's membership of a category stereotyped as more likely to offend, e.g. black or young or long-haired people.

This same schema, combining extended powers with new safeguards based on record-keeping monitored by internal discipline, runs through all the main sections of PACE. It can be seen in the provisions on powers to arrest suspects, to enter and search their premises and seize evidence, and to detain them for questioning.

The detention and questioning sections contain a particularly complex set of safeguards, resting on the custody officer (CO), a new police specialism with a duty to supervise the detention of suspects (s.36). The CO (normally a sergeant) has the duty of informing a new detainee of his rights (to see a solicitor, to have someone informed of his arrest, and to consult the Codes of Practice), and has to maintain a custody record on which is entered all significant events in the period of detention. A complex timetable of reviews of the necessity of detention, and of processes which can extend it in exceptional cases up to an absolute maximum of ninety-six hours is elaborated.

The interpretation of PACE at common law

PACE clearly extends the key investigative powers of the police, subject to a regime of internal disciplinary safeguards for each power. In addition some general safeguards are introduced. One is the possible exclusion of evidence obtained in violation of PACE procedures. Confessions are admissible only if the prosecution can show they were not obtained by oppression, or by any methods rendering them unreliable (s.76). Judges are obliged to warn juries of the dangers of convicting a mentally handicapped person on the basis of a confession (s.77). A more general discretion is provided for judges to exclude evidence if it appears that 'the circumstances in which the evidence was obtained' mean it would have 'an adverse effect on the fairness of the proceedings' (s.78). This rather loose discretion (a watered-down version of an amendment introduced by Lord Scarman) falls far short of the tough exclusionary rule hankered after by civil libertarians (Sieghart, 1985; Sanders, 1988).

However, one of the surprises of experience since PACE has been the much tougher attitude adopted by the judiciary towards police breaches of the Codes than their permissive toleration of violations of the old Judges' Rules. Although there is some unevenness in the reaction of individual judges, a thorough review of the post-PACE common law on the pivotal detention and questioning provisions concludes that 'the judges now see themselves as having a disciplinary and regulatory role in maintaining the balance between the powers of the police and the protection of suspects' (Feldman, 1990, p. 469; see also: Zuckerman, 1987; May, 1988; Birch, 1989; Choo, 1989). It is not yet clear, however, to what extent police practice responds to this tougher judicial approach to abuses of power.

PACE also contains a number of more general provisions aimed at enhancing police accountability, notably through the requirement to consult community views (s.106), and the reforms of the complaints system, particularly the establishment of the Police Complaints Authority. Research on these innovations suggests they do bring some advantages, but fall far short of meaningful accountability or a system for redressing individual grievances which satisfies most complainants (Morgan, 1989; Maguire and Corbett, 1991). In addition to the research evaluations of these accountability sections, there has been a plethora of empirical evaluations of the core aspects of PACE (and much more is on-going). These will be reviewed in the next section.

PACE in practice: the research verdict

Empirical studies of police work prior to PACE suggested that the powers of the police were formulated in so loose a fashion, and interpreted so permissively by the judiciary, that police practice frequently departed from principled statements of the 'rule of law' (McBarnet, 1981a, b and c). Of particular concern was the evidence of discriminatory use of police powers, as outlined in Chapter 4. This underlay much of the civil libertarian opposition to PACE. It was feared that the police would exceed their new extended powers just as they had prior to PACE. The safeguards were expected to be given the Nelson touch, relying as they did on police internal discipline and judicial discretion. These fears were exacerbated by the evidently jaundiced views expressed towards the cumbersome paper-work of the safe-guards, not only in the police rank and file but even many senior officers (Reiner, 1991, pp. 144–60).

The controversial character of the Act ensured that a considerable body of evaluative empirical research, commissioned by a variety of bodies, has been accumulated on the effects of PACE. The main sources are the Economical and Social Research Council (ESRC), which in 1986 launched an extensive initiative to monitor PACE, and the Home Office Research and Planning Unit. Much work is still going on, especially to assess the impact of recent changes in the Codes of Practice. The new Royal Commission on Criminal Justice, launched under the chairmanship of Lord Runciman in the wake of the Guildford Four and Birmingham Six miscarriage of justice revelations, is also assembling a research programme. Despite this growing volume of material, the jury is still out about the overall impact of PACE.

The evidence so far suggests a much more complex picture than implied by the polarised polemics which attended the birth-pangs of PACE. Research has thrown up more questions calling for further research and analysis, rather than definitive conclusions.

PACE certainly seems to have had a profound effect on the nature and outcomes of police handling of suspects. Routine practice has incorporated much of the rituals and procedures of the Codes of Practice, and many indices of suspects' access to rights indicate improvement. On the other hand, assimilation of the PACE rules into police culture and working practices has been uneven and incomplete. Much is ritualistic and presentational and affects little of substance in the experience of suspects. Furthermore, there are signs that some early changes may have been an impact effect of new procedures, and that old working practices are creeping back in.

On the plus side, research evidence suggests the following:

1. Suspects are almost invariably informed of their rights on reception at the police station (Sanders *et al.*, 1989; McKenzie *et al.*, 1990; Morgan *et al.*, 1990; Sanders and Bridges, 1990).
2. As a result, the proportion receiving legal advice has increased between two and four times, and is now about a quarter of all suspects (Maguire, 1988; Brown, 1989; Sanders *et al.*, 1989; Morgan *et al.*, 1990; Dixon *et al.*, 1990).
3. The special extended powers available for 'serious arrestable offences' (on the authority of senior officers or in some cases a magistrate's court) are obtained relatively infrequently, in

about 2 per cent of cases (Brown, 1989; Home Office Statistical Bulletin: *Statistics on the Operation of Certain Police Powers Under the Police and Criminal Evidence Act*, 14/01, 15 July 1991).
4. The extent of the use of dubious 'tactics' to extract incriminating statements by interrogation has declined (Irving and McKenzie, 1989a and b).
5. Tape-recording of interviews seems to have reduced arguments about what occurred in them, and is now welcomed by police who were long opposed to it (Willis *et al.*, 1988).
6. The average period of detention in police stations has declined a little (from about 6 hours 20 minutes, to about 5 hours 23 minutes, see Morgan *et al.*, 1990).
7. The Police Complaints Authority (PCA) supervision of the police investigation of complaints can be vigorous and active, especially in some serious cases (Maguire and Corbett, 1991).

There is also much evidence from the same research, however, which paints a more negative picture:

1. Detention is authorised almost automatically and invariably. The idea of the custody officer as an independent check on this has proved chimerical (McKenzie *et al.*, 1990).
2. The information to suspects about their rights is often given in a ritualistic and meaningless way. This may account for the overwhelming majority of suspects who do not take them up (Sanders *et al.*, 1989; Morgan *et al.*, 1990). It has been claimed also that 'ploys' are frequently used to dissuade suspects from taking up their rights (Sanders *et al.*, 1989), though the extent of this is debatable. Conversely, some recent research has suggested that the right to silence may benefit some serious offenders disproportionately (Williamson and Moston, 1990), although few offenders exercise it overall (McKenzie and Irving, 1988).
3. Later stages in the detention process (such as reviews, or regulating access to suspects by investigating officers) are less punctiliously followed than the reception rituals. Custody officers are also less scrupulous about monitoring pre-detention events (such as delay between arrest and arrival at police stations, see Morgan *et al.*, 1990).

4. PACE procedures can frequently be side-stepped by securing 'voluntary' compliance by suspects with police requests. Such 'consent' is especially important for the stop-and-search powers, where it is often circumvented (Dixon *et al.*, 1989, 1990; Bottomley *et al.*, 1991).

5. The use of 'tactics' in interrogation is increasing again, albeit not to pre-PACE levels (Irving and McKenzie, 1989a and b).

6. The average length of detention for more minor cases has increased since PACE (Morgan *et al.*, 1990).

7. However adequate PACE supervision of complaints investigations may be sometimes, public confidence and complainant satisfaction are disastrously low, while the rank-and-file police have simultaneously been alienated (Maguire and Corbett, 1989, 1991).

8. Consultative committees do more to impress police views on the public than vice versa, and act as a legitimating device more than a means of accountability (Morgan, 1989).

9. The socially discriminatory pattern of use of police powers remains as marked as before. The burden of police powers still falls disproportionately on the young, economically marginal, ethnic minority males, who are the overwhelming majority of those who are arrested and detained (Morgan *et al.*, 1990).

PACE: an interim conclusion

The resilience of the social pattern of policing and its basic practices in the face of PACE is due to the unchanging role of the police, primarily as regulators of public space and those who live their lives there predominantly. PACE can do little to alter the impact of this on the culture and organisation of policing.

None the less the Act *has* impacted on police practices, albeit unevenly and patchily. This is because of the symbolic consequences of the legislation, which puts safeguards on a statutory basis which carries more weight in police culture than the less formal Judges' Rules did. It is also because of the tougher line taken by the courts, the partial opening-up of the back-stage areas of policing by the recording requirements, and the deterrent value of internal disciplinary sanctions (however little these may be appreciated by outsiders). The legislation has achieved far more than its civil libertarian critics initially expected, if far less than they would wish.

Deterrence, symbolism, organisational and training changes are all important in understanding how PACE has affected police culture and practice. If powers are precisely rather than permissively formulated, procedures to render visible occasions of use are constructed, and supervisors and courts are determined to police the police, change can occur in line with the law. Thus the booking-in procedures, which are precise, relatively visible to supervisors, and clearly enjoined in training, are religiously followed. However, the danger of precisely formulated rules is also evident here. They can be satisfied by ritualistic observance with little meaning, defeating their intended objectives.

Given the low visibility and hence inevitable discretion of much routine police work, the key changes must be in the informal culture of the police, their practical working rules. These may be penetrated and altered, but are not determined, by official policy, through symbolism, training, organisation and discipline. But they are not determined by the formal rules. Police culture is fundamentally a function of the structurally determined social role of the police, which has not altered in any fundamental way. Policing in a hierarchical and divided society will never be even in its impact, and the socially discriminatory use of police powers will continue. Thus legal regulation alone will always be inadequate to secure legitimacy and genuine consent. This is true also of the mechanisms for rendering the police accountable, to which we turn.

Controlling the controllers: developments in police accountability

The basic objectives and rules of criminal procedure are framed by parliament in its enactment of substantive and procedural law. The issue of accountability is the question of how to keep police practice, in particular the operation of discretion, within that broad framework and in line with communal values. This itself resolves into three analytically distinct functions: (1) a 'judicial' function of determining whether specific police actions have breached legal or procedural rules; (2) a quasi-'legislative' function of setting priorities in the allocation of resources between different legitimate policing duties; and (3) an 'executive' one of managing the performance of these duties in as efficient and effective a way as possible. Debates about accountability revolve around how satisfactorily existing mechanisms perform these functions. Underlying these debates are conceptions of who should ultimately have the power of decision when there is a conflict of viewpoints, what is the scope of issues over which accountability is appropriate, and in terms of what political conceptions of justice should policing arrangements be evaluated. Conventional police rhetoric makes much of the democratic character of the British police (Pike, 1985; Oliver, 1987). As Robert Mark put it:

> The fact that the British police are answerable to the law, that we act on behalf of the community and not under the mantle of government, makes us the least powerful, the most accountable and therefore the most acceptable police in the world. (Mark, 1977, p. 56)

This illustrates the central role played in police ideology by the notion of accountability to the courts, which is one part of the present mechanism for performing the 'judicial' function of assessing alleged breaches of the law and disciplinary rules. The other part is the complaints process.

The prime channel of accountability of the police in Britain is supposed to be 'the law'. In concrete terms, there are four ways in which the courts may operate to regulate police conduct (Clayton and Tomlinson, 1987): (1) in serious complaints alleging criminal misconduct the Director of Public Prosecutions may recommend prosecution; (2) civil action can be brought for damages in cases of wrongful arrest, trespass, assault, etc.; (3) a writ of habeas corpus can be sought for illegal detention; and (4) judges have discretion to exclude evidence obtained in violation of due process of law. In practice none of these is fully satisfactory. The DPP has stated that it is the policy of his department to demand stricter standards of evidence before recommending the prosecution of police officers than of other suspects, because of the difficulty of persuading juries not to give special credence to police testimony (Loveday, 1983, pp. 42–3). The burden of proof in civil actions is the lesser standard of 'balance of probabilities' but the problems of cost, time and access to lawyers mean that such actions are rarely resorted to (and rarely successful). The same is true of habeas corpus. Before PACE judicial decisions whittled away the control functions of judicial discretion to exclude evidence. In *Sang*'s case in 1979 Lord Diplock stated: 'It is not part of the judge's function to exercise disciplinary powers over the police or prosecution as respects the way in which evidence to be used at the trial is obtained by them.' We have seen above that judicial attitudes to breaches of PACE have often been more robust, although this has been uneven, and many critics would still welcome a tougher rule for excluding evidence obtained improperly.

The complaints system

After many years of pressure to introduce an independent element into the assessment of complaints against the police, resisted by most police opinion, the Police Act 1976 established the Police Complaints Board. (For an excellent critical account of the history of attempts to reform the complaints process see Maguire, 1991.) The Board received a copy of the investigating officer's report on any complaint made under the procedures instituted by section 49 of the Police Act 1964, together with a memorandum stating whether the Deputy Chief Constable had decided to bring disciplinary charges against the officer. After studying the papers, the Board could recommend and, if necessary, direct that disciplinary charges be brought.

The Board – a political compromise – was greeted with dismay by both the police and civil libertarians. The latter deplored the impeccably establishment character of the Board's members, the lack of independent *investigative* powers, and the greater facilities for police officers to sue complainants for libel which was won by the Police Federation during the political wrangling preceding the Act.

The Board's 1980 Triennial Report set out several recommendations to improve its functioning. The most important suggested that in the crucial area of complaints alleging police assault its powers were severely limited:

> Assaults which are alleged to have occurred during arrest or while in custody are unlikely to be witnessed by civilians, and where there is a denial supported by one or more police colleagues and no corroborative evidence to support the allegation, neither criminal nor disciplinary action against a police officer is likely.

The Board recommended the establishment of a national specialist team of investigating officers, recruited from all forces on a 2–3 year secondment, who would look into allegations of assault resulting in serious injury, and be responsible to an independent, experienced lawyer or judge. This proposal was rejected by a Home Office working party. None the less, pressure seemed to be mounting for a more vigorous and independent scrutiny of allegations of serious police misconduct. The RCCP had argued strongly that public confidence in its safeguards required the implementation of the Police Complaints Board's proposals (para. 4.119). The Board's new Chairman, Sir Cyril Philips (formerly chairman of the RCCP), committed himself to a tougher policy, declaring that 'the existing Board had kept so low a profile that it has climbed into a ditch' (*The Guardian*, 19 March 1981). The Scarman Report and the Commons Select Committee on Home Affairs strongly argued for the independent investigation as well as adjudication of complaints. Finally, in a surprising but very welcome volte-face, the Police Federation retracted its opposition to independent investigation shortly before Scarman reported, as did a few Chief Constables. Since then the Police Federation has pressed the case that nothing short of a system of completely independent investigation and adjudication of complaints would satisfy the public, but in exchange police officers should have full legal representation.

Despite this pressure PACE did not establish a completely independent system. Rather, it replaced the Complaints Board with a new Police Complaints Authority, which is required to supervise the investigation of complaints alleging death or serious injury, and empowered to do so in any other case where it considers this is in the public interest. Some categories of complaint (to be determined by the Home Secretary) should always be brought to the Authority's attention. When supervising an investigation, the Authority has power of veto over the appointment of the investigating officer, and can issue directions. It also receives the report of the investigation, and has to certify whether it is satisfied with the quality of it. The Act establishes procedures for resolving minor complaints informally, if complainants agree to this. It also strengthens police rights; for example, by guaranteeing legal representation in cases where an officer might lose his job or rank. While enhancing the degree of independent scrutiny of complaints (and police rights) the reforms fall far short of a fully independent system. That a scheme involving completely independent investigators can work (in the sense of not impeding ordinary police work while sometimes reaching conclusions which are different from those of internal inquiries) is attested by overseas experience (Loveday, 1988; Goldsmith, 1991). For example, since 1981 Toronto has had a Public Complaints Commissioner with a non-police team of investigators, with encouraging initial results (*First Annual Report of the Office of the Public Complaints Commissioner*, Toronto, June 1983; a more sceptical assessment of the long-term impact is given in McMahon and Ericson, 1984).

It is unlikely that pressure in the area of complaints will cease until such a scheme is established here. Research on the new procedures since PACE suggests that the Police Complaints Authority and the system as a whole lack the confidence of both complainants and the police (Brown, 1987; Maguire and Corbett, 1989, 1991; Reiner, 1991, pp. 286–300). However, the much maligned Police Complaints Authority, and the new procedures for informal resolution of minor complaints work reasonably well given the severe resource constraints (Maguire and Corbett, 1991; Corbett, 1991). None the less, it seems clear that only a fully independent system would secure the confidence of the public or the rank-and-file police (Chesshyre, 1989).

Police authorities

The thorniest issues of police accountability arise in relation to the quasi-legislative and executive functions of determining the priorities and efficiency of force policy. For all the rhetoric about the democratic accountability of the British police they have become virtually impervious to any control by elected political bodies, and are adamant in remaining so.

The Police Act 1964 defines the general duty of the police authority as being 'to secure the maintenance of an adequate and efficient police force for the area' (section 4.l). The precise relationship constitutionally and in practice between police authority, Chief Constable and Home Office is a complex and much debated matter (Marshall, 1965, 1978; Loveday, 1983, 1984, 1985, 1991; Waddington, 1984b). Although the 1964 Act purports to clarify and rationalise the situation, it fails to do so. Its statements are self-contradictory or vague at the crucial points. The police authorities are explicitly empowered to appoint the Chief Constable, to secure his retirement (subject to the Home Secretary's agreement) 'in the interests of efficiency', and to receive an annual report from him. They may also ask him to submit further reports on 'matters connected with the policing of the area' (Section 12.2). However, the Chief Constable can refuse to give such a report if he deems it inappropriate, and the dispute is to be referred to the Home Secretary as arbiter. Nor is the 1964 Act clear about the possibility of the police authority being able to instruct the Chief Constable on general policy concerning law enforcement in the area (as distinct from the immediate, day-to-day direction and control of the force which is clearly precluded). Again, in cases of conflict it is for the Home Secretary to arbitrate. But the Act's thrust was to limit responsibility for 'operational' matters to the Chief Constables (Jefferson and Grimshaw, 1984a, Ch. 2). Lustgarten (1986) elegantly but devastatingly explodes this hackneyed, untenable distinction between 'operational' and 'policy' matters. These categories necessarily overlap and are arbitrary and tendentious classifications, without a basis in the Act itself.

Altogether, the Act, together with the organisational changes in policing already discussed (amalgamation, technological advance, professionalisation, growth of the police lobby), strengthened the power of the Chief Constable and the Home Office at the expense of the local authority. The police authorities pay the piper (or more precisely share policing costs with central government) but do not call any tunes. They determine the force's establishment and rank structure, and appoint the Chief Constable (both subject to Home Office approval). But the Chief Constable has sole responsibility for deployment of the force, as well as for appointment, promotion and discipline. The authority can dismiss the Chief Constable for good cause, but subject to Home Office veto. The evidence is that many police authorities do not even use the limited powers envisaged by the Act, deferring normally to the Chief Constable's 'professional' expertise (Brogden, 1977; Regan, 1983; Morgan and Swift, 1987; Reiner, 1991, Ch. 11). This is even more true of the Joint Boards which replaced the Metropolitan authorities abolished by the 1985 Local Government Act (Loveday, 1987, 1991).

Since the late 1970s there have been several initiatives from the Left campaigning for police authorities to exercise their dormant powers as well as seeking an expansion of these. The police retort has been that policing should be kept out of politics, a disingenuous plea in view of their own politicisation. Jack Straw, Labour MP for Blackburn, introduced an unsuccessful Private Member's Bill on police authorities in November 1979. This aimed to increase the influence of police authorities (to be democratically elected by the local community, removing the JP element) over general policy issues (e.g. the balance between panda cars and foot patrol, whether to have an SPG, etc.) as distinct from day-to-day operational decisions which would remain the Chief Constable's prerogative (albeit with the authority using more energetically its existing powers to call for after-the-event reports). The authority would also have control of appointments, promotion and dismissal of ranks above superintendents (whose responsibilities are now frequently equal to those of Chief Constables a decade ago). As safeguards against corruption, the Bill proposed that a Chief Constable could delay any suggested policy change for six months, and could appeal to the Home Secretary to over-rule the police authority.

Particular controversy has arisen over the Metropolitan Police, for whom the authority is the Home Secretary, so that Londoners do not have even the limited form of financial accountability available in the provinces. In March 1980 Jack Straw introduced another unsuccessful Bill aiming to create a Greater London police authority to control a reorganised force, from which the national policing functions now carried out by Scotland Yard would be hived off into a new National Police Agency. The lack of local accountability in London is now recognised as anomalous even by most Chief Constables (Reiner, 1991, Ch. 11).

After the sweeping Labour victories in the May 1981 local government elections, the GLC established a Police Committee with a strong support unit to monitor police policy. In the early 1980s several London boroughs, aided by GLC funds, have established local 'monitoring groups'. Many provincial councils also moved into radical Labour hands in 1981, and there followed some much publicised battles between the police authorities and Chief Constables, especially in Greater Manchester and Merseyside (Loveday, 1985; McLaughlin, 1990).

The 1984 miners' strike stimulated even sharper conflicts, with several Labour dominated police authorities protesting their lack of control over the manner of policing the strike or the extent to which the national operation produced a potentially disastrous depletion of resources for local policing needs (Fine and Millar, 1985; McCabe *et al.*, 1988; Green, 1991). South Yorkshire police authority attempted to curb its Chief Constable's spending on the miners' dispute, but was stopped by a High Court ruling. On 17 September 1984, the police authority instructed the South Yorkshire Chief Constable to disband the mounted police unit, and most of the dog section. They justified this on financial grounds, although the Chief Constable (and most of the press) saw it as retaliation for the controversial use of horses in controlling pickets (*The Times*, 18 September 1984, p. 2). The next day the Home Secretary warned the authority that it might be acting in contravention of the Police Act 1964 (*The Times*, 19 September 1984, p. 2). Overall the miners' strike indicated that police authorities can largely be ignored if Chief Constables and the Home Office are in agreement over the conduct of a national policing operation which uses the mutual aid system drawing on local forces.

Developments since the 1984–5 miners' strike have continued this trajectory of centralisation, reducing the role of local police authorities to virtual insignificance. PACE introduces a statutory requirement (s.106) that consultative arrangements be established in each force area. Whilst apparently enhancing local accountability, pressure was exerted by the Home Office for these to take the uniform shape of consultative committees, illustrating how the growing number of nominally advisory Home Office circulars have come to be effectively regarded as binding by most forces (R. Morgan, 1987; Morgan and Maggs, 1985). They also function as a key means of legitimating the constitutional status quo (Morgan, 1989). The Local Government Act 1985 which abolished the six Metropolitan councils replaced their police authorities, which had been the heartland of the campaign for greater accountability, replacing their police authorities by more quiescent joint boards. It also enhanced the Home Secretary's control over financial resources in these forces (Loveday, 1987, 1991).[10]

In the highly significant Court of Appeal judgment in *R* v. *Secretary of State for the Home Department ex.p. Northumbria Police Authority* [1988] 2 *Weekly Law Reports* 590, it appeared that local police authorities had no power to challenge policy decisions by a Chief Constable if he secures Home Office support, even if this involves spending matters. Home Office Circular 40/1986 had stated that where Chief Constables were not permitted by their police authorities to purchase CS gas or plastic bullets for training in riot control, they could obtain these from a central store if the HM Inspector of Constabulary felt this to be necessary. The Northumbria Police Authority sought a judicial review of this circular as outside the Home Secretary's powers under the 1964 Police Act, which places primary responsibility for 'maintaining an adequate and efficient' police force on the authority (s.41). The Court of Appeal rejected this argument, both because it held that the Home Secretary had power under the Royal Prerogative to do what he felt necessary for preserving the Queen's Peace, and because it interpreted the Home Secretary's powers to supply common services under s.41 of the Police Act, and to use his powers so as to promote general police efficiency (s.28), as enabling him to over-ride the police authority's views on necessary expenditure and equipment. This seems to underline the impotence of local police authorities *vis-à-vis* the other two legs of the tripartite system of police governance, making them a fig leaf of local influence in a highly centralised, *de facto* national structure (Reiner, 1991, pp. 25–8).

In the late 1980s and early 1990s a number of other developments have continued this clear centralising trend. Talk of a 'hidden agenda' of regionalisation or even a national force is common amongst the police elite. The overall pattern is one in which the government increasingly achieves effective central control of policing, but by proxy rather than the overt creation of a national force. Its instruments for this are Her Majesty's Inspectorate of Constabulary (HMI), the Association of Chief Police Officers (ACPO), the Met., and the creation of specialist national policing units.

The cutting edge of the thrust to greater centralisation has been the government's tightening control of the police purse-strings. Concern about 'value for money' from policing, as from all public services (although rather less stringently) was a major theme of the Thatcher government throughout the 1980s. Home Office Circular 114 of 1983 signalled the government's intention to make additional police resources conditional on evidence that existing resources were being used as efficiently, effectively, and economically (the dreaded three Es) as possible. The even tougher Circular 106 of 1988 cast a chill over police managers and staff associations which has continued ever since. Under its strict guidelines, which required Chief Constables to specify the objectives which are to be met by each new post asked for, police forces throughout the country have fared disappointingly in their bids for increased strength. The alarm which has permeated policing circles at all levels is indicated by the unprecedented joint study of the threat to 'traditional policing' which was sponsored in 1989 by all three staff associations (*Operational Policing Review*, Surbiton: Joint Consultative Committee of the Police Staff Associations, 1990).

The new financial regime is not only tighter but more centralised. New powers to cap local government are being used as a means not only of restricting locally funded capital expenditure by police forces, but of inducing forces to achieve economies by standardised purchasing of equipment and central-ised buying arrangements (*Police Review*, 9 March 1990, pp. 462–3; 20 April 1990, p. 786). Local accountability has been eroded, sometimes with the perverse consequence of encouraging local authorities to bid for extra resources whether these are needed or not, as the funding will largely come from central government. The Audit Commission, the independent body established by the government to monitor local authority spending, has itself argued that: 'The balance has now tilted so far towards the centre that the role of the local police authorities in the tripartite structure has been significantly diminished. Accountability is blurred and financial and management incentives are out of step' (Audit Commission, 1990a).

The role of HM Inspectorate of Constabulary has been considerably enhanced in recent years as the linchpin of a more centralised coordination of standards and procedures (Campbell, 1991). This process began in the early 1980s with the financial management initiative, and has developed apace. As Mollie Weatheritt, deputy director of the Police Foundation, put it:

> Inspections have become more analytical and probing and the inspector's role has become not only a much more overtly proactive one but also much more closely and explicitly linked to the policy concerns of the Home Office. Since 1984, forces have been required to submit more detailed, purposefully organised information to HMIs before the latter make their formal inspection. (Weatheritt, 1986, pp. 107–12)

In 1987, the HM Inspectorate launched a complex computer-based management information system, the Matrix of Police Indicators. This is used by HMIs in preparation for inspections. Inspections are evidently no longer the perfunctory affairs of police legend, but involve the collation of considerable data on a standardised basis, shaping police activity into centrally determined channels.

The scope and profile of the work of the Inspectorate is clearly extending as the government's grip over policing has tightened. In 1988 'the continuing expansion of the role of the Inspectorate led to the creation of an additional HM Inspectorate Region, and the consequent appointment of a further HM Inspectorate and support staff' (*Report of Her Majesty's Chief Inspection of Constabulary 1988*, London: HMSO, July 1989, p. 12). This now brings the number of Inspectorate regions to six. In late 1989, a Home Office Treasury report was launched, aimed explicitly to enhance the role of the HMI as the vehicle of a more standardised system of resource allocation (Jordan, 1991).

It is not only the number of inspectors which has increased. Until recently the Inspectorate was something like a House of Lords for the police. It was a place to which distinguished former

Chief Constables could aspire after completing long and worthy operational careers, or, occasionally, to which less successful ones could be kicked upstairs. The change in the role of the HMI from dignified to effective has been accompanied by a change in the character of appointments to it. Several recent appointments have been relatively young Chief Constables, in the prime of their careers, and with the prospect of advancement in terms of operational command still ahead of them.

The most significant of these appointments has been Geoffrey Dear, who in December 1989 announced his resignation from being Chief Constable of the West Midlands to become an HMI. Mr Dear was not only the Chief Constable of one of the largest provincial forces, but commonly regarded as heir apparent to Sir Peter Imbert as Metropolitan Commissioner. His move to the Inspectorate was generally interpreted as a clear indication of the Home Office's concern to beef up the status and role of the Inspectorate by moving younger 'star' chief officers into it.

Other recent developments which have enhanced the profile of the Inspectorate have included the decision for the first time to publish HMI reports, after their presentation to the Home Secretary (*Police Review*, 30 March 1990). The HMI has also begun to inspect aspects of the work of the Metropolitan Police, hitherto exempt from the external inspection process (*Reports of Her Majesty's Chief Inspector of Constabulary 1988 and 1989*, London: HMSO, 1989 and 1990, pp. 13 and 15).

The Home Office has also encouraged ACPO to develop a much higher profile and expand its role in recent years, as a means of enhancing the standardisation and centralisation of policing. ACPO first made a significant impact on public debate about policing when it established and operated the National Reporting Centre as a means of coordinating the massive national mutual aid policing operation during the 1984–5 miners' strike. It was widely argued that ACPO was acting as a medium of government control of policing, or at least as a proxy for it.

Successive Home Secretaries have encouraged ACPO to become the body for harmonising policies between forces. In 1989 Douglas Hurd called on them 'to deliver effectively co-ordinated operational action'. Failing this, he implied, the present structure of local policing might be replaced by either regional forces or a single national force. To deliver this enhanced function the Home Office agreed to increase funding for the ACPO secretariat, which was to become more professionalised and streamlined. It had until the 1960s been run entirely by serving chief officers, and until 1989 remained a shoestring operation managed by retired police officers. In October 1989 ACPO appointed a firm of management 'headhunters' to find a suitable candidate for the Home Office funded post of general secretary, which was to enjoy a salary comparable with that of serving chief officers. The new secretariat would be responsible for establishing a policy analysis unit. Although ACPO rules required the post to be offered first to the membership, in the event a civilian was appointed: Marcia Barton, former secretary of the official side of the Police Negotiating Board.

In addition to the growth in importance in recent years of HMI and ACPO as coordinating bodies between the Home Office and individual Chief Constables, there has been a proliferation of specialist national policing units. The Met. has figured importantly in this process. The last few years have seen the formation of national or regional intelligence units to deal with a variety of issues ranging from drugs to football hooliganism and acid house parties. In July 1989 Sir Peter Imbert delivered a much publicised Police Foundation lecture in which he advocated the establishment of a national FBI style force to combat major crime. Speaking at the Superintendents Association Conference in September of that year, Douglas Hurd supported a modified version of that idea, a national criminal intelligence unit to combat organised crime.

The issue was debated within ACPO and the Home Office throughout 1990. It received an extensive airing at the ACPO summer conference in June 1990. A national operational CID remained controversial amongst Chief Constables, but the executive coordinator of the existing regional crime squads announced that a national criminal intelligence unit would be operational by 1991. This would integrate the work of existing units such as the National Football Intelligence Unit and regional criminal intelligence offices. It seemed that the weight of influential opinion in ACPO was swinging round to the nationalisation idea, and it was widely anticipated that the new national intelligence unit would be the embryo of an eventual operational CID at national level (*Police Review*, 15 June 1990, pp. 1180–1).

Other proposals in recent years along these lines have included a Home Office suggestion for a national air support unit, and a European drugs and organised crime unit. One of the key sources of the impetus towards centralised units and the tighter national control of policing generally is the belief that it is an essential requirement of European integration after 1992. More generally there has been concern about the growth of international crime leading to a perceived need for higher level national (and indeed international) police bodies to cope with it (Anderson, 1989; Dorn *et al.*, 1991a and b).

The Met. is in the forefront of advancing national developments. The advocacy of Sir Peter Imbert, the Metropolitan Commissioner, started the ball rolling for the national FBI debate. His former deputy, Sir John Dellow (then ACPO president), and John Smith, then Assistant Commissioner in charge of specialist operations in the Met. (and now Imbert's Deputy), were prominent champions of the national CID idea at the June 1990 ACPO Conference. ACPO itself, Interpol, and the main national crime intelligence units are physically based on Scotland Yard. In August 1990 it was announced that the head of the Metropolitan Anti-Terrorist Squad, Commander Churchill-Coleman, would henceforth have responsibility for all major terrorism investigations throughout the country. The Met. is obviously a focal point for the national policing units which are likely to develop.

Another important source of the nationalisation trajectory in the late 1980s was the growing debate about the quality of senior officers, their selection, and training. During 1989 a 'moral panic' about policing clearly began to spread in establishment circles, stimulated both by the bumper crop of scandals, and declining faith in the capacity of the police to control crime. The government rapidly turned to the senior ranks of the service as convenient scapegoats. A chorus of opinion developed blaming the shortcomings of police management and calling for the creation of a new 'officer class'. This received a considerable impetus when it became known that the Prime Minister, Mrs Thatcher, was an enthusiast for the idea (*Police Review*, 9 February 1990, pp. 264–5).

Concern about the quality of police leadership has been a major source of the impetus towards centralisation in recent years. In December 1988 the House of Commons Home Affairs Committee (HAC) announced an inquiry into higher police training and the Police Staff College at Bramshill. The HAC chairman John Wheeler is one of the leading exponents of greater police centralisation, and has advocated a new structure of six regional forces controlled from the centre, to replace the tripartite system. It was perhaps no surprise when the HAC Report in March 1989 attributed most of the shortcomings of police leadership to lack of adequate central control leading to a deficient career structure and uncoordinated training.

The HAC proposals recommended a number of measures to enhance the extent of rational central control over the careers and training of senior officers, such as making successful completion of the Senior Command Course at Bramshill a condition of promotion above Assistant Chief Constable rank. Its proposals primarily involve a formal ratification of the status quo, in which the Home Office already exercises a considerable measure of control over who becomes a Chief Constable (Reiner, 1991, Ch. 5). The career patterns of Chief Constables clearly show them to be 'cosmopolitans' not 'locals' (in Robert Merton's terminology). The Police Federation's caustic portrayal of high-flyers as 'butterfly men' is not that far off the mark (*Police*, August 1989, pp. 3–6).

The one proposal of the HAC Report which would dramatically alter the picture was its final one:

> The ACPO ranks of the police service should be established as a central service grade within the Home Office as a cadre of professional officers holding the historic office of constable but available for appointment to the developing tasks of a modern police services, both in central posts and in existing constabularies.

This clear and explicit nationalisation of the senior ranks of the police was immediately rejected by the Home Office in its initial reaction to the Report (which welcomed the other recommendations). The Home Office argued that it would endanger the tripartite system where responsibility for chief officer appointments rests with police authorities.

The reality is, however, that the Home Office already has the power to approve the short list of candidates interviewed by police authorities, as well as to veto the police authority's selection, according to the 1964 Police Act. It is clear that even in the period before the Second World War, the Home Office could exercise considerable influence over chief officer appointments (for a vivid example, see St Johnston, 1978, pp. 61–3).

The development of a cadre of potential chief officers is informal, and their allocation to particular forces is uncertain because of the role of police authorities. It is this which leads many chief officers to regard it as a 'lottery', and frustrates the centralists. In general, however, it has seemed to suit the Home Office better to have a system which it can heavily influence but not totally control than to make its power plain.

It could be that this situation is changing as the trend towards more overt centralisation gathers pace. One straw in the wind has been the saga over the appointment of the new Chief Constable of Derbyshire. This is the first time that the Home Office has openly demonstrated its control over the short-listing and appointment process. In April 1990 the Derbyshire Police Authority appointed the Deputy Chief Constable, Mr John Weselby, as Chief Constable, despite the fact that the Home Office had indicated at the short listing stage that Mr Weselby would not be approved. The only apparent ground for this veto was the good relationship enjoyed by Mr Weselby with the police authority (*Police Review*, 20 April 1990, pp. 784–5). The police authority sought a judicial review of the Home Office's action, but before this could proceed Mr Weselby withdrew his candidature. The post then went to Mr John Newing, a Metropolitan Police Deputy Assistant Commissioner. Although there have been some previous disputes between the Home Office and police authorities about the short listing of candidates, this was 'the first occasion on which the two sides disagree publicly' (*Police Review*, 18 May 1990, p. 999).[11]

Although not leading to public disputes, there have been difficulties in finding suitable candidates for other chief officer posts (*Police Review*, 9 March 1990, p. 473; 18 May 1990, p. 990). Anxiety about a dearth of suitable candidates is not confined to the Home Office or police authorities. In April 1990 an ACPO working party on 'Providing the Future Chief Officers of Police' reported. It recommended a number of proposals aimed at ensuring an adequate supply of high quality senior officers, and constructing a system of national standards under the supervision of the HM Inspectorate. Prospective high-flyers would be 'starred' during their probationer training and then monitored by the Inspectorate as they moved through various stages including Home Office Extended Interviews and Bramshill course assessments (*Police Review*, 27 April 1990, pp. 832–3). Existing systems for selecting and advancing high-flyers, such as the Graduate Entry Scheme (revamped in 1989 as the Accelerated Promotion Scheme for Graduates), were held to be inadequate. From the point of view of the influential advocates of an externally recruited 'officer class', however, these reforms are likely to be dismissed as mere tinkering with a basically inadequate system. Whatever the outcome of this debate, the extent of central control over chief officer careers is going to become more prominent and overt (Reiner, 1991, Chs 2, 11, 13).

Greater centralisation is not a new development but the accentuation of a process that goes back to the initial creation of policing on a uniform basis throughout the country, the 1856 County and Borough Police Act. Since then every major piece of legislation concerning the police has imposed greater uniformity on policing. Nor is this just a question of the overt level of formal organisation of the police. Historical work, notably Jane Morgan's important study of the policing of industrial conflict and the labour movement in the first four decades of this century (J. Morgan, 1987), shows that the Home Office was often closely involved in the day-to-day operations of policing disputes. The 1984–5 miners' strike was far from being a new departure. National labour disputes and other serious public disorders have been a major impetus towards nationalisation of policing through this century.

Routine crime has also been a stimulus to greater centralisation, and to the more efficient coordination of the 'war against crime' which it is expected to provide. This was the rationale used by the 1962 Royal Commission Report to justify its advance towards greater control by the Home Office, although it balked at the overt national force advocated in Professor Goodhart's influential dissenting memorandum. However, what Professor Goodhart and others forecast in 1962 has come about. Rejecting a *de jure* national police force, we have ended up with the substance of one, but without the structure of accountability for it which the explicit proposals embodied. You cannot have accountability for something that it not supposed to be there.

Arguably, attempts to relocalise control now are like pushing a stream uphill. As 'law and order' has become increasingly politicised it becomes more unlikely that any government would wish to relinquish control over it. The only feasible way for this to be accomplished would be another radical departure from British tradition. The functions of the police would have to be split between more serious crime and disorder, which would become the province of national policing units (as in the 'third force' option for public disorder, which all Chief Constables currently oppose), and routine patrol and crime investigation, which would be handled by localised and less prestigious police. This solution, found in many countries, is certainly on the agenda of commentators at both ends of the political spectrum.

Short of this functional reallocation, the nationalising trend cannot really be reversed. Only by recognising it and accepting it can some accountability over national policies be achieved. Partly, this accountability must be to parliament. But, beyond that, John Alderson's suggestion during the miners' strike should be seriously considered: 'a national (emergency) police committee' comprising the Home Secretary, representatives of local police authorities, ACPO, and arguably the Police Federation (*The Guardian*, 13 September 1984, p. 16). This should not only be an emergency committee, but responsible for reviewing and formulating national policies and guidelines for policing. (These would also be discussed in parliament, of course, though detailed work would be done by the committee.)

It is unlikely, however, that such a proposal would be politically feasible, any more than local control would be, in the present climate. Why should the government relinquish a position which gives it power without responsibility? This is after all an ancient if rather unroyal prerogative. The myth of a tripartite structure of governance for essentially local policing, with constabulary independence for operational decisions, is useful for legitimating a system of *de facto* national control.

CHAPTER 7

CONCLUSION: *FIN DE SÌECLE* BLUES
Policing an anxious millennium

It is important that members of the public should have a realistic appreciation of what police can or cannot achieve . . . so too it is necessary that police officers' expectations . . . are shaped upon the reality of the present and not upon some imprecise aspiration of perfection based on either past or present phantasies.
(Sir Kenneth Newman, *Report of the Commissioner of Police of the Metropolis for the Year 1983*, London, June 1984, p. 3).

The police were founded primarily to deal with the conflicts of an emerging industrial capitalism, and in the face of considerable political opposition from diverse directions. The need to overcome this widespread mistrust was appreciated by the architects of the British tradition, Peel, Rowan and Mayne, and they shaped the strategies of the police accordingly. The sources of the English police image of impersonal and non-partisan legal authority, reliance on minimal force, and cultivation of a service role – now encapsulated in the shibboleth of 'policing by consent' – lie not in social consensus but conflict. During the first century and a quarter of the 'new police' there occurred a successful process of legitimation and depoliticisation. This was the product of the police tactical tradition instituted in the early nineteenth century, together with a wider process of pacification and incorporation of the working class into the political and social order of growing liberal-democratic capitalism.

During the 1970s a process of renewed politicisation was manifested in growing debate about police malpractice, and an apparent change of overall tactics towards a more coercive, 'fire brigade' style. This was commonly interpreted, especially on the Left, as a calculated shift in strategy. Anxiety about changing police practices has prompted a developing civil libertarian concern about limiting police powers and rendering the police more accountable. On the other hand, throughout the 1970s the police lobbied with increasing vociferousness for more powers to deal with 'the fight against crime', and to resist 'political' control. The pressure of these contradictory lobbies produced the Royal Commission on Criminal Procedure and the Police and Criminal Evidence Act 1984.

If the reasoning behind the post-1964 trends in police tactics is examined, however, it becomes less plausible to see them as a coherent and deliberate strategy. Many changes, notably the development of 'fire brigade' policing out of the Unit Beat reorganisation, were the unintended consequence of reforms aimed at achieving quite different results. Others, such as the use of more coercive tactics in crowd control and crime fighting, were largely reactive, *ad hoc* and unimaginative responses to pressing problems. As Sir Kenneth Newman explained it:

> The short-term reaction to rising crime rates is a tendency in policy-makers to favour the use of the criminal justice process for the repression of criminal conduct. This, the crime control model, has a relatively prominent police profile incorporating assertive patrol activity, high level visibility, extensive use of stop-and-search powers, the likelihood of abrasive street contacts and, on occasions, a casual attitude towards civil rights. (*Report of the Commissioner of Police of the Metropolis for 1983*, London, 1984, p. 7)

As Sir Kenneth's denunciation implied, this understandable, if counter-productive, knee-jerk response of increasing repressiveness to deal with deviance is now widely recognised to be a blind alley. However, much of the critical concern about police deviance has simply mirrored it. As I argued in the last chapter, the 'rational deterrence model is not likely to be more successful in policing the police than in policing crime'.

An adequate approach to police reform must be grounded in

an understanding of police culture and practices, not a simplistic view that if only the right authorities were in charge all would be well. But both police and popular culture embody views of policing and its purposes which are at odds with the reality of police work. They exaggerate the extent to which policing is concerned with serious criminal offences, and overestimate the capacity of the police to deal with criminality by detection and deterrence. Most demands for police interventions in practice are calls for the resolution of a diffuse range of minor conflicts, disorders and disputes – a 'peace-keeping' function (Banton, 1964). The legal powers possessed by the police (especially the capacity to use legitimate force) are the reasons for calling the police in an emergency, rather than, say, a priest, psychiatrist or marriage guidance counsellor. There is scope for discussion about whether 'peace-keeping' interventions are adequately and fairly handled, especially in the case of violent domestic disputes. What there can be no doubt about is that concentration on the crime-fighting image of the police has distracted attention from exploration of how the effectiveness of the craft of 'peace-keeping' can be defined, measured or cultivated by training and supervision (for some useful exploratory discussions of this problem, see Muir, 1977; Bittner, 1983; Fielding, 1984; Bayley and Bittner, 1984.)

On the crime side of police work, all the research in Britain and the United States emphasises the central role of the public (as victims and witnesses) in uncovering and clearing up offences. Only in a relatively small number of atypical (although prominent) major cases does detective work have any resemblance to popular images.

During the 1970s and early 1980s, debate about police powers and accountability unfortunately became polarised between a law and order and a civil libertarian lobby, both of which ignored the weaknesses of the 'rational deterrent' model (more sanctions = less offending) as a means of policing either crime or the police. The relationship between formal police powers and the extent of either ordinary crime or police malpractice is tenuous and uncertain. The point has come to be accepted in large part by the police, but it has yet to be taken on board by discussions about controlling the police.

Scarman to Newman

The Scarman Report on the Brixton disorders became the focal point for a multi-faceted and fundamental reorientation of police thinking. The message of Scarman was far from entirely new. Indeed, he explicitly drew on Sir Richard Mayne's 1829 instructions to the New Metropolitan Police. Much of the philosophy he outlined echoed Reith's 'Nine Principles of Police' (Reith, 1956, pp. 287–8) which emphasise as the fundamental principle of policing: 'the process of transmuting crude physical force, which must necessarily be provided in all human communities for securing observance of laws, into the force of public insistence on law observance'.

This same conception animated Lord Scarman's discussion of the 'two principles of policing' (paras 4.55–4.60). Scarman adopted Mayne's 1829 definition of the functions of the police being 'the prevention of crime . . . the protection of life and property, the preservation of public tranquillity'. These were to be achieved having regard to two fundamental principles: 'consent and balance' and 'independence and accountability'. The nub of Scarman's approach was that he emphasised the priority of maintaining public tranquillity over law enforcement. Law enforcement must sometimes be sacrificed in the interest of public tranquillity. Skilful and judicious discretion – 'the art of suiting action to particular circumstances' – may be the better part of valour.

Guided by these principles, Lord Scarman made several criticisms of the police both as background and immediate precipitants of the Brixton disorders. Overall, he judged 'the history of relations between the police and the people of Brixton during recent years has been a tale of failure' (para. 4.43). Both police and local leaders 'must accept a share of the blame' (para. 4.46). Whilst not condoning the disorders or all police practices, Lord Scarman did outline how the deprivations, frustrations and racial tensions of inner-city life ensure that the 'recipe for a clash with the police is therefore ready-mixed' (para. 2.37). The hostility and suspicion of blacks towards the police was fanned by harassment, misconduct and 'the ill-considered, immature and racially prejudiced actions of some officers' (paras 4–61–4.68). But above all it was aggravated by 'unimaginative and inflexible' tactics, in particular stop-and-search sweeps which antagonised the very many innocent people who fell victim to these. These operations culminated in the notorious 'Swamp '81' which was the immediate trigger for the riots, a classic illustration of law enforcement at the expense of the maintenance of public tranquillity.

Lord Scarman made numerous recommendations for improving policing so as to prevent reoccurrences of the disorders. Very broadly these can be divided into 'people' and 'system' factors (Sherman, 1983a). 'People' factors involve changing individual police characteristics, while 'system' factors refer to the internal and external structure of social relationships of the police organisation. Sherman's study suggested that police–black relations in the United States had improved since the riots, despite no general improvement in the economic or social plight of the majority of blacks, primarily due to changes in police behaviour. This was not mainly due to 'people' factors, such as new recruitment policies: trying to attract more blacks and graduates, screening out people with overt prejudices, etc., more and better training, or encouraging higher education for police. There is no evidence that black officers behave less aggressively to black suspects than do white officers (Alex, 1969). Nor is there evidence that officers with higher education are significantly different in behaviour (Jacobs and Magdovitz, 1977; Sherman, 1978b). Such policies are none the less worth pursuing. First, they are desirable in themselves in making the police fully representative of the community. Second, changing the proportion of black, women and higher educated police may dilute the whole ethos of the organisation away from the racially prejudiced and macho culture, described in Chapter 3.

The really effective changes in the US were brought about by 'system' not 'people' factors. The crucial cause was the rise of black political power. Between 1968 and 1980 the number of black elected officials increased ten times over. Many police policy changes – for example, over shootings – occurred in cities with black mayors. Internal discipline and restrictions on discretion increased, not only due to new political leadership, but because the Supreme Court expanded citizens' rights to sue police departments or police chiefs personally for misconduct of their officers, if this could be shown to result from organisational custom or practice. But the basic change, encapsulating all the separate 'people' and 'system' factors, has been 'a change in the very philosophy of police work, away from a rigidly mechanistic conception of enforcement of every law to a more malleable conception of keeping the peace' (Sherman, 1983a, p. 230; Skolnick and Bayley, 1986, give several illuminating case studies of such success stories; a more pessimistic view is offered in Dunne, 1991).

It is this same basic shift which Lord Scarman recommended as the core of his proposals. The more specific proposals of his Report incorporated many of the features which contributed to the American change: the 'people' factors most obviously (paras 5.6–5.32), but also tightening discipline in relation to racially prejudiced or discriminatory behaviour (paras. 5.41–5.42), increasing consultation (paras 5.55–5.71), increasing accountability through lay station visitors (paras 7.7–7.10), more independent investigation of serious complaints (paras 7–11–7.29) and narrowing the scope of highly discretionary powers (paras 7.2–7.6). In the absence of the possibility of black political control as in US cities, Scarman's recommendations were the nearest it was possible to get in terms of a clear signal to police forces of the need for reform. Certainly the Newman strategy in London, and similar initiatives elsewhere, echoed many elements of Scarman's recommendations, and were further encouraged by HMI and the Home Office.

The prioritisation of public tranquillity over law enforcement, the criticism of an 'unimaginative and inflexible' use of 'heavy' police tactics, aroused the ire of many police officers as well as some of the conservative press (e.g. see Reiner, 1991, pp. 118–25). From the Right Scarman was attacked for advocating differential law enforcement standards in black communities, and in effect protecting muggers from policing. This attack on Scarman was quite misconceived. What Lord Scarman advocated was an equalisation of law enforcement in the face of clear evidence of discriminatory treatment of various kinds. The Right-wing reaction rests on an untenable denial of the necessary and desirable existence of discretion in law enforcement.

Scarman's analysis and prescriptions for policing also drew fire from the Left, for three main reasons. One was its espousal of statutory consultation, rather than control of policing by elected authorities, as the main vehicle for enhancing accountability. In Chapter 6, I argued that while no adequate case *in principle* against control of policy by democratically elected authorities has been made, it does not follow that this is the wisest strategy to pursue from the point of view of improving policing. In other areas of social policy which are controlled by local elected representatives, say education or housing, it is by no means obvious that the directions pursued have been notably 'closer to the people' than policing (David, 1977).

The evidence from other countries suggests, furthermore, that the structure of formal control and accountability bears no close or clear relation to the quality of policing. The most exhaustive comparative study of police and government so far undertaken suggests that 'Accountability to a community does not depend on particular mechanisms but on the spirit activating the political system as a whole' (Bayley, 1983, p. 149; see also Bayley, 1985). The bottom line issue in police reform is how to make an impact on the working rules of rank-and-file culture. Scarman believed a low-profile consultative approach might be more effective, especially in association with the other changes he advocated, such as the lay visitors scheme to open up the back-stage aspects of police operations.

The second strand of Left-wing criticism of Scarman was his alleged failure to recognise that the 'hard' or 'militaristic' elements in police strategy are intrinsically incompatible with 'community policing'. 'Scarman's recommendations were inevitably contradictory, with coercive police measures unproblematically juxtaposed with measures designed to rescue consent' (Joshua *et al.*, 1983, p. 200). Far from treating this issue 'unproblematically', Lord Scarman agonised at length about it. He argued plausibly against his critics that 'policing is . . . too complex a job to be viewed in terms of a simplistic dichotomy between "hard" and "soft"' (para. 5.46). The crucial question is not the existence of 'hard' or 'militaristic' elements in policing strategy but how the mix is decided, and by whom. The ideal of 'policing by consent', to which everyone now pays lip-service, cannot mean complete acquiescence. In a totally harmonious society there would be no need for police. Policing is centrally about the way in which conflicts which potentially involve the use of force are to be handled (at a first-aid level, not necessarily fully resolved). The paradox is that while the ultimate police resource is the legitimate use of force, policing is more successful the less it has to be resorted to. But minimal force does not mean no force. How far force is necessary is only partly a function of police skill in defusing potentially violent confrontations. It also depends on the amount of violence offered against the police.

There is an important issue here which critics of the police have not reflected on sufficiently. In violent confrontations, a 'non-militaristic' response by police (i.e. one where they do not have adequate training, manpower, coordination and defensive or even offensive equipment) may mean that injuries will be multiplied (Waddington, 1991; but for a critical analysis of this view see Jefferson, 1990 for a cogent account of the dangers of paramilitarism). This does not just mean injuries to the police, but also to others who will suffer from undisciplined and excessive violence from constables who lose their cool or their courage. If the use of violence by the police is necessary, it must be handled efficiently rather than aggravated by incompetence or default. The very hard issue of how to cope with collective disorder is simply dodged by most critics. Using routine police for riot control (as in England) has the advantage of conferring on their riot-control activities any legitimacy built up by ordinary police work. It carries the danger that public hostility (and the psychological effects on police officers) due to the policing of public order confrontations may carry over into a delegitimation of routine police operations. Which effect is greater is a matter of judgement, and it may be that the combining of all functions in the same police body is now a factor undermining overall police legitimacy (Morris, 1985). The weight of police opinion continues to deny this (Reiner, 1991, pp. 178–9). However, the thrust of much critical comment seems to deny legitimacy to *any* public order strategy, condemning alike both the explicit 'third force' approach and the training of ordinary police units in riot control tactics. This lack of clarity about what would constitute an acceptable public order strategy vitiates much criticism of the policing of the 1984 miners' strike and other such conflicts.

The final element of the Scarman Report which attracted much anger from the Left was the denial that racism was 'institution-alised within police practice or in British society as a whole'. Scarman explicitly defined 'institutional racism' as discrimination which occurs 'knowingly, as a matter of policy' (para. 2.22). Critics argued that there was plentiful evidence of the dis-criminatory impact of official policies (of the police and other institutions), albeit often unwitting. This may have become a widely accepted usage (I used it myself in Chapter 4), but it is not Lord Scarman's definition. The critics fail to provide evidence of institutional police racism in his specified sense of deliberately adopted policy. In the broader meaning of institutional racism as the unintended consequence of organisational policies, Scarman's analysis of the disastrous impact of such strategies as stop and search was eloquent testimony to his awareness of the problem. But Scarman was above all concerned to reform police practice, and recognised that this cannot be done in the face of a closing of ranks brought about by attacking the 'integrity and impartiality of the senior direction of the force' (para. 4.62). His interpretation of institutional racism as a subjective, rather than objective concept allowed him to avoid imputations of personal and deliberate bias to the force as a whole. But his proposals were calculated to deal with both the widespread rank-and-file racial prejudice and the (unwitting or not) discriminatory impact of policies like 'Swamp '81'.[1]

Scarman was the trigger for a reorientation of policing on a wide front. Indeed by the late 1980s, his ideas had become the predominant conception of policing philosophy amongst Chief Constables (Reiner, 1991, Ch. 6). Scarman's principles first had practical impact through their influence on Sir Kenneth New-man's strategy for policing London, which he developed after becoming Metropolitan Commissioner in October 1982. This was the prototype of similar programmes around the country.

Newman's strategy was intended to be a fundamental reorien-tation of policy and organisation, aimed at achieving the same success in legitimation as Rowan and Mayne's original formula-tion, but in the face of new problems. This momentous historical role was explicitly avowed. Newman himself described the changes as 'the most sweeping in the Met.'s more-than-150 years history' (*Strategy '84*, 10 February 1984, p. 1). The stimulus for the reorientation of strategy was threefold: the crisis in legitimacy and public confidence, the unsatisfactory performance in terms of preventing or clearing up crime, and the clear indication from the Home Office that further resources would not be available unless efficiency was demonstrated. The latter message was un-equivocally embodied in the very significant Circular 114, 'Manpower, Effectiveness and Efficiency in the Police Service', which the Home Office issued on 30 November 1983, and its even tougher successor, Circular 106 of 1988. Circular 114 stated firmly that no increases in police resources and establishment would be sanctioned unless the Home Secretary was satisfied that the best possible use was being made of existing manpower. These circulars, coming hot on the heels of the riots and Scarman, were the final catalysts for a wonderful concentration of chief officers' minds on the tasks of reform.

The central premise of Newman's programme was that crime control cannot be a strategy for the police alone, but does and must closely involve the public (this is clearly informed by the research work on police effectiveness outlined in Chapter 4). To encourage this Newman placed great emphasis on the idea of a 'notional social contract'. The traditional notion of preventive policing was extended 'from a focus upon the individual offence and offender to more active consideration of the preconditions for offences and thought for the potential victim of crime' (*ibid.*, p. 8).

The vehicles for the 'notional contract' and 'preventive policing' aspects of the strategy were primarily the stimulation of greater public involvement, and the 'multi-agency' approach to social control. Among the key devices for public involvement were Scarman-style consultative committees (with lay station visitors reporting back to them), 'neighbourhood watch' ventures, crime prevention panels, victim support schemes, greater use of the Special Constabulary (and attempts to recruit more blacks into it). By June 1984 the Met. claimed that there were 390 neighbourhood watch programmes (and 590 more being set up), 19 crime prevention panels, 27 victim support schemes, and 21 consultative committees. These initiatives have been subjected to rigorous independent evaluations (Morgan and Maggs, 1984; Morgan, 1989; Kemp and Morgan, 1989; Bennett, 1990). This development of an independent evaluative research tradition was itself a significant index of commitment to reform. However, thus far most of the independent (as distinct from in-house) assessments have been negative (Weatheritt, 1989; Morgan and Smith, 1989).

The 'multi-agency' approach involves police collaboration with other agencies, 'social, economic, cultural and educational', to develop solutions which

> address the root causes rather than the symptoms of crime. The assumption is that through better understanding of all the facets of any type of anti-social behaviour, the community, including the police, should be able to produce constructive, co-operative ventures to prevent or reduce the phenomenon, so avoiding costly reactive policing. (*Report of the Commissioner of Police of the Metropolis for the Year 1983*, p. 8).

The other side of Newman's 'notional contract' involved changes in policing. The key targets were more careful and precise management of resources and the co-option of all ranks and sections into the overall strategy. Newman was a keen exponent of professional management techniques for policing (Butler, 1984). Prime among these was the idea of 'management by objectives' whereby each district and work unit was supposed to have more precisely delineated and feasible specific objectives, the accomplishment of which could be rigorously evaluated. (The related but distinct idea of 'problem-oriented policing' has also had distinguished advocates; see Goldstein, 1990.) Within existing manpower limits more officers (including supervisory ranks) were to be put back on to the streets through re-examination of working methods. Scarce detective skills were more carefully employed by 'case-screening' techniques to grade the potential of detection, and those cases with low ratings allocated to beat officers for investigation and victim support. The aim was that the neighbourhood officer, with local contacts, may succeed where the CID would fail, while in any event the system would raise the status and morale of beat officers, and improve the attention given to the victim. Consideration was also given to the problem which bedevilled so many previous innovations: how to incorporate the rank and file. A new 'code of ethics' was formulated, and very active steps are taken to spread the ideas through the force. A 'corporate management' style of involving the rank and file in the formulation of objectives and the targeting of areas for priority attention was aimed at.

Beyond 'Plus': cycles of reform

In the first edition of this book, I concluded with an optimistic assessment of the Scarman/Newman strategies of reform.

> The 'softly, softly' approach to police reform . . . far from being a sop, may be the most feasible chance for improving the standards of policing. To rebuild an ancient edifice brick by brick requires time and patience. But it is more likely to succeed than either calling it names or charging at it head-first. (1st edition, pp. 211–12)

However, it was also stressed that the success of the strategy was threatened by two contradictory pressures. One was the all-out opposition of a broad rejectionist front on the Left, based on the GLC Police Committee and some of the Metropolitan authorities, which adopted a style of undiluted attack that threatened to alienate the police from reform initiatives (*ibid.*, pp. 210–11). This radial rejectionism has been displaced by Neil Kinnock's 'new realism', as outlined below.

The other danger was increasing social polarisation due to the social and economic policies of the Thatcher government. I argued that the worst enemies of the police bid for legitimation were not their overt critics, but their apparent benefactors – a 'law and order' government which was unconcerned about destroying the social preconditions of consensus policing and the virtues of the British police tradition. The Conservative government's social and economic policies generated rapidly increasing inequality, long-term unemployment and political polarisation. The vaunted return to 'Victorian values' was above all a return to the spectre of the 'two nations' invoked by Disraeli, and of levels of crime, violence and disorder unprecedented since the nineteenth century. The policies which had achieved police legitimation in the days of Queen Victoria were successful only because of the wider processes incorporating the working class into the social and political order. The past decade has witnessed an accelerating deincorporation of more and more layers of society.

The young 'never-employed', especially concentrated amongst ethnic minorities, are swelling the ranks of the 'police property' groups who have always been the hard core of opposition to policing. The 1980s have seen inequality and social divisions grow considerably, reversing the long historical process of increasing social integration. In 1979 the top 20 per cent of households earned 37 per cent of post-tax income, but by 1988 this had grown to 44 per cent. At the same time, the share of the poorest 20 per cent fell from 9.5 per cent to 6.9 per cent (Will Hutton, *The Guardian*, 7 January 1992, p. 2). The implications of deepening social divisions for policing problems are now widely recognised by Chief Constables themselves (Reiner, 1991, Ch. 9).

These hostile conditions undermined the success of the Newman strategy for London. The reoccurrence of even more serious rioting at Broadwater Farm and elsewhere in 1985 (Gifford, 1986) underlined the continuing alienation between many young and black people and the police, and also brought to the surface the gulf which existed between many of the police rank and file and the Scarmanesque philosophy of the Commissioner.

After a decade of Scarmania, public confidence in the police is lower than at any time since they were first established throughout the country in the latter half of the nineteenth century. This has been registered in the evidence of a plethora of polls and surveys in recent years. The late 1980s seemed to witness a haemorrhage of public confidence in the police (although some caution is required in the interpretation of polls seeking to measure public views of the police, Hough, 1989). With roseate spectacles it might be possible for the police to take comfort from the high public standing they continue to enjoy in absolute terms, or compared to other public institutions. The 1988 British Crime Survey (BCS), for example, found that 85 per cent of the public rated the police as very or fairly good in the job they did, a vote of confidence with which most institutions would be delighted (Mayhew *et al.*, 1989). But the evidence suggests that this still robust general rating of the police conceals a dramatic decline in confidence. The BCS itself has charted a steady fall during the 1980s, with 92 per cent rating the police as good or very good in the first survey in 1982, compared to the 85 per cent found in the third and most recent sweep, 1988 (compare Hough and Mayhew, 1983 and 1985, with Mayhew *et al.*, 1989).

The year after the last BCS, 1989, was a vintage one for police scandals, notably the release of the Guildford Four by the Court of Appeal. Since then the police (as well as the criminal justice system more broadly) have been hit by a succession of similar scandals – the vindication of the Birmingham Six and the Maguires, the troubles of the West Midlands Serious Crimes Squad, the referrals back to the Court of Appeal of Judith Ward, and of the three men convicted for the murder of PC Blakelock at Broadwater Farm, and numerous other revelations and allegations of malpractice.

These have been reflected in a precipitous decline in poll ratings of the police since 1989. The contrast is sharpest with the more distant postwar period, often regarded as a 'Golden Age' for the police. A Mori poll for Newsnight 1989 found that only 43 per cent today have 'a great deal of respect' for the police, compared with 83 per cent of a national sample asked the same question in 1959 for the Royal Commission on the Police. At the other extreme, 14 per cent had 'little respect', compared to only 1 per cent on 1959. Before this recent fall in generalised approval ratings, surveys had for several years provided particular pointers to an erosion of support for the police. Those who tend to be at the receiving end of police powers – the young, male and economically marginal in the inner cities – have been shown as generally critical of the police in survey after survey. Perhaps even more significant a harbinger of the recent collapse of general support has been the poll evidence of an increasing perception of specific police abuses (such as corruption, excessive force, or racial discrimination) even by the 'respectable' majority of the population.

The other source of the decline in public confidence is the apparent failure of the police to deliver effectively the protection which their own propaganda had promised. Recorded crime rates have increased inexorably since the mid-1950s, and since the mid-1970s have entered a phase justifiably described as a 'hyper-crisis' (Kinsey *et al.*, 1986). In the last two years there has been a record-breaking increase in the official crime statistics almost every quarter. While the BCS and other crime surveys show that part of the apparent increase is the product of greater reporting and recording, rather than actual commission of offences, much of the rise reflects a real growth of victimisation. Public confidence is eroded by the combination of apparent police ineffectiveness and revelations of malpractice.

Newman's successor, Sir Peter Imbert, has continued to pursue a strategy aimed at securing the relegitimation of the police in the face of the many factors which have eroded it. In essentials this is similar to Newman's strategy, and certainly incorporates the Scarman spirit. Imbert has, however, generally received a warmer response from the media (e.g. Appleyard, 1987; Tendler, 1987; Stalker, 1987; *Sunday Times*, 1987; Wheatcroft, 1987; Darbyshire, 1988; Rose, 1989, 1990a). Newman's espousal of the jargon of management theory and a rather academic style was criticised as a factor in the failure of his ideas to win the hearts and minds of the police on the streets. Imbert has carried more street credibility, having a much more populist personal style, and a career rooted in the toughest aspects of operational policing (he first achieved popular renown as the Special Branch detective who arrested the Balcombe Street bombers). Imbert's approach has always emphasised openness to the media, as his co-operation with Roger Graef's 'fly-on-the-wall' TV series showed when he was Chief Constable in Thames Valley. Imbert has been widely credited with introducing a new spirit of *glasnost* at Scotland Yard (Imbert, 1989). Above all he has tried to deal with the crucial problem of achieving rank-and-file support for reform by the 'Plus' programme he initiated (under the immediate direction of Commander Alec Marnoch, one of the most humane and progressively minded of all senior police officers). This has concentrated on a massive commitment to a series of consciousness raising seminars aiming to involve all Met. personnel in a change to a new ethos of service to the community.

Imbert's strategy has coincided with the advent of 'new realism' in the Labour Party under Neil Kinnock and it faces much less radical opposition than Newman's did. Since the end of the miners' strike in 1985, the leadership of the Labour Party has tried hard and successfully to rebuild its bridges with the police at all levels. As the special relationship with the Tories has gone sour due to the government's increasing financial stringency, the police have been receptive to these overtures. In recent years there have been such unlikely signs of this *rapprochement* as Police Federation leaders appearing on a Labour platform immediately before the crucial Mid-Staffordshire by-election in March 1990, and Shadow Home Secretary Roy Hattersley berating the Tories for restricting expenditure on the police and pledging Labour to increase it. While there has not been a swapping of positions on the police between the parties, there has certainly been an attenuation of partisan discord. Indeed, if anything the police fear a Conservative 'hidden agenda' of incipient privatisation and/or nationalisation as much as they previously feared Labour's stance on accountability to local authorities (Rawlings, 1991).

The present Labour position is only subtly distinct from that of the police elite (for an accessible account see Sheerman, 1991; there are many parallels between this statement of Labour policy and the police contributions to the *Policing* symposium, 'The Way Ahead' in which it appears). The victory of realism over rejectionism is evident in the new Labour policy document, *A Safer Britain*. Instead of the keystone being a concern to rein in the police through enhanced accountability, the central theme is crime prevention. There are of course still differences from either Tory or police versions of crime prevention. Local authorities, not the police themselves, are to be the primary agency coordinating crime prevention strategy. Social crime prevention receives as much emphasis as situational, target-hardening measures. But the police receive their due weight as essential partners in crime prevention initiatives, and beat policing is accorded paramount importance.

More familiar radical concerns are reflected in concern about racism and sexism within the force. However, these are not emphasised any more than in the statements of many of today's police leaders. Accountability is discussed as a matter of restoring the tripartite system enshrined in the 1964 Police Act, redressing the centralising tendencies of the Tory years. At the same time the need for effective national agencies for new forms of organised and international crime is recognised. So is the necessity for national oversight of policing standards by a beefed-up HM Inspectorate of Constabulary. (This is no more than a continuation of themes found in the 1964 Police Act.)

The new language of managerialism is prominent in Labour

thinking now, as it is in Conservative and police pronouncements (although the Tory 'officer class' obsession is dismissed as retrograde). None the less, a concern for ensuring high quality police management is expressed in terms reminiscent of much senior police talk. However, what comes over as the clearest new thread of argument is the rhetoric of consumerism, which has become the most prominent panacea in current Conservative and police thinking as well.

Consumerism has rapidly become the keynote of all agendas for reform in public services. Both Conservative government (the Citizen's Charter) and Labour opposition (the Quality Commission) offer their rival versions. The police elite themselves have rapidly latched on to this new language as a way of founding a new ethic of service to revive their flagging status, and a way of circumventing the more political forms of accountability which once threatened.

This is evident in the first major national response by the police to the perceived crisis of public confidence. In 1990 there appeared the *Operational Policing Review*, the report of a wide-ranging study of policing problems launched by an unprecedented collaboration of the three staff associations: the Police Federation, the Superintendents' Association, and the Association of Chief Police Officers (ACPO). The police assessment of the implications of their own study was that the priorities of police and public were out of kilter. The public expressed a preference for a community-oriented, service style of policing rather than an enforcement-based approach. The ensuing 'Statement of Common Purpose and Values' enshrines a philosophy of policing in which the watchword is service. It is amplified by a 'Strategic Policy Document on Quality of Service' endorsed by the three staff associations.

All these ventures are following in the footsteps of the Met.'s pioneering Plus programme. These initiatives are to be evaluated by regular surveys, and these are also to be a major determinant of priorities. The public are regularly spoken of as the 'customers' of the service, with the paramount concern being to satisfy their requirements. This is summed up in an article by the present HM Chief Inspector of Constabulary. He calls for 'a service culture', which insists that all officers . . . measure up to the requirement of the customer' (Woodcock, 1991, p. 82).

Towards 2001

Playing Sad While Bobby Sang the Blues.
        (Kris Kristofferson: *Me and Bobby McGee*)

There are many welcome aspects of the emerging consensus around a service-based, consumerist approach to policing. Certainly it is infinitely preferable to the tough 'law and order' promises and practices of the early 1980s which constituted much of the initial police reaction to spiralling crime and disorder. Nevertheless, it is doubtful that they will restore the police to their former beloved and respected place in popular esteem.

What is missing from any of the approaches is a fundamental sociological analysis of the role of the police, and of the sources of their present plight. Common to all the solutions considered is an unquestioned assumption that their falling public status is caused by a decline in police standards, manifested in less effective and more abusive policing.

Certainly there is a plethora of scandals revealing serious police malpractice. But do these indicate that the standard of integrity of the British police force has fallen? The extent of police abuse at any time is unascertainable, and for obvious reasons there is likely to be a substantial dark figure of hidden police deviance. What we do know is that in the 'Golden Age' of the mid-century, when the police were symbols of national pride, there was extensive and routinised wrong-doing behind the scenes. This is clear from police memoirs (e.g. the very revealing vignettes of life in the Manchester police in the 1930s and 1940s found in Mark, 1978) and from oral histories of policing (e.g. Brogden, 1991). It is also evident in the serious miscarriages of justice in that period which are now established beyond reasonable doubt (such as the cases of Timothy Evans and Derek Bentley).

What prevented these abuses from being revealed at the time was the much more deferential culture of the social strata at the receiving end of policing, and of the media and the educated middle class. Complaints were less likely to be made (rather than sullenly put up with as yet another unpleasant fact of life), and they were far less likely to be given credence by opinion-formers if they were expressed. It is plausible that what appears to be a growing amount of police malpractice is largely just a greater likelihood of it coming to light, due to a much more deep-seated cultural change: the progressive erosion of deference in the postwar period, what has been described as a process of 'desubordination' (Miliband, 1978).

Even if some of the increase in police scandals is really a reflection of more abuses of power by the police, it is too simplistic to see this as due to a unilateral decline of standards of legalism in the police. Police tactics have always constituted an array of more or less coercive methods graduated according to the perceived scale of trouble they have to deal with (which the controversial ACPO Tactical Options Manual makes explicit but did not conjure up *ab initio*). As crime and disorder have grown, so the police have moved up the scale of coerciveness in their strategy.

The increase in crime and disorder problems which the police have confronted in recent years has profound social causes. Amongst these are the growing social and economic divisions and deprivation of the last decade, which have swelled the numbers of those who in Victorian times would have been called the 'dangerous classes' and today are referred to as the 'underclass' (Dahrendorf, 1985). These have always constituted the prime business of the police, and have been aptly labelled 'policy property'. As their 'property' and problems have increased so the police are driven higher up the scale of coerciveness in their menu of tactics. This is liable to generate more malpractice. In turn it is liable to reinforce tendencies to cynicism and authoritarianism in police culture. But these are the symptoms of the problem, not its prime mover. Consequently solutions aimed primarily at changing the police will miss the mark.

At the bottom of the more benign solutions considered above is a systematic failure to confront the question of what policing really is. The consumerist approach in particular implies that the police can and should be whatever market surveys reveal consumer preferences to be. But what is the 'service' which the police have historically been organised to deliver? What is the 'service' which clients effectively demand when they call for the police? Research suggests that it is characteristically disorder or crime, even though the police typically seek to resolve conflict without recourse to their legal powers of coercion. The police are the specialist repository domestically of the state's monopoly of legitimate force, and the 'service' they are predominantly called upon to provide is 'the capacity for decisive action' (Bittner, 1974, p. 35).

The police are thus inherently a 'dirty work' occupation, in Everett Hughes' term (Hughes, 1961). It is only in the most exceptional circumstances, such as the consensus climate of postwar Britain, that the police can be regarded widely as anything other than a regrettable necessity. This has always been the status of the police in even the most pacific and law-abiding countries of the world. However, there are only flashes of recognition of this in British police thinking. One rare example is a reflective passage at the end of a paper by the current HM Chief Inspector of Constabulary:

> I am sure that the real test of a police service is confidence in what would happen if your own son was arrested, confidence that he would get treated in such a manner that, while he might have a sense of grievance over the event, he would be left with a grudging respect for those who worked with the system. (Woodcock, 1991, p. 181).

For the most part, however, the fashionable languages of managerialism and consumerism overlook the fact that policing is not about the delivery of an uncontentious service like any other. Their business is the inevitably messy and intractable one of regulating social conflict. They cannot control, but rather are buffeted by, the prevailing currents in society, the concept Mrs Thatcher vainly sought to banish. The pressures of this underlie the demoralised condition of the British police as they enter the last decade of the millennium.

The end product of reform cannot realistically be the restoration of the previous status of the police as beloved symbols of national pride. The pedestal on which they stood in mid-century was based on unique circumstances, in particular the consensus climate of Britain during and after the Second World War. PC George Dixon was not the norm for the British bobby, but their finest hour.[2] As Britain enters more firmly into Europe our police will come to be seen increasingly in a similar light, in a matter-of-fact way as performing important functions: regulating public space, and processing that minority of crimes which can be cleared up, acting as the initial filter into the criminal justice system. Hopefully, they will be seen as providing these specific services as efficient and fair professionals. Hopefully, they will be respected for this by the majority of the public. But they will not regain their erstwhile national mascot status. They will have become a demystified, mundane institution of government, not sacred totems of the collective conscience.

NOTES

Chapter 1

1. Some have tried to distinguish variants of the orthodox approach. Manning's admirably lucid account of the rise of the police distinguishes between 'teleological' and 'incrementalist' readings (Manning, 1977, pp. 41–2). Brogden's rigorous analysis of the political economy of policing contrasts two conservative models of police history: the 'theological' or 'Reithian', and the 'institutionalist' versions (Brogden, 1982, pp. 173–80). The difficulty in drawing such fine distinctions becomes apparent when we notice that Reith, the incarnation of the theological position in Brogden's classification, is portrayed as 'temperate and less crudely ethnocentric' by Manning. By contrast, Critchley is lumped in as an example of the 'teleological' view by Manning, but dubbed as 'the soberest of police historians' and a characteristic 'institutionalist' by Brogden. In truth, the social and political perspectives and the implicit models of historical explanation shared by all the conservative writers may vary in emphasis and detail, but only within the limits of broadly common assumptions.
2. It might be argued that political disorders outside London are not relevant to the Metropolitan Police Act. But they clearly contributed to respectable contemporaries' fears for the social order which underlay passage of the Act. They are certainly emphasised in the revisionist accounts. These also emphasise the importance of the Irish and Colonial models (Brogden, 1987; Palmer, 1988).
3. Readers of Griffith's (1977) critique of the political partiality of the judiciary may not think this claim amounts to much. It should also be noted that in the formative years of the new police, far from

parliament being the *vox populi*, the overwhelming majority of the population were not enfranchised.

4. The grant was increased in 1874 to half these costs (which it remained until 1985, when the Local Government Act increased it to a symbolic majority of 51 per cent). The 1856 Act distinguished two kinds of local police authority: (1) Watch Committees in boroughs, which were committees of the town council; (2) county forces were the responsibility of magistrates in Quarter Sessions. The Local Government Bill 1888 established Standing Joint Committees consisting of one-third magistrates, and two-thirds elected councillors, the structure which survived until 1964 (and was extended to all police authorities by the Police Act 1964). The nominal powers of Watch Committees over appointment, promotion, discipline and the administration of the force in general far outstripped those of the county authorities. The 1856 Act also began the process of encouraging amalgamation of smaller forces. The 226 forces of 1856 had been reduced to 183 by the Second World War as a result of this and later legislative inducement.

5. Hart (1978), Bailey (1981a), Philips (1983), Ignatieff (1983), D. Jones (1983), Styles (1987), Gatrell (1988), Hay and Snyder (1989) Knafla (1990), and Emsley (1983, 1991) all address this revisionist position and offer a critique – or autocritique – from somewhat different perspectives. Whereas (with the exceptions of Hart and Radzinowicz) the 'orthodox' historians worked outside academia, the revisionists are mainly professional historians or academics in related fields. Their work is thus hedged in by more caution and qualification in style of presentation. None the less, certain commonalities, sharply contrasted with the orthodox view, can be discerned in Silver's seminal (1967) essay (which spearheaded the new approach with its subtle and stimulating account of police origins), Foster (1974), Storch (1975, 1976, 1977, 1980), Palmer (1976), Bunyan (1977), Spitzer and Scull (1977a and b), Cohen (1979), Philips (1980), the essays collected in Greenberg (1981, Part 3), Fitzgerald *et al.*, (1981) and Brogden (1982, 1987). It is out of these that I shall construct the model of a revisionist perspective. Harring (1983) is an American counterpart. It is found in its purest form in Scraton (1985).

6. I am tempted to suggest that a high Storch:Reith ratio in the index is a good guide to a book's degree of commitment to revisionism, except that this is distorted by critical references to Reith which inflate the denominator.

7. The 'structuralist' *vs.* 'instrumentalist' debate is fully addressed in the essays in Greenberg (1981, Part 3).

8. Watts-Miller raises this intriguing possibility.

   The Metropolitan Police, Radzinowicz and others tell us, soon became an 'accepted institution'. This ignores continuing criticism and government attempts to stifle it. . . . Although central control kept the capital in more 'reliable' hands, it is open to question if a Bill such as Peel's could have passed after 1832, or 1835, the 'Magna Carta' of local self-government. All that is certain is Parliament's refusal to accept the 'accepted institution' outside London. (Watts-Miller, 1987, p. 51)

9. Silver indicates the powerful support for this argument during the Reform Bill conflicts, including the King and the Duke of Wellington.

   Wellington argued after the Reform Bill was passed: 'From henceforth we shall never be able to carry on a government without the assistance and support of a military body. If we cannot have a regular army in such a state of discipline and efficiency as that the King can rely on them, we must and we shall have a National Guard in some shape or other.' (Cited in Silver, 1971, p. 185)

10. As Watts-Miller puts it trenchantly: 'The executive of a modern state is also a committee to mismanage the affairs in common of the bourgeoisie' (Watts-Miller, 1987, p. 58).

11. Under their ex-military Chief Constables, a few rural constabularies did initially adopt a paramilitary model, quite distinct from the borough forces or rural constabularies of a later period (Philips, 1977, pp. 76–8; Steedman, 1984, pp. 21–7).

12. Having explored the familiar caveats about official crime statistics, Gatrell concludes that the simultaneous changes in the criminal justice apparatus (more police and public prosecutions) would lead to the expectation of rising crime rates in this period. On the standard labelling theory grounds then, the falling crime rates in this period should be seen as under-recording the true decline. At any rate they give credence to the falling crime rate as reflecting a real trend. Many other ideological and economic factors apart from police effectiveness were responsible for this decline, whether these are seen (with the revisionists) as the 'soft' social control of the working class, or (in the more orthodox account) moral and political integration (Gatrell, 1980, pp. 252–61). But Gatrell suggests the plausibility of giving the gradually professionalised and rationalised police and criminal justice system some weight in the process (*ibid.*, p. 259).

13. I call this neo-Reithian in order to emphasise the virtues of that ideal of pacific policing by popular consent which Reith attributes to the British police. However, as an account of history Reith requires drastic critical revision to recognise the structured conflicts which surrounded policing in a class-divided society (and continue to do so).

Chapter 2

1. Some other police forces have equal claims to a commanding place in their country's popular culture, for example the FBI (Powers, 1983). Canadians often point out that their most characteristic national emblem is the Mountie (Walden, 1982). But in each case it is an elite force that is accorded prestige. The 'Yard' plays the same role in British popular mythology, but the mundane bobby is also a cornerstone of national pride, unmatched by the treatment of any other country's routine patrol force.

2. Too much weight should not be placed on this survey based on a self-selected sample of readers of *The People*. But it is worth noting (as Gorer does) that *The People* has a wide readership, and a disproportionately working-class one.

3. Shaw and Williamson's class I includes the Registrar General's classes 1 and 2; while their class 111 includes R–G classes 4 and 5.

4. This is the standard Weberian distinction. Weber emphasises that the nature of legitimacy 'subjectively . . . may vary, especially as between "submission" and "sympathetic agreement"' (Weber, 1964, p. 327). In other words, seeing an authority (like the police) as legitimate does not necessarily imply agreement with the concrete content of rules or their specific enforcement. It only means acceptance on some minimal basis of the authority's right to make or enforce rules. (For a recent critical exposition of the Weberian analysis of legitimacy see Beetham, 1991.)

5. The stance of compromise and co-option between classes, rather than outright conflict, was a wider historical pattern in English political development. 'Governing in the context of rapidly growing industrial capitalism, the landed upper classes . . . avoided serious defeat by well-timed concessions. This policy was necessary in the absence of any strong apparatus of repression' (Moore, 1967, p. 39). It can be added that the absence of a strong apparatus of repression was itself a tactical choice deeming it (against strong countervailing arguments) to be the course of political wisdom (Silver, 1971).

6. My understanding of the legitimation of the British police owes much to the seminal study of the contrasting creation of different patterns of police authority in London and New York by Miller (1977).

7. Other sectors of the criminal justice system, notably the police courts, performed similar broad social welfare functions in order to secure legitimacy for their crime control role (Davis, 1984).

8. I am using the Weberian concept of bureaucracy as the pursuit of administrative rationalisation in an organisation. This is to be

contrasted with the pejorative image of red tape, bungling and faceless oppressors, although these may well be dysfunctional consequences of the Weberian model (Albrow, 1970).

9. The West Yorkshire police issued 'personal protective equipment', i.e. cricket boxes and jock straps. Class discrimination within the police was complained of when it was discovered that the ones for sergeants and inspectors were bigger than for constables!

10. 'It is the generation who were pot-smoking, student demonstrators of the late 1960s, which is now acquiring positions of influence and power. . . . The real failure in "community" or "public-relations" has not been in the inner-cities, amongst alienated youth – little attention has been paid to their complaints in the past – but has been amongst the middle classes' (Waddington, 1982a, pp. 18–20; see also *Police*, March 1983, pp. 3–4). The view that a highly educated society is harder to police because more people challenge police authority is common amongst police officers (Reiner, 1978a, p. 222, 1991, Chs. 7–9).

11. In the last couple of years more critical attitudes to the police have spread from the liberal press to papers like *The Times* and even *The Telegraph*, erstwhile true-blue police groupies. There are signs that Conservative politicians and commentators are seeking to make the police scapegoats for the apparent failures of Tory law and order promises. This is evident for example in the recent 'officer class' debate (Reiner, 1991, pp. 33–4, 348–53).

Chapter 3

1. See Westley (1970), Banton (1964), Skolnick (1966), Bittner (1967a and b, 1983), Reiss (1971), Rubinstein (1973), Cain (1973), Manning (1977, 1979), Chatterton (1976, 1979, 1983, 1989), Muir (1977), Van Maanen (1973, 1974, 1983), Manning and Van Maanen (1978), Holdaway (1977, 1979, 1983), Punch (1979a, 1983b), Lundman (1980), Brown (1981), Ericson (1982) and Fielding (1981, 1984, 1989) and Fielding *et al.* (1989) for just a few examples of this very rich research tradition, based mainly on participant observation.

2. Her critique is in many respects similar to Gouldner's (1968) debate with Becker (1963, 1967) and the 'labelling' perspective in general, which Skolnick and the other interactionist studies of rank-and-file policing were part of. Her arguments pointing to the need for a structuralist analysis of the operation of police discretion, rather

than a culturalist one, is developed in Shearing (1981a and b), Ericson (1982) and Brogden (1983a and b). The most comprehensive and sophisticated presentation of this structuralist account is the rigorous attempt to develop a Marxist analysis of police culture and operations in Grimshaw and Jefferson (1987).

3. The police world remains aggressively a man's world, notwithstanding equal opportunities legislation in the United States and Britain. In America despite the Equal Employment Opportunity Act 1972 women remain grossly underrepresented in most forces (Heidensohn, 1989). Although some forces have sent women on routine patrol for many years now, they still face formidable barriers of an informal kind in 'breaking and entering' into this male preserve (Ehrlich, 1980). British research has also found unequivocal evidence of both informal and formal discrimination against women, in flagrant breach of the law (PSI, 1983, vol. II, pp. 163–8, vol. IV, pp. 91–7; Bryant *et al.*, 1985; Jones, 1986, 1987; Hanmer *et al.*, 1989; Young, 1991; Fielding and Fielding, 1992; Walklate, 1992). To talk of policemen is thus not shorthand but for the most part a literal description.

4. The dangers to police officers are not small. In the United States between 1968 and 1977, 1,094 police officers were killed on duty. (There were 686,000 police officers in the USA in 1977.) More than three times as many civilians were killed by police in the same period (Walker, 1983; Geller, 1983). In London, 4,444 officers were assaulted on duty in 1981, and 3,141 in 1982, out of a force of 26,350 (*Report of the Commissioner of Police of the Metropolis 1982*, pp. 20, 79). Cain found that about a third of her sample of city police had been injured on duty (Cain, 1973, pp. 192–5).

5. The sense of policing as a mission is conveyed in the most high-blown style by the 'FBI Pledge for Law Enforcement Officers' in which the new agent vows to 'always consider the high calling of law enforcement to be an honorable profession', and which portrays the policeman as a latter-day saint and saviour of mankind (Niederhoffer, 1967, pp. 24–5).

6. It also serves to resolve the 'Dirty Harry' problem, whereby 'policing constantly places its practitioners in situations in which good ends can be achieved by dirty means.' This is 'a genuine moral dilemma . . . from which one cannot emerge innocent no matter what one does' (Klockars, 1980, p. 33). Cynicism is a clearly possible psychological result.

7. I well remember the experience in 1971 (soon after I began research on the police) of attending a conference where, after the learned seminars, a local officer took me, two other sociologists, and two out-

of-town policemen to a local drinking club. There were about fifty men there, and just three women – two strippers and the barmaid. To the amazement of the observing but not participating sociologists, at the end of the evening the three policemen had managed to walk off with the three women, who they had been assiduously chatting up while fending off earnest discussion of police sub-cultural normative patterns.

8. The very disturbing racist flavour of these comments is sharply reminiscent of the notorious Hendon police cadet essays leaked by John Fernandes, a black lecturer, who lost his job as a consequence (Taylor, 1983).

9. I was delighted when my 1978 book appeared to find that the local force newspaper *Newsbeat* printed cartoons illustrating each type, indicating that they were recognisable to police officers. (These cartoons were reprinted in *Police Review*, 15 December 1978, p. 1849, and 22/29 December 1978, p. 1884.)

10. When I met them again some years later my 'ideal-type' professional had become a chief superintendent and my 'new centurion' a detective constable.

11. This partly results from a methodological problem with Wilson's (and some of the other) studies cited in this section. Departmental 'style' is inferred from data on police practices, and then used in a circular way to explain them. The only independent evidence about policies is attitudinal statements of the philosophies of chief officers. But there is no indication of how these views were translated into concrete policy decisions which effectively shaped the pattern of practices. A study of managerial decision-making in practice suggests that formally stated intentions of chief officers often fail to be translated into authoritative law enforcement policies (Grimshaw and Jefferson, 1987, Part IV).

Chapter 4

1. Because the types are not hermetically sealed entities, departmental policy can encourage one or other outcome as the normal response, as Wilson (1968a) implied in his analysis of varieties of organisational styles.

2. In addition to the experimental studies reported in the text, there have been attempts to discover the relationship between aggregate levels of crime and policing (McDonald, 1976, Ch. 6; Carr-Hill and Stern, 1979; Morris and Heal, 1981, pp. 16–18). These find a

positive relation between police force size and crime rate, which they attribute to the recording phenomenon: the more police, the more crime recorded.

3. The crucial information was usually provided by victims, but another important source of clear-ups was professional security personnel such as store detectives (Bottomley and Coleman, 1981, pp. 45–6).

4. While *increases* in policing may not do much to reduce crime, there are some intriguing, if tenuous, indications that visibly significant and sustained *reductions* in police services could result in increased crime and lower clear-ups. The evidence from police strikes is often adduced, but is rather more mixed than *causes célèbres* like Liverpool or Boston 1919 and Montreal 1969 imply (Ayres and Wheelen, 1977; Reiner, 1978a, p. 5). But during the prolonged depletion of manpower from ordinary police duties (including in some areas Regional Crime Squads) in the 1984 miners' strike, there were growing complaints from many police authorities of increasing crime rates and falling clear-up rates. Whether this really happened is called into question by the only research on the subject (Waddington, 1986c).

5. For similar Canadian evidence, see Lee (1981) and Ericson (1982).

6. For a disturbing and vivid account of a particular controversial incident illustrating this, see Franey (1983), which gives details of the joint police/DHSS (1982) operation in Oxford which involved the mass arrest of 283 homeless people for alleged fraud in claiming rent allowance for lodgings they were not living in (104 were subsequently released without charge after several hours' detention). The Thames Valley Chief Constable's later justification of what he called 'Operation Major' invoked the image of widespread serious criminality among those charged, but actually only cited the case of one burglar (Christian, 1983, pp. 130–2).

Chapter 5

1. This overlooks a fundamentally different perspective, which is probably the predominant one amongst media professionals themselves. With regard to news production it is what has been called the 'cock-up' theory (Murdock, 1982). In relation to crime fictions it is the view of them as mere innocent 'entertainments'. The common theme to these practitioners perspectives is the denial of coherent or consistent social or political implication, either on the grounds that the media 'tell it like is', or that they are 'only' stories. I assume

that media presentations are never innocent of social and political implications, though not conscious or intentional for the most part. Furthermore, although neither monolithic nor unchanging, the meanings of media accounts are structured by industrial and ideological pressures and processes.

2. This distinction is somewhat tenuous, and is based on the pretensions of producers. The edges are fuzzy. Crime fictions have often been at the frontiers of realism in style, while 'real-life' police are undoubtedly affected by media images. When I went on patrol in 1980 in the precinct of Los Angeles where Joseph Wambaugh's novel *The Choirboys* (and its film spin-off) was set, many officers wore belt-buckles sporting the legend 'I am a Choir-Boy'. (I was not, sadly, invited to any 'choir practice'.) The confusion in modes was brought out by frequent conservative complaint that G.F. Newman's 'Law and Order' drama quartet (with its ultra-cynical view of criminal injustice) was especially pernicious because of its quasi-documentary style. The Roger Graef documentaries on the Thames Valley police (especially the later *Operation Carter* segments) with their fly-on-the-wall camera technique were conversely criticised by some police viewers as misleading because officers being filmed tended to ham-act for the cameras to portray the expected image.

3. The Police Federation magazine *Police* frequently draws attention to the tendency of the media to mention a police background in reports of deviance as a way of adding piquancy. A gem is the following nomination for the 'Wicked Ex-Copper of the Year Award' of a *Western Daily Press* report: 'SADISTIC TORTURE BY AN EX.PC. . . . Former policeman Jeffrey Griffith, aged 32, was jailed for six years yesterday for his sadistic torture of two naked vice girls. [Pause to admire the sheer professionalism of a reporter who gets the three Ps: Police, Perversion and Prostitution into his opening sentence. The story goes on (and wait for it)] . . . Griffith, now a car dealer, but formerly a policeman in his native Barbados.'

4. One particularly important kind of fiction this leaves out is children's literature. A fascinating study examined the images of the police contained in children's stories. One of the most interesting aspects of this is the frequent message that the police (however laughable, lovable or large-footed) are essential for social order. In Enid Blyton's *Mr Plod and Little Noddy*, for instance, when Mr Plod is injured the Toytown populace bemoan their plight: 'Who is going to protect us against robbers?' asks Miss Fluffy Cat, and Mr Wobbly Man echoes her concern. The inconceivability to most modern people of social order without police presumably owes a lot to repetition of such stories (Morrison, 1984).

5. *T.J. Hooker* is a variant of the vigilante mould in being a detective who chose to return to uniform. This also gives him more opportunity to combine some friendly 'community policing' with the action-man routines. His credo (which I cite in the text) is a clear inversion of the old counter-culture quip (used for example in the 1970 *The Strawberry Statement* about police brutality at a Columbia University sit-in): 'You know the difference between a radical and a liberal? A radical is a liberal who's been hit by a cop's night-stick.'

6. *Juliet Bravo* symbolises a new fashion for female cop heroes, also found in ITV's *The Gentle Touch* series, and the American *Cagney and Lacey*, as well as the mid-1970s *Police Woman* series. None of these are 'community police' in the Dixon sense, although *The Gentle Touch* comes closest, with the exception of its emphasis on detective rather than uniform work. *Cagney and Lacey* are really a community of two within the male police world, confronting a variety of work but usually of the procedural type. *Police Woman* specialised in 'undercover cop' stories where a female infiltrator was called for, and was primarily an action series. *Prime Suspect* (1991) featured a senior woman detective heading a major murder inquiry, and focused primarily on problems of sexism in the police.

7. The same device of the socially invisible uniformed lackey was exploited by G.K. Chesterton in a Father Brown story where the murderer is a similarly unnoticed postman, as well as in the clichéd denouement: 'The butler done it.'

8. One-off plays like Allen's are, of course, outside the limits of the crime genre. More critical views of policing have regularly been presented in mainstream fiction, from Balzac onwards (Miller, 1981).

9. The crime genre, especially its law enforcement side, more than any other popular entertainment form, has always presented itself as topical and as bringing the public the facts 'hot from the headlines'. Although with differing devices for conveying verisimilitude (all of which have a very short shelf-life rendering yesterday's forms palpably artificial) police movies have always striven for what counted as 'realism'. So it is no puzzle that the police genre should so quickly register changing styles and debates in the police.

Chapter 6

1. Brogden (1982) suggests, for instance, that 'Selective harassment of the residual population is the price paid for . . . a professional and

legally accountable police organisation rather than a democratic and publicly accountable one' (p. 250). It is not clear that democratic control by the majority would be an effective guarantee against harassment of minorities. Likewise Christian (1983) argues that the powers proposed by the Police Act are unacceptable to 'the community' and 'a majority of people would reject these powers' (p. 191). The footnote supporting this referred to 'a poll of black people carried out by London Weekend Television's *Black on Black*' (p. 192). In fact, polls of the 'public' showed majority support for the suggested police powers. It is of enormous significance that this support is not shared by black people, but however much of a warning to the police this should be, nothing is served by rhetorical identification of black people as 'the public' or 'community' as a whole.

2. One intriguing way of achieving this is Goldsmith's suggestion of using collective bargaining techniques to win the support of police associations (Goldsmith, 1990).

3. It should be noted that there are inconsistencies in the precise characterisation of these changes. 'Fire brigade' policing is a *reactive* style in which police actions are geared to responding to emergency requests for service. The 'militaristic' and 'coercive' styles are largely pre-emptive, encouraging police-initiated actions such as stop-and-search tactics and information gathering. The analyses vary also in the assignment of causal priority. Hall *et al.*, 1978 see crime waves as due to police production of moral panic, while Lea and Young, 1984, and Kinsey *et al.*, 1986, see police militarisation as a futile response to rising crime.

4. Both the police and their critics often tend to exaggerate the efficacy of technology. A nice example of its subjection to human limitations is that the Metropolitan Police computer can now give patrol officers the precise map reference for responding to incidents. The utility of this is rather limited by the fact that the computer references are to the AA *Greater London Atlas*, while police stations and cars use the *Geographer's AZ*, which has incompatible references! (*Police*, September 1984, p. 6).

5. As Sir Cyril Philips commented, some critics seem 'compulsively committed to frontal assaults', but these carried 'the danger of frightening the police into closing ranks' (Bennett, 1983, p. 173).

6. In two sophisticated and complexly argued articles, and an important book, Jefferson and Grimshaw (1982, 1984a and b) claim that even this is not adequate to achieve justice. They argue that democratic electoral control of police decision-making would not achieve the declared end of 'equal rights' unless a socialist conception of rights

animates policy, rather than the 'individualistic' one which is embodied in liberal notions of legality. This thesis is based upon an interpretation of the 'individualist' view of equal rights as equal outcomes: 'this would entail deploying resources so as to equalise victimisation rates – as between groups of citizens – and to equalise offender rates' (1982, p. 106). They are probably right in arguing that such an equalisation of law enforcement outcomes is not attainable short of a wider socialist transformation. But the liberal conception of equal rights surely means less than this: the equalisation of treatment and 'inputs' from law enforcement agencies. In an unequal society this will still mean an inequality of outcome. The evidence of research, for example on race and the police, suggests that there is considerable scope for improvement even with reference to this more limited liberal goal, which is, at least in principle, attainable in a capitalist society. It is this more limited goal of equalisation of treatment which motivates much of the concern about policing. In their 1984 article, Jefferson and Grimshaw illustrate their thesis with reference to the racial attacks issue. But surely the (rightly very disturbing) claim made by Asians and blacks is that the police do not give them *equal* attention and concern compared with white victims, not that the police have a responsibility to achieve equalisation of victimisation rates.

7. Several texts give detailed accounts of the PACE provisions, e.g. Bevan and Lidstone, 1991; Freeman, 1985; Zander, 1991 (first edn. 1985). Useful anthologies of critical essays include: *Public Law*, Symposium Autumn 1985; Baxter and Koffman, 1985; Benyon and Bourne, 1986.

8. The reference is to the 1971 film in which Clint Eastwood as Detective Harry Callahan is faced with the choice of violating procedures or failing to apprehend a palpably dangerous psychopathic murderer.

9. There is also the problem that tactics which may be rational for an individual officer (say widespread use of stop-and-search powers to boost his personal arrest figures) may be irrational and counterproductive for the whole organisation, if many officers act in the same way thus alienating the public and reducing overall clear-up rates. The restriction of individual action in line with the interests of the organisation is a prime task of police management.

10. Since the 1985 Local Government Act the share of central government has gone up from 50–51 per cent, symbolising that Act's transfer of power to the centre (Loveday, 1987).

11. Ironically, the Chief Constable who was subsequently appointed, John Newing, has tended to support the local authority rather than

the Home Office over subsequent disputes arising from critical
Annual Reports by HM Inspector of Constabulary.

Chapter 7

1. It is clear unfortunately that Scarman's claim that racial prejudice
   was not to be found amongst policy-makers, but was a purely rank-
   and-file phenomenon, is altogether too sanguine about Chief
   Constables (Reiner, 1991, pp. 204–10).
2. I say this with regret, as a long-time fan of Dixon and his mythic
   contemporaries such as PC 49 and Fabian.

REFERENCES

Ackroyd, C., J. Rosenhead and T. Shallice (1980) *The Technology of Political Control*, London: Pluto Press.

Adlam, R. (1981) 'The police personality', in D. Pope and N. Weiner (eds), *Modern Policing*, London: Croom Helm.

Adlam, R. (1987) 'The special course', *Policing*, 3:3.

Albrow, M. (1970) *Bureaucracy*, London: Macmillan.

Alderson, J. (1979) *Policing Freedom*, Plymouth: Macdonald & Evans.

Alderson, J. (1984) *Law and Disorder*, London: Hamish Hamilton.

Alex, N. (1969) *Black in Blue*, New York: Appleton, Century, Crofts.

Alex, N. (1976) *New York Cops Talk Back*, New York: Wiley.

Anderson, M. (1989) *Policing the World*, Oxford: Oxford University Press.

Antunes, G. and E.S. Scott (1981) 'Calling the cops', *Journal of Criminal Justice*, 9:2.

Appleyard, B. (1987) 'Private man, public eye', *The Times*, 19 March, p. 14.

Ascoli, D. (1979) *The Queen's Peace*, London: Hamish Hamilton.

Audit Commission (1990a) *Footing the Bill: Financing provincial police forces*, London: HMSO.

Audit Commission (1990b) *Effective Policing: Performance review in police forces*, London: HMSO.

Ayres, R. and T. Wheelen (1977) *Collective Bargaining in the Public Sector*, Gaithersburg, Md.: International Association of Chiefs of Police.

Bailey, V. (1980) 'Crime, criminal justice and authority in England', *Bulletin of the Society for the Study of Labour History*, 40, Spring.

Bailey, V. (1981a) *Policing and Punishment in the Nineteenth Century*, London: Croom Helm.

Bailey, V. (1981b) 'The Metropolitan Police, the Home Office and the threat of outcast London', in V. Bailey (1981a) *Policing and Punishment in the Nineteenth Century*, London: Croom Helm.

Baldwin, J. and M. McConville (1977) *Negotiated Justice*, Oxford: Martin Robertson.

Baldwin, J. and M. McConville (1979) *Jury Trials*, Oxford: Oxford University Press.

Baldwin, R. (1987) 'Why accountability?', *British Journal of Criminology*, 27:1.

Baldwin, R. (1989) 'Regulation and policing by code', in M. Weatheritt (ed.), *Police Research: Some future prospects*, Aldershot: Avebury.

Baldwin, R. and R. Kinsey (1982) *Police Powers and Politics*, London: Quartet.

Baldwin, R. and R. Leng (1984) 'Police powers and the citizen', *Howard Journal of Criminal Justice*, 23:2, June.

Ball, J., L. Chester and R. Perrott (1979) *Cops and Robbers*, Harmondsworth: Penguin Books.

Banton, M. (1964) *The Policeman in the Community*, London: Tavistock.

Banton, M. (1973) *Police–Community Relations*, London: Collins.

Banton, M. (1974) 'The keepers of the peace', *New Society*, 5 December, p. 635.

Banton, M. (1983) 'Categorical and statistical discrimination', *Ethnic and Racial Studies*, 6:3, July.

Baxter, J. and L. Koffman (1983) 'The Confait inheritance – forgotten lessons?', *Cambrian Law Review*, 14.

Baxter, J. and L. Koffman (eds) (1985) *Police: The constitution and the community*, Abingdon: Professional Books.

Bayley, D. (1983) 'Accountability and control of police: some lessons for Britain', in T. Bennett (ed.) *The Future of Policing* (Cropwood Papers 15), Cambridge: Institute of Criminology.

Bayley, D. (1985) *Patterns of Policing*, New Brunswick: Rutgers University Press.

Bayley, D. and E. Bittner (1984) 'Learning the skills of policing', *Law and Contemporary Problems*, 47.

Bayley, D. and H. Mendelsohn (1968) *Minorities and the Police*, New York: Free Press.

Becker, H. (1963) *Outsiders*, New York: Free Press.

Becker, H. (1967) 'Whose side are we on?', *Social Problems*, 14:3.

Beetham, D. (1991) *The Legitimation of Power*, London: Macmillan.

Bennett, T. (1979) 'The social distribution of criminal labels', *British Journal of Criminology*, 19.

Bennett, T. (ed.) (1983) *The Future of Policing* (Cropwood Papers 15), Cambridge: Institute of Criminology.

Bennett, T. (1989) 'The neighbourhood watch experiment', in R. Morgan and D. Smith (eds) *Coming to Terms With Policing*, London: Routledge.

Bennett, T. (1990) *Evaluating Neighbourhood Watch*, Aldershot: Gower.

Benstock, B. (ed.) (1983) *Essays on Detective Fiction*, London: Macmillan.

Bent, A. (1974) *The Politics of Law Enforcement*, Lexington, Mass.: D.C. Heath.

Benyon, J. (ed.) (1984) *Scarman and After*, Oxford: Pergamon.

Benyon, J. and C. Bourne (eds) (1986) *The Police: Powers, Procedures and Proprieties*, Oxford, Pergamon.

Bernstein, S., T. Platt, J. Frappier, G. Ray, R. Schauffler, L. Trujillo, L. Cooper, E. Currie and S. Harring (1982) *The Iron Fist and the Velvet Glove: An analysis of the US police*, 3rd edn, Berkeley, California: Center for Research on Criminal Justice.

Bevan, V.T. and K. Lidstone (1991) *The Investigation of Crime: A guide to police powers*, London: Butterworth.

Binder, A. and P. Scharf (1982) 'Deadly force in law enforcement', *Crime and Delinquency*, 28.

Birch, D. (1989) 'The PACE hots up: confessions and confusions under the 1984 act', *Criminal Law Review*.

Bittner, E. (1967a) 'The police on Skid Row: a study in peacekeeping', *American Sociological Review*, 32.

Bittner, E. (1967b) 'Police discretion in the emergency apprehension of mentally ill persons', *Social Problems*, 14.

Bittner, E. (1970) *The Functions of the Police in Modern Society*, Chevy Chase, Md.: National Institute of Mental Health.

Bittner, E. (1974) 'Florence Nightingale in pursuit of Willie Sutton: a theory of the police', in H. Jacob (ed.), *The Potential for Reform of Criminal Justice*, Beverly Hills: Sage.

Bittner, E. (1983) 'Legality and workmanship' in M. Punch (ed.). *Control in the Police Organization*, Cambridge, Mass.: MIT Press.

Black, D. (1970) 'Production of crime rates', *American Sociological Review*, 35.

Black, D. (1972) 'The social organization of arrest', *Stanford Law Review*, 23.

Black, D. and A.J. Reiss Jr (1970) 'Police control of juveniles', *American Sociological Review*, 35.

Bloch, P. and D. Anderson (1974) *Policewomen on Patrol*, Washington, D.C.: Police Foundation.

Blom-Cooper, L. (1984) 'Criminal justice in 1984', *Criminal Justice*, 2:2, June.

Blom-Cooper, L. and R. Drabble (1982) 'Police perception of crime', *British Journal of Criminology*, 22:1, April.

Blumberg, A. (1979) *Criminal Justice*, New York: Franklin Watts.

Bogolmony, R. (1976) 'Street patrol: the decision to stop a citizen', *Criminal Law Bulletin*, 12:5.

Boostrom, R. and J. Henderson (1983) 'Community action and crime prevention', *Crime and Social Justice*, 19, Summer.

Bopp, W. (ed.) (1971) *The Police Rebellion*, Springfield, Ill.: C.C. Thomas.

Bottomley, A.K. (1973) *Decisions in the Penal Process*, Oxford: Martin Robertson.

Bottomley, A.K. and C. Coleman (1981) *Understanding Crime Rates*, Farnborough: Gower.

Bottomley, A.K. and K. Pease (1986) *Crime and Punishment: Interpreting the data*, Milton Keynes: Open University Press.

Bottomley, A.K., C. Coleman, D. Dixon, M. Gill and D. Wall (1991) *The Impact of PACE: Policing in a Northern Force*, University of Hull: Centre for Criminology and Criminal Justice.

Bottoms, A.E. (1990) 'Crime prevention facing the 1990s', *Policing and Society*, 1:1.

Bottoms, A.E. and S. Stevenson (1990): 'The politics of the police 1958–1970', in R. Morgan (ed.) *Policing, Organised Crime and Crime Prevention* (British Criminology Conference Papers 4), Bristol University: Centre for Criminal Justice.

Bowden, T. (1978) *Beyond the Limits of the Law*, Harmondsworth: Penguin.

Bowling, B. and W. Saulsbury (1991) 'Racial attacks and the multi-agency approach', paper to the British Criminology Conference, 25 July, University of York: Department of Social Policy.

Box, S. (1981) *Deviance, Reality and Society*, New York: Holt, Rinehart & Winston (1st edn 1971).

Box, S. (1983) *Power, Crime and Mystification*, London: Tavistock.

Box, S. (1987) *Recession, Crime and Unemployment*, London: Macmillan.

Box, S. and K. Russell (1975) 'The politics of discreditability', *Sociological Review*, 23:2.

Boydstun, J.E. (1975) *San Diego Field Interrogation Study: Final report*, Washington, DC: Police Foundation.

Bradley, D., N. Walker and R. Wilkie (1986): *Managing the Police*, Hemel Hempstead: Harvester Wheatsheaf.

Bradley, D., N. Walker and R. Wilkie (1987): 'Beyond managing by objectives', *Policing*, 3:1.

Brewer, J. and J. Styles (eds) (1980) *An Ungovernable People*, London: Hutchinson.

Brewer, J.D. (1991): 'Policing in divided societies', *Policing and Society*, 1:3.

Brewer, J.D., A. Guelke, I. Hume, E. Moxon-Browne and R. Wilford (1988): *The Police, Public Order and the State*, London: Macmillan.

Brewer, J.D. and K. Magee (1990): *Inside the RUC*, Oxford: Oxford University Press.

Bridges, L. (1983a): 'Policing the urban wasteland', *Race and Class*, Autumn.

Bridges, L. (1983b) 'Extended views: the British left and law and order', *Sage Race Relations Abstracts*, February.

Bridges, L. and T. Bunyan (1983) 'The Police and Criminal Evidence Bill in Context', *Journal of Law and Society*, Summer.

Broderick, J. (1973) *Police in a Time of Change*, Morristown, N.J.: General Learning.

Brodeur, J.P. (1983) 'High policing and low policing: remarks about the policing of political activities', *Social Problems*, 30:5, June.

Brogden, A. (1981) 'Sus is dead, but what about Sas?', *New Community*, IX:1, Spring/Summer.

Brogden, M. (1977) 'A police authority – the denial of conflict', *Sociological Review*, 25:2.

Brogden, M. (1981) 'All police is conning bastards', in B. Fine, A. Hunt, D. McBarnet and B. Moorhouse (eds) *Law, State and Society*, London: Croom Helm.

Brogden, M. (1982) *The Police: Autonomy and consent*, London and New York: Academic Press.

Brogden, M. (1983a) 'The myth of policing by consent', *Police Review*, 22 April.

Brogden, M. (1983b) 'From Henry VIII to Liverpool 8: the complex unity of police street powers', *International Journal of Sociology of Law*, Winter.

Brogden, M. (1987): 'The emergence of the police: the colonial dimension', *British Journal of Criminology*, 27:1.

Brogden, M. (1991): *On the Mersey Beat: An oral history of policing Liverpool between the wars*, Oxford: Oxford University Press.

Brogden, M. and D. Graham (1988) 'Police education: the hidden curriculum', in R. Fieldhouse (ed.), *The Political Education of Servants of the State*, Manchester: Manchester University Press.

Brogden, M., T. Jefferson and S. Walklate (1988): *Introducing Policework*, London: Unwin.

Brogden, M. and M. Wright (1979) 'Reflections on the social work strikes', *New Society*, 53.

Brooks, T.R. (1965) 'New York's finest', *Commentary*, 40, August.

Brown, A. (1988) *Watching the Detectives*, London: Hodder & Stoughton.

Brown, D. (1987) *The Police Complaints Procedure: A survey of complainants' views*, London: HMSO.

Brown, D. (1989) *Detention at the police station under the Police and Criminal Evidence Act 1984*, London: HMSO.

Brown, D. (1991) *Investigating Burglary: The effect of PACE* (Home Office Research Study 123), London: HMSO.

Brown, D. and S. Iles (1985) *Community Constables: A study of a policing initiative*, Research and Planning Unit Paper 30, London: Home Office.

Brown, J. and G. Howes (eds) (1975) *The Police and the Community*, Farnborough: Saxon House.

Brown, L. and A. Willis (1985) 'Authoritarianism in British police recruits: importation, socialisation or myth?', *Journal of Occupational Psychology*, 58:1.

Brown, M. (1981) *Working the Street*, New York: Russell Sage.

Bryant, L., D. Dunkerley and G. Kelland (1985) 'One of the boys', *Policing*, 1:4.

Bull, R. and P. Horncastle (1989) 'An evaluation of human relations training', in R. Morgan and D. Smith (eds) *Coming to Terms With Policing*, London: Routledge.

Bunyan, T. (1977) *The Political Police in Britain*, London: Quartet.

Bunyan, T. (1981) 'The police against the people', *Race and Class*, 23:2/3, Autumn/Winter.

Bunyan, T. and M. Kettle (1980) 'The police force of the future is now here', *New Society*, 21 August.

Bunyard, R. (1978) *Police: Organisation and command*, Plymouth: Macdonald & Evans.

Burrows, J. and H. Lewis (1988) *Directed Patrolwork: A study of uniformed policing*, London: HMSO.

Burrows, J. and R. Tarling (1982) *Clearing Up Crime*, London: Home Office Research Unit.

Butler, A.J. (1982a) 'An examination of the influence of training and work experience on the attitudes and perceptions of police officers', Ms., Bramshill: Police Staff College.

Butler, A.J. (1982b) 'Effectiveness, accountability and management: the challenge of contemporary police work', in C. Jones and J. Stevenson (eds) *Yearbook of Social Policy in Britain 1980–1*, London: Routledge.

Butler, A.J. (1984) *Police Management*, London: Gower.

Butler, A.J. (1985) 'Objectives and accountability', *Policing*, 1:3.

Butler, A.J. (1986) 'Purpose and process', *Policing*, 2:2.

Cain, M. (1973) *Society and the Policeman's Role*, London: Routledge & Kegan Paul.

Cain, M. (1977) 'An ironical departure: the dilemma of contemporary policing' in K. Jones (ed.) *Yearbook of Social Policy in Britain*, London: Routledge & Kegan Paul.

Cain, M. (1979) 'Trends in the sociology of police work', *International Journal of Sociology of Law*, 7:2.

Cain, M. and S. Sadigh (1982) 'Racism, the police and community policing', *Journal of Law and Society*, 9:1, Summer.

Campbell, D. (1980) 'Society under surveillance', in P. Hain (ed.) *Policing the Police 2*, London: Calder.

Campbell, D. (1991) 'Police G7 that's promising action', *The Guardian*, 7 August.

Carr-Hill, R. and N. Stern (1979) *Crime, the Police and Criminal Statistics*, London and New York: Academic Press.

Carrier, J. (1988) *The Campaign for the Employment of Women as Police Officers*, Aldershot: Avebury.

Carter, A. (1982) 'The wonderful world of cops', *New Society*, 23 September.

Cashmore, E. and E. McLaughlin (1991) *Out of Order? Policing black people*, London: Routledge.

Cawelti, J.G. (1976) *Adventure, Mystery and Romance*, Chicago: Chicago University Press.

Chambliss, W. and M. Mankoff (eds) (1975) *Whose Law, What Order?*, New York: Wiley.

Chandler, R. (1944) 'The simple art of murder', *Atlantic Monthly*, December. (Reprinted in R. Chandler (1964) *Pearls Are a Nuisance*, London: Penguin.)

Chapman, B. (1970) *Police State*, London: Macmillan.

Chapman, D. (1968) *Sociology and the Stereotype of the Criminal*, London: Tavistock.

Chatterton, M. (1976) 'Police in social control', in J. King (ed.), *Control Without Custody* (Cropwood Papers No. 7), Cambridge: Institute of Criminology.

Chatterton, M. (1979) 'The supervision of patrol work under the fixed points system', in S. Holdaway (ed.) *The British Police*, London: Edward Arnold.

Chatterton, M. (1983) 'Police work and assault charges', in M. Punch (ed.) *Control in the Police Organization*, Cambridge, Mass.: MIT Press.

Chatterton, M. (1987a) 'Assessing police effectiveness: future prospects', *British Journal of Criminology*, 27:1.

Chatterton, M. (1987b) 'Front-line supervision in the British police services', in G. Gaskell and R. Benewick (eds) *The Crowd in Contemporary Britain*, London: Sage.

Chatterton, M. (1989) 'Managing paperwork', in M. Weatheritt (ed.) *Police Research: Some future prospects*, Aldershot: Avebury.

Chatterton, M. and M. Rogers (1989) 'Focused policing' in R. Morgan and D. Smith (eds) *Coming to Terms With Policing*, London: Routledge.

Chesshyre, R. (1989) *The Force*, London: Sidgwick & Jackson.

Chibnall, S. (1977) *Law and Order News*, London: Tavistock.

Chibnall, S. (1979) 'The Metropolitan Police and the news media', in S. Holdaway (ed.) *The British Police*, London: Edward Arnold.

Choo, A. (1989) 'Improperly obtained evidence: a reconsideration', *Legal Studies*, 9:3.

Christensen, J., J. Schmidt and J. Henderson (1982) 'The selling of the police: media, ideology and crime control', *Contemporary Crises*, 6.

Christian, L. (1983) *Policing By Coercion*, London: GLC Police Committee and Pluto Press.

Christopher, S. (1990) 'The who and why of police assaults', *Police Review*, 98.

Clarens, C. (1980) *Crime Movies*, New York: Norton.

Clark, J.P. (1965) 'Isolation of the police: a comparison of the British and American situations', *Journal of Criminal Law, Criminology and Police Science*, 56:3.

Clarke, A. (1982) *Television Police Series and Law and Order* (Popular Culture Course Unit 22), Milton Keynes: Open University.

Clarke, A. (1983) 'Holding the blue lamp: television and the police in Britain', *Crime and Social Justice*, 19, Summer.

Clarke, A. and I. Taylor (1980) 'Vandals, pickets, and muggers', *Screen Education*, 36, Autumn.

Clarke, R. and M. Hough (1980) *The Effectiveness of Policing*, Farnborough: Gower.

Clarke, R. and M. Hough (1984) *Crime and Police Effectiveness*, London: Home Office Research Unit.

Clarke, R. and P. Mayhew (eds) (1980) *Designing Out Crime*, London: Home Office Research Unit.

Clayton, R. and H. Tomlinson (1987) *Civil Actions Against the Police*, London: Sweet & Maxwell.

Clutterbuck, R. (1980) *Britain in Agony*, Harmondsworth: Penguin.

Cochrane, R. and A.J. Butler (1980) 'The values of police officers,

292 References

recruits and civilians in England', *Journal of Police Science and Administration*, 8.

Cohen, P. (1979) 'Policing the working class city', in B. Fine, R. Kinsey, J. Lea, S. Piciotto and J. Young (eds) *Capitalism and the Rule of Law*, London: Hutchinson.

Cohen, S. (1972) *Folk Devils and Moral Panics*, London: Paladin (2nd edn, 1980, Martin Robertson, Oxford).

Cohen, S. (1979) 'The punitive city', *Contemporary Crises*, 3:4.

Cohen, S. and A. Scull (eds) (1983) *Social Control and the State*, Oxford: Martin Robertson.

Cohen, S. and J. Young (eds) (1973) *The Manufacture of News*, London: Constable (2nd edn, 1981).

Collins, H. (1982) *Marxism and Law*, Oxford: Oxford University Press.

Colman, A. (1983) 'Rejoinder', *Sociology*, August.

Colman, A. and L. Gorman (1982) 'Conservatism, dogmatism and authoritarianism in British police officers', *Sociology*, February.

Colquhoun, P. (1797) *Treatise on the Police of the Metropolis*.

Colquhoun, P. (1806) *Treatise on Indigence*.

Corbett, C. (1991) 'Complaints against the police: the new procedure of informal resolution', *Policing and Society*, 2:1.

Coulter, J., S. Miller and M. Walker (1984) *State of Siege: Miners' strike 1984*, London: Canary Press.

Cox, B., J. Shirley and M. Short (1977) *The Fall of Scotland Yard*, Harmondsworth: Penguin.

Crawford, A., T. Jones, T. Woodhouse and J. Young (1990) *The Second Islington Crime Survey*, London: Middlesex Polytechnic Centre for Criminology.

Cray, E. (1972) *The Enemy in the Streets*, New York: Anchor.

Critchley, T.A. (1970) *The Conquest of Violence*, London: Constable.

Critchley, T.A. (1978) *A History of Police in England and Wales*, London: Constable (1st edn, 1967).

Cumming, E., I. Cumming and L. Edell (1964) 'The policeman as philosopher, guide and friend', *Social Problems*, 12:3.

Currie, C. (1986) 'Divisional command', *Policing*, 2:4.

Dahrendorf, R. (1985) *Law and Order*, London: Sweet & Maxwell.

Darbyshire, N. (1988) 'No hiding place at the Yard', *Daily Telegraph*, 30 July, p. 9.

Davey, B.J. (1983) *Lawless and Immoral: Policing a country town 1838–57*, Leicester: Leicester University Press/New York: St Martin's Press.

David, M.E. (1977) *Reform, Reaction and Resources*, London: NFER.

Davies, J. (1990) *Youth and the Condition of Britain*, London: Athlone.

Davis, J. (1980) 'The London garotting panic of 1862', in V. Gatrell, G. Parker and B. Lenman (eds) *Crime and the Law*, London: Europa.

Davis, J. (1984): 'A poor man's system of justice: the London police courts in the second half of the nineteenth century', *The Historical Journal*, 27:2.

Davis, K. (1969) *Discretionary Justice*, Urbana, Ill.: University of Illinois.

Davis, K. (1975) *Police Discretion*, St Paul, Minn.: West.

Day, P. and R. Klein (1987): *Accountabilities*, London: Tavistock.

Dean, M. (1982) 'The finger on the policeman's collar', *Political Quarterly*, 53:2.

Ditton, J. and J. Duffy (1983) 'Bias in the newspaper reporting of crime news', *British Journal of Criminology*, 23:2, April.

Dixon, D. (1990) 'Consent and the legal regulation of policing', *Journal of Law and Society*, 17:3.

Dixon, D., A.K. Bottomley, C.A. Coleman, M. Gill and D. Wall (1989) 'Reality and rules in the construction and regulation of police suspicion', *International Journal of the Sociology of Law*, 17.

Dixon, D., A.K. Bottomley, C.A. Coleman, M. Gill and D. Wall (1990) 'Safeguarding the rights of suspects in police custody', *Policing and Society*, 1:2.

Dominick, J. (1978) 'Crime and law enforcement in the mass media', in C. Winick (ed.) *Deviance and Mass Media*, Beverly Hills: Sage.

Donajgrodski, A.P. (ed.) (1977a) *Social Control in Nineteenth Century Britain*, London: Croom Helm.

Donajgrodski, A.P. (1977b) ' "Social police" and the bureaucratic elite', in A.P. Donadjgrodski (ed.) (1977a).

Dorn, N., K. Murji and N. South (1991a) 'Mirroring the market? Police reorganisation and effectiveness against drug trafficking', in R. Reiner and M. Cross (eds) *Beyond Law and Order: Criminal justice policy and politics into the 1990s*, London: Macmillan.

Dorn, N., K. Murji and N. South (1991b) *Traffickers: Drug markets and law enforcement*, London: Routledge.

Dove, G. (1982) *The Police Procedural*, Bowling Green, Ohio: Bowling Green Popular Press.

Dove, G. and E.F. Bargainnier (eds) (1986) *Cops and Constables: American and British fictional policemen*, Bowling Green, Ohio: Bowling Green Popular Press.

Downes, D. and T. Ward (1986) *Democratic Policing*, London: Labour Campaign For Criminal Justice.

Dummett, M. (Chairman) (1980a) *Southall 23 April 1979*, London: NCCL.

Dummett, M. (Chairman) (1980b) *The Death of Blair Peach*, London: NCCL.

Dunne, J.G. (1991) 'Law and disorder in Los Angeles', *New York Review of Books*, XXXVIII: 15 and 17.

Edwards, S. (1989) *Policing 'Domestic' Violence*, London: Sage.

Ehrlich, S. (1980) *Breaking and Entering: Police women on patrol*, Berkeley: University of California Press.

Ekblom, P. and K. Heal (1982) *The Police Response to Calls from the Public*, Research and Planning Unit Paper 9, London: Home Office.

Emsley, C. (1983) *Policing and its Context 1750–1870*, London: Macmillan.

Emsley, C. (1987) *Crime and Society in England 1750–1900*, London: Longman.

Emsley, C. (1991) *The English Police: A political and social history*, Hemel Hempstead: Harvester Wheatsheaf.

Ericson, R. (1981) *Making Crime: A study of detective work*, Toronto: Butterworth.

Ericson, R. (1982) *Reproducing Order: A study of police patrol work*, Toronto: University of Toronto Press.

Ericson, R. (1991) 'Mass media, crime, law and justice: an institutional approach', *British Journal of Criminology*, 31:3.

Ericson, R., P. Baranek and J. Chan (1987) *Visualising Deviance: A study of news organisation*, Milton Keynes: Open University Press.

Ericson, R., P. Baranek and J. Chan (1989) *Negotiating Control: A study of news sources*, Milton Keynes: Open University Press.

Ericson, R., P. Baranek and J. Chan (1991) *Representing Crime: Crime, law and justice in the news media*, Milton Keynes: Open University Press.

Evans, P. (1974) *The Police Revolution*, London: Allen & Unwin.

Everson, W. (1972) *The Detective in Film*, New York: Citadel.

Farrington, D. and E. Dowds (1985) 'Disentangling Criminal Behaviour and Police Reaction' in Farrington, D. and Gunn, J. (eds) *Reactions To Crime: The public, the police, courts and prisons*, Winchester: Wiley.

Farrington, D., B. Gallagher, L. Morley, R.J. St Ledger and D.J. West (1986) 'Unemployment, school leaving and crime', *British Journal of Criminology*, 26:4.

Feldman, D. (1990) 'Regulating treatment of suspects in police stations: judicial interpretations of detention provisions in the Police and Criminal Evidence Act 1984', *Criminal Law Review*.

Ferdinand, T. and E. Luchterhand (1970) 'Inner city youths, the police and justice', *Social Problems*, 17, Spring.

Field, J. (1981) 'Police, power and community in a provincial English town: Portsmouth 1815–75', in V. Bailey (ed.) *Policing and Punishment in Nineteenth Century Britain*, London: Croom Helm.

Field, S. (1990) *Trends in Crime and Their Interpretation: A study of recorded crime in post-war England and Wales* (Home Office Research Study 119), London: HMSO.

Field, S. and P. Southgate (1982) *Public Disorder*, London: Home Office Research Unit.

Fielding, N. (1981) 'The credibility of accountability', *Poly Law Review*, 6:2, Spring.

Fielding, N. (1984) 'Police socialisation and police competence', *British Journal of Sociology*, 35:4.

Fielding, N. (1988) *Joining Forces*, London: Routledge.

Fielding, N. (1989) 'Police culture and police practice' in M. Weatheritt (ed.) *Police Research: Some future prospects*, Aldershot: Avebury.

Fielding, N. (1991) *The Police and Social Conflict*, London: Athlone.

Fielding, N. and J. Fielding (1992) 'A comparative minority: female recruits to a British constabulary force', *Policing and Society*, 2:3.

Fielding, N., C. Kemp and C. Norris (1989) 'Constraints on the practice of community policing', in R. Morgan and D. Smith (eds) *Coming to Terms with Policing*, London: Routledge.

Fine, B. and R. Millar (1985) (eds) *Policing the Miners' Strike*, London: Lawrence & Wishart.

Fisher, C. and R. Mawby (1982) 'Juvenile delinquency and police discretion in an inner-city area', *British Journal of Criminology*, 22:1, January.

Fisher, Sir H. (1977) *The Confait Case: Report*, London: HMSO.

Fiske, J. and J. Hartley (1978) *Reading Television*, London: Methuen.

Fitzgerald, M., G. McLennan and J. Sim (1981) *Intervention, Regulation and Surveillance* ('Issues in Crime and Society', Block 2:3), Milton Keynes: Open University.

Fogelson, R. (1977) *Big-City Police*, Cambridge, Mass.: Harvard University Press.

Forrester, D., M. Chatterton and K. Pease (1988) *The Kirkholt Burglary Prevention Project* (Crime Prevention Unit Paper 13), London: Home Office.

Foster, J. (1974) *Class Struggle in the Industrial Revolution*, London: Methuen.

Foster, J. (1989) 'Two stations: an ethnographic study of policing in the inner city', in D. Downes (ed.) *Crime and the City*, London: Macmillan.

Foucault, M. (1977) *Discipline and Punish*, Harmondsworth: Penguin/New York: Pantheon.

France, A. (1894) *Le Lys Rouge*, Paris.

Franey, R. (1983) *Poor Law*, London: Campaign for Homeless People,

Child Poverty Action Group, Claimants' Defence Committee, National Association of Probation Officers, National Council for Civil Liberties.

Freeman, M. (1981) 'Controlling police discretion', *Poly Law Review*, 6:2, Spring.

Freeman, M. (1984) 'Law and order in 1984', *Current Legal Problems 1984*.

Freeman, M. (1985) *The Police and Criminal Evidence Act 1984*, London: Sweet & Maxwell.

Friedrich, R. (1979) 'Racial prejudice and police treatment of blacks', in R. Baker and F.A. Meyer Jr (eds) *Evaluating Alternative Law Enforcement Policies*, Lexington, Mass.: Lexington.

Fyfe, J. (1981) 'Race and extreme police–citizen violence', in R. McNeely and C. Pope (eds) *Race, Crime and Criminal Justice*, Beverly Hills: Sage.

Garofalo, J. (1981) 'Crime and the mass media: a selective review of research', *Journal of Research in Crime and Delinquency*, 18:2, July.

Garrison, J. (1984) 'Greenboro and after', *New Society*, 9 August.

Gash, N. (1961) *Mr Secretary Peel*, London: Longman.

Gatrell, V. (1980) 'The decline of theft and violence in Victorian and Edwardian England', in V. Gatrell, B. Lenman and G. Parker (eds) *Crime and the Law*, London: Europa.

Gatrell, V. (1988) 'Crime, authority and the policeman–state 1750–1950', in F.M. Thompson (ed.) *The Cambridge Social History of Britain*, Cambridge: Cambridge University Press.

Gatrell, V. and T. Hadden (1972) 'Nineteenth-century criminal statistics and their interpretation', in E. Wrigley (ed.) *Nineteenth Century Society*, Cambridge: Cambridge University Press.

Geary, R. (1985) *Policing Industrial Disputes*, Cambridge: Cambridge University Press.

Geller, W. (1983) 'Deadly force: what we know', in C. Klockars (ed.), *Thinking About Police*, New York: McGraw Hill.

Gifford, Lord (1986) *The Broadwater Farm Inquiry*, London: Broadwater Farm Inquiry.

Gill, P. (1987) 'Clearing up crime: the big "con"', *Journal of Law and Society*, 14:2.

Gill, M. and R. Mawby (1990) *A Special Constable*, Aldershot: Avebury.

Gilroy, P. (1982) 'The myth of black criminality', in M. Eve and D. Musson (eds) *Socialist Register 1982*, London: Merlin.

Gilroy, P. (1983) 'Police and thieves', in Centre for Research on Contemporary Cultural Studies, *The Empire Strikes Back*, London: Hutchinson.

Gilroy, P. (1987) *There Ain't No Black in the Union Jack*, London: Hutchinson.

Goldsmith, A. (1990) 'Taking police culture seriously: police discretion and the limits of law', *Policing and Society*, 1:2.

Goldsmith, A. (ed) (1991) *Complaints Against the Police: The trend to external review*, Oxford: Oxford University Press.

Goldstein, H. (1977) *Policing a Free Society*, Cambridge, Mass,: Ballinger.

Goldstein, H. (1990) *Problem-Oriented Policing*, New York: McGraw Hill.

Goldstein, J. (1960) 'Police discretion not to invoke the criminal process: low-visibility decisions in the administration of justice', *Yale Law Journal*, 69.

Goldthorpe, J., C. Llewellyn and C. Payne (1980) *Social Mobility and Class Structure in Modern Britain*, Oxford: Oxford University Press.

Gordon, P. (1983) *White Law*, London: Pluto.

Gordon, P. (1984) 'Community policing: towards the local police state', *Critical Social Policy*, 10, Summer.

Gorer, G. (1955) *Exploring English Character*, London: Cresset.

Gouldner, A. (1968) 'The sociologist as partisan', *The American Sociologist*, May.

Graber, D.A. (1980) *Crime News and the Public*, New York: Praeger.

Graef, R. (1989) *Talking Blues*, London: Collins.

Grant, L. (1992) 'Not one of the boys in blue', *The Independent on Sunday*, 26 January, p. 20.

Green, P. (1991) *The Enemy Without: Policing and class consciousness in the miners' strike*, Milton Keynes: Open University Press.

Greenberg, D. (ed.) (1981) *Crime and Capitalism*, Palo Alto, Calif.: Mayfield.

Greene, J.R. and S.D. Mastrofski (eds) (1988) *Community Policing: Rhetoric or reality?*, New York: Praeger.

Greenwood, P., J. Chaiken and J. Petersilia (1977) *The Criminal Investigation Process*, Lexington, Mass.: D.C. Heath.

Greer, S. (1987) 'The rise and fall of the Northern Ireland supergrass system', *Criminal Law Review*.

Greer, S. and R. Morgan (eds) (1990) *The Right to Silence Debate*, Bristol University: Centre for Criminal Justice.

Gregory, F. (1985) 'The British police system', in J. Roach and J. Thomaneck (eds) *Police and Public Order in Europe*, London: Croom Helm.

Grella, G. (1970) 'Murder and manners: the formal detective story', *Novel*, 4:1.

Griffith, J. (1977) *The Politics of the Judiciary*, London: Fontana.

Grigg, M. (1965) *The Challenor Case*, Harmondsworth: Penguin.

Grimshaw, R. and T. Jefferson (1987) *Interpreting Policework*, London: Unwin.

Gross, B. (1982) 'Some anti-crime proposals for progressives', *Crime and Social Justice*, 17, Summer.

Gutzmore, C. (1983) 'Capital, "black-youth" and crime', *Race and Class*, 25:2, Autumn.

Hain, P. (ed.) (1979) *Policing the Police*, London: Calder.

Hain, P. (ed.) (1980) *Policing the Police 2*, London: Calder.

Hain, P. (1984) *Political Trials in Britain*, Harmondsworth: Penguin.

Hall, S. (1973) 'The determination of news photographs', in S. Cohen and Y. Young (eds) *The Manufacture of News*, London: Constable.

Hall, S. (1979) *Drifting into a Law and Order Society*, London: Cobden Trust.

Hall, S., C. Critcher, T. Jefferson, J. Clarke and B. Roberts (1978) *Policing the Crisis*, London, Macmillan.

Halloran, J., P. Elliott and G. Murdock (1970) *Demonstrations and Communication*, Harmondsworth: Penguin.

Halpern, S. (1974) *Police Association and Department Leaders*, Lexington, Mass.: D.C. Heath.

Hanmer, J. R. Radford and E.A. Stanko (eds) (1989) *Women, Policing and Male Violence*, London: Routledge.

Harring, S. (1983) *Policing a Class Society*, New Brunswick, N.J.: Rutgers University Press.

Harris, T.J. (1987) *Courtroom's Finest Hour in American Cinema*, Metuchen, N.J.: Scarecrow Press.

Hart, J. (1951) *The British Police*, London: Allen & Unwin.

Hart, J. (1955) 'Reform of the borough police 1835–56', *English Historical Review*, 70.

Hart, J. (1956) 'The County and Borough Police Act 1856', *Public Administration*, 34.

Hart, J. (1978) 'Police', in W. Cornish (ed.) *Crime and Law*, Dublin: Irish University Press.

Harvey, L., P. Grimshaw and K. Pease, (1989) 'Crime prevention delivery: the work of crime prevention officers', in R. Morgan and D. Smith (eds) *Coming to Terms with Policing*, London: Routledge.

Hauge, R. (1965) 'Crime and the press', in N. Christie (ed.) *Scandinavian Studies in Criminology 1*, London: Tavistock.

Hay, D. (ed.) (1975a) *Albion's Fatal Tree*, Harmondsworth: Penguin.

Hay, D. (1975b) 'Property, authority and the criminal law', in D. Hay (1975a).

Hay, D. (1980) 'Crime and justice in eighteenth and nineteenth century England', in N. Morris and M. Tonry (eds) *Crime and Justice 2*, Chicago: Chicago University Press.

Hay, D. and F. Snyder (eds) (1989) *Policing and Prosecution in Britain 1750–1850*, Oxford: Oxford University Press.

Haycraft, H. (1941) *Murder for Pleasure*, New York: Appleton, Century.

Haycraft, H. (ed.) (1946) *The Art of the Mystery Story*, New York: Grosset & Dunlap.

Heal, K., R. Tarling and J. Burrows (eds) (1985) *Policing Today*, London: HMSO.

Heidensohn, R. (1989) *Women in Policing in the USA*, London: The Police Foundation.

Heidensohn, F. (1992) *Women in Control? The role of women in law enforcement*, Oxford: Oxford University Press.

Hewitt, P. (1982) *The Abuse of Power*, Oxford: Martin Robertson.

Hillyard, P. (1981) 'From Belfast to Britain', in *Politics and Power 4: Law, Politics and Justice*, London: Routledge.

Hillyard, P. (1982) 'The media coverage of crime and justice in Northern Ireland', in C. Sumner (ed.) *Crime, Justice and the Mass Media* (Cropwood Papers 14), Cambridge: Institute of Criminology.

Hirst, M. (1991) 'What do we mean by quality?', *Policing*, 7:3.

Hirst, P.Q. (1975) 'Marx and Engels on law, crime and morality', in I. Taylor, P. Walton and J. Young (eds) *Critical Criminology*, London: Routledge. (Reprinted from *Economy and Society*, 1973.)

Hirst, P.Q. (1979) 'Law, socialism and rights', in P. Carlen and M. Collinson (eds) *Radical Issues in Criminology*, Oxford: Martin Robertson.

Hobbs, D. (1988) *Doing the Business: Entrepreneurship, the working class and detectives in the East End of London*, Oxford: Oxford University Press.

Hobsbawm, E. (1959) *Primitive Rebels*, Manchester: Manchester University Press.

Hobsbawm, E. (1964) *Labouring Men*, London: Weidenfeld & Nicolson.

Hobsbawm, E. (1968) *Industry and Empire*, London: Penguin.

Hobsbawm, E. (1969) *Bandits*, London: Penguin Books.

Hobsbawm, E. and G. Rude (1969) *Captain Swing*, London: Penguin.

Holdaway, S. (1977) 'Changes in urban policing', *British Journal of Sociology*, 28:2.

Holdaway, S, (ed.) (1979) *The British Police*, London: Edward Arnold.

Holdaway, S. (1983) *Inside the British Police*, Oxford: Basil Blackwell.

Holdaway, S. (1986) 'The Holloway incident', *Policing*, 2:2.

300   *References*

Holdaway, S. (1989) 'Discovering structure: studies of the British police occupational culture', in M. Weatheritt (ed.) *Police Research: Some future prospects*, Aldershot: Avebury.

Holdaway, S. (1991) *Recruiting a Multi-Ethnic Police Force*, London: HMSO.

Holdaway, S., C. Spencer and D. Wilson (1984) 'Black police in the UK' *Policing*, 1:1.

Horton, C. (1989) 'Good practice and evaluative policing', in R. Morgan and D. Smith (eds) *Coming To Terms With Policing*, London: Routledge.

Horton, C. and D. Smith (1988) *Evaluating Police Work*, London: Policy Studies Institute.

Hough, M. (1980) *Uniformed Police Work and Management Technology*, London: Home Office Research Unit.

Hough, M. (1987) 'Thinking about effectiveness', *British Journal of Criminology*, 27:1.

Hough, M. (1989) 'Demand for policing and police performance: progress and pitfalls in public surveys' in M. Weatheritt (ed.) *Police Research: Some future prospects*, Aldershot: Avebury.

Hough, M. and P. Mayhew (1983) *The British Crime Survey*, London: Home Office Research Unit.

Hough, M. and P. Mayhew (1985) *Taking Account of Crime: Key findings from the second British crime survey*, London: HMSO.

Hughes, E.C. (1961) 'Good people and dirty work', *Social Problems* 10:1.

Humphry, D. (1979) 'The complaints system', in P. Hain (ed.) *Policing the Police 1*, London: Calder.

Hurd, G. (1979) 'The television presentation of the police', in S. Holdaway (ed.) *The British Police*, London: Edward Arnold.

Ianni, E.R. and R. Ianni (1983) 'Street cops and management cops: the two cultures of policing', in M. Punch (ed.) *Control in the Police Organization*, Cambridge, Mass.: MIT Press.

Ignatieff, M. (1978) *A Just Measure of Pain*, London: Macmillan.

Ignatieff. M. (1979) 'Police and people: the birth of Mr. Peel's blue locusts', *New Society*, 49.

Ignatieff, M. (1983) 'State, civil society and total institutions', in S. Cohen and A. Scull (eds) *Social Control and the State*, Oxford: Martin Robertson. (Originally in M. Tonry and N. Morris (eds) *Crime and Justice*, 3, Chicago: Chicago University Press, 1981.)

Imbert, P. (1989) 'Glasnost at the Yard', *Police Review*, 1 December.

Inciardi, J. and J.L. Dee (1987) 'From the Keystone Cops to Miami Vice: images of policing in American popular culture', *Journal of Popular Culture*, 21:2.

Irving, B. and I. McKenzie (1989a) *Police Interrogation*, London: Police Foundation.

Irving, B. and I. McKenzie (1989b) 'Interrogating in a legal framework', in R. Morgan and D. Smith (eds) *Coming to terms with policing*, London: Routledge.

Irving, B., C. Bird, M. Hibberd and J. Willmore (1989) *Neighbourhood Policing: The natural history of a policing experiment*, London: Police Foundation.

Jacob, H. and M. Rich (1980) 'The effects of the police on crime: a second look', *Law and Society Review*, 15:1.

Jacob, H. and M. Rich (1981) 'The effects of the police on crime: a rejoinder', *Law and Society Review*, 16:1.

Jacobs, J. and J. Cohen (1978) 'The impact of racial integration on the police', *Journal of Police Science and Administration*, 6:2.

Jacobs, J. and S. Magdovitz (1977) 'At LEEP's end? A review of the Law Enforcement Education Programme', *Journal of Police Science and Administration*, 5:1.

Jacobs, P. (1966) *Prelude to Riot*, New York: Vintage.

Jefferson, T. (1987) 'Beyond paramilitarism', *British Journal of Criminology*, 27:1.

Jefferson, T. (1988) 'Race, crime and policing: empirical, theoretical and methodological issues', *International Journal of the Sociology of Law*, 16:4.

Jefferson, T. (1990) *The Case Against Paramilitary Policing*, Milton Keynes: Open University Press.

Jefferson, T. and R. Grimshaw (1982) 'Law, democracy and justice', in D. Cowell, T. Jones and J. Young (eds) *Policing in Riots*, London: Junction Books.

Jefferson, T. and R. Grimshaw (1984a) 'The problem of law enforcement policy in England and Wales: the case of community policing and racial attacks', *International Journal of Sociology of Law*, 12, May.

Jefferson, T. and R. Grimshaw (1984b) *Controlling the Constable: Police accountability in England and Wales*, London: Muller.

Jefferson, T., E. McLaughlin and L. Robertson (1988) 'Monitoring the monitors: accountability, democracy and police watching in Britain', *Contemporary Crises*, 12:2.

Jeffery, K. and P. Hennessy (1983) *States of Emergency*, London: Routledge.

Johnson, B. (1976) 'Taking care of labour', *Theory and Society*, 3:1.

Johnston, L. (1987) 'Controlling the police', *Review* 3:1.

Johnston, L. (1988) 'Controlling policework: problems of organisational reform in large public bureaucracies', *Work, Employment and Society*, 2:1.

Johnston, L. (1991) 'Privatisation and the police function: from "new police" to "new policing"', in R. Reiner and M. Cross (eds) *Beyond Law Order: Criminal justice policy and politics into the 1990s*, London: Macmillan.

Johnston, L. (1992) *The Rebirth of Private Policing*, London: Routledge.

Jones, D. (1982) *Crime, Protest, Community and Police in Nineteenth Century Britain*, London: Routledge.

Jones, D. (1983) 'The new police, crime and people in England and Wales 1829–88', *Transactions of the Royal Historical Society*, 33.

Jones, M. (1980) *Organisational Aspects of Police Behaviour*, Farnborough: Gower.

Jones, M. and J. Winkler (1982) 'Policing in a riotous city', *Journal of Law and Society*, 9:1, Summer.

Jones, P. (1981) 'Police powers and political accountability', in *Politics and Power 4: Law, Politics and Justice*, London: Routledge.

Jones, S. (1983) 'Community policing in Devon and Cornwall', in T. Bennett (ed.) *The Future of Policing* (Cropwood Papers 15), Cambridge: Institute of Criminology.

Jones, S. (1986) 'Caught in the act', *Policing*, 2:2.

Jones, S. (1987) *Policewomen and Equality*, London: Macmillan.

Jones, S. and M. Levi (1983) 'The police and the majority: the neglect of the obvious', *Police Journal*, LVI:4.

Jones, S. and E. Silverman (1984) 'What price efficiency?' *Policing*, 1:1.

Jones, T., B. McLean and J. Young (1986): *The Islington Crime Survey*, Aldershot: Gower.

Jordan, P. (1991) 'The Home Office Treasury study: the development of police management information systems', *Research Bulletin 31*, London: Home Office.

Joshua, H., T. Wallace and H. Booth (1983) *To Ride the Storm: The 1980 Bristol 'riot' and the state*, London: Heinemann.

Judge, A. (1972) *A Man Apart*, London: Barker.

Judge, A. (1983) 'A small gale in Fleet Street', *Police*, May, pp. 12–14.

Kahn, P., N. Lewis, P. Livock and P. Wiles (1983) *Picketing*, London: Routledge.

Kelling, G. (1983) 'On the accomplishments of the police', in M. Punch (ed.) *Control in the Police Organization*, Cambridge, Mass.: MIT Press.

Kelling, G., T. Pate, D. Dieckman and G. Brown (1974) *The Kansas City Preventive Patrol Experiment*, Washington, D.C.: Police Foundation.

Kemp, C. and R. Morgan (1989): *Behind the Front Counter: Lay visitors to police stations*, Bristol University: Centre for Criminal Justice.

Kerr, P. (1981) 'Watching the detectives', *Prime-Time*, 1:1, July.

Kettle, M. (1980) 'The politics of policing and the policing of politics', in P. Hain (ed.) *Policing the Police 2*, London: Calder.

Kettle, M. (1981a) 'A conflict of evidence', *New Society*, 1 January.

Kettle, M. (1981b) 'Controlling the police', *New Society*, 8 January.

Kettle, M. and L. Hodges (1982) *Uprising! The police, the people and the riots in Britain's cities*, London: Pan.

King, P. (1984) 'Decision-makers and decision-making in the English criminal law 1750–1800', *Historical Journal*, 27:1.

Kinsey, R. and R. Baldwin (1982) *Police Powers and Politics*, London: Quartet.

Kinsey, R., J. Lea and J. Young (1986) *Losing the Fight Against Crime*, Oxford: Blackwell.

Klockars, C. (1980) 'The Dirty Harry problem', *The Annals, 452*, November. (Reprinted in Klockars, 1983.)

Klockars, C. (ed.) (1983) *Thinking About Police*, New York: McGraw-Hill.

Klockars, C. (1985): *The Idea of Police*, Beverly Hills: Sage.

Klug, F. (1982) *Racist Attacks*, London: Runnymede Trust.

Knafla, L.A. (ed.) (1990) *Crime, Police and the Courts in British History*, London: Meckler.

Knight, S. (1980) *Form and Ideology in Crime Fiction*, London: Macmillan.

Lacey, N., C. Wells and D. Meure (1990) *Reconstructing Criminal Law*, London: Weidenfeld & Nicolson.

La Fave, W. (1962) 'The police and non-enforcement of the law', *Wisconsin Law Review*, January and March.

La Fave, W. (1965) *Arrest*, Boston, Mass.: Little, Brown.

Lambert, J. (1970) *Crime, Police and Race Relations*, Oxford: Oxford University Press.

Lambert, J. (1986) *Police Powers and Accountability*, London: Croom Helm.

Landau, S. (1981) 'Juveniles and the police', *British Journal of Criminology*, 21:1, January.

Landau, S. and G. Nathan (1983) 'Selecting delinquents for cautioning in the London metropolitan area', *British Journal of Criminology*, 23:2, April.

Langbein, J. (1983) 'Albion's fatal flaws', *Past and Present*, 98.

Larson, R. (1976) 'What happened to patrol operations in Kansas City?', *Journal of Criminal Justice*, 3:4.

Laurie, P. (1970) *Scotland Yard*, London: Penguin.

Lea, J. (1986) 'Police racism: some theories and their policy implications', in R. Matthews and J. Young (eds) *Confronting Crime*, London: Sage.

Lea, J. and J. Young (1982) 'The riots in Britain 1981', in D. Cowell, T. Jones and J. Young (eds) *Policing the Riots*, London: Junction Books.

Lea, J. and J. Young (1984) *What is to be done about law and order?*, Harmondsworth: Penguin.

Lee, J.A. (1981) 'Some structural aspects of police deviance in relations with minority groups', in C. Shearing (ed.) *Organisational Police Deviance*, Toronto: Butterworth.

Lee, M. (1901) *A History of Police in England*, London: Methuen.

Leigh, L. (1977) 'The Police Act 1976', *British Journal of Law and Society*, 4:1, Summer.

Leigh, L. (1981) 'The Royal Commission on Criminal Procedure', *Modern Law Review*, May.

Leigh, L. (1985) *Police Powers in England and Wales*, 2nd edn, London: Butterworth.

Leigh, L. (1986) 'Some observations on the parliamentary history of the Police and Criminal Evidence Act 1984', in C. Harlow (ed.) *Public Law and Politics*, London: Sweet & Maxwell.

Leon, C. (1989) 'The special constabulary', *Policing*, 5:4.

Leon, C. (1990) 'The special constabulary: an historical view', *Journal of the Police History Society*, 5.

Leon, C. (1991) 'A study of the special constabulary', Ph.D. thesis, School of Humanities and Social Science, Bath University.

Levi, M. (1977) *Bureaucratic Insurgency*, Lexington, Mass.: D.C. Heath.

Levi, M. (1987) *Regulating Fraud*, London: Tavistock.

Lidstone, K. (1981) 'Investigative powers and the rights of the citizen', *Criminal Law Review*, July.

Lidstone, K. (1984) 'Magistrates, the police and search warrants', *Criminal Law Review*, August.

Linebaugh, P. (1991): *The London Hanged: Crime and civil society in the eighteenth century*, London: Allen Lane.

Lipset, S.M. (1969) 'Why cops hate liberals, and vice versa', *Atlantic Monthly*. (Reprinted in W. Bopp (ed.) *The Police Rebellion*, Springfield, Ill.: C.C. Thomas, 1971.)

Loveday, B. (1983) 'The role of the police committee', *Local Government Studies*, January/February.

Loveday, B. (1984) 'The role of the police committee: constitutional arrangements and social realities, a reply to Dr Waddington', *Local Government Studies*, September/October.

Loveday, B. (1985) *The Role and Effectiveness of the Merseyside Police Committee*, Liverpool: Merseyside County Council.

Loveday, B. (1987) 'The joint boards', *Policing*, 3:3.

Loveday, B. (1988) 'Police complaints in the USA', *Policing*, 4:3.

Loveday, B. (1991) 'The new police authorities', *Policing and Society*, 1:3.

Lundman, R. (1974) 'Routine police arrest practices', *Social Problems*, 22. (Reprinted in Lundman (ed.) 1980.)

Lundman, R. (1979) 'Police work with traffic law violators', *Criminology*, 17. (Reprinted in Lundman (ed.), 1980.)

Lundman, R. (ed.) (1980) *Police Behaviour*, New York: Oxford University Press.

Lundman, R., R. Sykes and J.P. Clark (1978) 'Police control of juveniles', *Journal of Research in Crime and Delinquency*, 15. (Reprinted in Lundman (ed.) 1980.)

Lustgarten, L. (1982) 'Beyond Scarman: police accountability in Britain', in N. Glazer and K. Young (eds) *Ethnic Pluralism and Public Policy*, London: Heinemann.

Lustgarten, L. (1986) *The Governance of the Police*, London: Sweet & Maxwell.

McBarnet, D. (1976) 'Pre-trial procedures and the construction of conviction', in P. Carlen (ed.) *Sociological Review Monograph: The sociology of law*, Keele: Keele University.

McBarnet, D. (1978a) 'The police and the state', in G. Littlejohn, B. Smart, J. Wakeford and N. Yuval-Davis (eds) *Power and the State*, London: Croom Helm.

McBarnet, D. (1978b) 'False dichotomies in criminal justice research', in J. Baldwin and A.K. Bottomley (eds) *Criminal Justice*, Oxford: Martin Robertson.

McBarnet, D. (1979) 'Arrest: the legal context of policing', in S. Holdaway (ed.) *The British Police*, London: Edward Arnold.

McBarnet, D. (1981a) *Conviction*, London: Macmillan.

McBarnet, D. (1981b) 'Balance and clarity: has the Royal Commission achieved them?', *Criminal Law Review*, July.

McBarnet, D. (1981c) 'The Royal Commission and the Judges' Rules', *British Journal of Law and Society*, 8:1, Summer.

McBarnet, D. (1982) 'Legal form and legal mystification', *International Journal of the Sociology of Law*, 10.

McCabe, S. and F. Sutcliffe (1978) *Defining Crime*, Oxford: Basil Blackwell.

McCabe, S., P. Wallington, J. Alderson, L. Gostin and C. Mason (1988) *The Police, Public Order and Civil Liberties*, London: Routledge.

McCarthur, C. (1972) *Underworld USA*, London: Secker & Warburg.

McConville, M. (1983) 'Search of persons and premises: new data from London', *Criminal Law Review*.

McConville, M. and J. Baldwin (1981) *Courts, Prosecution and Conviction*, Oxford: Oxford University Press.

McConville, M. and P. Morrell (1983) 'Recording the interrogation: have the police got it taped?', *Criminal Law Review*.

McConville, M., A. Sanders and R. Leng (1991) *The Case for the Prosecution: Police suspects and the construction of criminality*, London: Routledge.

MacDonald, I. (1973) 'The creation of the British police', *Race Today*, 5:11, December.

McDonald, L. (1976) *The Sociology of Law and Order*, London: Faber.

Mack, J. (1976) 'Full-time major criminals and the courts', *Modern Law Review*, 39.

McKenzie, I. and P. Gallagher (1989) *Behind the Uniform*, Hemel Hempstead: Harvester Wheatsheaf.

McKenzie, I. and B. Irving (1988) 'The right to silence', *Policing*, 4:2.

McKenzie, I., R. Morgan and R. Reiner (1990) 'Helping the police with their inquiries: the necessity principle and voluntary attendance at the police station', *Criminal Law Review*.

McLaughlin, E. (1990) 'Community, policing and accountability: a case study of Manchester 1981–88', Ph.D. thesis, Faculty of Law, University of Sheffield.

McMahon, M. and R. Ericson (1984) *Policing Reform*, University of Toronto: Centre of Criminology.

McNee, D. (1979) 'The queen's police keepeth the peace', *The Guardian*, 25 September, p. 25.

McNee, D. (1983) *MeNee's Law*, London: Collins.

Maguire, M. (1988) 'Effects of the "PACE" Provisions On Detention and Questioning', *British Journal of Criminology* 28:1.

Maguire, M. (1991) 'Complaints against the police: the British experience', in A. Goldsmith (ed.) *Complaints Against the Police: The trend to external review*, Oxford: Oxford University Press.

Maguire, M. and C. Corbett (1989) 'Patterns and profiles of complaints against the police', in R. Morgan and D. Smith (eds) *Coming To Terms With Policing*, London: Routledge.

Maguire, M. and C. Corbett (1991) *A Study of the Police Complaints System*, London: HMSO.

Maitland, R. (1885) *Justice and Police*, London: Macmillan.

Mandel, E. (1984) *Delightful Murder*, London: Pluto Press.

Manning, P. (1977) *Police Work*, Cambridge, Mass.: MIT Press.

Manning, P. (1979) 'The social control of police work', in S. Holdaway (ed.) *The British Police*, London: Edward Arnold.

Manning, P. and J. Redlinger (1977) 'Invitational edges of corruption', in P. Rock (ed.) *Politics and Drugs*, Rutgers, N.J.: Dutton. (Reprinted in Klockars (ed.), 1983.)

Manning, P. and J. Van Maanen (eds) (1978) *Policing: a view from the street*, Santa Monica, Calif.: Goodyear.

Manwaring-White, S. (1983) *The Policing Revolution*, Hemel Hempstead: Harvester Wheatsheaf.

Marenin, O. (1983) 'Parking tickets and class repression: the concept of policing in critical theories of criminal justice', *Contemporary Crises*, 6:2.

Marenin, O. (1985) 'Police performance and state rule', *Comparative Politics*.

Mark, R. (1977) *Policing a Perplexed Society*, London: Allen & Unwin.

Mark, R. (1978) *In the Office of Constable*, London: Collins.

Marshall, G. (1965) *Police and Government*, London: Methuen.

Marshall, G. (1973) 'The government of the police since 1963', in J. Alderson and P. Stead (eds) *The Police we Deserve*, London: Wolfe.

Marshall, G. (1978) 'Police accountability revisited', in D. Butler and A.H. Halsey (eds) *Policy and Politics*, London: Macmillan.

Martin, J.P. and G. Wilson (1969) *The Police: A study in manpower*, London: Heinemann.

Matza, D. (1969) *Becoming Deviant*, Englewood Cliffs, N.J.: Prentice Hall.

Mawby, R. (1979) *Policing the City*, Farnborough: Gower.

Mawby, R. (1991a) 'Community involvement in criminal justice', in R. Reiner and M. Cross (eds) *Beyond Law and Order: Criminal justice policy and politics into the 1990s*, London: Macmillan.

Mawby, R. (1991b) *Comparative Policing Issues*, London: Unwin.

Mawby, R. and I.D. Batta (1980) *Asians and Crime*, London: National Association for Asian Youth.

Maxfield, M. (1984) *Fear of Crime in England and Wales*, London: Home Office Research Unit.

May, R. (1988) 'Fair play at trial: an interim assessment of s.78 of the Police and Criminal Evidence Act 1984', *Criminal Law Review*.

Mayhew, P., D. Elliott and L. Dowds (1989) *The 1988 British Crime Survey*, Home Office Research Study III, London: HMSO.

Merricks, W. (1981) 'How we drew the thin blue line', *New Statesman*, 9 January.

Meyer, M. (1980) 'Police shootings at minorities: the case of Los Angeles', *The Annals*, 452, November.

Meyers, R. (1981) *TV Detectives*, San Diego, Calif.: Barnes.

Meyers, R. (1989) *Murder on the Air*, New York: The Mysterious Press.

Midwinter, E. (1968) *Law and Order in Early Victorian Lancashire*, York: St Anthony's Press.

Miliband, R. (1978) 'A state of desubordination', *British Journal of Sociology*, 29:4.

Miliband, R. (1982) *Capitalist Democracy in Britain*, Oxford: Oxford University Press.

Miller, D.A. (1981) 'The novel and the police', *Glyph*, 8. (Reprinted in G. Most and W. Stowe (eds) *The Poetics of Murder*, New York: Harcourt, Brace, Jovanovitch, 1983).

Miller, W. (1977) *Cops and Bobbies*, Chicago: Chicago University Press.

Minto, G. (1965) *The Thin Blue Line*, London: Hodder & Stoughton.

Mitchell, B. (1984) 'The role of the public in criminal detection', *Criminal Law Review*, August.

Monkkonen, E. (1981) *Police in Urban America 1860–1920*, Cambridge: Cambridge University Press.

Moore, Jr, B. (1967) *The Social Origins of Dictatorship and Democracy*, London: Penguin/Boston: Beacon.

Moore, C. and J. Brown (1981) *Community versus Crime*, London: Bedford Square Press.

Moore, M. and G. Kelling (1983) ' "To serve and protect": learning from police history', *The Public Interest*, 70, Winter.

Morgan, J. (1987) *Conflict and Order: The police and labour disputes in England and Wales 1900–1939*, Oxford: Oxford University Press.

Morgan, R. (1987) 'Police accountability: developing the local infrastructure', *British Journal of Criminology*, 27:1.

Morgan, R. (1989) 'Policing by consent: legitimating the doctrine', in R. Morgan and D. Smith (eds) *Coming To Terms With Policing*, London: Routledge.

Morgan, R. and C. Maggs (1984) *Following Scarman?*, Bath University: Social Policy Papers.

Morgan, R. and C. Maggs (1985) *Setting the PACE*, Bath University: Social Policy Papers.

Morgan, R. and D. Smith (eds) (1989) *Coming To Terms With Policing*, London: Routledge.

Morgan, R. and P. Swift (1987) 'The future of police authorities: members' views', *Public Administration* 65:3.

Morgan, R., R. Reiner and I. McKenzie (1990) *Police Powers and Policy: A study of custody officers*, Final Report to the Economic and Social Research Council.

Morris, P, and K. Heal (1981) *Crime Control and the Police*, London: Home Office Research Unit.

Morris, T. (1985) 'The case for a riot squad', *New Society*, 29 November.

Morrison, C. (1984) 'Why PC Plod should come off the beat', *The Guardian*, 30 July, p. 8.

Most, G. and W. Stowe (eds) (1983) *The Poetics of Murder*, New York: Harcourt, Brace, Jovanovich.

Muir, Jr, K.W. (1977) *Police: Streetcorner politicians*, Chicago: Chicago University Press.

Mullin, C. (1989) *Error of Judgment: The truth about the Birmingham bombings* London: Chatto & Windus.

Muncie, J. (1984) *'The Trouble with Kids Today'*, London: Hutchinson.

Murdock, G. (1982) 'Disorderly images', in C. Sumner (ed.) *Crime, Justice and the Mass Media* (Cropwood Papers 14), Cambridge: Institute of Criminology.

Murdock, G., P. Schlesinger and H. Tumber (1989) 'The media politics of crime, law and justice', paper presented to the British Criminology Conference, Bristol Polytechnic, 20 July.

Newburn, T., D. Brown, D. Crisp and P. Dewhurst (1991) 'Increasing public order', *Policing*, 7:1.

Newman, G.F. (1982) *Operation Bad Apple*, London: Methuen.

Newman, G.F. (1983) *Law and Order*, London: Granada.

Niederhoffer, A. (1967) *Behind the Shield*, New York: Doubleday.

Niederhoffer, A. and A. Blumberg. (eds) (1976) *The Ambivalent Force*, 2nd edn, Hinsdale, Ill.: Dryden Press.

Norris, C. (1989) 'Avoiding trouble: the police officer's perception of encounters with the public', in M. Weatheritt (ed.) *Police Research: Some future prospects*, Aldershot: Avebury.

Northam, G. (1988) *Shooting in the Dark*, London: Faber.

Oakley, R. (1989) *Employment in Police Forces: a survey of police forces*, London: Commission for Racial Equality.

Oaks, D. (1970) 'Studying the exclusionary rule in search and seizure', *University of Chicago Law Review*, 37, Summer.

Oliver, I. (1987) *Police, Government and Accountability*, London: Macmillan.

Operational Policing Review (1990) Joint Consultative Committee of the Police Staff Associations, Surbiton, Surrey: The Police Federation.

Packer, H. (1968) *The Limits of the Criminal Sanction*, Stanford: Stanford University Press and Oxford University Press.

Palmer, J. (1976) 'Evils merely prohibited', *British Journal of Law and Society*, 3:1, Summer.

Palmer, J. (1978) *Thrillers*, London: Edward Arnold.

Palmer, S.H. (1988) *Police and Protest in England and Ireland 1780–1850*, Cambridge: Cambridge University Press.

Pandiani, J. (1978) 'Crime time TV: if all we knew is what we saw', *Contemporary Crises*, 2.

Park, W. (1978) 'The police state', *Journal of Popular Film*, VI:3.

Parrish, J.R. and M. Pitts (1990a) *The Great Cop Pictures*, Metuchen, N.J.: Scarecrow.

Parrish, J.R. and M. Pitts (1990b) *The Great Detective Pictures*, Metuchen, N.J.: Scarecrow.

Pearson, G. (1983) *Hooligan*, London: Macmillan.

Pearson, G., A. Sampson, H. Blagg, P. Stubbs and D. Smith (1989) 'Policing racism', in R. Morgan and D. Smith (eds) *Coming to Terms with Policing*, London: Routledge.

Percy-Smith, J. and P. Hilliard (1985) 'Miners in the arms of the law: a statistical analysis', *Journal of Law and Society*, 12:3.

Philips, C. (1982) 'Politics in the making of the English police', in *The Home Office*, London: RIPA.

Philips, D. (1977) *Crime and Authority in Victorian England*, London: Croom Helm.

Philips, D. (1980) 'A new engine of power and authority: the institutionalisation of law enforcement in England 1780–1830', in V. Gatrell, B. Lenman and G. Parker (eds) *Crime and the Law*, London: Europa.

Philips, D. (1983) 'A just measure of crime, authority, hunters and blue locusts; the 'revisionist' social history of crime and the law in Britain 1780–1850', in S. Cohen and A. Scull (eds) *Social Control and the State*, Oxford: Martin Robertson.

Pike, M. (1985) *The Principles of Policing*, London: Macmillan.

Piliavin, I. and S. Briar (1964) 'Police encounters with juveniles', *American Journal of Sociology*, 70.

Polanyi, K. (1944) *The Great Transformation*, Boston, Mass.: Beacon.

Policy Studies Institute (PSI) (1983) *Police and People in London*, vol. I, D.J. Smith, 'A survey of Londoners'; vol. II, S. Small, 'A group of young black people'; vol. III, D.J. Smith, 'A survey of police officers'; vol. IV, D.J. Smith and J. Gray, 'The police in action', London: PSI.

Pope, D. and N. Weiner (eds) (1981) *Modern Policing*, London: Croom Helm.

Porter, B. (1987) *The Origins of the Vigilante State*, London: Macmillan.

Porter, D. (1981) *The Pursuit of Crime*, New Haven: Yale University Press.

Powers, R.G. (1983) *G-Men: Hoover's FBI in American popular culture*, Carbondale, Ill.: Southern Illinois University Press.

Powis, D. (1977) *The Signs of Crime*, London: McGraw Hill.

Pratt, M. (1980) *Mugging as a Social Problem*, London: Routledge.

Punch, M. (1979a) *Policing the Inner City*, London: Macmillan.

Punch, M. (1979b) 'The secret social service', in S. Holdaway (ed.) *The British Police*, London: Edward Arnold.

Punch, M. (ed.) (1983a) *Control in the Police Organization*, Cambridge, Mass.: MIT Press.

Punch, M. (1983b) 'Officers and men', in Punch (ed.) (1983a).

Punch, M, (1985) *Conduct Unbecoming: The social construction of police deviance and control*, London: Tavistock.

Punch, M. and T. Naylor (1973) 'The police: a social service', *New Society*, 24.

Radzinowicz, L. (1948–69) *A History of English Criminal Law*, vol I 1948: II 1956; III 1956; IV 1968, London: Stevens.

Radzinowicz, L. and R. Hood (1985) *A History of English Criminal Law*, vol. 5: *The Emergence of Penal Policy*, London: Stevens.

Rawlings, P. (1991) 'Creeping privatisation? The police, the Conservative government and policing in the late 1980s', in R. Reiner and M. Cross (eds) *Beyond Law and Order: Criminal justice policy and politics into the 1990s*, London: Macmillan.

Regan, D. (1983) *Are the Police Under Control?* (Research Reports Paper I), London: Social Affairs Unit.

Reiner, R. (1978a) *The Blue-Coated Worker*, Cambridge: Cambridge University Press.

Reiner, R. (1978b) 'The new blue films', *New Society*, 30 March.

Reiner, R. (1980a) 'Fuzzy thoughts: the police and law and order politics', *Sociological Review*, 28:2, March.

Reiner, R. (1980b) 'Forces of disorder', *New Society*, 10 April.

Reiner, R. (1981a) 'The politics of police power', in *Politics and Power*, vol. 4: *Law, Politics and Justice*, London: Routledge.

Reiner, R. (1981b) 'Black and blue: race and the police', *New Society*, 17 September. (Reprinted in New Society Reader, *Race and Riots '81*.)

Reiner, R. (1981c) 'Keystone to Kojak: the Hollywood cop', in P. Davies and B. Neve (eds) *Politics, Society and Cinema in America*, Manchester: Manchester University Press.

Reiner, R. (1981d) 'A mysterious affair', *New Society*, 7 May.

Reiner, R. (1981e) 'The law-enforcers', *The Movie*, 77, 19 June. (Reprinted in A. Lloyd (ed.) *Movies of the Seventies*, London: Orbis, 1984.)

Reiner, R. (1984) 'Is Britain turning into a police state?', *New Society*, 2 August.

Reiner, R. (1985) 'The police and race relations', in J. Baxter. and L. Koffman (eds) *Police: The constitution and the community*, London: Professional Books.

Reiner, R. (1988a) 'British criminology and the state', *British Journal of Criminology*, 29. (Reprinted as P. Rock, (ed.) *The History of British Criminology*, Oxford: Oxford University Press.)

Reiner, R. (1988b) 'Keeping the Home Office happy', *Policing*, 4:1.

Reiner, R. (1989a) 'Race and criminal justice', *New Community*, 16:1.

Reiner, R. (1989b) 'The politics of police research', in M. Weatheritt (ed.) *Police Research: Some future prospects*, Aldershot: Avebury.

Reiner, R. (1990) 'Crime and Policing', in S. Macgregor and B. Pimlott (eds) *Tackling the Inner Cities*, Oxford: Oxford University Press.

Reiner, R. (1991) *Chief Constables*, Oxford: Oxford University Press.

Reiner, R. (1992a) 'Police research in the United Kingdom: a critical review' in N. Morris and M. Tonry (eds) *Modern Policing*, Chicago: Chicago University Press.

Reiner, R. (1992b) '*Fin de siècle blues*: the police face the millenium', *Political Quarterly*, 63:1.

Reiner, R. and M. Cross (eds) (1991) *Beyond Law and Order: Criminal justice policy and politics into the 1990s*, London: Macmillan.

Reiner, R. and L. Leigh (1992) 'Police power' in G. Chambers. and C. McCrudden (eds) *Individual Rights in the UK Since 1945*, Oxford: Oxford University Press/Law Society.

Reiner, R. and J. Shapland (eds) (1987) 'Why police? Special issue on policing in Britain', *British Journal of Criminology*, 27:1.

Reiss, Jr., A.J. (1968) 'Police brutality', *Trans-action*, 5. (Reprinted in Lundman (ed.), 1980.)

Reiss, Jr., A.J. (1971) *The Police and the Public*, New Haven: Yale University Press.

Reith, C. (1938) *The Police Idea*, Oxford: Oxford University Press.

Reith, C. (1940) *Police Principles and the Problem of War*, Oxford: Oxford University Press.

Reith, C. (1943) *British Police and the Democratic Ideal*, Oxford: Oxford University Press.

Reith, C. (1948) *A Short History of the Police*, Oxford: Oxford University Press.

Reith, C. (1952) *The Blind Eye of History*, London: Faber.

Reith, C. (1956) *A New Study of Police History*, London: Oliver & Boyd.

Reynolds, G. and A. Judge (1968) *The Night the Police Went on Strike*, London: Weidenfeld.

Roberts, B. (1982) 'The debate on "Sus"', in E. Cashmore and B. Troyna (eds) *Black Youth in Crisis*, London: Allen & Unwin.

Roberts, D. (1984) 'Tape-recording the questioning of suspects', *Criminal Law Review*, September.

Roberts, R. (1973) *The Classic Slum*, London: Penguin.

Robinson, C. (1978) 'The deradicalisation of the policeman', *Crime and Delinquency*, 24:2.

Robinson, C. (1979) 'Ideology as history', *Police Studies*, 2:2, Summer.

Robinson, C. and R. Scaglion (1987) 'The origins and evolution of the police function in society: notes towards a theory', *Law and Society Review*, 21:1.

Rock, P. (1973) 'News as eternal recurrence', in S. Cohen and J. Young (eds) *The Manufacture of News*, London: Constable.

Rock, P. (1977) 'Law, order and power in late seventeenth- and early eighteenth-century England', *International Annals of Criminology*, 16. (Reprinted in S. Cohen and A. Scull (eds) 1983.)

Rollo, J. (1980) 'The special patrol group', in P. Hain (ed.) *Policing the Police*, 2, London: Calder.

Rolph, C.H. (ed.) (1962) *The Police and the Public*, London: Heinemann.

Rose, D. (1989) 'An opening at the Met.', *The Guardian*, 8 November, p. 25.

Rose, D. (1990a) 'Forces of change', *The Guardian*, 21 February, p. 23.

Rose, D. (1990b) 'The law faculty', *Weekend Guardian*, 2 June, pp. 4–6.

Roshier, R. (1973) 'The selection of crime news by the press', in S. Cohen and J. Young (eds) *The Manufacture of News*, London: Constable.

Roshier, R. (1989) *Controlling Crime*, Milton Keynes: Open University Press.

Rosow, E. (1978) *Born to Lose*, New York: Oxford University Press.

Rossi, P., R. Berk and B. Eidson (1974) *The Roots of Urban Discontent*, New York: Wiley.

Royal Commission on the Police (1962) *Final Report*, Cmnd 1728, London: HMSO.

Royal Commission on Criminal Procedure (1981) *Report and Law and Procedure*, Cmnd 8092, London: HMSO.

Rubinstein, J. (1973) *City Police*, New York: Ballantine.

Ruchelman, L. (ed.) (1973) *Who Rules the Police?*, New York: New York University Press.

Ruchelman, L. (1974) *Police Politics*, Cambridge, Mass.: Ballinger.

Rude, G. (1964) *The Crowd in History*, New York: Wiley.

Rude, G. (1970) *Paris and London in the Eighteenth Century*, London: Collins.

Ruehlman, W. (1974) *Saint With a Gun*, New York: New York University Press.

St Johnston, E. (1978) *One Policeman's Story*, Chichester: Barry Rose.

Sanders, A. (1988) 'Rights, remedies and the Police and Criminal Evidence Act', *Criminal Law Review*.

Sanders, A. and L. Bridges (1990) 'Access to legal advice and police malpractice', *Criminal Law Review*.

Sanders, A., L. Bridges, A. Mulvaney, B. Crozier (1989) *Advice and*

Assistance at Police Stations and the 24-Hour Duty Solicitor Scheme, London: Lord Chancellor's Department.

Sanders, W. (1977) *Detective Work*, New York: Free Press.

Savage, S. (1984) 'Political control or community liaison?', *Political Quarterly*, 55:1, January–March.

Savage, S. and Wilson, C. (1987) 'Ask a policeman: community consultations in practice', *Social Policy and Administration*, 21:3.

Sayers, D.L. (ed.) (1928) *Tales of Detection*, London: Everyman.

Scarman, Lord (1981) *The Scarman Report: The Brixton disorders*, Cmnd 8427, London: HMSO. (Reprinted by Penguin Harmondsworth, 1982.)

Scraton, P. (1985) *The State of the Police*, London: Pluto.

Scraton, P. (ed.) (1987) *Law, Order and the Authoritarian State*, Milton Keynes: Open University Press.

Shadoian, J. (1977) *Dreams and Dead Ends*, Cambridge, Mass.: MIT Press.

Shapland, J. and D. Hobbs (1989) 'Policing on the ground', in R. Morgan and D. Smith (eds) *Coming to Terms With Policing*, London: Routledge.

Shapland, J. and J. Vagg (1987) 'Using the police', *British Journal of Criminology*, 27:1.

Shapland, J. and J. Vagg (1988) *Policing by the Public*, London: Routledge.

Shaw, M. and W. Williamson (1972) 'Public attitudes to the police', *The Criminologist*, 7:26.

Shearing, C. (1981a) 'Subterranean processes in the maintenance of power', *Canadian Review of Sociology and Anthropology*, 18:3.

Shearing, C. (ed.) (1981b) *Organisational Police Deviance*, Toronto: Butterworth.

Shearing, C. (1981c) 'Deviance and conformity in the reproduction of order', in Shearing (ed.) (1981b).

Shearing, C. (1984) *Dial-A-Cop: A study of police mobilisation*, University of Toronto: Centre of Criminology.

Shearing, C. and J. Leon (1978) 'Reconsidering the police role: a challenge to a challenge of a popular conception', *Canadian Journal of Criminology and Corrections*, 19.

Shearing, C. and P. Stenning (eds) (1987) *Private Policing*, Beverly Hills: Sage.

Sheerman, B. (1991) 'What labour wants', *Policing*, 7:3.

Sheptycki, J. (1991) 'Innovations in the policing of domestic violence in London, England', *Policing and Society*, 2:2.

Sherman, L. (1978a) *Scandal and Reform: Controlling police corruption*, Berkeley, Calif.: University of California Press.

Sherman, L. (1978b) *The Quality of Police Education*, San Francisco: Jossey-Bass.

Sherman, L. (1980) 'Causes of police behaviour: the current state of quantitative research', *Journal of Research in Crime and Delinquency*, 17:1.

Sherman, L. (1983a) 'After the riots: police and minorities in the US 1970–1980', in N. Glazer and K. Young (eds) *Ethnic Pluralism and Public Policy*, London: Heinemann.

Sherman, L. (1983b) 'Reducing police gun use', in M. Punch (ed.) *Control in the Police Organization*, Cambridge, Mass.: MIT Press.

Sherman, L. (1992) 'Attacking crime: police and crime control', in M. Tonry and N. Morris (eds.) *Modern Policing*, Chicago: Chicago University Press.

Sherman, L. and R. Berk (1984) 'The specific deterrent effects of arrest for domestic assault', *American Sociological Review*, 49, April.

Sherman, L., C. Milton and T. Kelley (1973) *Team Policing*, Washington, D.C.: Police Foundation.

Sherr, A. (1989) *Freedom of Protest, Public Order and the Law*, Oxford: Basil Blackwell.

Sichel, J. (1978) *Women on Patrol*, Washington, D.C.: US Department of Justice.

Sieghart, P. (1985) 'Sanctions against abuse of police powers', *Public Law*, Autumn.

Silberman, C. (1978) *Criminal Violence, Criminal Justice*, New York: Vintage.

Silver, A. (1967) 'The demand for order in civil society', in D. Bordua (ed.) *The Police*, New York: Wiley.

Silver, A. (1971) 'Social and ideological bases of British elite reactions to domestic crises 1829–1832', *Politics and Society*, 1, February.

Sim, J. (1982) 'Scarman: the police counter-attack', in M. Eve and D. Musson (eds) *Socialist Register 1982*, London: Merlin.

Sinclair, I. and C. Miller (1984): *Measures of Police Effectiveness and Efficiency* (Research and Planning Unit Paper 25), London: Home Office.

Skogan, W. (1990) *The Police and Public in England and Wales: A British crime survey report*, London: HMSO.

Skolnick, J. (1966) *Justice Without Trial*, New York: Wiley.

Skolnick, J. (1969) *The Politics of Protest*, New York: Bantam.

Skolnick, J. (1972) 'Changing conceptions of the police', *Great Ideas Today*, Chicago: Encyclopaedia Britannica.

Skolnick, J. and D.H. Bayley (1986) *The New Blue Line*, New York: Free Press.

Skolnick, J. and D.H. Bayley (1988) *Community Policing: Issues and practices around the world*, Washington D.C.: National Institute of Justice.

Smith, A.T.H. (1987) *Offences Against Public Order*, London: Sweet & Maxwell.

Smith, D.A. and J.R. Klein (1984) 'Police control of interpersonal disputes', *Social Problems*, 31:4, April.

Smith, D.A. and C.A. Visher (1981) 'Street-level justice: situational determinants of police arrest decisions', *Social Problems*, 29:2, December.

South, N. (1988) *Policing for Profit*, London: Sage.

Southgate, P. (1982) *Police Probationer Training in Race Relations*, London: Home Office Research Unit.

Southgate, P. (ed.) (1988) *New Directions in Police Training*, London: HMSO.

Southgate, P. and P. Ekblom (1984) *Contacts Between Police and Public*, London: Home Office Research Unit.

Southgate, P. and P. Ekblom (1986) *Police-Public Encounters* (Home Office Research Study 90), London: HMSO.

Sparks, R. (1992) *Television and the Drama of Crime*, Milton Keynes: Open University Press.

Sparks, R., H. Genn and D. Dodd (1977) *Surveying Victims*, London: Wiley.

Spencer, S. (1985) *Police Authorities During the Miners' Strike*, London: Cobden Trust.

Spencer, S. (1992) *Called to Account*, London: National Council for Civil Liberties.

Spitzer, S. and A. Scull (1977a) 'Privatisation and social control', *Social Problems*, 25.

Spitzer, S. and A. Scull (1977b) 'Social control in historical perspective', in D. Greenberg (ed.) *Corrections and Punishment*, Beverly Hills: Sage.

Stalker, J. (1987) 'A safe pair of hands at the yard', *Evening Standard*, 27 July, p. 7.

Stalker, J. (1988) *Stalker*, London: Harrap.

Stanworth, P. (1984) 'Elites and privilege', in P. Abrams and R. Brown (eds) *UK Society*, London: Weidenfeld & Nicolson.

Stanworth, P. and A. Giddens (eds) (1974) *Elites and Power in British Society*, Cambridge: Cambridge University Press.

Stead, P. (ed.) (1977) *Pioneers in Policing*, Montclair, N.J.: Patterson Smith.

Stead, P. (1985) *The Police of Britain*, New York: Macmillan.

Steedman, C. (1984) *Policing the Victorian Community*, London: Routledge.

Steer, D. (1980) *Uncovering Crime* (Royal Commission on Criminal Procedure Research Study 7), London: HMSO.

Stenning, P. and C. Shearing (1984) 'Corporate justice', *Australian and New Zealand Journal of Criminology*, 17, June.

Stephens, M. (1988): *Policing: The critical issues*, Hemel Hempstead: Harvester Wheatsheaf.

Stevens, P. and C. Willis (1979) *Race, Crime and Arrests*, London: Home Office Research Unit.

Stevens, P. and C. Willis (1981) *Ethnic Minorities and Complaints Against the Police*, London: Home Office Research Unit.

Stevenson, J. (1977) 'Social control and the prevention of riots in England 1789–1829', in A.P. Donajgrodski (ed.) *Social Control in Nineteenth Century Britain*, London: Croom Helm.

Stevenson, J. and C. Cook. (1977) *The Slump*, London: Cape.

Stinchcombe, A. (1963) 'Institutions of privacy in the determination of police administrative practice', *American Journal of Sociology*, 69:2.

Stoddard, E.R. (1968) 'The informal code of police deviancy: a group approach to blue-coat crime', *Journal of Criminal Law, Criminology, and Police Science*, 59:2.

Storch, R. (1975) 'The plague of blue locusts: police reform and popular resistance in Northern England 1840–57', *International Review of Social History*, 20.

Storch, R. (1976) 'The policeman as domestic missionary', *Journal of Social History*, IX:4, Summer.

Storch, R. (1980) 'Crime and Justice in nineteenth-century England', *History Today*, 30.

Storch, R. (1989) 'Policing rural southern England before the police: opinion and practice 1830–1856' in D. Hay and F. Snyder (eds) *Policing and Prosecution in Britain 1750–1850*, Oxford: Oxford University Press.

Styles, J. (1977) 'Criminal records', *Historical Journal*, 20:4.

Styles, J. (1982) 'An eighteenth-century magistrate as detective', *Bradford Antiquary* (n.s.), 47.

Styles, J. (1983) 'Sir John Fielding and the problem of criminal investigation in eighteenth-century England', *Transactions of the Royal Historical Society*, 33.

Styles, J. (1987) 'The emergence of the police: explaining police reform in eighteenth- and nineteenth-century England', *British Journal of Criminology*, 27:1.

Sumner, C. (ed.) (1982a) *Crime, Justice and the Mass Media* (Cropwood Papers 14), Cambridge: Institute of Criminology.

Sumner, C. (1982b) ' "Political hooliganism" and "rampaging rioters":

the national press coverage of the Toxteth "riots"', in Sumner (ed.) (1982a).

Sunday Times (1987) 'A thinking man's copper to cool the hottest beat', *Profile*, 2 August, p. 12.

Sykes, R. and J. Clark (1975) 'A theory of deference exchange in police–civilian encounters', *American Journal of Sociology*, 81.

Sykes, R., J. Fox and J. Clark (1976) 'A socio-legal theory of police discretion', in A. Blumberg and A. Niederhoffer (eds) *The Ambivalent Force*, 2nd edn, Hinsdale, Ill.: Dryden.

Symons, J. (1972) *Bloody Murder*, London: Penguin.

Takagi, P. (1974) 'A garrison state in "democratic" society', *Crime and Social Justice*, Spring–Summer.

Tarling, R. (1988) *Police Work and Manpower Allocation* (Research and Planning Unit Paper 47), London: Home Office.

Tarling, R. and J. Burrows (1985) 'The work of detectives', in K. Heal, R. Tarling and J. Burrows (eds) *Policing Today*, London: HMSO.

Taylor, I. (1980) 'The law and order issue in the British general election and Canadian federal election of 1979', *Canadian Journal of Sociology*, 5:3, Summer.

Taylor, I. (1981) *Law and Order: Arguments for socialism*, London: Macmillan.

Taylor, I., P. Walton and J. Young (1973) *The New Criminology*, London: Routledge.

Taylor, L. (1984) *In the Underworld*, Oxford: Basil Blackwell.

Taylor, P. (1983) 'How Hendon police cadets are wooed away from racialism', *Police*, August.

Tendler, S. (1987) 'Approaching with due caution', *The Times*, 28 July, p. 8.

Thomas, T. (1988) 'The Police and Criminal Evidence Act 1984: the social work role', *Howard Journal of Criminal Justice*, 27:4.

Thompson, E.P. (1968) *The Making of the English Working Class*, London: Penguin.

Thompson, E.P. (1971) 'The moral economy of the English crowd', *Past and Present*, 50.

Thompson, E.P. (1975) *Whigs and Hunters*, London: Penguin.

Thompson, E.P. (1980) *Writing by Candlelight*, London: Merlin.

Thompson, E.P. (1992): *Customs in Common*, London: Merlin.

Thurmond Smith, P. (1985) *Policing Victorian London*, Westport, Conn.: Greenwood.

Tierney, J. (1989) 'Graduating in criminal justice', *Policing*, 5:3.

Trojanowicz, R. and B. Bucqueroux (1990) *Community Policing*, Cincinnati, Ohio: Anderson.

Tuck, M (1989) *Drinking and Disorder: A study of non-metropolitan violence* (Home Office Research and Planning Unit Study 108), London: HMSO.

Tuck, M. and P. Southgate (1981) *Ethnic Minorities, Crime and Policing*, London: Home Office Research Unit.

Tullett, T. (1981) *Murder Squad*, London: Granada.

Tumber, H. (1982) *Television and the Riots*, London: British Film Institute.

Turk, A. (1982a) *Political Criminality*, Beverly Hills, Calif.: Sage.

Turk, A. (1982b) 'Policing in political context', in R. Donelan (ed.) *The Maintenance of Order in Society*, Ottawa: Canadian Police College.

Tuska, J. (1978) *The Detective in Hollywood*, New York: Doubleday.

Uglow, S. (1988) *Policing Liberal Society*, Oxford: Oxford University Press.

Unsworth, C. (1982) 'The riots of 1981', *Journal of Law and Society*, 9:1, Summer.

Van Maanen, J. (1973) 'Observations on the making of policemen', *Human Organisation*, 32.

Van Maanen, J. (1974) 'Working the street', in H. Jacob (ed.) *The Potential for Reform of Criminal Justice*, Beverly Hills, Calif.: Sage.

Van Maanen, J. (1978) 'Watching the watchers', in P.K. Manning and J. Van Maanen (eds) *Policing*, Santa Monica, Calif.: Goodyear.

Van Maanen, J. (1983) 'The boss', in M. Punch (ed.) *Control in the Police Organization*, Cambridge, Mass.: MIT Press.

Vennard, J. (1984) 'Disputes within trials over the admissibility and accuracy of incriminating statements', *Criminal Law Review*.

Vick, C. (1981) 'Police pessimism', in D. Pope and N. Weiner (eds) *Modern Policing*, London: Croom Helm.

Vincent Jones, P. (1986) 'The hippy convoy and criminal trespass', *Journal of Law and Society*, 13:3.

Vogler, R. (1991) *Reading the Riot Act*, Milton Keynes: Open University Press.

Waddington, P.A.J. (1982a) 'Why the "opinion-makers" no longer support the police', *Police*, December.

Waddington, P.A.J. (1982b) 'Conservatism, dogmatism and authoritarianism in the police: a comment', *Sociology*, November.

Waddington, P.A.J. (1983a) *Are the Police Fair?* (Research Paper 2), London: Social Affairs Unit.

Waddington, P.A.J. (1983b) 'Beware the community trap', *Police*, March, p. 34.

Waddington, P.A.J. (1984a) 'Black crime, the "racist" police and fashionable compassion', in D. Anderson (ed.) *The Kindness that Kills*, London: SPCK.

Waddington, P.A.J. (1984b) 'The role of the police committee:

constitutional arrangements and social realities', *Local Government Studies*, September/October.

Waddington, P.A.J. (1986a) 'Defining objectives', *Policing* 2:1.

Waddington, P.A.J. (1986b) 'The objectives debate', *Policing* 2:3.

Waddington, P.A.J. (1986c) *The Effects of Manpower Depletion during the NUM Strike 1984–5*, London: Police Foundation.

Waddington, P.A.J. (1987) 'Towards paramilitarism: dilemmas in policing civil disorder', *British Journal of Criminology*, 27:1.

Waddington, P.A.J. (1991) *The Strong Arm of the Law*, Oxford, Oxford University Press.

Wakeford, J. and J. Urry (eds) (1973) *Power in Britain*, London: Heinemann.

Walden, J. (1982) *Visions of Order*, Toronto: Butterworth.

Walker, M. (1992) 'Do we need a clear-up rate?', *Policing and Society*, 2:4.

Walker, S. (1977) *A Critical History of Police Reform*, Lexington, Mass.: D.C. Heath.

Walker, S. (1980) *Popular Justice*, New York: Oxford University Press.

Walker, S. (1983) *Police in America*, New York: McGraw Hill.

Walklate, S. (1992) 'Jack and Jill join up at Sun Hill: public images of police officers', *Policing and Society*, 2:3.

Wall, D. (1987) 'Chief Constables: a changing elite', in R. Mawby (ed.) *Policing Britain*, Plymouth Polytechnic: Department of Political and Social Sciences.

Wall, D. (1989): 'The Selection of Chief Constables in England and Wales 1835–1985' M.Phil. thesis, University of York: Department of Social Policy.

Walsh, J.L. (1977) 'Career styles and police behaviour', in D.H. Bayley (ed.) *Police and Society*, Beverly Hills: Sage.

Walters, R. (1975) *The Establishment of the Bristol Police Force*, Historical Association, Bristol Branch: University of Bristol, Department of History.

Wambaugh, J. (1971) *The New Centurions*, London: Sphere/New York: Dell.

Wambaugh, J. (1973) *The Blue Knight*, London: Sphere/New York: Dell.

Wambaugh, J. (1976) *The Choir-Boys*, London: Futura/New York: Dell.

Ward, T. (1986) *Death and Disorder*, London: Inquest.

Watson, C. (1971) *Snobbery With Violence*, London: Eyre & Spottiswoode.

Watts-Miller, W. (1987) 'Party politics, class interest and reform of the police 1829–56', *Police Studies*, 10:1.

Weatheritt, M. (1983) 'Community policing: does it work and how do we know? A review of research', in T. Bennett (ed.) *The Future of Policing* (Cropwood Papers 15), Cambridge: Institute of Criminology.

Weatheritt, M. (1986) *Innovations in Policing*, London: Croom Helm.

Weatheritt, M. (ed.) (1989) *Police Research: Some future prospects*, Aldershot: Avebury.

Webb, J. (1959) *The Badge: The inside story of the Los Angeles police department*, London: W.H. Allen/New York: Prentice-Hall.

Weber, M. (1964) *The Theory of Social and Economic Organisation*, Glencoe: Free Press (original translation 1947).

Weinberger, B. (1981) 'The police and the public in mid-nineteenth-century Warwickshire', in V. Bailey (ed.) *Policing and Punishment in Nineteenth-Century Britain*, London: Croom Helm.

Weinberger, B. (1991) *Keeping the Peace? Policing strikes in Britain 1906–1926*, Oxford: Berg.

Weinberger, B. and H. Reinke (1991) 'A diminishing function? A comparative historical account of policing in the city', *Policing and Society*, 1:3.

Weiner, A. (1973) 'Crime wave: the TV cops', *New Society*, 12 December.

Wells, R. (1991) 'Implementation and non-implementation of the 1839–40 policing Acts in East and West Sussex', *Policing and Society*, 1:4.

Werthman, C. and I. Piliavin (1967) 'Gang members and the police', in D. Bordua (ed.) *The Police*, New York: Wiley.

Westergaard, J. and H. Resler (1975) *Class in a Capitalist Society*, London: Heinemann and Penguin.

Westley, W. (1970) *Violence and the Police*, Cambridge, Mass.: MIT Press.

Wheatcroft, G. (1987) 'Polishing up the image of the police', *Daily Telegraph*, 3 August, p. 12.

Whitaker, B. (1964) *The Police*, London: Penguin.

Whitaker, B. (1979) *The Police in Society*, London: Eyre Methuen.

White, J. (1986) *The Worst Street in North London*, London: Routledge.

Williamson, T. and S. Moston (1990) 'The extent of silence in police interviews', in S. Greer and R. Morgan (eds) *The Right To Silence Debate*, Bristol University: Centre for Criminal Justice.

Willis, C. (1983) *The Use, Effectiveness and Impact of Police Stop and Search Powers*, London: Home Office Research Unit.

Willis, C., J. Macleod and P. Naish (1988) *The Tape-Recording of Police Interviews with Suspects* (Home Office Research Study 97), London: HMSO.

Willis, T. (1983) 'Is PC Dixon on the way back?', *TV Times*, 26 November–2 December.

Wilson, I. (1981) 'Political awareness in policing', in D. Pope and N. Weiner (eds), *Modern Policing*, London: Croom Helm.

Wilson, J.Q. (1968a) *Varieties of Police Behavior*, Cambridge, Mass.: Harvard University Press.

Wilson, J.Q. (1968b) 'Movie cops: romantic vs. real', New York, 19 August. (Reprinted in A. Blumberg and A. Niederhoffer (eds) *The Ambivalent Force*, Hinsdale, Ill.: Dryden.)

Wilson, J.Q. (1975) *Thinking About Crime*, New York: Vintage.

Wilson, J.Q. and B. Boland (1978) 'The effects of the police on crime', *Law and Society Review*, 12:3.

Wilson, J.Q. and B. Boland (1981) 'The effects of the police on crime: a response to Jacob and Rich', *Law and Society Review*, 16:1.

Wilson, J.Q. and G. Kelling (1982) 'Broken windows', *The Atlantic Monthly*, March.

Winick, C. (ed.) (1978) *Deviance and Mass Media*, Beverly Hills: Sage.

Woffinden, B. (1989) *Miscarriages of Justice*, London: Coronet.

Woodcock, J. (1991) 'Overturning police culture', *Policing*, 7:3.

Woolf, Lord Justice (1991) *Prison Disturbances April 1990*, Cmnd. 1456, London: HMSO.

Worsley, P. (1964) 'The distribution of power in industrial societies', *Sociological Review Monographs: The Development of Industrial Societies*.

Wren-Lewis, J. (1981–2) 'TV coverage of the riots', *Screen Education*, 40, Autumn/Winter.

Wright, M. (1982) *Making Good*, London: Burnett.

Young, J. (1971) 'The role of the police as amplifiers of deviancy', in S. Cohen (ed.) *Images of Deviance*, London: Penguin.

Young, M. (1991) *An Inside Job: Policing and police culture in Britain*, Oxford: Oxford University Press.

Zander, M. (1974) 'Are too many professional criminals avoiding conviction?: A study of Britain's two busiest courts', *Modern Law Review*, 37.

Zander, M. (1979a) 'What is the evidence on law and order?', *New Society*, 13 December.

Zander, M. (1979b) 'The investigation of crime: a study of cases tried at the Old Bailey', *Criminal Law Review*.

Zander, M. (1981) 'Royal Commission: no grounds for suspicion', *The Guardian*, 12 January.

Zander, M. (1982) 'Police powers', *Political Quarterly*, 53:2, April–June.

Zander, M. (1991) *The Police and Criminal Evidence Act 1984*, 2nd edn, London: Sweet & Maxwell.

Zuckerman, A.A.S. (1987) 'Illegally obtained evidence: discretion as a guardian of legitimacy', *Current Legal Problems 1987*, London: Stevens.

INDEX